A Journey into Accounting Thought

This book explores the role of accountants in business and society. The final work of Louis Goldberg, Professor Emeritus at the University of Melbourne, it aims to raise awareness of the existence and importance of fundamental issues that are often ignored or by-passed in contemporary discussion of accounting.

The sixteen chapters assess exactly what accountants do in carrying out their work. They are structured in four central parts, addressing:

- Historical context and background considerations.

- The most important perceptions and concepts that govern the main functions of accountants.

- The constraints of current orthodox accounting endeavour, including an examination of the tripodal cluster of expressions of current orthodox accounting behaviour: the fundamental accounting equation, the procedure of double entry and the balance sheet.

- The extent to which advances in recent decades can be applied to the search for answers to the problems that have arisen, and the future challenges which face accounting.

The work concludes by posing a challenge to future accountants: the author suggests the possibility of developing a structure of accounting with the requisite strength and flexibility to face whatever changes lie ahead.

Essential reading for scholars or historians of accounting, this work will also interest philosophers and practising accountants.

Louis Goldberg was G.L. Wood Professor of Accounting at the University of Melbourne and Head of Department from 1958 to 1973. He was elected to the Academy of Social Sciences in Australia; assigned life membership of the Academy of Accounting Historians and the Accounting Association of Australia and New Zealand; and appointed to the general division of the Order of Australia (AO) in 1987.

Stewart A. Leech is Professor of Accounting and Business Information Systems at the University of Melbourne, a Fellow of the Institute of Chartered Accountants in Australia and a Fellow of CPA Australia. He was Professor of Accounting and Head of the School of Accounting and Finance at the University of Tasmania prior to his appointment at Melbourne in 2000.

Routledge studies in accounting

1 A Journey into Accounting Thought
Louis Goldberg
Edited by Stewart A. Leech

A Journey into Accounting Thought

Louis Goldberg

Edited by Stewart A. Leech

London and New York

First published 2001
by Routledge
11 New Fetter Lane, London EC4P 4EE

Simultaneously published in the USA and Canada
by Routledge
29 West 35th Street, New York, NY 10001

Routledge is an imprint of the Taylor & Francis Group

Typeset in Baskerville by Exe Valley Dataset Ltd, Exeter
Printed and bound in Great Britain by
TJ International Ltd, Padstow, Cornwall

British Library Cataloguing in Publication Data
A catalogue record for this book is available
from the British Library

Library of Congress Cataloguing in Publication Data
A catalogue record for this book has been requested

ISBN 0–415–26021–3

Contents

PART III
Constraints   201

PART IV
Loosening shackles   303

Editor's foreword

This book is the result of my discussions with Lou Goldberg during the last ten years of his life. The work is his thoughts about accounting and the future of accounting expressed in his own words. I believe he always intended for me to be a co-author, which accounts for the way the manuscript is written. Lou liked to write in the first person, and the words 'we' and 'our' are used many times.

My adopted role as 'editor' was an interesting one. It was not easy to edit the words that Lou wanted to use – after all, he was honoured by the University of Melbourne with a Litt.D. in 1967. Thus, my role of 'editor' was rather to give advice, edit the manuscript in the way Lou wanted it edited, and to argue gently on many occasions.

While I had an influence on some chapters and provided references and paragraphs in selected sections, most of this book was not only Lou's work but also written as he wanted to write it. I was a colleague who was willing to listen, argue, assist and collaborate. The sessions we had discussing the work were an enjoyable and rewarding experience. I am sure that many accounting historians, philosophers and others will enjoy this book as well.

Acknowledgements are due to several people who were involved with the manuscript. Thanks are due to the late David Solomons, Lee Parker, George Findlay, Geoff Harris and Garry Carnegie for their helpful comments on various drafts, to Michael Sullivan for proof-reading, to Geoff Burrows for assistance with the bibliography, and to Annmaree Sharkey who provided expert assistance with word-processing. The highest praise and thanks must go to Suellen Lampkin, who typed the original manuscript, undertook continual editing and formatting, assisted with constructing the bibliography and was involved with the book over the entire ten-year period. There may be others who are unknown to me who read the manuscript or assisted in other ways. If so, may I apologise in advance for any omission in acknowledging your assistance.

PROFESSOR STEWART A. LEECH

Part I
Background

1 Introductory overview

What cannot be understood cannot be managed intelligently.

(Dewey 1928: 3)

Whatever it is that accountants do, and whatever means, procedures, techniques or technology they use to do it, it is a human activity that is concerned with human activity. This is the essential and pervading proposition of this work. It is not a new proposition, but it seems that many writers and practitioners carry out their tasks without adequately appreciating the implications of accepting it. The emphasis placed on it in this work seeks to redress this neglect so far as possible. We believe that, despite the enormous changes in technology in recent years, and its great advances in earlier centuries, the kernel of accounting endeavour is, as it has always been, activities carried out by and for people.

This work is written as an exploration and exposition of ideas. Our objective has been to enquire into and assess what accountants do in carrying out their functions as accountants. The principal methods used are observation, reflection and analysis. This is in some contrast to many treatises on accounting which usually, to a greater or lesser extent, are exercises in revelation and advocacy of a system of ideas which are presented as authoritative propositions with (if such a personification may be metaphorically applied) an ambition to become dogma.

Our purpose has been to raise the awareness of accountants (and, we hope, others) of the existence and importance of fundamental issues which are often ignored or bypassed in much of the earlier and current discussion in the literature of accounting. We believe that all of these issues are significant, and that some, at least, are urgent and warrant immediate attention. We recognize that they may be regarded as controversial and in some respects contrary to the current 'conventional wisdom', but we consider that this does not constitute sufficient reason for not raising them now.

However, controversy for the sake of drawing attention has not figured in our objectives. We have aimed at providing at least some constructive suggestions arising from our analysis; we suggest these as pointers of direction of improvement rather than as complete solutions to problems. If they are taken up as such, the ensuing examination, elaboration and adaptation to specific situations will, we believe, improve the performance, status and social credibility of accountants as vocational practitioners. But this is up to them, and depends on their attitude and reliance on their own acumen in formulating and implementing appropriate (and sometimes courageous) decisions in whatever kind of society they find themselves.

We are aware that accountants are looking for solutions to problems which, as time goes on, seem to become more numerous, more complicated and more perplexing almost day by day. We consider, however, that it is important to understand the questions that should be asked before providing solutions to them. If the questions are not understood adequately, they cannot be framed properly; if they are not properly formulated, any answer to them surely cannot have long-term benefit, if it has any at all.

In this exercise in inquiry we may be taken into territory which is unaccustomed for writers on accounting to visit or take their readers to, but our intention has been to go wherever our methods lead us and to see what is there, even if we do not see it all. We are looking for questions which not only accountants may ask of others or others may ask of accountants, but, perhaps most important, which accountants should be asking of themselves.

One of the great difficulties in embarking on a project of this nature is that many of the topics to be discussed are interrelated and could be examined within several categories of classification. Classifying them at all involves some arbitrariness, and is subject to the attitude and purpose of the classifier. We should recognize that classifying in itself does not create anything; it merely brings some things into a perceived relationship with some others. The perception of the relationship is subjective and its acceptance or rejection signifies a subjective or 'value' judgement. In many instances, the things so classified have multiple relationships, whence it follows that often more than one basis of classification can be applied to sets of phenomena or occurrences or, even, of concepts.

Similarly and analogously, many of the topics to be discussed in this work are pervasive throughout the field under examination, so that some aspects arise for consideration at several points and there may seem to be repetition and/or discontinuity in places. Perhaps none of them is exhaustively treated even if all the partial discussions were to be brought together. We do not claim to have treated any of these topics exhaustively, but we suggest that we are providing some new and clearly marked signposts of directions in which further exploration may be productive and useful.

The work is set out in four parts, in the first of which we raise what we regard as background considerations, so to speak, for the discussion of basic ideas in accounting, and their implications, which comprise the subject-matter of subsequent parts. In this part, after a brief discussion of the term 'accounting' (Chapter 2), in which some of the more obvious ambiguities and difficulties in its use are pointed out, we suggest in Chapter 3 that various approaches are possible in examining the constituents of the subject of enquiry, and briefly indicate a link between two of these approaches which are worthy of emphasis. A few observations are made in Chapter 4 on the function and purpose of classification in an analytical approach, and in Chapter 5 some comments are proffered on accounting regarded as a field of knowledge.

Part II presents our view of the most important perceptions and concepts which govern the main functions of accountants in their vocational work. In Chapter 6 we examine what we regard as the most significant concept in the area of our attention, namely, the unit of experience. This, we believe, turns out to be the individual human being; that is, a living, sentient organism, which is a distinguishable unit with the capacity of being a member of a group of similar organisms with some kind of common objectives or mutual relationships (including, in many instances, interdependence). Whatever interpretation is put upon 'accounting' and whatever approach is used in its exploration, it has to do with the activities of beings who (or which) are capable of carrying out these activities. As we see it, while the primary and fundamental unit of experience in and for accounting is the individual human being, individuals can act together in groups; they can be in conflict with others as groups; they can create a concept or set up a banner as a symbol of their communal allegiance and do all sorts of things to make it a symbol of power or influence. But despite all this, we believe that the experiences of people are inescapably those of the individuals as individuals, and that the experience of each individual is, at bottom, privy to that individual alone. Further, the beliefs and attitudes of individuals are developed by experiences throughout their own lives to any given moment. The utmost any of us can currently say about anything is that, in the light of our experience to date (which includes not only our own activities and our perceptions of those of others around us, but our own reading and thinking and any internal experiences of pain or pleasure or 'spiritual' uplifting and the like) such a thing is *as we see it, here and now.* Perhaps this is the most that can ever be irrefutably said, or the strongest view that can or should be proffered with confidence.

Virtually no human being can survive a completely solitary life for long after birth, but, on the contrary, lives as a member of a social group and, in some instances, of several groups with differing common interests. Since much of the accounting process is intended to be communicative, in the next chapter (7) we discuss some of the important aspects of the function and process of communication between such units of experience, with particular attention to the place of language and its often implicit conceptual acceptances. Whatever we may think about the processes of accounting, or the functions of accountants, there can be no doubt that their communicative aspects form a large, inherent and inevitable part. Even if one thinks only of an accounting proposition without recording it in any form, one is engaged in a part of the process of communication; and this is so even if the one person is both formulator and recipient of the unrecorded proposition. In other words, one can communicate with oneself in thought as well as in more permanent ways.

Then follows a discussion of the kinds of activity of our units of experience which are of essential interest in the area of accounting. These are occurrences and 'ventures' of various kinds (Chapter 8) and are seen in Chapter 9 to be expressions of relationships which can be distinguished from each other for some degree of analytical exploration. For millennia human progress – or at least what we all have come to regard as progress – has depended upon the interaction of people within groups: families, tribes, communities, nations, professional and international associations. Duties and responsibilities, as well as rights and privileges, attach to each member of a group. Some of the principal relationships between people with which accountants are vocationally concerned are discussed in Chapter 9. Accountants, no less than others, belong to groups.

While accountants are concerned with processes of communication about occurrences impinging upon, and activities carried out by, units of experience (individual or groups of human beings), their functional activities, that is, the accounting procedures, are addressed in each instance to a particular unit of operation which becomes a focus of attention. A unit of operation may comprise the activities and relationships of a specific human being or a group of people, or a conceptual institution or organization recognized as a separate person through a legal or social fiction, for example, a company or a trust, or a hypothetical entity set up by accountants. However, whatever unit of operation may be set up, what accountants are actually dealing with are the activities and relationships, and their results, of real human beings, that is, of units of experience. Some aspects of such a unit of operation are considered in Chapter 10.

In any sphere of human activity people are continually making decisions of various kinds and at various levels. The occurrences which comprise the subject-matter of accounting procedures are the results of and/or the precursors to decisions. While the expression 'decision-making' or an equivalent has been widely used in accounting literature in recent decades, it seems desirable to examine from our own viewpoint what is actually involved in arriving at a decision or, for instance, whether 'making' a decision necessarily entails its implementation. The function of arriving at a decision is explored in Chapters 11 and 12, since we believe that many of the procedures of accounting are inevitably bound up with these functions of decision-making.

In Part III we critically examine the tripodal cluster of expressions of current orthodox accounting endeavour. These are the so-called fundamental accounting equation, the procedure of double entry, and the balance sheet or any equivalent report. For many years now, the exposition in the study of both the procedural aspects and the theoretical composition of accounting has been traditionally approached through an accounting equation set out in a mathematical form of equating monetary values for assets with either ownership plus liabilities or (what the sum of these two amounts to) 'equities' or claims upon the assets. Upon this basis the superstructure of both procedure and theory has been developed. While the components of such an equation have often been scrutinized and discussed at great length by accounting writers, little attention appears to have been given to one particular element in it. This element is examined, together with some of its implications, in Chapters 13, 14 and 15, involving a reassessment not only of the double-entry process of thought about many of the problems that face accountants in their day-to-day activities, but also of the function and usefulness of the major reports.

This leads us to a further discussion in Chapter 16 (Part IV) of decisions in the light of this reassessment, and to a consideration of the extent to which advances in recent decades can be applied to the search for answers to the problems that have arisen.

We see the central problem facing both academic and practising accountants as that of being able to see each occurrence as it happens, to examine it and clarify the relationships between human beings which it affects within the particular context of accounting. Accountants may need to exercise some intellectual courage to broaden this context from its present relatively narrow parameters, to include social components which will enable them to develop a structure with the requisite strength and flexibility to face successfully whatever changes will be encountered. Therein lies the accounting challenge.

2 'Accounting' and the activities of accountants

To run a factory properly you need:

(1) An accountant
(2) Another accountant

(Two are necessary because accountants never agree, and it is desirable to see both sides of everything. An accountant left alone soon pines away and dies.)

(Spode 1934: 34)

The term 'accounting'

It seems appropriate to begin an exploration of accounting by paying a little attention to the term itself, which will lead to a consideration of what accountants do, or purport to do, or are thought to do, in their vocational capacity.

The word 'accounting' will be recognized by some as a participle of the verb 'to account'. It may be and, indeed, often is used in more than one sense. Anybody who purports to say what accounting 'is' at all times and places and in all circumstances becomes exposed to a charge of omni-science or omnipotence which are not characteristics of any ordinary human being. The term is a symbol created by human beings in order to convey ideas between human beings, and these ideas are several, changeable and often nebulous rather than specific, universal and limpid in the minds of the people seeking to express them.

'Accounting' is the symbol we use to suggest to our audience that we are thinking about a set of practices or activities which are distinguishable in some way from other practices and activities. What are the characteristics by which the distinction can be made and sustained?

The usages to be examined may be approached by posing some questions. If, when the question is asked: 'What do accountants do?', the answer is given: 'They do accounting', or if 'What are you studying?' is followed by 'I am studying accounting', or if 'What is your occupation?' elicits the reply 'I practise accounting as my vocation', the answer suggests the sense to be explored. More than one meaning may well be involved in these usages. Sometimes the context serves to clarify the intention of the user, but often it does not, or not precisely enough to ensure accurate communication, for it is easy for a symbol, such as a word of generalization or abstraction, to be taken – by the reader or hearer who receives it – in a sense different from that intended by the writer or speaker, unless the intention is not only clearly intimated in the first place, but reiterated and emphasized on other occasions as well. 'Accounting', when used as a noun, may be intended to suggest a kind of activity, a field of study, that is, an intellectual discipline, or a form of professional practice.

If we are interested in 'accounting' as a field of study, we are concerned with understanding both how and why accountants do what they do in the way they do it, and, perhaps, in some aspects of the study, why they ought to be doing something different. This involves seeking a rationale for the activities of accountants, and raises questions of what constitutes a satis-factory explanation of something so that it can be accepted by recipients and, in relevant cases, adopted by them in the furtherance of the field of study.

To say that accounting is 'what accountants do' – or even, perhaps, what they should do, which introduces the notion of criteria by which their performance might be judged – is essentially a tautology, and, on the face of it, not very useful as an intellectual instrument. Alternatively, we may wish to suggest to our audience that we are thinking about an area of study which comprises a set of concepts (or ideas or thoughts), techniques (or procedures or systems), rationales (lines of argument) and rules (or guides to or standards of performance) which are normally considered apposite to carrying out the activities which comprise the practice of accounting. This meaning is not merely allied to the previous one, it is dependent upon it. It is this aspect which warrants exploration.

As a form of professional practice, the sense of the term takes on some aspects of both of the two senses already distinguished. At this level of meaning the activities being considered are those of people who perform them not only as human activities but vocationally; they are not casual or occasional but regular and continuous, and carry with them a responsibility attaching to the social recognition of a group of people who profess to possess and apply advanced knowledge and useful skills. That knowledge and those skills are commonly presumed to have been mainly developed through the intellectual discipline of their study of the field(s) related to their activities.

'Accounting' may be regarded as the symbol for 'what accountants think' or 'what accountants think about'. If this view is adopted, we then have to ask: What do accountants – as accountants, of course – think about? Do they think about a process, or sets of procedures, or about the social environment in which they operate as accountants, including such things as the legal and fiscal features of the environment and the impact of what they do within the organization they operate in and the society in which they live? They do think of these matters, of course, in a fashion; they are to some extent part of most courses of instruction. But do they think about them in search of any effect which their activities, as accountants, may have on the social environment as well as the influence which that environment has on their activities?

In any set of circumstances, other than a static society, the social environment is necessarily changing, and most accountants probably realize this whenever they pause to think about it. There seems to be a widespread attitude that accounting practice has to conform to the requirements of the changing environment in which its practitioners find themselves. This is only natural and laudable. But a somewhat neglected question that may well be raised is: What influence have the practices of accountants had on the social environment? How has this influence – slight or great as it might be – been generated and exerted, and how strong has it been? Has it been an influence for good, according to whatever criteria – and there may, of course, be several – are used to form a judgement of this sort?

The term is also sometimes used in the sense of an explanation such as in 'accounting for' some action or attitude or state of affairs, where it means, virtually, explaining or attributing influences or causal factors; for example, the frequently used saying, 'there is no accounting for tastes' is an idiomatic way of saying that the different tastes of people cannot be easily explained by logical argument. And sometimes somebody is called on to provide an 'accounting' for his or her actions, which may be anything from a cursory to a complicated explanation of a sequence of circumstances which may or may not contain or refer to any of the kinds of activities usually thought of in relation to accountants. By intending this usage, a book title such as 'Accounting for Accounting' would not necessarily be meaningless or tautological, but without some clarification it would probably be open to misinterpretation.

The word can also be used as an adjective, and there are subtle differences in connotation in this use which could easily be overlooked or ignored unless one is well aware of them. For instance, 'an accounting book' may be a book about accounting (whatever that may be considered to be), that is, the expression *indicates* the subject-matter of the content of the book, whereas 'a red book' or 'a thick book' *describes* some aspect of its physical qualities rather than its content. On the other hand, 'an accounting book' may be used in the sense of a record of occurrences or transactions in a form which makes it identifiable as a record of statements or propositions commonly made by or for someone accustomed to the techniques and practices of 'accountants'; in this sense, while the term 'accounting book' still refers to the content, that content is not so much about 'accounting' as evidence of 'accounting practice'.

Similarly, a work including in its title an expression such as 'accounting method', 'accounting principles', or 'accounting theory', would normally be interpreted, at least at first sight, as comprising a study of, respectively, the methods or practices applied, or the 'principles' adhered to or recognized, or the 'theory' envisaged or propounded, by accountants in their vocational activities. In each case the word 'accounting' would be taken to have behind it the notion of vocational behaviour of those people we know as account- ants. In other words, in this kind of usage the noun to which 'accounting' is attached is modified to pertain to what accountants do or should do in their capacity as accountants.

When W.A. Paton wrote on *Accounting Theory* (1922), he was concerned with expounding a set of ideas which he thought accountants ought to abide by or conform to in carrying out their professional activities. Implicit in the title was the notion of a set of ideas applicable to the vocational activities of the people we know as accountants. When Stephen Gilman produced a work entitled *Accounting Concepts of Profit* (1939), he set out to examine the notional content, as he saw it, of the methods and procedures by which accountants usually (or most frequently) calculated the periodical net financial result of operations of commercial units. He was concerned, as a critical analyst, with the ideas which, in his view, governed the practices of accountants. In cases such as these, a more stringently correct, if somewhat pedantic, adaptation would be the substitution of 'Accountants' for 'Accounting', in the sense of 'pertaining to' or 'envisaged by' or 'applied by' accountants as professional people. Paton was writing about a theory for accountants to make use of; Gilman was examining concepts according to which accountants measured or ought to measure financial net results.

While a formal definition is not considered essential, or, indeed, desirable, at this stage, the word is used to signify activities which, (a) are carried out by human beings, (b) reflect relationships between human beings, and (c) in general, are intended (or presumed to be intended) to be of benefit to human beings.[1]

The main purpose of this discussion is to suggest that communication about what accountants do, what they think about, what they may think they think about, and what others think they do and think about, is open to widespread misinterpretation and lack of community of ideas; much of the so-called theory or rationale of accounting practice turns out to be at cross- purposes because of insufficient attention to basic conceptual or intellectual

---

1 For a brief discussion of problems involved in defining terms see: Appendix to this chapter, taken from Goldberg 1965: 24–7. It may be noted in passing that, in the development of our language, the symbol we use for a particular notion is not always what we would expect to find as most appropriate for it etymologically. For instance, the word 'dunce' which signifies someone slow at learning or unintelligent has come into the language from the name of a very learned cleric of the thirteenth century, named Duns Scotus. The word originally meant one who was well versed in the views of the Scottish cleric, then opponents of the views of his followers used it as a term of scorn to indicate a narrow pedant; both of these interpretations fell into disuse but the word became the indicator of a dullard, the meaning which it conveys in current language. Thus, while the etymological origins of our words are always interesting and useful, their subsequent history has in some cases made for a strange and unexpected transition in meaning.

propositions. Our objective is to bring some of these into the open for examination and exploration.

Perhaps the one thing we can be reasonably confident of without adopting a dogmatic attitude is that the term has some relation to accounts in the sense of stores of information, which are human artifacts and not natural phenomena; with this as base, we can begin to explore.

One object of carrying out the processes and procedures of accounting is to get appropriate 'pictures' of what is going on in the social unit with which the accountant is concerned, that is, what the people who comprise the unit and/or have relations with it have been doing and are doing, and even, in some cases, what they may or should do in the future. In preparing these 'pictures' the accountant is involved in a task of communication and is thereby concerned with bringing people's minds together.

The activities of accountants

However an accountant's functions are interpreted, they are concerned with the activities of people and with the results of those activities. In any organization of people, for instance, the accountant comes in contact, directly or indirectly, with other members of the organization.

One of the current responsibilities of an accountant is to 'translate' those activities into a form in which they can be measured, summarized and related to other activities where such relations appear to be significant. 'Significance' raises questions of criteria by which it can be indicated: significance for whom?; in respect of what?; for what purpose or objective? Some aspects of this are discussed in later chapters. Among the basic, traditional activities of accountants are recording, reporting, interpreting and validating.

Recording

Recording includes not only making durable records in books or on cards or papyri (as the ancient Egyptians did) or clay tablets (as in ancient Sumeria) or in computer files, but also the designing, installation and implementation of systems appropriate to the purpose for which the recording is required. It is, in a sense, the initial and pervasive activity in accounting. However, before a record can be made, a decision is necessary on what is to be recorded. The decision is based on observing activities of people other than the recorder according to certain selected criteria. Since none of the subsequent functions could be exercised without records, the recording process and the resulting records warrant some attention.

As we contemplate the enormous, almost endless, variety of the kind of things that form the subject-matter for accounting records, some characteristics which may suggest themselves have to be discarded.

Since we are dealing with the making of records, is writing a necessary characteristic? If we think of writing in a narrow sense only, the answer must be 'No', for accounting records include not only handwritten or typewritten entries in bound or loose-leaf books or on cards, but also such various exhibits as incisions on clay tablets, as in ancient Sumeria, notches on pieces of wood, as in medieval tally sticks, holes in paper tape, and punched cards, magnetic ink characters and encoding on magnetic tape or disk as in computer hardware. It has even been suggested that knots in pieces of cord, as in the Ryukyu Islands, constituted accounting records (Jacobsen 1988: Paper 213).

The position is somewhat different if we broaden our notion to 'writing or equivalent'. The question then arises as to whether the record is to be capable of being permanent; not whether it is in fact permanent but whether it could be permanent, that is, whether or not it is naturally destructible before its intended purpose has been served. Is an ephemeral record – writing on a scrap of paper – any less an accounting record because it does not happen to be preserved for subsequent perusal?

If we consider that an accounting record does not necessarily have to be permanent, why not go further and say that such a record may be mentally contemplated and not put on visual or other reproducible record at all and still be an accounting record? In a traditional accounting system, one can dictate, say, a journal entry, and one can hear it, without any means of transmission other than the sound waves between speaker and listener; one could inwardly visualize a whole ledger, if one wished, without putting pen to paper or finger to keyboard. Of course, it is normally much easier to think in terms of accounting records if one has actually seen one or an illustration of one in a written, typed, encoded, notched or incised form, but the existence of these forms of record does not preclude the possibility of either some other visual form or a non-visual form.

This suggests that permanence (relative permanence at best) or even the potentiality of permanence is not an essential characteristic of an accounting record. It may be not only ephemeral but incorporeal or intangible in the sense that it has no physical embodiment in transferable material substance. This is what concepts are made of.

However, if an accounting record is to be subsequently useful it must be capable of enduring for some time, and, in particular, long enough to satisfy the requirements of a piece of evidence. It has to be recognizable by somebody other than its maker. At the same time we must acknowledge that, when we look for evidence of patterns or even of the existence of accounting records, we must (in our present stage of non-telepathic human development) consider only those records which have survived and do survive because they have been embodied in some form of visible or reproduceable corporeality.

Accounting records are generally thought of as having monetary attributes. But such monetary attributions are not essential to all accounting records. It is quite common, for instance, to have inventory records in terms of 'physical' units or quantities for exercising control over the stocks and movement of commodities. Whatever the underlying objective of keeping such records, the quantitative terms in which they are kept are obviously not monetary ones. Similarly, a fixed asset register may have the major and most significant proportion of its information in descriptive rather than monetary terms, while a company's register of share issues and transfers of shares between its members is not maintained in monetary terms. It may be argued that these non-monetary records are not accounting records in any proper sense, but records of management. It is submitted, however, that whatever else they may be in addition, they are in fact accounting records if for no other reason than that they record matters which accountants must take cognizance of if they are to carry out their functions effectively and that their installation and proper maintenance often constitute part of an accountant's responsibility.

An example of a non-financial accounting function is given in Captain Scott's account of his first voyage to the Antarctic:

> A ship's steward is a specially important individual in an exploring vessel; he has to keep the most exact account of the stores that are expended, and of those that remain; he has to see that provisions are properly examined and properly served out, and that everything is stowed below in such a manner that it is forthcoming when required. I had difficulty in filling this post . . . but eventually I decided to give it to C. R. Ford . . . He soon mastered every detail of our stores, and kept his books with such accuracy that I could rely implicitly on his statements. This . . . was no small relief when it was impossible to hold a survey of the stores which remained on board.
>
> (Scott 1905, I: 55)

Scott was literally commander not only of the expedition but also of the resources or stores; and Ford was literally involved in a stewardship function as the keeper of records and preparer of statements.

In essence, an accounting record is composed of symbols which represent some perceived things or services. The representation may be pictographic, or verbal, but in either case it has to be communally accepted as 'standing for' (that is, expressing a reference to) the same particular commodity or kind of service each time it is used; in other words, stable symbols are necessary.

A further feature is that the record is usually expressed in some quantitative terms; its subject-matter is quantifiable, whether in monetary terms or in some non-monetary measure. The quantity may be indicated on the basis of a one-to-one matching of individual items with individual symbols, e.g., five units of a particular commodity represented in the record by five symbols of the same shape, such as crosses or circles, or by using the abstract concept of number, where the symbol 'four', '4' or 'iv' is used with any other symbol which represents the particular kind of 'factual' or 'actual' or perceived thing which is its referent.

This may be thought to constitute a wide interpretation of accounting recording, and to impinge upon the area of statistics, and perhaps this is true; but if the boundaries of two disciplines or areas of activity overlap this need not be any reason for alarm or even dispute, so long as the people involved are not imbued with an overwhelming jealousy in respect of a tightly drawn professional domain. It is better, surely, to have a 'two-men's land' in which work can be done cooperatively than a no-man's land in which no work at all is possible and over which opponents fire bullets of disapproval at each other. There are, however, certain other characteristics of accounting records which normally distinguish them from purely statistical records; the relationship and distinction between accounting and statistics have long been known. (Cf. Rorem 1927)

What, then, apart from these features, are the essential characteristics of accounting records, that is, those which are common to all accounting records and without which an accounting record could not be said to exist?

It is submitted that accounting records are expressions of occurrences – things that happen – which can be quantified in such a way that they can be related to other occurrences. The words 'events' and 'transactions' have also been suggested to describe this basic subject-matter of accounting records. 'Transactions' has a somewhat narrower connotation than is desired, since it implies the existence of two parties between whom or in relation to both of whom an activity takes place and is recorded accordingly. 'Events' could be satisfactory except that it has an element of ambiguity, and is therefore open to some misinterpretation in that, in a historical sense, it may be taken to comprise a number of separate occurrences; thus, in, say, a work of history a battle is often stated to be an event, whereas, from the point of view with which we are presently concerned, it would be composed of a considerable number of occurrences, each distinct from the others but related to them in some overall pattern. It is upon each of these occurrences that primary attention is directed in accounting activity.

Another point is that some of these occurrences may be 'mental', so to speak, rather than 'physical' happenings. Thus, the allocation of cost of, say, a piece of operating equipment to particular jobs or processes or periods represents somebody's personal assessment, somebody's judgement, rather than an accurate observation of a 'physical' happening, but is no less an accounting occurrence to be recorded than the acquisition of the equipment in the first place, or the sale of finished, manufactured products. One writer has suggested that the allocation of cost is one of '. . . the kinds of things associated with conventional accounting that would not be reported under a pure events approach' (Cushing 1989b: 32–3). However, we suggest that at least some of Cushing's so-called 'non-events' are, indeed, purposive occurrences for accounting procedures (see Chapter 8).

Accountants, then, are dealing with occurrences when they are carrying out their recording function, and the occurrences they record are usually expressible in quantitative terms. These quantitative terms need to be specific if discrete occurrences are to be sensibly related to each other in an accounting record. At least two things are implied in this. First, the record made by an accountant is more than a recital of a happening; it is more than just a chronicle or bald factual statement that such and such a thing happened. Many statements of past occurrences that would be material for the making of a historical record would not be material for an accounting record. At the same time, any accounting record that has been preserved may become material for the narration or interpretation of history. Secondly, statements of occurrences in terms of more or less than something else, or in any other comparative terms, are not traditional accounting records because of their lack of specific quantitative expression. Whatever the quantitative measure may be, whether it be pounds, dollars, francs, kilogrammes, ounces, metres, bushels, acres, or cowrie shells or whales' teeth, the numbers involved in any occurrence ordinarily have to be specific if it is to be treated as the basis for an accounting record.

Thus, when we say that we are going to consider what accountants do, and then go on to say that one of the things they do is carry out the function of recording, we are, in effect, asserting a piece of prior knowledge, namely, that accountants record, and, further, we are averring that this function is significant, that is, valuable for our purpose. The knowledge may be our interpretation of our observations. Or it may be part of a definition, and the judgement of value may be part of our experience or insight. This point is raised only to suggest that in any 'objective', scientific, unbiased set of observations there is a subjective, judgemental component. Admitting this does not deny or confirm the possible accuracy or fairness of the task undertaken: it simply recognizes an inescapable human factor – inescapable, at least, until research can be initiated and undertaken by robots.

This discussion suggests that the term 'accounting record' may apply to a wide range of records, in which symbols are used to represent activities of people, and relationships between people arising from such activities. The resulting record may vary from a mere memento to a sophisticated, co-ordinated system of interrelated symbols.

One significant aspect of recording that is apt to be overlooked is that, while records exhibit what has occurred, they are, when made consciously and deliberately, intended for some use in the future. It is possible, however, that uses other than those envisaged may emerge in that future. Such unforeseen uses constitute much of the stuff of interpretation, and, so, of history.

A word of caution is desirable. What accountants do is not necessarily what the observer, or anybody else, may consider they ought to be doing. What accountants ought to be doing is a separate question altogether and is based on an avowal or acceptance of criteria of conduct derived from somebody's norms of activity; it is, in this sense, an ethical question, one of mores. It is an important matter, but one that should not be confused with that of observing what they do in fact. Some aspects of it are discussed in later chapters. Hence, observations of the functions of accountants and the way in which they carry them out should not be taken to commit the observer to a necessary acceptance of the virtue or sanctity of either those functions or the mode of their performance. The primary task of an accountant is to observe, and as an observer an accountant has no judgements to express. If and when an accountant does express any views about goodness or badness, virtue or vice, integrity or peccability, it is as a moralist – perhaps a standard-bearer for a cause – and such views, as suggested, are more than observations of fact: they are based on a personal scheme of values.

Despite the logical, yet speculative, possibility of functions anterior to the making of records, the evidence for the actual making of a record lies in the record itself. It is only from available records that inference can be made about the physical and intellectual process involved.

Observing and selecting

While making an accounting record, in the sense of using symbols on a non-ephemeral material to ensure subsequent communication, may well appear to be the essential initiating function of accountants, the determining of what is to be put into such a record is functionally anterior to the making of the record itself.

It is carried out as an intellectual activity in which selection is made, out of the multifarious occurrences taking place continuously all around us, of those which, according to certain criteria, are deemed to be appropriate for subsequent accounting procedures.

It seems that the selection criteria include a recognition of the creation or variation of a relationship between two or more human beings ('units of experience' as discussed in Chapter 6), identification of the parties to the relationship, and, usually, its measurement in terms of some mutually acceptable unit.

The earliest known records to which these criteria apply appear to be those of people of the Middle East of some 10,000 years ago (cf. D. Schmandt-Besserat, 1992). There may have been earlier ones on less durable materials than the clay which has preserved these records for us. But if they do not now exist we cannot use them except in imagination and speculation. It seems reasonable to suggest that the intention behind making any record is that it shall last at least as long as the relationship which it records.

Several aspects of the criteria are discussed later (Chapters 8 and 9, for instance); we point out here that the limit, so to speak, for any of these criteria is the social character of the relationship under consideration. Such relationship is, ultimately, always one between human beings, whether direct, as in a trading transaction, or indirect, as between a human being and the community to which he or she belongs, such as a right to exercise a dog in public park land, or a right to vote.

Whether a relationship is an accounting one often depends on whether it is measurable in an accepted and recognized unit, but whether this measurability is in the sense of according specific numbers in measuring, is open to examination and exploration.

Various features of this underlying function of selecting are considered at several appropriate points in later chapters. The topic is introduced at this stage to recognize its primacy and pervasiveness as a function in accounting procedures.

Reporting

The function of reporting includes a matching of recorded data in an arrangement perceived or presumed to be relevant to the recipient of the report. Classification of data is usually carried out as part of the recording process, and some reports are virtually copies or versions of or extractions from part of the accounting records themselves. However, data can be classified in various ways, and reports may be required to exhibit relationships which are not readily apparent in the classified records.

Accounting reports may vary from an *ad hoc* statement of, say, a day's output of a specific manufacturing process or the quantity of energy used by a particular instrument, to the annual report to shareholders of a multinational enterprise or the budget of the most sophisticated social or political organization.

Reporting is, essentially, a purposive process of communication in which the preparer of a report is deemed to be different and separate from the recipient.

Any user of an accounting report usually has some expressible purpose in view; if not, it is difficult to justify its production. Even if it were merely for intellectual enjoyment, there would have to be certain criteria for a report to be satisfactory according to the user's standard of intellectual enjoyment. This would also apply if the object were aesthetic satisfaction, although the criteria for this requirement are, admittedly, beyond our present means to formulate; but even if this were the objective, the criteria would have to satisfy the user, not the preparer.

From the user's point of view, there is, surely, no such thing as a 'general purpose financial report'. The idea of general purpose in this context appears to be an expression of relative inadequacy on the part of the preparer to cope with the requirements of a multitude of particular purposes of a variety of users. It is, so to speak, a refuge of weakness, not of strength; necessary and unavoidable at present, perhaps, but no less a refuge. It would be well if those who develop standards of reporting would recognize this and apply their talents accordingly. It might well affect the product they wish to make acceptable.

It is worth noting that, in general, accounting reports are derived from data in accounting records, and the trail of preparation and arrangement of information in these records is usually clear and readily traceable. Complicating or obscuring the trail almost invariably suggests either incompetence or an intention to mislead.

Reporting covers the responsibility for design and preparation of reports, whether regular or *ad hoc*, in order to inform people involved in making further decisions about the types and scope of the activities being reported upon. The recipients may include people who entrust resources to others for management use or disposal, people who, in a governmental capacity, direct, supervise or modify the activities of others, and, at times, people who are making surveys or seeking information for specific or general social purposes. To a great extent, such reports are based on and derived from accounting records, but some may be derived, at least in part, from other sources. Oral reports are sometimes made, but these usually carry little or no evidential credence; if a report is to have value as evidence, it needs to be in some lasting visible or orally reproducible form.

Interpreting

It seems only natural that accountants should be widely regarded as competent interpreters of reports prepared and presented as the technical and vocational output of other accountants. For instance, providers (lenders and investors) of resources to others to deploy usually require reports showing how the deployers have used the resources entrusted to them. Both lending and investing are based on trust.

In this respect, the most prominent area to which accountants have paid attention has been that of periodical financial statements of corporations, companies and other organizations which are presented to the providers of resources, such as shareholders, members and individual or institutional lenders. These statements form an important and integral part of the reports which the executive officers of an organization provide as a customary and legal requirement.

A considerable number of numerical relationships (or 'ratios') have been developed between particular 'items' in the conventional financial statements (such as the balance sheet and profit and loss or income statement) which are often considered to throw light on financial position and prospects of socially recognized institutions and organizations. These have doubtless proved valuable in innumerable cases as clear forewarning of likely financial difficulties unless action is taken to avoid them. Nevertheless, such measurements are based on information in the financial statements, and, in the absence of any other reliable evidence, the validity of such interpretation depends on the reliability of the figures provided in the reports as prepared from the records.

Some aspects of this problem are discussed in later chapters. At this point it should be noted that, however valid an analysis of past performance may be, the future is always unknown, even though it can be imagined. Further, the processes of reporting and interpreting are based upon the trust placed by the recipient of the report on the honesty and competence of the preparer and presenter and their recognition of the use to which the reports are to be put.

Validating

Validating or verifying information contained in accounting reports is a widely recognized function of professional accountants, who are presumed to have the required expertise to form a reliable judgement on the validity and veracity of the information transmitted in accounting reports as instruments of communication. The most prominent public accountancy firms have large auditing staff divisions, and the duties and responsibilities of auditors have attracted social and legal attention for at least a century. The practice of the function itself, however, goes back many centuries.

Without becoming engrossed in the details of this important function or its development, a few observations seem apposite here. Consideration of this function reveals a paradox, perhaps two paradoxes. An accounting record is made in the first place because of a recognition or supposition of human frailty: it is made because evidence may later be required of something that was agreed upon, or was intended at the time it was made. The frailty envisaged may be one of memory or one of lack of resistance to temptation (often manifested as dishonesty). The validating function is carried out in order to test the competence and honesty of people who are entrusted by others to carry out activities. Thus, while they are entrusted with responsibilities, their performance can only be monitored by a process of checking to observe whether the presumed competence and honesty have in fact been exercised. In short, validating (which includes auditing) is based on the paradox that, in essence, one does not fully trust the people that one trusts.

Further, in seeking to validate accounting reports and records, the monitor (or investigator or auditor) looks for evidence which may, in fact, invalidate them. The search is for error, either intentional (which suggests dishonest or fraudulent intent) or unintentional (which may suggest human incompetence or weakness in a recording system).

Hence, this function is often a difficult and delicate one, and, at the same time, an exceedingly important one, since it is necessary to apply it to all but the very least significant of social activities in our current culture.

These functions, which are characteristic of the activities of accountants, can also be looked at as those of instituting and implementing systems for producing adequate and relevant information. As an area of study, accounting is often referred to as being concerned with information systems.

Accountants are generally regarded as experts in financial matters, probably because the data that their information systems handle, both as input and output, are traditionally expressed predominantly in monetary terms. Accountants are often called on to advise on the investment of financial resources. Members of other professions, such as bankers and stockbrokers, also proffer financial advice, and these people usually have studied accounting and are well acquainted with it.

Accountants are also called upon to act as trustees of estates, executors of wills, liquidators or receivers of companies or similar social units or enterprises. The performance of this kind of function requires sound knowledge of the relevant law and expertise in the management of a variety of resources in order to deploy them to the best advantage of the respective beneficiaries.

If we consider the function of financing to be that of obtaining (or arranging to obtain) and deploying monetary resources (or their equivalent), then the functions of financing and accounting are so closely interrelated that it is scarcely possible to conceive of the one being carried out by anybody without a substantial knowledge and appreciation of the other. Perhaps accounting is the wider, in that it is not or should not necessarily be confined by definition to financial resources, although these are what they are most acquainted with, at least so far in the history of its development. The essential point to recognize at the moment, however, is simply that accountants are presently presumed to be knowledgeable in financial matters and are frequently consulted as experts in them.

To understand what accountants do requires an examination of the concepts which underlie their activities, whether they recognize them consciously or not. For what they do constitutes a process of converting concepts into activities. We often have to infer the concepts from the activities or from the results of activities, for example, from the nature and content of the records made, or the reports prepared, by accountants or their subordinates. To some extent the concepts are enunciated in the literature of accounting or the law of the land, and these affect and largely control the attitudes and, hence, the activities of accountants.

A matter of technology

In broad terms, the foregoing discussion portrays the traditional activities or functions of accountants, with which most accountants would be familiar and, probably, in agreement. In one respect, however, another possibility has been hinted at, namely, that non-financial and even non-quantifiable data may be appropriate for the attention of accountants. Recent developments in information technology strengthen this possibility to warrant close attention from accountants in broadening their vocational activities.

In recent decades many accountants, both practitioners and researchers, have advocated changes to accounting in response to changes in technology. Geerts and McCarthy (1991) have pointed to a distinction, made by McCrae in 1976, between 'accounting technology' and 'accounting systems'. McCrae (1976) wrote:

> The technology of accounting is concerned with the physical artifacts which are employed to process accounting data. These artifacts range all the way from quill pens to remote controlled computers. Accounting systems are concerned with the classifying and structuring of accounting data . . . It is possible to change the accounting technology without changing the accounting system and vice-versa.

and

> The clear distinction between system and technology is important since
> many accountants suffer from the delusion that because they have
> changed the accounting technology they must automatically have
> effected dramatic changes in the accountancy system. This is not so.
>
> (p. 39)

Geerts and McCarthy (1991) concluded that: 'The major alterations called
for by McCrae have, by and large, not yet materialized in the modern EDP
environment' (p. 160).

Elliott (1991), addressing the issue of 'The Subject Matter of Accounting'
states: 'Strategic use of information technology has caused colossal
changes in business, but we accountants have not reacted to it yet' (p. 3),
and '. . . our industrial-era accounting paradigm is actually holding us
back' (p. 2).

These are but a few examples of concerns expressed by academics and
practitioners alike about the need to reconsider 'accounting'. For one
reason or another, accounting systems (to use McCrae's term) appear to
have changed very little in response to substantial advances in the use of
computers over the last forty years. What lies behind this term 'accounting
system'? Accounting systems have been implemented on computers since
the late 1950s – the way data are put in has changed, the processing is
faster, and the reports that are produced may appear a little different in
form (if not in content). However, it is a matter of observation that
accountants still use systems based on the double-entry system. In fact,
most, if not all, of the accounting systems implemented on computers are
'general ledger based'. The ledger account may have changed form – some
systems produce a T account, others a version of a ledger account in a
different format – but the underlying concept appears to be the same as
that used by accountants and others long before the advent of computers.

Throughout this work we are interested in the disquiet being expressed
about the appropriateness of accounting operations in a modern computerized environment. While we do not deal directly with technology, we
are concerned about changes which are likely to have (and to have had) an
impact on accounting. Over several centuries successions of accountants
have developed a systematic infrastructure for the processing of information. They are, broadly speaking, acquainted with the available technology
and processes for carrying out their functions and meeting their functional
responsibilities, and are capable of devising, installing and conducting or
supervising appropriate procedures for particular circumstances. Up to
date their operation of this infrastructure has been restricted by their
acceptance of limitations in their conceptual outlook, so that the kind of
information that they have permitted themselves to handle in or through
this familiar infrastructure has itself been restricted by adherence to this
conceptual outlook.

We suggest that accountants should now become prepared to broaden their attitude and approach from a monetary one to broach wider issues, that is, they need to reformulate some of the basic questions they have been asking. Broadly, they should start to ask what kind of information is needed for a serious approach to the problems facing man as a social animal and all men (and women and children, too) as members of a global community. On the basis of answers to the kind of information required, they should be able and prepared to set up, install and operate the systems required to provide the information and to convey its meaning, relevance and importance to those who will use it. They are in a good position to build on the infrastructure with which they are familiar and bring within their data-processing activities and capabilities any non-monetary information essential to the making of socially and culturally desirable decisions; thus, they have an opportunity to devise a means of getting wise decisions for mankind, not merely profitable ones on a relatively short-sighted interpretation of profit or loss. Perhaps they can become the wise people who enable good decisions to be made for the society of which they are a vital contributing part. To get to this position, however, they have to see things as they actually are, not hampered by intellectual blinkers which blot out anything that may seem, to the orthodox, to be peripheral influences. They must not accept the restriction that a social factor is none of their concern or responsibility, or that, in expressing a professional view, they cannot go beyond the boundaries defined by an entrenched and currently sanctified criterion.

The accounting community

In broad terms, the accounting community comprises several sub-groups of functionaries:

1 Practitioners
   (a) Employees and 'staff', who act, by whatever description, and with whatever range of technology, as preparers of records and reports, interpreters, and/or validators of communication of accounting information. These are the people who have direct contact with non-accountants and carry (or endure) the cultural image of accountants within the society to which they belong.
   They may comprise employees within an organized group operating as an extractive, manufacturing, distributive, financial, fiscal, consult-ative, administrative, governmental, educational, religious, charitable or other recognizable unit of socio-economic activity, ranging from a sole trader to a national or multi-national organization.
   (b) Public accountants who offer professional accounting services to those who desire them or are obliged by regulation (e.g. public com-panies or municipal and other statutory bodies in relation to inde-pendent auditing) for a fee determined by contract between the parties or by regulation. The kind of activities provided by this sub-group has

over a long period been varied with considerable broadening in recent decades; as clients have expanded beyond local and national boundaries, the activities in some of the larger public accounting firms have also developed internationally.

2 Administrators and professional monitors

Virtually all these practitioners are or aspire to become members of a professional group which assures and safeguards the capacity of recognized members to have attained a level of acceptable performance. The activities of these organizations – institutes, societies, associations (or equivalent) – of accountants are usually steered on an honorary basis by well-respected members of the particular professional body, but administered in detail by salaried staff often specialized for their respective tasks. The people engaged in conducting the affairs of these bodies undertake responsibilities for monitoring the activities of their members in accordance with a code of ethics and standard of professional performance accepted by members on admission. Through such professional bodies, members are provided with a social recognition of professionalism in their customary functions and usually with provision of activities and resources designed to help them in their professional development.

3 Educators

Since admission to membership of a recognized professional body depends upon an expertise in and knowledge of accounting procedures and related disciplines, each professional body has minimum educational qualifications for admission to membership. During the twentieth century there has been a trend from specialist schools and tutors for specific examinations for each professional body towards the provision of courses in accounting and related studies at a tertiary college and university level for preparation, at least in considerable part, for admission to professional accounting bodies. Details vary, but in several countries now a university degree including a substantial acquaintance with the breadth and depth of accounting procedures and knowledge is a preliminary requirement for professional recognition. For some professional bodies, further experience in and acquaintance with particular aspects, such as a 'professional year' based on active experience in accounting practice, is required before admission. Some professional bodies require evidence of some continuing, further educational endeavour by members to maintain active membership. In some countries, some professional bodies exist as specialist groups, such as management accountants, chief financial officers, financial analysts and the like, which cater for additional requirements of specialist groups.

4 Legislators and regulators

Several aspects of accounting practice have long been subject to statutory requirements. For instance, in Britain and other countries influenced by the British legal system, the minimum amount of information to be disclosed in periodical reporting by directors of companies registered under company legislation has been prescribed since the companies acts of the mid-nineteenth century; these have applied, most notably, to the form and content of the balance sheet and to the auditing opinion relating to it and other financial statements presented publicly to shareholders.

During the mid and latter part of the twentieth century, much of the responsibility for enunciating, broadening and deepening these require-ments shifted from politicians and governmental bureaucrats to people from within the accounting profession. This development has varied somewhat from country to country, but in broad terms, many of the nations which recognize the profession and practice of accountancy have also a body of people who devote much of their time and energy towards establishing, or adapting from other countries, standards of reporting by directors of public companies to their shareholders, with the backing of legal enforcement. In some countries this influence has extended to cover some governmental, as well as private sector, activities. Further, in several respects international standards have been devised and adopted for application internationally.

The kind of activity required for this type of endeavour involves a strong ethical attitude and a desire to eliminate wrong-doing. This is often accompanied by a tendency towards adopting an ideal of absolute good which is difficult to apply and, even, to identify in a community of people with interacting and sometimes conflicting interests.

Appendix to Chapter 2[1]

On the Dangers of Definition

In embarking upon an enquiry into the scope of accounting, it might, at first sight, seem logical that the first step should be to define accounting. To be sure, this would provide a neat and tidy approach, and is a suitable method of opening for a text-book in which the exposition comprises a development of the implications of the definition(s) initially propounded. Indeed, quite a large number of text-books in accounting, as in other fields of study, do proceed along these lines.

However, there are several reasons for avoiding this procedure in the present case. In the first place, the present work is not and does not purport to be a text-book in accounting procedures; it is not a book in which rules are laid down for students (or practitioners) to follow; it does not purport to be a book of authority in the sense that the author is attempting to teach something categorically to the reader. Rather is it a joint adventure to be undertaken by both writer and reader, in which the

---

1   Reprinted from Goldberg, 1965, pp. 24 ff.

former can only point out paths along which he thinks the reader may wish to travel; paths which may lead anywhere – or nowhere. It is intended to explore some of these paths to some extent, but it is not pretended that even those paths have been followed as far as they will go, nor that alternative routes do not exist. It is hoped, therefore, that the dogmatism which often results from initial formal definition may be avoided.

Secondly, if a definition is to be relevant at all, it delimits the scope of discussion, whether it is submitted for that purpose or not. To put it metaphorically, a definition erects a wall around a field of discussion and, if one does not agree with the definition presented, one often finds oneself outside the wall, shut out from at least a large part of the discussion; alternatively, if one agrees in part with the definition, one may find oneself shut inside the wall with no means of getting out or even of obtaining a view of the country which lies outside. As John Stuart Mill pointed out long ago, "[i]t is not to be expected that there should be agreement about the definition of anything, until there is agreement about the thing itself." (Mill, 1884, p. 1) Let us first strive to reach agreement about the thing – in this case, accounting – and the definition may well follow.

Thirdly, there appears to be some doubt among logicians themselves as to what comprises a definition and what its purpose is. For instance, Susan Stebbing discusses such various types of definition as extensive definition, ostensive definition, biverbal definition, definition *per genus et differentiam*, analytical definition of an expression, definite description and genetic definition; some of these, although recognized by some logicians, are, in her opinion, inadmissible as valid definitions (Stebbing, 1946, p. 422 ff.). And on the question whether we define expressions or what the expressions stand for, she contends that the view of many logicians that it is the latter that is defined is mistaken; she agrees with Mill that "all definitions are of names, and of names only." (Mill, 1886, p. 93) Mill further points out that "in some definitions, it is clearly apparent that nothing is intended except to explain the meaning of the word, while in others, besides explaining the meaning of the word, it is intended to be implied that there exists a thing corresponding to the word. . . . There are, therefore, expressions commonly passing for definitions which include in themselves more than the mere explanation of the meaning of a term.' (Mill, 1884: 93–94) And although Stebbing is in agreement with this position in her discussion on definition, she begins her chapter on the theory of definition by stating that

> definition is an aid to clear thinking and, therefore, to the communic-
> ation of thought . . . We can define words only when we understand
> them. We understand a word when we know what it is to which a word
> refers or when we can use it significantly in combination with other
> words. (Stebbing, 1946, p.421)

However, if we understand what a word refers to, does not this reference introduce the "thing," that is, an object or concept or person outside the word itself? Is not the important matter that of communicating thoughts about things rather than about words?

Further, we are concerned with the question: What is accounting?, and a definition at this stage would of necessity presuppose the course and result of subsequent discussion. Admittedly, of course, we must have some general notion of what the principal term – accounting – relates to; one would not expect to find, in a work on accounting, a discourse on ballroom dancing or the care of tropical fish, although, it seems only fair to warn the reader, our enquiry may indeed take us into some strange and unwonted territory (that is, strange for accountants). Some idea of the field of accounting procedures is presumed, however, and it is hoped that there are few reasonably educated adults in our society who have not some such idea – even if many people at present do think of accounting merely as the distasteful task of adding up columns of refractory figures in nauseating books and documents.

Another reason for avoiding a definition at this stage is that accounting may be defined differently by various persons according to the particular point of view. We shall have to consider some of these points of view because the point of view colours the form and direction of discussion, but an initial definition from a particular point of view would necessarily ignore or at least underemphasize other points of view which may, in fact, be just as legitimate as the point of view adopted.

The process of definition (especially definition *per genus et differentiam*) is largely a part of the process of classification, and when a definition is offered the basis of classification is often presupposed. Frequently, given a certain basis of classification, the definition of terms within that classification must conform to a pattern in accordance with it; with a different basis of classification, a different definition is almost inevitable.

All this does not mean that it is undesirable to define accounting at any stage or for any purpose. Nor does it mean that none of the terms used in the following discussion is to be defined. It means, simply, that definitions will be introduced only as considered necessary to enable the inquiry to go on, and that since 'the definition we set out with is seldom that which a more extensive knowledge of the subject shows to be the most appropriate' (Mill, 1886, p. 1) it is more fitting to postpone postulating any short definition of accounting at least until a later stage of the inquiry if, indeed, it is desirable at all. After all, the really important thing in any discussion is that all parties should make their arguments clear to the other (or others) so that each may be able to interpret them correctly and exercise appropriate judgement as to their validity; if a formal definition is necessary for this purpose, it should be used; if the objective can be reached without formal definition, then its use may be not merely unnecessary, but, in some cases, unduly restrictive.

3 Approaches

'O Star-eyed Science! hast thou wandered there,
To waft us home the message of despair?'
(Thomas Campbell, *Pleasures of Hope*, Part II, line 325)

Various approaches possible

In clarifying our thoughts about accounting, two different modes of approach may be helpful: what we might call a 'history' approach and a 'natural science' approach. Without professing or claiming great expertise in either history or natural science, the expressions are used here simply as labels for propositions and attitudes in looking for useful intellectual instruments to discuss ideas of or for accounting.

The history approach

'History' is at least four different things.

First, history is what happened in the past, that is, the actual occurrences that have taken place. What happens today will be the history of tomorrow.

Can we think fruitfully about accounting by analogy with this view of history? Perhaps a strict or complete analogy does not apply. However, as we have seen, 'accounting' does have multiple meanings and may evoke different responses and interpretations not only for or from different people but also in different contexts.

While accounting is of necessity interpreted as what accountants do, it is also concerned with what people other than accountants do, for what accountants do is to observe, and process their observations of, what other people do (including what they themselves may do in an 'other-than accounting' function). Both the observing and the processing of the observations need examination, for it is in the 'nature' of both of these that the distinctive characteristics of accounting inhere.

In exploring these matters we are also concerned with what accountants think they are doing and whether their practices conform to their ideas, and, further, with what non-accountants think accountants do. In other words, 'accounting' has a social context in which it has to be studied.

If we write down a statement like the following, probably most people would agree that it is an accounting proposition:

Statement of trading activity

Sale of 5 gadgets @ $120.00 each	$600.00
Cost of purchasing 5 gadgets @ $90.00	$450.00
Gross profit on purchase-cum-sale	$150.00

If, as is done by many people every day, such a calculation is made mentally, and not written down, is it any less an accounting proposition? We suggest that it would be an accounting proposition; a written or potentially 'permanent' record is not essential for the existence of some accounting, any more than a historical record, whether it be document, structure, painting, sculpture, artifact, archaeological or even geological remnant or the like, of something that has happened is essential for the *fact* of the happening. In other words, an oral statement that a particular gentleman had bought five gadgets at $90.00 and sold each one for $120.00, resulting in a (gross) increase in his resources of $150.00, would constitute an accounting statement, whether it is preserved in a recorded form or not.

However, unless there is some record, whether of the happening in history or of the thinking in accounting, its occurrence is not supported by any evidence, and thus cannot be directly proved or disproved to the satisfaction of our ordinary human observational and logical attitude. It is possible, nevertheless, that an accounting 'proposition' may sometimes be inferred from evidence of other propositions, just as, in historical investigation, the probable or likely occurrence can sometimes be inferred from available evidence of other occurrences.

Hence, when we say that accounting is necessarily concerned with the making of records, the necessity arises, not in relation to the occurrence or the existence of the record itself, but because of its evidential character and subsequent usefulness. Mental accounting is possible but, if it is purely ephemeral and leaves no trace, its occurrence can only be conjectured and, obviously, cannot be subject to examination, whether scientific or any other – at least not until our telepathic capacities are much more widely developed and accepted than they are at present.

Second, history comprises the records available of what happened. Many things that happened in the past are lost to our knowledge because no records of them were made or have survived; many things that happen today will leave no trace and will be irretrievably lost to tomorrow's historians. We have no way of assessing these lost happenings. Our knowledge of what has happened and our judgement of their significance is basically dependent on the records available for investigation and interpretation.

The evidence of accounting as an activity lies in records of the past. (If we regard 'the present' as a mere instant which continuously and immediately becomes the past, it can be ignored in this context.) Accounting evidence is thus historical evidence and the history may be long past or very recent. It may be of what people did or of what they thought. For instance, an accounting statement may be evidence of a speculative or imaginary calculation; it may be evidence of what somebody thought, but perhaps nobody ever acted upon. It would be an accounting record, the interpretation of which would require some knowledge of the circumstances and context in which it was made, if it were to be identified and classified properly.

Again, a statement such as a budget or a forecast of cash flows in a prospectus is evidence of what somebody at some time past thought about activities and the results of activities of people in the then future. It is no less an accounting record, and no less a historical record derived from the past. To assess it properly would again require knowledge and judgement.

Third, history *is*, for some, the interpretation of the records available, a reconstruction of the story. Perhaps this is what historians do as their primary function, and different historians have, in many instances, inter-preted the same records differently and thereby presented different histories to their respective audiences. This raises the question whether there ever is or can be a definitive set of occurrences which could not be observed differently by different observers. This is a very thorny question to which, in our view, a fully affirmative answer is unlikely. However, it does seem possible that, if observers with different attitudes or from different vantage points agree that certain occurrences took place, the credence in these occurrences is justifiably enhanced, despite likely differences in detail.

Fourth, history is sometimes (and, probably, too often) taken to be what some people think happened, or even what they think should have happened or might have happened according to exercise of judgement, imagination and/or prejudices of the 'historian'. Historians who go beyond simply chronicling occurrences have to exercise judgement, even in the mere selection of occurrences; if perceptive, they will recognize the possibility of some bias and, if honest and truthful, will bring it out into the open for examination rather than push it behind a curtain of ostentatious display of words or even of logic, and, if wise, will recognize the intrusion of imagination and reveal when their interpretation goes beyond the established facts of occurrence. It has also been pointed out that history doesn't make judgements; it is historians who make judgements.

The natural science approach

If we follow, say, the physical scientists and adopt a sub-molecular view that the internal constitution of all things is in atomic or sub-atomic activity, then a little thought suggests that the permanence of things is relative to the scale on which and the point from which it is viewed. A similar relativism arises for the biologist with a cellular and sub-cellular view. An insect or a moth whose life is measured (by humans) in hours might well consider as a permanent feature of its existence a flower which is in full bloom for a few days; for us humans, however, a flower is an ephemeral phenomenon. On the other hand, a sequoia tree, whose life spans several centuries or even a millennium or two, would surely be regarded by most humans as a permanent feature of their lives.

We do not suggest, and much less assert, that any such apparent permanence is illusory, for illusion is something different. Illusion also may well be relative, but this is another matter altogether. Illusion is a matter of error in identifying the nature or characteristics of what is perceived, whereas relative permanence is a matter of difference in measuring the duration of perceptible occurrences. What needs emphasis here is that the very notion of permanence is related to and depends upon a concept of time or duration and some scale of measurement of it.

On this view, physics, for example, becomes a study of activity and change rather than of states or stationary existence; in other terms, a consideration of 'becoming' rather than of 'being'. This does not mean that the 'state' or the 'being' is neglected, but that it is seen as a result of a continuous process and that it is never quite the same from instant to instant; it means, further, that its apparent sameness arises from the kind of observation *we* apply as observers and the terms of measurement *we* use in our observation. Presumably, something similar applies in many other areas of intellectual attention; for instance, in biology (and kindred disciplines) the cells and their substructure are forever changing, and are so changing for any living organism, from conception to beyond death, even to ultimate decay and decomposition and chemical re-composition.

Of course, there is nothing new in suggesting that one's view of permanence is relative. Accountants are familiar, as are many others in the community, with the difference between short-term and long-term expectations, hopes, fears, benefits, policies, strategies, and so on. Further, the notion of 'becoming' is not completely new in the study of accounting. It is now several decades since the view was advanced that the 'income statement' was a more significant report than the balance sheet because it purported to represent an ongoing activity whereas a balance sheet was 'merely' a presentation of a static position or an interruption in the flow of economic or business activity. Also, one often encounters writers who contrast 'stocks' and 'flows' in varying contexts, with a general, if not universal, emphasis on the greater significance of flows.

There may be, however, an even deeper and more pervasive significance of the idea of 'becoming' which is still to be explored in accounting. If we indeed follow in the path of the physicists and biologists we can conceive that everything accountants deal with in their recording function can be expressed as in a stage of becoming. Whatever happens to a debt – whether it is increased or decreased or merely gets older – is an example of becoming; whatever happens to equipment – whether it is used or merely stands unused but affected by time, weather or technological development – is an instance of becoming; monetary resources, inventories, buildings, even land, do not remain completely static. Some forces, natural and/or social, are operating to impose change upon all the things that accountants are required to deal with.

As hinted at in Chapter 2, an important task of an accountant is to recognize this process of change, to measure it by some appropriate criterion, to record the changes that take place and to report such changes from time to time, to ensure that the records and reports are valid and useful and to interpret them to others so that they may serve as instruments of information and communication in a simple or complex environment.

Underneath, or behind, their interpretation of becoming is a notion of some kind of causal influence, the idea that if something occurs there will ensue a particular consequence because of a causal relationship between the occurrence and the consequence. Whether this interpretation is regarded as instinctive (as we humans tend to do when considering the activities of non-human creatures) or deliberate and reasoned (as we tend to do for so many human activities, and in anthropomorphic views of animal behaviour) there is little, if any, behaviour that cannot be seriously observed without being subject to at least attempted causal interpretation. In short, we always seem to be asking 'why?'.

The link between approaches

At first sight, the two approaches may appear to produce two differing and possibly conflicting results. By analogy with history we reach an attitude whereby attention is to be focused on discrete occurrences and an attempt made to link them by discovering a relationship between them. By analogy with, say, physics our attention is to be concentrated on a process of becoming which in itself is continuous and in which the discreteness of 'separate' occurrences is possibly illusory. If a basis for a coherent view of accounting is to be found along these lines, these apparently divergent attitudes need to be reconciled. Accountants are concerned with both occurrences and the process of becoming.

On the one hand, the accounting records themselves are records (documents and accounts) of occurrences, that is, of things that happen, and each occurrence can be and is noted separately from all others; in any given case, accounting records are expressions of discrete but related occurrences. Taking 'account' of an occurrence may, of course, extend beyond what is normally thought of as the subject-matter of 'accounting'. If a piece of equipment is purchased, for example, the 'facts' to be recorded about the purchase may extend beyond, say, the date, purchase price and which accounts to debit and credit. The physical dimensions of the equipment, its provenance, and so on, may be regarded as necessary characteristics to be recorded about the purchase. Accountants may be only one group interested in deciding the pertinent 'facts' about an occurrence.

On the other hand, each asset or each liability or each item of 'equity' investment in terms of which the records are set up, is subject to the process of becoming, that is, of continuous change, whether it has physical existence, such as equipment or buildings, or arises from a social or legal relationship, amounting to rights, such as debtors, bills, loans, and virtually all liabilities.

The influence on assets and liabilities which we have called 'becoming' is an aspect or an effect of both time and occurrences. It may seem obvious and trite to say that time is the connecting link between occurrences, but it may not be strictly true if it is taken to mean that time is the only such link. For instance, there may be simultaneous occurrences which have to be accounted for in a distinctive way, and the link between them is something other than time. This link is closely related to and perhaps identical with intention or deliberateness, although sometimes occurrences arise out of 'accidental' or unforeseen circumstances; even these latter, however, affect the outcome of an intended activity.

This suggests that both time and intention link occurrences. Accountants account for occurrences not merely as happenings at discrete moments in time but also as expressions of intended activities. That is, they are concerned with interpreting occurrences as constituent members of distinguishable episodes or 'ventures' and it is this teleological view, so to speak, of episodes or ventures which is significant in accounting and which distinguishes accounting records from purely chronological statements of events. In other words, specific occurrences make sense only if they can be seen as part of a series which constitutes a venture, and the venture is an expression of becoming. In effect, the discerned occurrences may be part of the becoming, but not necessarily the whole of it. Thus, occurrences are discrete as observable 'facts' which may be recorded separately from each other, but, between related occurrences there is also a connecting tissue of 'becoming' which arises not only from just the passage of time itself but also from a ventural intention behind the occurrences. At the same time, it must be recognized that the ventures with which accountants are concerned have discernible beginnings and eventual ends, even though in some instances the end cannot be determinable in advance at any given time.

This topic of the basic raw materials for the processes of accounting is explored further in Chapter 8. In that discussion we argue that specific occurrences may have more than one natural characteristic, and may be a part or aspect of more than one venture.

Another point is that in making plans, estimates, budgets, forecasts or the like for the future, the kind of thinking most likely to be effective is a projection about the past from a supposed future point of time. Thinking about the future simply as the future without reference to *its* past is mere speculation and imagination. For instance, to say that sales in the next year or in five years' time would be $x is, by itself, close to meaningless. To get meaning, it must surely be related to something else which will have happened in the period between now and that future time. That is, we have to project our thinking forward to a point of time and look back from that point.

This way of looking at things has some interesting implications. It raises the question of making specific the assumptions under which we make our forecasts and plans; for example, one assumption might be that, say, there shall be no variation in import duty, another that there will be a rise in wage rates of so much at such a time, another that no new major competitive product will come on to the market, and so on. It raises the point that past performances should be examined in relation to past forecasts in order to ascertain any unfulfilled assumptions made in the past. Bygones may well be bygones, but history is still likely to be useful.

Thus, it raises the possibility of developing accounting systems to bring within their ambit such assumptions (implicit as well as explicit), and variations in result arising from the non-fulfilment of assumptions, and so to bring to notice circumstances which should be regarded as conditions for future performance. In fact, there are probably infinite circumstances which impinge upon the activities of any person or group of people; and, at any given moment, we cannot determine which of these will prove to be relevant in the future. However, we may be able to assess fairly reasonably those which have proved relevant in the past, even though we can only guess at those which will have proved relevant in a future past.[1] One of the functions of the accountant of the future may well turn out to be the clarifying of assumptions made by planners and decision-makers, together with the follow-up of actual events and testing the subsequent or ultimate validity of those assumptions. This, in effect, ties in with the need to provide feedback in an accounting system and gets very close to cybernetics.

Currently, accountants often use the assumptions prepared by other people, as for example, in formulating budgets. They rely on estimates from engineers, economists, statisticians and other professionals. These assumptions are included in 'financial models' implemented on spreadsheet (or other financial modelling) software. Assumptions about such factors as expected changes in prices of materials and other inputs, expected movements in wages, changes in taxes, and variations in sales forecasts are but a few of the assumptions that accountants currently use in formulating budgets. The changes that may have to be made to such assumptions, and therefore to budget estimates, over a period, as new evidence becomes available, is made relatively painless by the use of current technology, such as spreadsheet software on computers. Likewise, the testing of the validity of the assumptions, and their effects on budget estimates, is also made easier by using the spreadsheet software. It is now relatively easy for accountants not only to undertake 'what if' analysis (e.g. what if the price of materials rises by 5 per cent next quarter) but also to analyse 'what has been', and 'what might have been' if certain actions had been taken or other circumstances had prevailed.

Thus, one problem facing accountants is to devise a system that will incorporate plan and budget amounts, identify and record assumptions in

---

1   Relevance is further discussed in Chapter 12.

an appropriate manner, and produce what we might call 'assumption variances'. For a start, it may be necessary to have this outside the accounting system proper, but, if so, reconciliation should be possible and provided for as a stage in the development of an integrated system.

It should be noted that accountants are already addressing these issues. The advent of financial modelling software has meant that these tasks are now much easier technically than before, and the use of such software opens up possibilities for using the analysis of assumption variances for the preparation of future budgets. The automation of such tasks using available technology should ensure that the results of such analyses are integrated in the accounting records. At the same time, human ingenuity is being applied to increasing the complexity of the world in which more and more people have to live, so that by the time a solution to one problem or one set of problems is available, it has been succeeded by more than one other, which supersede and overshadow it.

Nevertheless, it will be recognized that, when any attempt is made to forecast a future position or outcome, this is just what a scientist sets out to do in the formulation of a hypothesis and the preparation of an experiment or a set of observations. The scientist is predicting the outcome of some specific activity; if the prediction is 'correct', that is, if the future result or outcome accords with the prediction, this evidence supports the likelihood of the hypothesis being reliable. Such reliability is strengthened by replication of the procedure. If the prediction is not correct in this sense, it is likely that the hypothesis will be re-examined and either modified or rejected.

This step of predicting is fundamental to the scientist's work, and there seems to be little difference between it and the kind of thinking we have just been considering in relation to planning and forecasting. One difference, however, is that in a humane society it is rarely possible in financial, economic or social planning to carry out controlled experiments, since the subject-matter is the activity of our fellow human beings, whose personal dignity is basic to the notion of humane-ness.

Some decades ago the philosopher, Bertrand Russell, made the following comments which are apposite to this view:

> What is important to the philosopher in the theory of relativity is the substitution of space-time for space and time. Common sense thinks of the physical world as composed of 'things' which persist through a certain period of time and move in space. Philosophy and physics developed the notion of 'thing' into that of 'material substance,' and thought of material substance as consisting of particles, each very small, and each persisting throughout all time. Einstein substituted events for particles; each event had to each other a relation called 'interval', which could be analysed in various ways into a time-element and a space-element. The choice between these ways was arbitrary, and no one of them was theoretically preferable to any other. Given two events A and B, in different regions, it might happen that according to

one convention they were simultaneous, according to another A was earlier than B, and according to yet another B was earlier than A. No physical facts correspond to these different conventions.

From all this it seems to follow that events, not particles, must be the 'stuff' of physics. What has been thought of as a particle will have to be thought of as a series of events. The series of events that replaces a particle has certain important physical properties, and therefore demands our attention; but it has no more substantiality than any other series of events that we might arbitrarily single out. Thus 'matter' is not part of the ultimate material of the world, but merely a convenient way of collecting events into bundles.

(Russell 1946: 860–1)

We should make it clear at this point that we do not believe that practising accountants, when they carry out their vocational activities, necessarily or usually operate as scientists. On the contrary, they apply their knowledge and their skills to deal with records of occurrences in accordance with rules of procedure laid down by or derived from procedures developed in earlier times or in other circumstances. It may not matter much, however, whether accountants see themselves as acting as scientists or not. Just as any other group of people, accountants can be regarded as a group within a community and their functional activities, so far as they are distinguishable, can be subject to scientific examination by, say, an anthropologist or other qualified social scientist.

An unenlisted approach

One of the features of accountants' performance in the twentieth century has been their conscious and expressed desire for direction from within their profession in the application of procedures to enable them to fulfil their economic responsibilities as specialist members of society.

A search for 'principles' appears to have started in the USA in the 1930s and has gone on, in a more or less metamorphosed state, to the formulation and imposition of international standards, not only for corporations publicly reporting to their investor members but also for government instrumentalities and even departments as well.

In very broad terms, what has been sought has been a basic and universally acceptable set of propositions – 'postulates' (e.g., Paton 1922: Ch. 20), 'principles' (e.g., Sanders *et al.* 1938: 1 ff.), 'axioms' (e.g., Ijiri 1965 and 1967: Chs 3, 4), 'standards' (e.g., Paton and Littleton 1940: Ch. I), 'concepts' (e.g., Paton and Littleton 1940: Ch. II) – from which prescriptions for practice can be derived through an agreed intellectual process. Professional adherence to these prescriptions passed from voluntariness (as with the 'recommendations' of the Institute of Chartered Accountants in England and Wales in their earliest phase) to (more recently) submission as legal requirements with severe penalties for non-adherence (as with the demand for mandatory compliance with its prescriptions by the Australian Accounting Research Foundation).

A prominent characteristic of these latter endeavours has been the zeal and energy applied by proponents of particular prescriptions and their vigorous advocacy, usually unmoved except by powerful lobbying by influential groups for an alternative. The common feature in all these appears to have been the conviction that the proponents of the basic propositions had access to, and were called upon to pronounce, absolute and undeniable truths from which, by a process of argument, with varying degrees of logical support, prescriptions for compulsory adherence could be derived. In this way, under the banner of achieving uniformity between differing situations, that is, in the name of 'consistency', the need for many individual practitioners to rise above the status of mere rule-followers could be avoided.

The prescribing bodies (or individuals, in some instances) took over the responsibilities, but not the incumbent risks, of forming judgements on many controversial accounting problems.

We do not follow this kind of approach in this work, but offer some comments on certain aspects where it appears pertinent to our exposition of ideas.

4   Classification

It is a fundamental principle in logic, that the power of framing classes is unlimited, as long as there is any (even the smallest) difference to found a classification upon. Take any attribute whatever, and if some things have it, and others have not, we may ground on the attribute a division of all things into classes; and we actually do so the moment we create a name which connotes the attribute. The number of possible classes, therefore, is boundless; and there are as many actual classes (either of real or imaginery things) as there are general names, positive and negative together.

(J.S. Mill 1884: 79)

A few points about classification

A little reflection suggests that the process of classifying is well-nigh ubiquitous in the activities of accountants, even though much of it may be done habitually and thus goes virtually unnoticed. A succinct description was provided by Wolf:

Classification is the process of recognizing classes or kinds, each class or kind consisting of members having certain characteristics in common. The members may themselves be classes or they may be individuals. In a complete system of classification the lowest classes (in which only individual members can be distinguished) are subordinated to higher ones, and these again to others still higher until the most inclusive category with which the science in question is concerned is reached.

(Wolf 1937: 777)

It seems reasonable to suppose that before one can get far in classifying, and, perhaps, before one begins to classify, one needs to have a concept of 'class'. Such a concept appears to be a part of the cultural heritage of any human society. The search for appropriate classes begins at an early age in our individual development. Perhaps, when a young child points to a cow and says 'Horsie!', it has in its mind some concept of quadruped, although it does not know the word; when it is corrected, this forms part of its education in the classifying process; gradually it learns to distinguish between various species of quadrupeds, in accordance with the criteria used in the community to which it belongs.

The process of classifying should be recognized as a subjective activity; it is something each one of us does every day, often almost automatically; with continued practice, we come to recognize quickly the characteristics in individual potential or prospective members of a class, which can be tested, by observation or measurement or other acceptable means, for meeting the criteria for inclusion in the class. However, it is not always automatic or quick. For instance, if we have the class of quadrupeds in mind, and, while we might quickly accept such creatures as cats, dogs, cows and horses, we might hesitate about, say, crocodiles or kangaroos (not to mention gorillas or crawling young humans), at least while we give the matter some thought.

The process of classifying consists of identifying one or more characteristics which a number of disparate occurrences or phenomena have in common and arranging the occurrences or phenomena according to such characteristic(s). The resulting classification portrays a complex set of occurrences or phenomena as a collection of smaller groups; each group consists of singular occurrences or phenomena with common characteristics within the group to the exclusion of occurrences or phenomena belonging to other groups or to none of them.

Classification is important in all our learning. The capacity to identify what is good for survival and what is dangerous to it seems to be part of any creature's natural learning equipment. Much of it may be what we humans call instinctive, but we do not know what part of it is, among many species, conscious and deliberate. This identifying of beneficial from dangerous or toxic materials or conditions is an elementary but basic form of what we call classification.

An infant exercises and develops early in life a power of distinguishing between materials or conditions that are comfortable and uncomfortable, desirable and undesirable, and so on. As a child, it is taught to distinguish between different animals, people, physical objects, modes of transport, scenes, and, in general, the several kinds of occurrences and phenomena in the world in which it finds itself and has to live. Thus, although the basic capacity may be instinctive or inherited, the exercise which develops that capacity to a high level of efficacy is a cultural endowment which may also vary between individuals according to their cultural environment. That is, in many, and perhaps in most, of the classifications we make, the bases and modes of distinguishing occurrences and phenomena are taught and learned, rather than observed and discovered or inferred. The requirement for order to be made out of a chaotic environment may be based on a survival attitude, but this is not apparent at the level to which humans have developed the practice of classifying.

Classifying is very much like sorting, and, in the process of sorting a collection of objects, several criteria can usually be applied. To take a few simple, homely instances, a pile of, say, buttons may be sorted according to the criteria of size, colour, material of which they are made, number of holes, and so on; a collection of coins according to country of issue, denomination, material, date of issue, condition, etc.; stamps according to country, date of issue, face value, design or theme, perforation, watermark, condition and the like. As the criteria are successively applied in the sorting process, the classifying becomes more refined, so to speak, and the apparent inchoate nature of the original pile of objects becomes transformed into a number of sets of approximately homogeneous or closely related members of smaller groups, each one of which can be described with some degree of precision.

Suppose that, as accountants, we are given the following expression of an occurrence:

John Doe bought a filing cabinet for $500.

In order to be able to classify the occurrence for recording, a number of questions, which will govern the identifying process, have to be asked.

Who is John Doe? Or, perhaps more precisely, what relationship does John Doe have to our 'client', that is the person or unit whose accounting processes are under consideration?

1   If John Doe is, say, a social acquaintance or a more or less generally known figure who has no relevant relationships with the person or unit concerned, no further questions need be asked and no accounting relationship arises. The statement is merely a piece of social or trivial gossip.
2   If he becomes the owner of the filing cabinet by acquiring it from our client, the occurrence is a sale, and he becomes a debtor, but we have to ask further:
3   Was the filing cabinet part of our client's merchandise, or part of unwanted equipment? That is, is it a sale by our client of trading merchandise or of equipment that has been retired from service?
4   Was the transaction for immediate or deferred settlement? If the former, it would be recorded as a cash sale; if the latter, John Doe's obligation to settle his debt would be formally recorded, that is, John Doe would be a debtor.

If John Doe is, in fact, our 'client' or a manager or representative acting on behalf of our client, we know who he is (that is, the answer to the initial question is, again, not merely a piece of social or trivial gossip, but involves an accountable relationship), and some other questions arise: as he becomes the owner, the occurrence is a purchase, and we have to ask further:

5   What are the conditions of purchase? If by immediate payment, the occurrence will involve a payment of cash; if payment is deferred he will need to acknowledge the seller as a creditor to whom he owes a

debt; if other conditions attach, as, for example, in an instalment purchase, appropriate treatment needs to be applied.

6   Was the filing cabinet for private use? If so, the occurrence should be treated as a charge to proprietor's drawings. If it was for commercial reasons, we have to ask:

7   Does John Doe deal in filing cabinets or does he need it as part of the office equipment? If the former, the occurrence is a trading occurrence, to be treated as a purchase of merchandise; if the latter, it is the acquisition of a long-term piece of equipment.

The resultant classification of the occurrence for accounting purposes reflects the raising of all these questions and their being answered (presumably) honestly and accurately.

With a little practice, classifying the vast majority of occurrences can become habitual and speedy, but there is one point that should not be overlooked, namely, that giving something a name or putting it into a class does not explain it or affect its character. Naming it and classifying it merely reflect one of our own characteristics – that of wanting to bring like things together in specific concordant organizational contexts in order to help us in likely or possible future activities. Thus the classification of John Doe as a debtor or creditor indicates a future activity of receipt or payment of resources; the classification of the filing cabinet as merchandise or longer-term equipment foreshadows either a sale in a relatively near future in the ordinary course of events or use as part of office furniture over a relatively longer period. In each case the notions of relationship and future activity are the significant concepts. In this way classification aids interpretation of a complex and, often, apparently chaotic world outside each one of us. But the very notions of both order and chaos lie within our own minds; they describe the way we see things from time to time and in particular sets of circumstances.

Nowadays classification is usually discussed in accounting literature, and practised in the workplace, in terms of the sorting of items for ledger or equivalent recording and/or the preparation of accounting reports. Such classification in the accounting process is imposed, so to speak, by a pre-designed chart of accounts, whether consciously and deliberately formulated in detail or not. The classification used is purposively based in accordance with the kind of reporting envisaged as an end-product.

However, this was not always so. Before the days of charts of accounts as we now know them, the classification of, for instance, ledger accounts was not necessarily report-driven; it was common to find bound ledgers with alphabetical indexes in which the account titles were listed together with the pertinent 'folio' or page numbers. The accounts were set up in the order in which they first occurred in journal (or equivalent) entries, and often, since the extent to which they would subsequently be used was difficult to gauge, the number of pages to be allocated to particular accounts was not easy to foretell. The advent of loose-leaf ledgers was a considerable advance in technology, despite the fears held at the time for the security of the information so recorded.

The classification is not made, as it commonly is in scientific activity, as an attempt to find a pattern towards explaining the observed phenomena. On the contrary, it is made for the purpose of measuring the totals of the several kinds of occurrences for collection, or for collation, or for settlement of indebtedness. The reason for the occurrences is not normally in question as an element in the technical aspects of the accounting process, but may become important in considering implications of policy or attitude which they depict.

Classification undertaken by accountants places constraints on interpreting the characteristics recorded about an occurrence. The interpretation, for accounting purposes, is seen quite clearly from the example of John Doe (above). However, there may be other individuals who wish to know about the occurrence of John Doe buying a filing cabinet who have a different view of the occurrence from that of accountants. The answers to the questions above that result in an accounting classification may not suit the needs of these others; they may wish to have either other facts about the occurrence and/or the same facts classified differently. For example, someone may wish to have the filing cabinet (and any further filing cabinets that may be purchased) classified by size, or number of drawers, or manufacturer, or colour, or location. Someone else may wish to know the replacement price, or the selling price, or the insured value, or the expected length of life of the cabinet(s). The imposition of the accountant's classification, usually by means of a pre-designed artifact, (the chart of accounts) for the purpose of recording the items in a ledger and the preparation of accounting reports, may preclude, or at least inhibit, others from having access to information which they need.

While accounting data are normally classified into *accounts* according to a recognized chart of accounts, such a chart is not required for recording some data about occurrences.

Classification of any sort is a reflection and an expression of a human attitude; it is a human invention, an artifact as much as any physical tool or instrument, but an artifact of and for the mind. In nature itself there is no such formal classification, but only similar or comparable characteristics (or component parts or elements or features, or call them what we will; the nomenclature is also a human device) and the discerning of any similarity or dissimilarity is a human activity. Classification tells us how someone looks at and thinks about a number or set of occurrences or phenomena; it tells us little about the things or phenomena themselves other than perceived resemblances between some of them. Classification is very much bound up with nomenclature, and the naming of occurrences or phenomena is an intellectual device; it, also, is an artifact. This is not to say that non-human creatures never classify: for example, many of them are well able to distinguish harmful from beneficial types of food or shelter; and this could be viewed as a kind of classification.

We should not pretend that we create anything by naming or classifying, except a way of looking at something; whether we use names or classes as part of a truly scientific series of observations or not, we do not thereby create anything within or outside the occurrences or phenomena; they remain unchanged by the human application of classificatory procedure. However, classifying may be a useful way of looking at some of the relationships between distinguishable occurrences or phenomena.

Any classification is carried out to help *us*, that is, humans, in our activities. The classification may help us in further investigation, or it may deter us, or it may influence us in hastening or postponing some activity; it may even incite us to try to influence future phenomena of the classes observed (as in the fight against disease), but it cannot in itself affect the phenomena already observed and classified.

Recognition of this in itself should serve to emphasize the limitations of much of the so-called empirical research in accounting that has been carried out in recent decades and has occupied so many columns of accounting literature with its reports. Many of these researchers give the impression of having mastered an investigative technique, usually borrowed from some other discipline, and then having sought a topic in or related to the field of accounting in order to apply it. In their findings, negative and tentative outcomes abound. It is as if an army of research technicians have been limping around in circles waving their intellectual armory in a frenzied display of futile offensives against an imaginary foe.

At the same time, however, it must be observed that applying a different classification may vary the overall 'picture', so to speak, of what is under consideration. Indeed, because we are used to classifying occurrences or phenomena in a particular way, the application of a different classification may well lead to a different human perception of the occurrences or phenomena; and a different classification may well lead to a different explanation or interpretation of the observed occurrences or phenomena.

In classifying, we are faced with an array of occurrences or phenomena which is bewildering in its apparent disarray or disconnectedness, that is, there seems to be a lack of relationships (a) between the occurrences or phenomena themselves and (b) between the occurrences or phenomena and our own experience. We classify in order to find these relationships, that is, classifying is a step in interpreting occurrences or phenomena for our intellectual comprehension or satisfaction. It is a process of identifying occurrences and phenomena and relating similar individual occurrences or phenomena to each other according to certain criteria which we set up as desirable or important *for our purpose*. In a sense, it is a process of descending the ladder of abstraction, approaching the specific referent, but never quite getting to the ultimate classes of one only occurrence or phenomenon in each case.

The choice of the grouping or classes is something between one class for the *whole* array of occurrences or phenomena, and one for *each* occurrence or phenomenon. The choice depends on the individual classifier and the

purpose in mind in forming the classification. Identifying the characteristics to be recorded about an occurrence or phenomenon should be
separated from the subsequent processing of data about those characteristics. Purposes may differ from one individual to another. The purpose of
classification imposes some restrictions on subsequent use of some data. It
is important to recognize that there may be more than one way of classifying characteristics, depending on the purpose or viewpoint. Thus, there are
two distinct stages in the development of a system to process data for
various users. First, the characteristics to be recorded need to be identified.
Secondly, the classification and other processing of data about the characteristics for specified purposes may be undertaken by or for particular
users. Accountants are *one* group (but *only* one group) of people who are
interested in both stages.

One problem with classification in accounting which arises, for example,
in preparing reports such as balance sheets, is that the information presented
is not always clearly restricted to serving only one purpose. Hence, in many
cases, more than one criterion may be justifiably thought to be applicable.
For instance, the characteristics themselves of some items appearing in a
balance sheet may vary according to the intentions of different people
concerned with their deployment. By way of illustration, investments in
certain types of bonds may be seen as having the characteristics of producing
a specific level of revenue (interest-bearing); their acquisition may have been
intended as a long-term source of revenue, and, hence, could properly meet
a criterion for classification as a long-term asset. At the same time, they may
well have such a ready market for conversion into cash resources that they
meet the criterion for classification as a claim to cash, and hence, as a current
or short-term asset. This potential function is not necessarily precluded from
the mind of the person responsible for the acquisition in the first place, that
is, the intention is not necessarily singular and dissociated from any other,
nor is any one aspect necessarily predominant over all the others. Indeed,
further potential or actual uses may be found for such an investment after it
has been acquired – as collateral security for borrowing, for instance. The
point at issue is that attempts to develop unchangeable categories for
classification are virtually bound to become unworkably restrictive in any but
a completely static environment.

As long ago as 1830 (and perhaps even earlier), Auguste Comte pointed
out that 'the principle of classification' was 'that the classification must
proceed from the study of the things to be classified and must by no means
be determined by *a priori* considerations' (Comte 1830).

And as Wolf further put it:

> Classification is one method, probably the simplest method, of dis-
> covering order in the world. By noting similarities between numerous
> distinct individuals, and thinking of these individuals as forming one
> class or kind, the many are in a sense reduced to one, and to that
> extent simplicity and order are introduced into the bewildering multi-

plicity of Nature. In the history of every science classification is the very first method to be employed; but it is much older than science. Every name, indeed almost every word, of a language is the expression of some implicit classification; and language is older than science. The classifications expressed in ordinary language are, however, the result of practical needs rather than of scientific interests, so that science has to correct them even when it starts from them.

(Wolf 1937: 778)

While classification in itself may not provide new knowledge, the search for relationships which it entails may lead to a recognition of otherwise unsuspected characteristics whose relationships with other occurrences or phenomena may prove of interest or value in the search for knowledge. Hence the scrutiny of characteristics for possible significant relationships is often a useful intellectual instrument.

Much may depend on an individual's interpretation of experience. Doubt or misconception of prevailing cultural explanation may arise from a conflict between elements contributing to one's experience.

It is important to recognize that any particular classification has its own specific purpose as its justification, which may not be equally appropriate for a different purpose. Classifying in itself is, in a sense, a limiting procedure, and the multiplicity of characteristics of any occurrence or phenomenon should remind us of the possibility, and, often, the desirability, for other useful classifications to be explored.

Classification, in the sense of a process (rather than that of the result of a process) can be used effectively as an intellectual instrument if it can be regarded as flexible, rather than rigid.

5 Accounting as a field of knowledge

That virtue only makes our bliss below,
And all our knowledge is, ourselves to know.
(Pope 1732, *Essay on Man*, Epistle IV: 184)

If we postulate accounting as a field of knowledge, we have to ask: How does a study of accounting increase our knowledge, and, even more challenging, what kind of knowledge is it?

As has already been suggested, a broad functional notion of accounting is that of what accountants do. This may include anything that accountants do when they act in accordance with widely accepted interpretations of their function; that is, any sort of activity which they carry out because of their known or expected vocational qualifications, experience and/or expertise. 'Accountants can do this – or ought to be able or are presumed to be able to do this properly – because they have a knowledge of accounting' is the kind of bench-mark assessment that could be applied.

It is a familiar observation that accountants work within a social setting and that what they do as accountants is concerned with the activities of other human beings. This does not preclude them from doing the same sort of things for themselves, as may be requisite, but when they do this they view their non-accounting activities as if they were undertaken by somebody else.

Academics teach or purport to teach; students learn or presumably or allegedly learn. This teaching and this learning constitute something which people in both of these groups, and other people as well, call 'accounting'. There is something a world of ideas or a type of activity or a conflation of both which many people agree to think and speak of as 'accounting knowledge' or 'knowledge about accounting'. Two questions arise: What is this accounting knowledge? How does it compare with other areas of knowledge?

To talk about an area (or some equivalent) of knowledge is, clearly, to use a metaphor, a usage we may not be able to avoid, but which we should recognize and remember. A metaphor is used to suggest, on the one hand, some sort of holism or homogeneity in what we are thinking about, and, on the other, some characteristics which distinguish what we are thinking about from other things which we might think about. It is an instrument of communication and helps people to think in similar terms or on the same level, so to speak (using another metaphor!), so that consensus can be relied upon for communicating effectively.

Since we probably have to use a metaphor, it might be profitable to seek a more apt one, for instance, that of a lake or a seemingly bottomless sea; and, further, we could recognize that knowledge, in such a metaphor, has an endless horizon. Such a figure of speech might suggest better the absence of boundaries when we study part of what we regard as knowledge and seek to extend it. Perhaps even a space of knowledge might be apt. What is needed is some image that does not cramp our endeavours and make us unduly subservient to prescribed or implied restrictions of thought. However, our knowledge has to have some relevance to our primary subject-matter, which, we propose, is human activity and its results. To explore this we need to reach some basis of communication of ideas and arguments.

It could be said that a study of accounting develops or increases a knowledge of how to record for various circumstances, and this would include a knowledge about design, installation and maintenance of recording and reporting systems. It would also include knowledge of the tools or instruments of recording, and of the criteria for selection of the occurrences to be recorded. Similarly, it would develop a knowledge of how, and how often, the reporting function can be and perhaps should be performed, how and to whom reports are and should be addressed, and the instruments used in the reporting process. It would encompass a knowledge of interpretation and validation of the records and reports. At all stages the purpose(s) of the functions and procedures would presumably be envisaged.

In the current technological climate, one function of accountants requires a knowledge about the design of recording systems. Concepts that were the basis for recording in bound or loose-leaf journals and ledgers, or card systems, may not be appropriate for data-base and other file systems used with computers. Methods of recording data often change independently of accounting requirements. For example, computer scientists have developed techniques associated with the conceptual design of recording systems (in general), as well as the computer hardware on which such systems may be installed. Data, of interest to accountants, may be only a part of a large collection of data recorded about occurrences or phenomena. Since a study of accounting develops or increases a knowledge of how to record data for some purposes, accountants should be aware of the work in other disciplines that affect their recording function.

The restrictive nature of conventional accounting was raised by Goldberg (1965) when he described the unit of activity for accountants as an 'event'. In Goldberg's words:

> Not all events are accountable in the sense that they are suitable objects for accounting procedures. At the same time, it is likely that *many more*

48   *Accounting as a field of knowledge*

> *events are suitable objects for accounting procedures than is generally recognized.*
>
> (p. 89, emphasis added)

and

> To tie accounting irrevocably to financial occurrences is too restrictive and not in accordance with the facts of accounting procedures as they are carried out at present.
>
> (p. 89)

Sorter (1969) also criticized conventional accounting ('the value approach') when he described the 'events approach' to accounting. According to Sorter:

> Proponents of the 'Events' theory suggest that the purpose of accounting is to provide information about relevant economic events that might be useful in a variety of possible decision models.
>
> (p. 13)

It is important to ask: What is the nature of events that are of concern to accountants? Several researchers have considered what constitutes an event (see, for example, Goldberg (1965), Johnson (1970) and Cushing (1989b)). Cushing (1989b) saw the 'definition' of an event as the fundamental difference between conventional accounting and the events approach. He states:

> A fundamental difference between events theory and value theory that has not been heretofore articulated concerns the definition of a relevant economic event. Although both approaches account for events, the definition of which economic events and attributes are relevant under value theory is prescribed by contemporary financial accounting standards established within the framework of the double-entry bookkeeping model. According to these standards, the events of primary relevance are transactions that involve an exchange of value, such that the measure of value in exchange represents the fundamental input to the accounting process. These standards also specify how the events data are to be aggregated and valued.
>
> In contrast the events approach is not tightly constrained by such restrictive notions about what kind of events and attributes are relevant. However, it is still essential under the events approach to establish criteria for the selection of events and attributes to be accounted for.
>
> (Cushing 1989b: 31)

Cushing then considered what would and what would not be included as an event under the 'events approach'. He conceded that, besides exchange transactions and other events that have financial implications, events of a non-financial character would be included 'under a broader concept of corporate accountability' (p. 32). He also identified a number of things 'associated with conventional accounting that would not be reported under a "pure" events approach' (pp. 32–3). Those items, such as accruals, cost and revenue allocations, depreciation, account classifications, valuations, consolidations, and judgements regarding values, involve some form of 'processing' or use of data about events, and do not meet the requirement of a 'pure' events approach that '. . . events and attribute selection . . . are independent of any particular view of how the events data should be processed' (p. 32). Whether we use the term 'event', or 'occurrence', or 'happening', does not matter for the purposes of this discussion. The ideas germane to the 'events approach' were seen to be relevant to those who also advocated a 'data base approach'.[1] The idea of separating the definition of data to be recorded (that is, the definition of the occurrences and their characteristics) from procedures that involve some kind of change or processing of the data is basic to the design and operation of data-base systems. Items such as accruals, cost and revenue allocations, depreciation and other 'non-events' defined by Cushing (1989b) are seen as procedures or the results of procedures used by accountants to achieve the objectives of their reporting function. We argue below (Chapter 8) that at least some of these so-called 'non-events' could be considered occurrences for accounting purposes. However, that does not detract from the argument that the separation of the responsibility for recording (including the criteria for the definition of occurrences and their characteristics) from the responsibility for reporting (including the procedures needed to draw conclusions from the data recorded about occurrences) may suggest that accountants should reconsider their purpose(s) in recording and reporting, and the infra-structure developed for carrying out these functions.

In all this, however, the discovery is about a man-made knowledge – it is a knowledge of how people act. It is also knowledge about an instrument, albeit a sophisticated and, in many of its uses, a social instrument.

It is important to recognize that, in its practice and in its procedures, accounting is seen as essentially a service industry: the records, reports, advice and recommendations which accountants produce professionally are provided in an attempt to assist others engaged in the processes of production, distribution, preservation and, perhaps, even consumption or enjoyment of resources of all kinds. To the extent that their output, if it could be satisfactorily measured, results in increasing net availability or decreasing net wastage of resources, accountants as a group might be regarded as being indirectly productive; this would be the hallmark of a socially useful service industry. To the extent that the endeavours and skills of accountants are directed towards assisting others to do otherwise, such as, for instance, to divert resources from a legitimately taxable status to a non-taxable one, they may well be regarded as socially non-productive and even, in extreme cases, destructive. It is questionable whether knowledge

---

[1]See, for example, Colantoni, Manes and Whinston (1971), Lieberman and Whinston (1975), Haseman and Whinston (1976), McCarthy (1979), Denna and McCarthy (1987), and Mepham (1988).

about an increasingly intricate set of obfuscating rules, regulations, decrees, or other forms of dogma, devised by humans to frustrate or oppress other humans, can contribute any kind of ultimately useful knowledge about either the people involved or the world in which they operate.

The test of knowledge is ultimately a subjective one. For each one of us what we accept into our corpus of experience is an addition to our body of knowledge, and what we accept is whatever we deem to be compatible or reconcilable with that accumulated experience; if we regard a proposition or an observation as incompatible or irreconcilable with what we already accept, our initial attitude, at least, is one of suspended scepticism or even outright refusal to believe. Usually a person's knowledge is gradually accumulated as experience grows in breadth and depth. In a broad sense, what we know is what we believe, and what we believe is what we know. Ultimate acceptance may depend on additional argument or the presentation of further observational evidence to remove the incompatibility or irreconcilability.

One way of regarding knowledge is that, for each one of us, it comprises those perceptions of that which is within ourselves, for example, thirst, pain, discomfort, pleasure and other sensations, and that which we can accept from outside ourselves into our experience. If this provides a basis or an incentive to take positive actions, such knowledge becomes belief.

While experience, and therefore knowledge, is private and individual, some aspects of both can be communicated to others, but only those which can be expressed in symbols which can be understood as having the same import for the recipient of a message as for its sender: symbols like gestures, words, figures, numbers, movements. This depends on consensus. Communication is further discussed in Chapter 7.

Events of the past three centuries or so have served to develop the view that, broadly speaking, the test of new 'scientific' knowledge is whether it can be used to predict outcomes. If the observable outcomes accord with those prognosticated, a hypothesis or process is accepted as a statement of knowledge in the corpus of human experience. On this score, accountants hardly seem to have taken more than the most timid steps of exploration.

Why do we make accounting records? A primary answer is that they are made as an aide-memoire, so to speak, so that we can take cognizance of:

(a) resources at our disposal from time to time,
(b) actual or potential, immediate and distant, commitments or restrictions on any deployment of such resources,
(c) the available record of means of deployment of resources in the past,

so that decisions on future deployment of resources may be based on knowledge, rather than ignorance, of as much relevant information as can be made available. In this work we envisage a wider, rather than a narrow interpretation of 'resources' so that a broader range of accountants' functions than is currently 'normal' is implied.

In this context, three aspects of an aide-memoire may be distinguished. First, the record serves as a reminder of something which should be done in the future as a consequence of the occurrence which is noted; for example, if something has been lent to a borrower, it serves as a reminder to have the loaned object or its equivalent returned. Second, as a record of something that has occurred, it may serve as evidence of the occurrence if such evidence is required. Third, it serves as a basis for further processing within a recording system, such as for billing customers, or for classifying and summarizing occurrences for preparation of periodical accounting reports.

This suggests that, while accounting records are made as evidence of people's actions and thoughts, no accounting reports – or, at least, no credible accounting reports – can be made except from the records which they purport to classify, summarize and illuminate. The distilling of this knowledge is the subject-matter of what has come to be known as analysis and interpretation of accounting reports.

The verificatory function is an appendage to the others, made necessary only because of a human propensity to err (or to differ from others), whether innocently or not, whether in respect of matters of principle or of procedure, whether on a matter of fact or of judgement or assessment.

Perhaps we should draw a distinction between accounting as an instrument of knowledge and accounting as a field of knowledge. As soon as we raise this possibility it is clear that the symbol 'accounting' is capable of being used in more than one sense. When used to suggest an instrument, it calls to mind an idea of a process or set of procedures – something that can be applied or carried out by operators, whereas, when used to signify a field, it summons up a notion of an established – or at least establishable – mine of information which needs only the right digging tools for it to be made available in all its richness for our benefit and delight.

As an instrument of knowledge, accounting, or, more correctly, the processes which we recognize as those normally carried out by accountants, may be used to reveal knowledge about operating units which cannot be revealed by any other means. But if we call this 'accounting knowledge' it is not knowledge *about* accounting but rather knowledge about something other than accounting which has been uncovered by means of an application of procedures familiar to and vocationally used by accountants. The uncovering of this knowledge may result in impacts on organizational and social functions.

Is a knowledge of these processes and procedures, then, enough to constitute a field of knowledge? Perhaps, if we were prepared to explore them at sufficient depth, they would turn out to be so; and perhaps in the course of doing this we might find many other things which would otherwise have escaped our scrutiny. It is our intention to explore some of the aspects of what is commonly called accounting to discover what we can, and bring it up from its underlying level for examination and, possibly, judgement. To pronounce judgement, however, requires the recognition and acceptance of criteria, and this, too, will have to be explored in due course. The main point to be made here is that wherever the thread leads we are required to follow it, so long as the thread continues to be identified with or related to accounting. Wherever it may go *to*, it must always be traceable *back to* accounting. This is the essential criterion of this exploratory journey.

Once we start thinking about knowledge, it soon appears that, in a basic sense, knowledge has no boundaries. We humans may classify our 'areas' of knowledge and give them names; we may think or feel that we perceive distinctions between them. But, as we explore them, we reach areas in which the distinctions become blurred; where, for instance, one could once distinguish between physics and chemistry, and biology, one can now explore physical chemistry, biophysics and biochemistry. Often the boundaries are not only flexible but fusible as well.

As already noted, what we call knowledge is for each of us what we accept into our whole body or 'universe', so to speak, of experience. If a proposition or piece of evidence is incompatible with our existing universe of experience, it will either be rejected as unbelievable or modify our experience by its acceptance, and this will occur irrespective of its source or nature. However, we must all come to this conviction as individual units of experience.

This may seem to be an unduly subjective view of knowledge, especially for anybody who believes that there is a world of knowledge waiting 'out there' to be discovered, and that this world of knowledge is finite and capable of being discovered by human effort. The evidence to date, however, surely points to an alternative view, namely, that the development of human knowledge has proceeded and accelerated through the development of the instruments devised through human endeavour, together with the preparedness of human beings to enlarge their experience through acceptance of 'new' knowledge. If either of these latter were terminated, surely the possibility of accessing new knowledge would be limited, if not ended.

Accounting may be viewed as, above all else, an instrument for recording how people act and how they think; in this guise, it is an instrument of historical interest and concern. But it is, at the same time, an instrument of communication, in that the purpose behind the making of such records is most frequently (but not inevitably) to make intelligible to intended recipients the symbols of activity which they are used to represent.

Thus, when we talk about accounting as a field of knowledge, the knowledge may include not only that of the kinds of instrument used and the way(s) in which they can be used, but also the kinds of human activity which their use can be applied to and their appropriateness and significance for such purposes. The boundaries of such an area of knowledge may well become diffused, and following them may take us to unusual, but interesting terrain.

One approach in considering accounting as a field of knowledge is through reflecting, in broad terms, upon the course of learning which accountants might undertake (or be subjected to) in their vocational development. In the initial, introductory stage, the learner discovers that the procedures of accounting are based upon a technique of recording which has to be mastered if subsequent stages are to be adequately understood and successfully applied. Whatever means are used in this stage of learning, whether it be by rote, as commonly used to be the case in most of the text-books before the twentieth century, or by interpretation and application of a basic simple, but not unsophisticated 'accounting equation' as has been the custom in more recent decades, or by imitation, as might occur in a 'purely' apprenticeship situation, the learner finds that an instrument of recording is available for use; the resulting record has the function of preserving information from a fate of irrecoverable ephemerality. The knowledge that the learner acquires in this stage is technical knowledge of the nature of the instrument and how and to what it can be applied more broadly. It is knowledge about a human, intellectual artifact, which may range from the simplest handwritten or tally-notched records to highly sophisticated computer-based installations.

In the next stage, the learner discovers or is instructed in the means of preparing reports, whether on a regular periodical cycle or an *ad hoc* requirement, from the information stored in the records. This reporting stage is, in effect, an instrument of communication, and is generally presumed to be applied for the benefit of recipients of information, usually specific in the case of *ad hoc* reports, sometimes specific for regular periodic reports, but often assumed in the most general and inchoate terms by the preparers in many instances of the latter. The spread of knowledge in this stage – if adequate attention is to be paid to it embraces some awareness and appreciation of the process of communication itself as well as the tenets of classification, format and content applicable under various legal, customary and usage requirements. Some aspects of judgement-forming are often involved in this stage of the learning process.

Conventionally, under double-entry procedures that are based on an accounting equation, the learner finds that the instrument of recording, whether it be handwritten books or a computer-based accounting system, requires that the data to be recorded be classified, usually as shown in a chart of accounts. A debit amount is assigned to one account and an equal credit amount to another. Recording in this way may be considered as, at least partly, a processing of data about occurrences. The resulting record is in a format that is suitable for further processing into accounting reports, but this may not suit the requirements of other potential users. Throughout this work, we raise questions about problems that may be faced by users of data about occurrences because of the intermingling by accountants of the recording and reporting functions.

As people skilled in preparing accounting reports, accountants are often presumed to be capable of interpreting reports prepared by others for recipients who are not so skilled. In this further stage, accountants have to put themselves in the position of the recipient and attempt to interpret the information contained in a set of reports to answer questions for the recipient's benefit. The nature of this benefit may vary considerably according to the circumstances and attitudes of the recipient or user. Not only are financial aspects involved, but such wide-ranging issues as environmental effects, economic activities, marketing, production, exporting or even consumption patterns or plans, communal health and waste disposal do not exhaust the possibilities of the implications that may have to be regarded as relevant in interpreting accounting reports in particular instances.

As an instrument, the process of interpretation requires a mastery of a technical application of analysis of data, and a number of relationships (or 'ratios') between commonly found components in many accounting reports have been formulated as useful in interpreting accounting information. But the validity of applying such ratios should be assessed by relating them to the actual use of the report by the recipient(s).

Hence, the knowledge pertaining to the function of interpretation comprises not only that of the instrument of analysis, but also at least some appreciation of broader social and communal influences which may affect any given instance. Much of this latter can only be developed with experience and application by the individual; only a nodding acquaintance with their existence and possible importance can be transmitted in any pre-professional studies. Nevertheless some indication of the sensitivity of the circumstances in which the instrument may be applied could well be provided during exercises in applying it and its possible or likely shortcomings made clear in given cases.

According to this approach, the field of knowledge of accounting turns out to be largely a knowledge about a social instrument and how it can be handled, accompanied by an appreciation of the variety of human activity and some of the results of human actions. It is, in effect, part of the study of human beings and some of their artifacts.

In the course of learning about interpretation (and, perhaps, to a smaller extent, in the course of preparation) of accounting reports, the aspiring accountant learns about situations involving deployment of resources and what sorts of deployment are, according to certain criteria, beneficial and which are detrimental. But these criteria are standards of human activity, not of inert things. Such human activity is not that of an accountant as such. It is the activity of entrepreneurs, directors, managers, employees, government officials, politicians, and, indeed, any of those people who have the capacity and responsibility for deploying resources. In short, the occurrences and phenomena which accountants are vocationally concerned with are the actions, and the results of actions, of people – of both ordinary people and extraordinary people, doing ordinary things or extraordinary things.

In this way, the functional activity of deploying resources may become and may be seen to be a 'natural' function for an accountant to undertake, especially in such capacity as a director, an executive of an organization, a liquidator or receiver, and the like. The knowledge or expertise is one of human action; this knowledge and expertise have been explored and developed through use of the conventional accounting process as an instrument, and, while it seems to be a natural or normal consequence of the knowledge and use of the instrument, it is not the field of knowledge of the instrument (or process) itself.

One of the astonishing developments in science in the twentieth century has been the recognition of the extension of the observable limits of existence; in sub-atomic physics, in microbiology, astrophysics, cellular biology, what were not so long ago thought to be the limits of observation have been shown to be complex structures of simpler and more elemental constituents, the existence and activities of which have either been observed or taken to be necessary to explain perceivable occurrences in nature.

Practically nothing of this sort has occurred in accounting. Accountants, whether academic or practising, have rarely attempted to analyse the *underlying* concepts on which their procedures are founded. For instance, much time and energy were devoted for some years in discussing the shortcomings of what became widely known as 'historical cost' reporting and in suggesting various methods of overcoming them; much warmth but little light was generated by the discussion, since most of the protagonists were engaged in advocating a specific point of view with its inevitable mode of 'solving' the problem and in decrying the features of the suggested remedies of their dissenting fellows. The issue is, so to speak, currently sleeping, and, if it has not already passed into a coma, it may well appear to have done so. It has lost its status symbol of fashionable glamour which its contributors enjoyed a few years ago. Very little, if any, attention was given to the problems inherent in all bases of reporting, some of which are discussed in Chapters 13, 14 and 15.

One important question arises regarding the nature of accounting knowledge. In the natural sciences, organic as well as inorganic, it has long been recognized that the subject-matter of each science (which is the subject-matter which each scientist studies) is capable of developing through a broadening and deepening investigatory process. New know-ledge is added to earlier knowledge by extending the boundaries of search; sometimes some aspects of earlier knowledge are shown to be in error, and therefore have to be replaced or corrected; sometimes they are shown to be of more limited application than was thought, so that while they may not be in error, their limitations have to be acknowledged. Beneath all the search in these areas of endeavour, however, is a universal conviction that there are 'laws' or 'principles' of uniformity, operating beyond the influence of the searchers themselves, to be discovered and laid bare to the scrutiny of the whole human race. This conviction has been supported by enormous discoveries and inventions during the last two centuries or so, to such an extent that almost any vocation or field of activity whose practitioners do not aspire to recognition in some measure as scientists or appliers of scientifically derived rules or standards tends to be regarded as one of the less respected social callings. In these scientific ranges of inquiry, the broadening and deepening of the knowledge can be tracked clearly as a progressive development in the direction of an 'ultimate' objective.

It can scarcely be said that the same applies to the knowledge of or about accounting. It is, of course, true that the current procedures and practices are more complicated than their respective counterparts of some decades ago, but the underlying concepts have scarcely changed at all. In fact, the search for accounting 'principles' which began consciously and deliberately in the English-speaking world in the 1930s has not yet produced any body of reliable knowledge which can serve as a basis for development comparable in any way with that of any of the natural sciences.

The widespread move towards standards has been one of prescribing treatments laid down by authoritarian groups of people who seek, with the best of intentions, to impose a uniformity of recognition and measurement of publicly reportable phenomena. They are more akin to the law from Mount Sinai or the bye-laws of a municipal council than to any scientifically expressed law or theory. The 'due process' by which these pronouncements are reached is not remotely like the processes by which any advance in scientific knowledge is made. It is, if anything, more like a politico/legal procedure. The so-called research which is claimed to lie behind such pronouncements is, broadly, neither conceptually fruitful nor empirically impartial. It is rarely subjected to open and widespread critical assessment by peer researchers; comments, indeed, may be made on an 'exposure draft', but these have to be directed to the standard-makers and may be totally ignored if unsupported by some influential interest more powerful than logic or if they do not contain anything that the standard-makers can themselves use in their favour. When it is issued, a standard is not a statement of a 'principle' or theory based on and supported by available unbiased and replicable evidence, but a pronouncement of a judgement arrived at by an approximation to consensus of a small group of people.

Further, there is not yet available an adequate or satisfying history of accounting practices, even in restricted specializations, nor does any history as yet show a *development* of thought about accounting which portrays a progressive 'internal' trend rather than a series of reactions to external changes. There is, indeed, a succession of issues which are discussed widely for a time and then die because an external influence changes and serves to displace one issue in its importance and/or urgency by another which attracts attention. These latter issues are often unrelated to those which they succeed and appear as problems arising from some legal, fiscal, political or social issue emanating from outside the domain of accounting itself.

It may well be asked: Why should, or how can, accounting information, which portrays past activity, be relevant to, and therefore useful for, determining what should be done now for effect in the future? (Whether the future is distant or near is not material at this point.)

There may be several appropriate answers, but the essence of most, if not all, is probably along these lines. What has happened in the past, and so recorded, *was* the result of decisions arrived at and carried out in the past. If all circumstances relating to such decisions are precisely the same now as they were when the decisions were implemented, we presume that the same decisions will have the same effects. Obviously, however, all the circumstances can never be precisely and universally the same. For one thing, time will have elapsed, and the lapse of time is recognized only by change of some sort, but many other influences, apart from the obvious time-change itself, will probably have altered. However, if we can discern enough of the changes, we can estimate the likely changed effects of decisions to be taken. It is a process of extrapolation, but not of blind or mindless extrapolation. The effects of variation in the influential circumstances of the past activity should be recognized and measured in some way (if precision is not possible or would be misleading or ineffectual the measuring may be in broad terms only) and allowance made in determining the decision to be arrived at. For instance, the people involved may be different between the two or more points of time, the kinds of resources may have changed, the social environment may have altered through political or economic developments, the earlier activity itself may have affected the circumstances surrounding the later decision-to-be-made, and so on. The possibilities of difference may appear to be endless. But this is where human judgement has to be exercised, and human judgement is based upon human experience and a human capacity to interpret that experience. And this capacity incorporates a possibility of flexibility rather than a strict adherence to a fixed and inevitable formula. The number of variables involved in many, if not most, decisions is usually very large, if not infinite, and, while it may not be beyond the capacity of a computer to handle them if appropriately programmed, it would be exceedingly difficult for a human programmer to construct the appropriate program. The number of discernible relevant variables may, of course, be much less, and manageable in a computer system, or by a human, for that matter, but the result would be an approximation to the 'ideal' formulation, and open to question accordingly.

As a rough schema, it may be said that accounting knowledge comprises:

(a) knowledge about what accountants do, that is, about
   (i) processes and practices which they devise and carry out;
   (ii) the environment, such as the social conditions, opportunities and restrictions applicable to the unit of operation (see Chapter 10) to which the processes and practices are devised and carried out; this would include the rules and standards that accountants observe and adhere to, and these obviously may vary from community to community;
(b) knowledge about the results of the application of the processes and practices, that is, the results of the application of (a) above, covering the results affecting not only
   (i) a specific unit which is the immediate focus of attention in a particular case, but also

(ii) broader, social circumstances such as economic, environmental, even, in some cases, political or cultural repercussions;

(c) knowledge about individual people and institutions involved in or responsible for effecting important changes in processes or practices or attitudes of thought about them; this would comprise biographical and historical knowledge;

(d) knowledge about what accountants think they do (which may differ, in some instances, from what they do or should do);

(e) knowledge about what non-accountants think accountants do (which may often turn out to be different from what accountants in fact do or consider they should do).

An alternative, or complementary, outline would be:

(1) Coverage:
Accounting knowledge is about the activities of people and the results of people's activities;
Based on perceptions of activities and results.

(2) Medium:
Processes and practices of accountants —
double entry or non-double entry records;
periodical and *ad hoc* reports;
cost accounting; management accounting; public sector accounting, etc.

(3) Instrument/Artifact:
Manual, involving pen, ink, pencil and paper or parchment (Middle Ages to modern period), clay tablets (Sumeria, Babylonia), papyri (Greek, Roman), quipu (Inca), tallies (Middle Ages to early modern), and the like;
Mechanical;
Electronic;
All these are means of processing data.
A question that arises here is whether the instrument (in this sense) affects the nature of the output, and, if so, how and to what purpose. For example, is a financial report produced by a computer system any *better* than one which *could be* prepared manually or mechanically? If so, in what specific way, and what are the respective direct and indirect costs and benefits of operation?

(4) Underlying characteristics:
Can accounting knowledge be shown to have been cumulative and developmental or has it been mainly supersessive, substitutive and rejective in response to the emergence of changing issues?
It may be pointed out in passing that if the object of any educational process is to teach the current 'state of the art' it is almost certain to become continuously obsolescent.

We seek to stress and reiterate that accounting is a human activity. Its 'principles' and its procedures have always been devised by humans. Any knowledge about it or emanating from it is transmitted between humans by means of communication. Hence, it might be argued that such mysteries as there may be in accounting are of human making and therefore should be capable of being understood, if only the evidence could be provided. This may well be valid, but at the same time it should be realized that it is based on an assumption or a presumption that every human being's thought processes, whenever or wherever they may have taken place, are inevitably capable of being replicated by some other human being somewhere, some time. In other words, the possibility of unique human thought or activity is denied. This, however, is unproven and, probably, incapable of proof. This should not deter anybody from seeking required evidence, but it should temper our confidence in being able to 'understand' all of even human activity and thought.

Other issues could be emphasized, such as accounting as an instrument of communication (which is considered briefly in Chapter 7), or as an instrument of control (which is not addressed specifically in this work). For such issues, a slightly different interpretation of 'accounting' might be warranted, but, whatever aspect is emphasized, the relation to human activity is, in our view, inescapable.

Part II

Perceptions and concepts

6   The unit of experience

> ... In estimating the prospects of investment, we must have regard ... to the nerves and hysteria and even the digestions and reactions to the weather of those upon whose spontaneous activity it largely depends.
>
> (Keynes 1936: 162)

Whatever interpretation is placed upon the term 'accounting', the notion of some kind of activity seems to be inescapable, whether it be physical (that is, 'bodily') or mental, or carried out through or with the aid of mechanical or electronic or other kinds of instruments. As soon as we consider activity, we are faced with determining the kind of unitary being who or which can be active. The position taken here is that this unit, which we call the unit of experience, is the individual human being. Each one of us can identify with such a unit and might well say something like the following:

> The most fundamental concept that I consider I have to accept is that I am a human being, with a capacity to perceive; this capacity has been developed through a continuity of experience throughout my life to date, and I believe that it has some limitations because I am a human being. This may not, in itself, be a simple or unsophisticated proposition, but, for me, it is basic.
>
> Each one's experience is essentially unique to one's self, but at the same time it has common elements or relationships with the experiences of some other human beings – and, possibly, of other, non-human, creatures. This means that I am the unit of my experience; I am also the total of my experience to date. Further, I am a self-conscious being and my experience has not yet been fully completed. I am able to discern changes in myself as a self-conscious, organic unit, and I perceive what I interpret to be changes in 'beings', both organic and inorganic, outside my 'self', that is, in my environment.
>
> I interpret my environment widely rather than narrowly, although the degree of width may vary according to changes in my state of health, state of mind, and the kind of experience I am undergoing at any given time. If, for example, I am concentrating on a particular

task, my awareness of some changes in my environment may well be lower than if I were not concentrating in this way.

From this I posit that from time to time and from place to place I have 'experiences', that is, I come into interactive relationships with other beings, some of whom (or which) I perceive as having similar perceptual capacities to my own, and any mutual experiences support this perception. The relationships vary in intensity and frequency, as well as in extent of similarity. I have greater empathy with some of my friends than with, say, a neighbour's pet cat, although the latter appears to be quite friendly. Such things as these are part of my perceptions.

In the present context we use 'unit of experience' to signify the individual human being who is distinguishable from all others by a capacity to have experiences which are uniquely his or her own. For each such individual, communication of some kind is necessary in any attempt to convey to any other similar individual any impression of or approximation to thoughts, feelings, connotations or attitudes comprising any particular experience. We use 'unit of experience' rather than an alternative such as, say, 'individual human being' because we consider that 'experience' carries a notion of activity and development which 'being' does not; equally, we regard 'person' as lacking the essential of human embodiment, both etymologically and in some of the legal and socio-political usages in at least the western culture with which we are most familiar.

The point then arises whether the absence of consciousness precludes experience. Apparently not completely, for an unconscious person may have experiences which would, or at least could, be observable if conscious, for example, breathing, perhaps healing or ageing, so that consciousness does not seem to be a necessary condition for being a unit of experience unless experience is defined as a conscious state of being or of change. Such a definition, however, might be too restrictive, and experience may be more usefully interpreted as any sort of change which impinges upon the unit.

Clearly, not all our experience comes from outside sources. Our discomforts, pains, pleasures, feelings and reactions are internal to each one of us and cannot be communicated directly to others; they can only be transmitted in a surrogate way by an arrangement of symbols. Each one of us can get only an approximation to another's experience through communication.

Another way of expressing this, perhaps rather more subjectively, would be as follows: While the individual is the unit of experience, that experience includes perceptions which that individual interprets as coming from sources outside the 'self'. More accurately and to put it in the first person singular, my experience includes perceptions which I interpret as emanating from outside myself, and I extrapolate from my interpretation to that of other people and, in some measure, of other (non-human) creatures. But when I consider myself more closely, I see that I can also perceive some things which are derived from within my own 'self', if 'self' is taken to be the being that I and all who recognize me take to be 'me', and the recognizability of whom is expressed by bodily characteristics which remain relatively constant, at least over a considerable period of my living existence – my stature, facial features, voice, mode of expression and the like – those characteristics which identify me. I presume or infer or am informed that others have sensory perceptions which emanate from me, just as I get them from others. In addition to these externally produced perceptions, I get perceptions whose source is within myself. I can experience pain in my leg or in my tooth, which is derived from some malaise within my psycho-physical system, and this pain is not transmissible to any other being. I may be able to describe it to another, such as a doctor or a dentist, who may be able to locate evidence of an inflammation, but the pain itself is not transmissible. I may be irritated enough to, say, kick my dog who may as a result yelp in pain, but it is his pain he is yelping about, not mine, and mine may not be (and in a just world would not be) assuaged, but even if such a boorish action does give me some relief it is likely to be a temporary diversion unless, by a miracle of coincidence, the act of kicking removes the cause of the pain. The point at issue, however, is that there is a perceiving part of me – no doubt somewhere in the brain – and there are other parts of me that produce or are responsible for producing sensations which can be perceived; perhaps that is what the nervous system is all about. But it adds up to this: that my experience is derived from both outside my 'self' and within my 'self'. How this experience accumulates in our first few years is for each of us (with few, if any, exceptions) shrouded in mists of forgetfulness.

Another point is that an individual human being or, for that matter, almost any other living creature, is a highly elaborate complex of living organisms or, perhaps more accurately, of living and dying organisms. And each one of these organisms – cells, tissues, neurons and so on can and does change; why, then, is it not a unit of experience? It probably could be for certain purposes, but the answer for us lies in the existence of a relationship which unites these organisms into a single representative of a particular species, so that the unit which we wish to consider is a member of a particular species. Thus the unit of experience for humanity is the individual man or woman or male or female child. If we were considering dogs or bees, the unit would be the individual dog or bee. Communication takes place, as a commonplace happening, between individual members of the species; in some cases, to a limited extent, between some members of one species and some members of another, for example, between humans and dogs.

While we say that the unit of experience and outlook is the individual sentient being, we are saying at the same time that no individual can know for sure what the emotion, outlook or experience of another is or has been; for only an approximation can be obtained through communication, and it requires great skill in the process of communicating to convey to another a close approximation to one's own experience or outlook. Some common basis is required, and this is laboriously developed throughout our learning years.

Acceptance of the individual as the unit of experience obviously does not exclude communication between individuals, because it is virtually impossible for a human being to survive for long without having any contact, direct or indirect, with others and still remain a sentient, thinking being. Acceptance of the self as a unit of experience is a matter of self-recognition rather than an aggrandisement of self-interest or of egocentricity as these are usually interpreted, although, if they could be divorced from their normal moral connotations, they could be useful words in our conceptual vocabulary. Unfortunately, they are so encrusted with value implications that their use would almost certainly lead to misinterpretations of our intended meaning. Self-recognition is not meant to refer to economically bounded or purely selfish attitudes or activities. It is, rather, intended to refer to a consciousness of self as a distinct sentient and thinking being. Emphasis upon the continuity of the individual as the unit of experience does not necessarily involve emphasis (to the exclusion of everything else) on greed or self-interest. Our experience informs us that there are other units of experience outside our own selves with whom we can communicate, and that this is the purpose of communication. Further, it suggests that such a sharing can augment one's own experience immensely. Care for others, thought for others, compassion, are rewarding processes of communication and contribute to the deepening, broadening and enriching of our own experience.

Neither does it exclude any common group experience; that is, experiences which several separate members of a group share and are able to recognize in each other's communications about them. However, even if an individual is or feels subservient to a group, that person still experiences the activities of living as an individual within the group, so that the 'common' experience is individually perceived; only through communication is its commonness among the several members of the group recognized. There may well be occasions when the judgement of an individual member of a group is affected by such membership, so that actions of 'the group' as a collection of people are different from what the individuals would have carried out if they had remained separate from each other, unaffected by the presence or activities or views of fellow members. But this does not mean that the experience of any member of the group is other than an individual experience; it means only that the experience is affected by the proximity (in space, time, thought and/or feeling) of other individuals who, in some respects, are able to communicate a contributing factor to the motivating force of the activities undertaken. The actual experience remains that of each individual, even though some individuals may feel that their individuality is being or has been submerged in a generalized group personality.

When we speak of the unit of experience we are at the same time implying a unit of attitude or outlook. We are what we are because of what we have been, and everything is what it is because of what it has been. This obviously recognizes and accepts a historical and causal sequence in experience, which may serve to clarify but not necessarily simplify our view of occurrences that take place. In human experiences both genetic and environmental influences contribute, the latter, in this context, including cultural influences.

This notion of the unit of experience is also important when we consider our understanding of explanation. We are generally satisfied with an explanation which fits in with our experience, which, in turn, is the sum total of the inherent and environmental influences which have produced the state of our being at any given time. Thus, as our experience grows, the criteria for accepting explanations of particular phenomena may alter: few adults believe in the Santa Claus that was a convincing personage in their early childhood, the 'rising' of the sun becomes comprehensible as a result of the rotation of a globular earth, a fever is interpreted as an invasion of the privacy of our bodies by some hostile micro-organisms even though we cannot see them without powerful optical aids. Such developments of understanding are a part of our normal education in the society to which we belong. In other communities and in other processes of education the beliefs and interpretations of similar or analogous phenomena would be different. But, whatever kind of basis we have for understanding, we cannot accept – and are often too ready to reject – an explanation which does not match our own experience up to date. Unfortunately, this can sometimes lead to a lack of mutual tolerance and to the adoption of an adversarial attitude which is prone to lead to disaster in relationships between groups as well as between individuals.

This leads to the suggestion that, while one's experience forms the basis for acceptance of explanations of various occurrences, it is at the same time an acceptance of what may be only one side or aspect of these explanations. An open mind is surely a desirable adjunct to anyone's experience in seeking understanding of occurrences and phenomena.

This view of the unit of experience is important because it implies that accounting activities are part of the experience of human beings acting either alone or in cooperation with (sometimes, perhaps, in antagonism to) other individuals or groups. But whether in cooperation or antagonism, the activities are of individual human beings. Each one of us could say: I am the unit of (my) experience, and I am the measure of it. Nobody else can have my experience, nor can I truly have the experience of anybody else. Approximations through communication may be possible but identity of experience is, so far in the history of human development, not possible.

The importance of recognizing, and, indeed, of emphasizing, the individual as the unit of experience lies in the effect it has of focusing attention upon the attitudes and activities of people rather than upon abstractions or figments. In other words, accountants are people, and what they account for are the activities of people and the results of the activities of people. For instance, it is not accounting, as a process or practice or discipline or a field of study, which does anything or which has objectives, aims or ideals or points of view, but accountants – and it is they who have thoughts and express concepts. If we use such an expression as 'concepts of accounting' we mean concepts which are related to the process of accounting; the relationship is not one of possession, that is, 'accounting' is not perceived as being able to possess anything, as humans can. These concepts are what accountants think of and express or try to formulate. Accounting is a process or a series of processes; the processes are carried out or designed or controlled by accountants; accountants are responsible for the processing; accountants have objectives, aims or ideals.

A further relevant point is that if one believes that there are (or could be) other lives for one, it is still only this life which one can participate in *now* and which one experiences before dying; the other lives are con-jectural, and even if one accepts them, this very acceptance is part of one's experience in this present life.[1] What we learn about the past, and what we conjecture about the future both become part of our experience here and now and contribute to the persons we take to be – each one of us – ourselves.

The insistent point is that the experience is, and cannot be other than, that of an individual, unitary, living being, capable, in a social role, of recognizing other like individuals with whom relationships can be estab-lished through means of communication. In short, the unit of experience for anybody interested in accounting is the cognitive, emotive, interactive human being. The reaction of an individual to an idea may affect that individual's subsequent experience, but it is still the experience of the individual, which can only be shared in a differing, usually diminished, but sometimes heightened, degree by anybody else.

Even the acceptance (or rejection) of a group of people – a club, a family, a tribe, a community, a nation, all of humanity, even all of the living creatures on earth – is an individual acceptance (or rejection) of each one of us, and cannot be otherwise. So, too, is the acceptance or rejection of any concept or idea or instrument of thought or action. If somebody else proffers an idea for consideration, it is accepted or rejected or modified by each individual whose attitude and action result from his or her experience up to that point.

It is important to say this in order to prevent, if possible, a distortion or misinterpretation of what we are saying. Our present primary purpose in discussing the unit of experience is explanation, rather than ethical or social suasion. Naturally, we hope the proposition will be accepted, but, if it is to be rejected, we believe it should be because it can be shown to be inadequate in explaining phenomena, or in contributing towards such an

---

[1] We use 'acceptance' as having a more subjective connotation than 'proof', but, in the ultimate analysis, proof itself may well turn out to be subjective and a form of acceptance.

explanation, and not because it may be thought to have ethical or unethical implications which are not intended.

The concept of the unit of experience is important in several respects. It is important in considering communication, when we examine the extent of agreement on the meaning and connotations of the symbol we use to convey perceptions between units of experience, when we look at the similarity and congruence of cultural experiences required for successful communication, or when we examine whether there is, say, an intention or commitment for one party to inform another or others when communicating. Aspects of this are raised in Chapter 7. It is also important in considering what we mean by understanding something, that is, the criteria by which we are prepared to judge evidence presented to us for acceptance and belief. Acceptance or rejection of, for example, specific authority (or sceptical suspension about it) is part of one's attitude based on experience. It is important to perceive and preserve the recognition and acceptance of each individual's corpus of experience.

The words 'unit' and 'experience' have been used advisedly here: 'unit' to reflect and emphasize the notions of wholeness and integration of an individual human being, 'experience' to reflect the sum total of the vicissitudes that each individual human being alone has lived through up to any given point in time. The use of such a term is an attempt to suggest what is often called 'reality'. On either side of it, and perhaps in any direction from it, lie the regions of abstraction.

The emphasis on the individual does not imply any insistence on, support for or argument against competition between people. Moreover, while it is a matter of self-awareness, this does not preclude recognition that cooperation with others is necessary for social living. Such social units are significant: human beings rarely function in isolation, but belonging to a group does not eliminate their self-awareness as individuals.

7 Communication

A word fitly spoken is like apples of gold in baskets of silver.
(Proverbs, XXV, 11)

Importance of communication

Since most accountants spend a good deal of their time and energy in preparing, arranging to prepare, analysing and/or interpreting reports developed from accounting records, a brief discussion of some of the essential characterisitics of human communicating is relevant to understanding what accountants do.

Communication has been succinctly described as 'the use of signs and symbols by which men influence each other' (Evans 1955: 4), and, while the delimitation of this description to human activity alone may be somewhat restrictive for some purposes, it is broad enough for acceptance when human activities are being considered.

Basically, the process of communication comprises the functions of preparing, formulating or 'encoding' a message, sending or transmitting it to another or others (or to oneself at a future time), and its reception by another who interprets or 'decodes' it.

The chief problem in this area of human activity is to provide more effective communication than we have now. For this, it is necessary to understand its present process and practice:

(a) what it comprises,
(b) how it works,
(c) where, and to what extent, it does not work effectively, which involves criteria of effectiveness, that is, the setting up of norms or standards of performance,
(d) what to communicate, that is, the message:

    (i)   from whom   symbols   encoders   interference
    (ii) by whom and/or by what channels   decoders   or 'noise'
    (iii) to whom   receptors

(e) the interpretation.

Communicating clearly involves more than one function. Even if only one person is concerned, as may happen if one writes something for future action, that person is performing two functions: (i) recording (sending) a message, and (ii) receiving the message in the future. The recording or sending is a function distinct from that of the subsequent reception. The distinction between these functions is, of course, more obvious when the sender and the receiver are different people.

If the meaning of the message received is not identical with that intended in the message sent, the reason(s) may be that there are faults in the encoding process (that is, in the symbols used), in the mode of transmission, (the channel by which it has been sent), in the means of decoding, or in the process of interpreting the message received.

If a particular attempt to communicate is to be successful, the symbols to be used in formulating (encoding) the message clearly have to convey the same meanings for both sender and receiver; the channels by which the message is transmitted have to be clear of any influences which may distort or modify the message, that is, clear of interference or 'noise', and the receptors (which may be anything from human eyes or ears to radio tele-scopes) in good working order. Further, the message has to be interpreted from the symbols in which it is received and decoded by the mental activity of the receiver; for example, the symbol 'chair sale' in the French language would convey a meaning of something like 'unclean meat' or 'dirty flesh', which would be very different from its meaning in the English language.

When we talk about accounting as a means of communication we are thinking of the records of activities and the reports prepared from time to time from those records; we are thinking of accountants as recorders and reporters of the activities of others. In this context the notion and expression of 'reporting' may, as suggested above, include analysis, interpretation and verification of information contained in the reports and the formulation of advice developed from these.

Within the usual current interpretation of accountants' functions an accounting report may be described as a communication between different persons or groups which includes or purports to include information comprising or based predominantly on financial data: in ordinary current usage, financial considerations, whether in content or purpose, are regarded as a major, and often predominant, influence in the preparation and use of accounting reports. This interpretation may be changing slightly in the direction of broadening from a narrow financial focus towards an acceptance of wider, social measures of performance; however, these have not yet become significant in the preparation of accounting reports.

The process of communication

A.J. Ayer expressed a seminal notion when he pointed out that we think that the physical world is public. If we allow for such difficulties as arise from defective sense organs, or lack of appropriate scientific instruments, or limitations on the ability to travel, 'we are all equally able to observe it and report upon it'. We can understand each other's reports because they refer to things we all have access to. When one describes a table to one's neighbour one is telling him what he (the neighbour) could, in principle, find out directly for himself, but, even if he does this, he does not have access to the describer's thoughts and feelings. 'Our experiences are private. We try to communicate them but we can never . . . be sure that we succeed. . . . We cannot communicate the content of our experiences but we can at least determine that they have the same structure' (Ayer 1955: 17).

Philosophically, one may be solipsist, but even the most dedicated and sincere adherent to solipsism could be so by concept only. If such a person set out to live practically according to such concepts, survival, and the capacity to contemplate such a philosophy, would be at risk very quickly. We do not act or live as solipsists, whatever we may think in our abstractions.

Intellectually, we all live in our own world of signs which puts boundaries on our interpretations of what we perceive. The boundaries are not completely fixed or inflexible, however, and we can vary our interpretations when we think it necessary or desirable. Further, a channel or medium of transmitting messages may operate to modify signals, and so improve or reduce the chances that an intended message will be adequately received by the intended receiver.

In accounting, most of the process of communicating appears to be one of transmitting information, but we should recognize that transmission of feeling and attitude also has a part. For instance, if the report of a company indicates a year of highly successful operations, it would be a very phlegmatic board of directors which would not seek to extract some favourable recognition from the result; and if the result is adverse, it would be unusually contrary to our knowledge of human nature to find the board accepting full responsibility without attributing at least some of it to adverse conditions over which the members of the board had little or no effective control.

Ayer also reminds us that even when the communication of information is intentional the intention may or may not be fulfilled, and, when it is not fulfilled, something different from the intended information may be communicated, and this may be information which the sender of the message does not have or, at least, is not consciously aware of having (Ayer 1955: 12–13).

Communication as a symbol is used, like so many of our words, to cover a wide range of connotations. As well as information, Ayer lists knowledge, error, opinions, thoughts, ideas, experiences, wishes, orders, emotions, feelings and moods, and such diverse experiences as of heat, motion, strength, weakness, and disease as being 'communicable' (Ayer 1955: 11–12).

However, in some of these instances, the process or activity suggested by the symbol 'communication' involves a transfer which leaves the transferor's capacity in some way diminished while that of the transferee is increased; the 'communication' of heat from one object to another is an example. In other instances, however, such as communication of information or ideas, the transfer does not diminish the transferor's supply of the commodity or the capacity to transfer it in any way; rather, the process is one of sharing, so that both sender and receiver may (or are intended to) partake equally of what is to become common to them. (Ayer 1955: 11–12).

Even further, we suggest that, in some cases the requirement to encode a message in order to communicate it to a receiver enriches the transferor's capacity to communicate. This may occur particularly where a receiver has difficulty in grasping an intended meaning clearly or precisely, and the sender has to try to overcome this by using alternative symbols more appropriate to the receiver's range of experience.

The way in which a person reacts to a symbol depends upon the symbol's relation to his or her remembered experience. If the symbol does not seem to be related to anything the recipient remembers (whether consciously or subconsciously) it will hold no meaning for that individual and, hence, no impact on his or her knowledge or feelings; it will not make any contribution to that person's fund of experience (Cf. Evans 1955: 5).

Agreement, between sender and receiver, upon the 'meaning' or significance of the signs and symbols used in the process of communicating depends upon expressing the relationship of the signs and symbols to the experience(s) to which they are taken to refer. Thus, successful communication requires, first, some commonness of experience between sender and receiver, and, secondly, agreement between them upon the relationship between the signs or symbols to be used to refer to such experiences.

Accountants (and others) decide upon the occurrences to be recorded and their characteristics. The decisions on what data are to be recorded will be made by communication between likely users. These data may include financial as well as other characteristics about occurrences. If the requirements of some users are not communicated effectively to those who decide on the data to be recorded, the intention of the users may not be fulfilled. Users may later use data from the data base, unaware of their different meaning. The information contained in reports prepared from such data may be misleading. Such a breakdown in communication could lead to different decisions being made from those which may have been made if more precise meaning of the required data had been conveyed in the first place. For example, the accountant in a manufacturing organization required, as one cost factor in estimating product cost, the dollar per power-unit of a particular machine and conveyed this requirement to the designer of a new data-base system; the characteristic 'power-unit' was included in the data specifications. The accountant had assumed the measurement was in kilowatts (kW) and the calculations of product cost were based on this measure. In fact, the measurement of power was in horsepower (hp), but this was not conveyed to the accountant, nor was it described as such in the data base. Since 1 kW=1.34 hp, the accountant's use of the data recorded about the characteristic 'power-unit' produced misleading information about product cost. Such difficulties can only be overcome through effective communication. It would be possible to store an explanation in the data base of how the depreciation and net asset value are calculated, which would help to overcome any misinterpretation of the figures. When the figures are needed by a user, the explanation would also be available.

It is often difficult to communicate successfully. It is one thing – and not always easy – to know what one means. It is another to know how to express it. And it is still another to realize that one's audience (actual or supposed receiver) may not appreciate one's meaning or understand one's expression of it in precisely the way one intended.

Most of us would probably agree with Ayer that 'we are often less well placed for testing some statements than we are for testing others', but when he goes on to say that '[i]n general, we are not so well placed for testing statements about the past and future as those who were, or will be, living at the relevant times' (Ayer 1955: 19), it is possible, and proper, to demur on at least some aspects of the past. For the number and variety of circumstances and occurrences at any point of time are so great that nobody can experience more than an infinitesimal portion of them; there is so little that can be known about what is happening, at any one instant, of what may or may not be relevant to our current and future activities, that only when some of these have worked through their consequences can we say that our activity or attitude would have been unaltered had we known then what we came to know later. The past has to be reconstructed from what has *survived* from that past, and not from *everything that happened* at the time; further, the past would undoubtedly have been different if all those living at any particular time had been aware of all that was happening in their world then. How often do we hear people say that if they had known what was happening at some time in their past they would have done something different from what they in fact had done?

Clearly, nobody can forecast with certainty what the future will unfold, and we must accept that nobody can enter another person's inner life except, possibly, under some hypnotic (or similar equivalent) influence. Nevertheless, we might well agree with Ayer's further claim that 'we are not so well placed for testing statements about another person's inner life as he is himself' (Ayer 1955: 19).

Symbols

Communicating is an *attempt* to bring into common agreement the perceptions of different people of their understanding of symbols of the language used between them. We cannot say that any given sign or symbol has a particular inherent or inevitable meaning. We can try to express the meaning it has for us and invite the reader or listener to agree that it fits in with his or her experience. If there is such agreement, then a successful communication can take place; if not, and to the extent not, then it cannot.

In the development of experience, oral symbols normally precede visual ones. For instance, the needs of young babies are expressed initially by their crying or whimpering. Communication begins with transmitting symbols. Use of a word (or other symbol) does not do anything to provide existence in anything except the word itself; its existence is constituted solely by its use as a symbol. Whatever it signifies, symbolizes or indicates, is what exists – if it exists – apart from the symbol. A smile may be a symbol of friendliness, but it exists only as a smile; it is not the friendliness itself. Indeed, as Shakespeare made Hamlet point out, 'one may smile, and smile, and be a villain'.

The range of symbols commonly used in human communication is quite wide. The following rough classification suggests this range.

Symbols	Non-verbal	Gestures e.g., smiles, nodding, frowns Sounds, e.g., groans, laughter, music
	Verbal	Non-written Speech, or the use of audible words
		Written Mathematical signs, but these are expressible in words; i.e., mathematical signs are a shorthand for words, not a substitute for them Music notation; musical scores Morse codes, etc., which are substitutes for words and letters Choreography Writing in its various forms, including hieroglyphics, typewriting, etc., which express words.

Words are important symbols. We use different words because we want them to refer to different things, whether these 'things' are thoughts in our minds or objects we can see or hear or feel. Many words and expressions which are first used with precise and specific meanings are often extended to multiple and/or even different meanings. The English language, at least, is continuously changing in the way many of its words are used and gain or lose acceptance.

For successful communication, symbols need to have referents which mean close approximations to the concepts or thoughts or perceptions of each party in communication. If words are used as symbols for concepts, the dilemma arises that the concept in one person's mind cannot be communicated to anybody else except by using symbols, especially words, in the attempt to convey the concept from one mind to another. This requires agreement upon the meaning of words or other symbols, but that agreement can only be attained, and communicated, through the use of words and/or other symbols. Thus the world of symbols is a self-perpetuating and inescapable universe by which humanity is surrounded and permeated in almost all its activities. As one writer once put it:

Dr Cherry reminds us that we cannot transmit our thoughts to each other. We can only evoke in each other whatever corresponds to the symbols which we use. The effect which our words have at the receiving end depend (sic) upon all those disparate factors which [comprise] the frame of reference of the receiver, personal to him, hidden from the sender, perhaps hidden from the receiver himself. The relevant parts must be made conscious and explicit, if communication is to be effective between those with different frames of reference; and this is one of the most important functions of communication itself.

(Vickers 1955: 81)

A few points about language

Several decades ago, one writer succinctly observed:

Language is first and foremost a means of transmitting information, and its study a branch of the study of symbols and of the signs and objects that they symbolize . . .

Language is also a form of social behaviour. If all normal humans talk, and only humans, they also talk to one another.

(Whatmough 1956: 22)

He regarded meaning as being conveyed by action, of which language was often just a verbal part; at the same time he recognized that humans often used language alone to convey meaning. He saw meaning as 'activity or expression directed to a goal . . .. subject to purpose and control (cybernetics), not something to which man is servile, but something by which he may both interpret and modify his environment' (Whatmough 1956: 68)

However, 'language' sometimes has wider connotations than the purely verbal ones. For instance in recent years 'body language' has become a subject of study of the gestures and physical body movements and attitudes observed in the search for hidden meanings lurking behind verbal expressions used in communicating. At the same time, it should be noted that the additional symbol 'body' has to be attached in order to indicate clearly the nonverbal characteristics that are being observed.

Whatmough added:

'Meaning' is what you do about a situation; what does it 'mean' to you? The question is answered by what you do, either by word of mouth, pen and ink, mere cerebral activity (provoked by perception and sensation), or by some more overt performances . . . In logic and mathematics only is it possible to assign a strictly defined, rigid, and unchanging meaning to a symbol. In language this is, fortunately, not so, and cannot be so.

(Whatmough 1956,: 71)

In amplification of this, he pointed out that, in symbolic logic, propositions, rather than words in themselves, have meaning, because only propositions can be true or false, and a proposition that is neither true nor false is meaningless. Ordinarily, however, in our language, single words may have symbolic values (that is, meanings) of their own, derived from observation of how they are used in different sentences which indicate their relationships to other words with which we are familiar. '[W]e say that we understand the meaning of a word if we know how to use it, or how it is used by others, in sentences of different environments' (Whatmough 1956: 71). Whatmough set up an important caveat when he pointed out that:

> . . . in linguistics, identity of meaning is only a convenient fiction, set up for use in analysis. The naughty child who says 'I'm hungry' just after supper because he does not want to go to bed, is not hungry in the same sense as a beggar or a tired laborer. But we assume that the meaning is the same in order to be able to identify the word as one and the same word wherever it occurs in the use of the language, notwithstanding that the meaning is not identical in every context or situation.
>
> (Whatmough 1956: 72)

However, when that author personified language by saying that it 'must strive toward equilibrium in meaning as in all its features, in order to serve the needs of communication', the metaphor disguises the complexity of the process by which our language changes. Words and expressions are, indeed, born, and in due course some die, that is, they become obsolete or fall into disuse; and the meanings of many change over time, some being broadened, some narrowed, and some, even, being virtually reversed in their usage. These variations can only take place through human action (or inaction or neglect), and it is in people's use of language that the impact of specific words and expressions is maintained or varied. Language is the instrument, humans are the players. And it is in the very course of 'serving the needs of communication', that is, the need for people to understand each other, that the changes in language occur. It is questionable whether equilibrium, in any broad sense, is aimed at when these changes are introduced by the initiators of new uses; some changes 'catch on', survive and travel and become part of the recognized language, while others are virtually still-born and disappear into an unidentifiable local oblivion.

It would seem, however, that Whatmough was not unaware of this complexity, for he pointed out that 'a language is never a completely stable system until it ceases to be spoken altogether'. By contrast, '[i]n logic stability is achieved only at the cost of inhibiting change, which sooner or later will burst the bounds of any system of logic' (Whatmough 1956: 72)

In many fields of human activity, those interested usually develop precise, singular meanings to identify substances, species, processes, formations, stages, and so forth, in the course of clarifying the significance of their activities, especially in communication with fellow students and practitioners.

Language is an instrument for identifying and classifying objects in the environment and within ourselves. It acts as a mould or set of moulds into which we can put our perceptions. But it could be and often is dangerous to have these moulds so inflexible that they govern the experiences and reject any which do not fit them. At the same time, it is possible to have an experience which one is not able to describe in accessible language; this does not necessarily mean that such experiences are not 'real', in the sense of being perceived by the individual who has the experience, but rather that that person does not have the kind or extent of communicative capacity to formulate and transmit appropriate messages about the experience. The deficiency may lie either in the education or training or state of mind of the individual or in the inadequacy of the language itself to provide appropriate symbols. The net result is that inexpressible experiences cannot be communicated.

Some of the most common and essential words in our language are subject to ambiguity. Consider, for example, just a few of the ways in which 'is' can be and often is used. When we say that 'Thomas is the brother of Jane', we are saying something to establish the identity of Thomas, by describing his relationship to Jane. If the recipient of this message does not know Jane, then the identifying of Thomas has to be attempted by some other statement, such as, for instance, 'Thomas is the man you met in the bank yesterday'. If we say 'Thomas is a stupid fellow' we are asserting an attribute attaching to him; it is a partial description of his characteristics and very different from an identification as in the previous usage of 'is'. If we say 'Thomas is here, as large as life' we are establishing that Thomas is a real person, that is, that he 'exists', and that his location has been identified, and these would be established even without the phrase 'as large as life'. In each of these cases the verb is used as a connecting link between the subject and the predicate of the sentence, but the nature of the connection varies from instance to instance.

These simple examples of the variety of usage of one of our most commonly used words may serve to caution us in our own preparation of messages when we try to convey precise information. The care devolving upon the sender becomes obvious, but the question also arises on the responsibility of the receiver. How much effort should the sender expect the receiver to apply in decoding the message transmitted? The question becomes significant in many varied circumstances, and is particularly important for accountants to consider seriously.

Accountants and accounting writers often share with many other people a lack of precision in the use of some words, especially:

(a) when one word is used to symbolize more than one different 'thing' e.g. capital;
(b) when a word or phrase that is available is not used to symbolize a different 'thing' e.g. using 'depreciation', which has more than one meaning, when allocation of cost is intended;

(c) using simple or familiar words but attaching unfamiliar meanings to them, that is, using commonlanguage words with multiple meanings or shades of meaning in a technical, restricted sense, especially in messages addressed to or reaching nonaccountants; even worse, using such words indiscriminately in varying senses according to context with insufficient indication of the intended sense in each case, e.g. almost any auditor's annual report to shareholders of an Australian publicly listed company.

One of the serious difficulties is that when specialists or technicians have to communicate with lay people they have to either use something like common-language terminology, so that the receiver can get an approximate understanding of their messages, or require the receiver to study and master the specialized or technical vocabulary which they, the specialists or technicians, use among themselves with some precision. The latter is an arduous task which many receivers are not likely to undertake properly without a desire to become specialists or technicians themselves. Further, in a field which changes rapidly, the specialized terminology may change frequently, or at least new terms are often coined to represent innovations, so that there is something like an inherent obsolescence in part of the terminology of a rapidly developing specialization or technology.

As an illustration of some of the ambiguities possible in the use of language, consider the following. If somebody sets out to give an account of accounting, the intention may be to provide a history of accounting practices or a description of them. If somebody is required to give an account of his financial dealings, this may represent a demand for a detailed listing of financial transactions or for a justification of them. If one were to say we cannot account for the tastes or the attitudes or the actions of accountants, one would be saying that there is no explanation for them or that there is no acceptable justification for them, (in the sense of proof of compliance with acknowledged criteria). The word 'account' symbolizes several different referents, and it is necessary to know something, and often a great deal, about the full context, (sometimes in addition to the accompanying words) in order to interpret the meaning specifically intended in each case. As C. Day Lewis once put it:

> As I understand it, perhaps the greatest problem now facing those sciences which cannot use the language of mathematics is the problem of finding a language more efficient to communicate their ideas. It is a problem greatly complicated, even for the mathematician, by the principles of Relativity, which demand that a statement about any course of events should admit the modifications necessary if it is to be true for any other observer stationed anywhere or moving in any direction at any speed. In the writings of scientists we frequently come across such phrases as 'Physiologists have no generally accepted way of talking about' so and so. They tell us that the exact *description* of their

thoughts is part of the discipline required for discovery; if we could find the right way to describe a given process, we should know more about the process. . .

(Lewis 1957: 17)

The use of verbal language not only transmits thoughts; it can create them. It can promote the association and development of ideas. It can also affect emotions in a similar way, and so can gesture and body language promote emotional reactions in another.

Ayer put the view that words are neither just 'reflexions of thoughts' nor 'emissaries which thought sends out, being itself unable to travel'. He suggested that thinking is 'a form of operating with signs' and insisted that:

> if the thought is to be a thought *of* something, or a thought *that* such and such is so it must be expressed in symbols of some sort . . . The thought which we are unable to put into words is vague and inchoate; the symbols in which it is embodied are fragmentary; they do not fit together, or not in any way that satisfies us. As we find more appropriate expression for it the thought itself becomes more definite. In the end one may say 'Yes, this is what I meant all along', but the fact is not that one had a meaning all along . . . The words say 'what we meant all along' because it is they that finally give its sense to the whole previous process of groping; we are satisfied with them in a way that we were not satisfied before. A part of this process may consist in fitting words to images; but then the images themselves are symbols. In identifying thinking with the use of signs . . . I do not wish to imply that these signs must necessarily be verbal.

(Ayer 1955: 22–4)

Also, as Ayer put it, if it makes sense to say that something is communicated, then it is, at least in principle, communicable. While recognizing this as a tautology, he pointed out that some things are harder to communicate than others, because either a suitable set of symbols has not been devised or mastered, or the intended receivers have not had the experience or the appropriate training to understand the transmitted message. He concluded, however, that 'in theory, all such deficiencies are capable of being remedied, although in some cases it may be practically unlikely that they ever will be' (Ayer 1955: 20).

He further observed:

> There are very many uses of language, prescriptive, ritualistic, playful, or performative, which are not factstating and cannot just be lumped together as forms of emotional expression. They have functions to fulfil, which have to be carefully distinguished and analysed for what they are, not fitted into a single preconceived scheme. . . . Many problems are linguistic, a matter of our having to be clear about the way in which words are used, or to prescribe the ways in which they should be used, but many, even in philosophy, are not, or at least not in any straight-

forward sense; and outside philosophy most are not. . . It sometimes happens that what appear to be practical disputes are really verbal; but very often it is the other way about.

This is not to say, however, that even in these cases linguistic analysis is trivial or useless. By itself, it does not solve the problems; but it can fulfil the extremely important function of enabling us to see more clearly what the problems are.

(Ayer 1955: 27–8)

As we see it, attention to words and verbal expression can often promote the framing of pertinent questions and the re-framing of imprecise or irrelevant or fruitless ones. Much of our present discussion is devoted to a search for appropriate expression of pertinent questions.

Levels of communication (A)

It is also of interest to note another early writer's list (Haldane 1955: 29) of classes or levels of communication relevant in studying biology, namely:

(a) between parts of the same cell;
(b) between cells in the same organism;
(c) between organisms of the same species;
(d) between organisms of different species.

While the level of communication that is relevant to a study of accounting is that between organisms of the same species, some aspects of intra-organism communication warrant a passing thought. For example, Haldane pointed out that muscle fibres which carry impulses from muscle to brain are more numerous than those carrying impulses from brain to muscle:

The muscle fibres are not slaves who cannot answer back. Engineers call this system feedback, neurologists proprioception. A not utterly dissimilar process in the body politic is called democracy.

Human beings have a most elaborate system of communication, including title deeds, conveyances, and so on, to establish claims to inanimate objects. Birds do so by singing. For many mammals 'my' is a single sensory quality like 'red' or 'sour'.

Philosophically this form of communication is important because it is, among other things, a communication between *X* in the past and *X* in the future, as when I make a note in my diary, or, perhaps, a note in my brain which is the physical basis of memory.

(Haldane 1955: 33)

Some of the communication between different species was regarded by that writer as equivalent to human lying, such as camouflage (moths that look like the bark of a tree, insects that look like twigs or sticks, and the like) or lures (fish with appendages which act as bait for unsuspecting prey, plants which entice insects into their ambit in order to capture them for food, and so on). He observed that, using this point of view, 'human anglers are liars, but net fishermen are not' (Haldane 1955: 40).

Some inter-species communication is cooperative, as when small song-birds of different species combine to try to drive away a larger predator such as an owl, or when flowers are coloured or scented to attract insects or other creatures which will collect and distribute their pollen as part of their feeding habits (Haldane 1955: 40).

After observing that hiding could be regarded as negative communication and that most animals, 'whether predator or prey, should not be too conspicuous', he commented that 'the colours of animals represent a compromise between the needs for making truthful communications to members of their own species, and false ones to those of others' (Haldane 1955: 41).

Communication between non-human creatures should not be regarded as irrelevant to human communication, not even that between different species. For one thing, much human communication, rather than conveying information, is still at the animal level, serving to alter the mood and, so, the actions, of recipients, as often happens in advertising, political oratory, religious ritual, and love-making. But, while this is basically animal communication about our emotions and aspirations, there is, of course, also specifically human communication about facts in the external world of each of us. (Haldane 1955: 42) It may be noted that Haldane agreed that in thought and memory the self communicates with the self (Haldane 1955: 42).

If we attempt to make an analogy with Haldane's classification in terms of social communication, we might arrive at something like the following:

1   Between parts of the same cell, such as between members of a small group of workers on a job or project; for example, between pilot, navigator and other members of the crew involved in flying an aircraft, or between the individuals (crane operator, wharf-hand, deck-hand, etc.) making up a team in loading and unloading a ship or freight truck. The individuals need to be able to communicate with each other on a fairly intimate basis, by word, instrument and/or gesture, to ensure the safe completion of the task.

2   Between cells in the same organism. 'Organism' may not be the perfect word to describe the relevant social unit, but an example would be communication between, say, sales officers and production managers or quality controllers within the same business unit to improve or ensure customer satisfaction; another might be strategic conferences between divisional representatives of a large organization.

3   Between organisms of the same species. Again, the word 'organism' may be open to some reservations, but an example would be the communication necessary in negotiations between a trade union and an employer to resolve a difference of attitudes; or diplomatic discussions on an international level; or the communication or 'commerce'

that occurs in the everyday activity of buying and selling of commodities or services.

4   Between organisms of different species. Here, the analogy takes us to
communication between humans and non-human creatures, as when a
stockman directs his sheep dog to apply its efforts to herding a flock of
sheep into a specific compound, or when a bullock driver used to direct
his team of animals to pull a load in the direction and to the distance
he required, or when a jockey urges his mount to greater effort as they
near the finishing post, or when a circus trainer gets animals to
perform their droll exploits.

A little reflection suggests that, no matter what level of communication
we contemplate, the conveyance of meaning, whatever interpretation we
put upon this word, depends upon a common sharing between sender and
receiver of the appropriate means of encoding and decoding a message;
that is, there needs to be some commonness of language between the two
parties, and this is so whatever might comprise the language and whatever
the message might be. Further, the greater the degree of this commonness,
the greater the likelihood that the intention of a sender will be 'correctly'
understood by a recipient, so long as that intention is not to mislead, that
is, in the absence of deliberate lying.

The meaning which will be attached by any unit of experience to the
symbols in any message depends upon what has previously happened to
each unit to comprise that experience. Since the experience of each unit is
peculiar to that individual, we can never be absolutely certain that the
symbols used by any two or more units of experience will mean precisely
the same for both or all of them. The best we can hope for is that
inferences or activities, the same as or similar to those intended by the
sender, will ensue after the receiver has interpreted the message; this is a
matter of empirical observation, which in turn is subject to the vagaries of
interpretation.

Data base communication

In undertaking a recording function, accountants are involved in communicating their needs to others who also participate in deciding what data
to record about occurrences. The characteristics to be recorded about each
occurrence must be specified, as well as the possible relationships that are
perceived to exist between occurrences and their characteristics. These
relationships will depend, at least in part, on the procedures to be used
later to produce reports. Each individual who participates in the designing
of systems is a distinct unit of experience, and each may have a particular
purpose in defining the data to be recorded; in an organization-wide data-
base system, for example, different users may have different views of the
data. If these different views are taken into account, and integrated into
one logical model, this would help to minimize redundant data by record-

ing them in one place only, thereby reducing possible inconsistencies. Further, it would enhance the accessibility and sharing of data between various users; it would help to install controls on one set of records to ensure security and privacy; and it would separate the description of data from the subsequent processing by users. For example, a supplier's details (name, address, telephone number, etc.) would be normally recorded once only. Such details may be used by many different users of the data base; a clerk may access the supplier's details in order to telephone about a particular order; a computer program may access the supplier's details to direct the printing of the name and address on a purchase order; another computer program may access the details to direct the printing on an invoice. Each access of the details is for a different purpose, but is to the one set of details. Subject to appropriate security and privacy controls, a user can share the records with another user. Any change in the data-base record is made once only, thus diminishing the opportunity for inconsistencies through such changes. If part of the details have to be kept secure or private, the controls will apply to one set of records. This 'data-base approach' can be contrasted with (earlier) computer-based (and manual) file management systems where such details may have to be recorded several times – once for each user. In such systems, the description and recording of the data would depend on their use for a specific purpose. For example, a person responsible for controlling inventory would keep one set of records of suppliers; another, responsible for paying suppliers from invoices received, would keep a separate set. If the supplier were to change address, inconsistencies would occur if the address were updated in one file only.

In undertaking a reporting function, accountants devise procedures that transform data about occurrences into a different form. It is generally presumed that accounting reports are intended to be useful, but that usefulness will, ultimately, depend on how successful accountants are in communicating with the users of the reports. In this case, the communication with users includes being able to (i) understand the requirements of those users; (ii) produce reports that meet those requirements; and (iii) analyse and interpret the results contained in the reports so that users may understand the implications of the decisions they presumably wish to make.

A potential problem may arise in using a data base through misinterpretation of the meaning of a characteristic that has been recorded initially for a different purpose. For instance, when the data base is designed, the decisions on the characteristics to be recorded will be derived from an integration of users' requirements, or users' views of the data, thereby eliminating overlapping or redundancy in recording of data. However, users' requirements change, and cannot be predicted entirely. A user may search through the data base for a particular characteristic for a new specific use, and find the datum (or 'data item') that is appropriate. However, that datum may have been recorded in the data base with a particular purpose or meaning different from that understood by the current user; or it may be the result of a procedure that has processed data and stored the results in the data base. For example, an accounting procedure which calculates depreciation and deducts the accumulated depreciation from the amount of the asset provides a net asset 'value'. The depreciation may be calculated by using one of several methods and the resulting net asset amount will differ accordingly. The numbers shown for 'depreciation' and 'net value' of the asset may mean one thing to accountants familiar with calculations of depreciation but may be misinterpreted by, say, an environmentalist attempting to use the data for making very different decisions from those envisaged by an accountant. In any event, the 'value' cannot, typically, be verified by reference to independent commercial evidence.

The design of a data base depends on possible users being able to communicate their present and future requirements. The designers, often including accountants, have to identify possible users and understand their needs. Prediction is a major problem: how do users know what data are needed for decisions to be made in the future? While a data base can be designed to reflect the communication of requirements from users, it must be flexible to allow for changes in those requirements. However, all that can be done *at present* is to ensure that the data base will reflect the requirements of users as accurately as possible. The process of communication between users and designers is clearly important in undertaking this task. So far as possible, it should be ensured that any changes affecting the use of data in a data base should be the subject of continuous communication between relevant parties concerned.

The problem of precision in the use of words to describe characteristics of occurrences or the result of a procedure may be illustrated by the example already referred to. A data base may include records about individual assets in relation to which one item for data may be under the word 'depreciation'. The data so recorded will be in terms of the prevailing currency. What meaning does the word 'depreciation' convey to subsequent users of the data? To the accountants who were involved in devising the procedures that calculated the depreciation, the meaning, in a procedural sense, may be quite clear. For example, the depreciation of asset A was based on the straight-line method with an expected life of five years; but that of asset B on sum-of-the-digits method; and so on. Another user, wishing to establish the 'value' of the assets to the organization for a specific purpose, scans the data base and finds the word 'depreciation'. To that user, it may mean 'wear and tear' or 'amount spent on maintenance' or some other meaning that fits his or her own experience. Certainly, without further investigation or explanation, there is no indication that the data calculated for depreciation of each asset may be on varying bases or values. The use of such data by users who do not understand their precise meaning may lead to inappropriate decisions.

The challenges facing accountants in designing and using a data base lie in (a) the definition of occurrences and their characteristics and (b) the use of the data that are recorded.

Decisions must be made on what occurrences to record, and the description of their characteristics must be precise enough to ensure that the meaning of the resulting data is understood by potential users. If a characteristic is described by one technical word, as often happens, a user needs to have adequate facilities available to describe the intended meaning for the user. For example, 'help' or 'explanation' facilities can be provided to aid a user unsure of the precise meaning of a characteristic so that he or she could request, from the computerized data base system, a precise description of the characteristic and, if appropriate, how the data were compiled.

Levels of communication (B)

One writer has observed that what an individual actually perceives is always what that person is interested in. He described perceiving as 'the process of translating messages from the special senses (seeing, hearing, touching, tasting, smelling) to indicate to the receiver that something is there, at the moment, in the world around him, which is important for him to notice' (Bartlett 1962: 147).

Our interests continue for us so long as we live: some of them grow – perhaps, in some instances, to the extent of obsession; some decrease, perhaps to extinction, at least at the conscious level; some wax and wane according to changing circumstances or opportunity; but, so long as one is alive and conscious, there is something to be perceived and what is perceived is what is of interest or concern to the perceiving individual.

This implies that perceiving is, of necessity, a conscious activity, and perhaps this is so; but if it is, we need to recognize that another kind of activity also occurs, namely, that of non-conscious or at least non-deliberate noticing of some things outside or inside the unit of experience, which is somehow stowed in the storehouse of the mind. These occurrences or 'noticings' contribute to the sum of the experience of the unit equally with the conscious, deliberate perceptions and may affect the attitudes of people in unexpected ways.

Our present context, however, does not require analysis of this aspect of mental operation, since we are concerned with the process of communication and the perceptions of the receiver of messages. At the same time, however, it would be wise to recognize that the interpretation of messages may also be influenced by attitudes developed by occurrences not carried forward into current consciousness or memory.

Various bases may be used for classifying perceptions, and one relevant for present purposes is that of relative abstraction. Many of our perceptions may be thought of as different degrees or at different levels of abstraction. At one level is the perceiving of something (or somebody) as a unique object of attention. For example, I am sitting at this table at this time – and at no other table or time. This table can be described by its features and its location; this time can be expressed by a specific date and a specific hour. The occasion is unique. But if I wish to communicate anything about this table I must be satisfied (a) that the intended audience uses the same word as I do, not only as the symbol for the article that I designate 'table', but also that that audience shall use the same words as I do to convey the meaning of whatever it is I want to say about the article, and (b) that the audience has the same understanding of space (location) and time as I have (or purport to have) in communicating about the table.

However, the word 'table' symbolizes a *class* of things within which are subclasses or subsets, such as dining tables, dressing tables, office desks, coffee tables, and so on. To communicate successfully about 'this' table requires an identifying description which will distinguish it from all other tables – and not only from those in other classes of table, but from all others in its own class. We *perceive* specific tables in specific locations at specific times. The specificity of each of these elements or characteristics is what we experience.

It is part of our experience that we are 'educated' (using this term in a wide sense) from early stages of our development to enable us to generalize most of the objects we perceive in our everyday lives; much of the social usefulness of communication depends upon this ability to form and accept such generalization.

If something is completely unique it cannot be described, because we do not have the words or other symbols to be able to communicate anything about it. Description and depiction depend upon agreement on and acceptance of the symbols we use, and that means that anything we wish to describe or depict must have some characteristics which can be compared or identified with those of other objects or sensations that have come within our experience. Consider a table that is regarded as being of unique design; there is no other table exactly or, perhaps, even remotely the same. If it can be described by using accepted symbols, it has something in common with the things that those symbols are symbols of. It may be unique as a table, but it is not completely unique as a 'thing' because it has some characteristics in common with something else that exists and can be described. For example, it may be designed as a flying cockatoo or a floating cloud, but those words themselves display its lack of *complete* uniqueness, since they are symbols of something which we can observe and describe.

Similes and metaphors are used in speech and in literature to promote communication of what would otherwise be uncommunicable, and their usefulness in this function depends upon the similarity between the experiences of the sender and the receiver of the messages comprising the communication. A 'good' description, that is, one based on accurate adherence to acceptable expression of experiences common to both or all parties, permits, at least, an approximation and, in hopeful anticipation, a close approximation, in the perceptions of the receiver, to those of the sender. The test of closeness of the approximation is usually in the hands of the sender of the message, who alone is able to gauge whether the response of the receiver tallies, and the extent to which it tallies, with the response anticipated in the composition and transmission of the message.

We should also recognize that the way in which a system of communication operates can influence perceptions and memory. As Bartlett put it:

> It is easy to show by experiment that what is perceived, and still more what is remembered, are largely shaped by the names that are used at the time. Some of these names can indicate whole classes of objects, or any instance of a whole class, or they may call attention to characteristics and properties that can belong to all sorts of different objects (like 'roundness' or 'colour' or 'truth' or 'beauty'). When this happens the names are often said to indicate that whoever uses them has a 'concept' or a 'general notion'. As concepts are achieved and are distinguished one from another, new words and names are developed, and then again these help to improve the understanding of the concepts and notions.
>
> (Bartlett 1962: 150)

We can, and do, attach names to all sorts of things that come to our attention; indeed, we use names for all our verbal communications (which is, in effect, a tautology: words are words). Tautology or not, however, we do have different levels of naming. We use names to symbolize particular, individual objects of our attention; for instance, Charles the First of England symbolizes a different human being from Charles the First of Naples and Sicily; the degree of possible ambiguity if the respective countries were not included would depend upon the context of the communication and the similarity of the experiences of the respective parties in the communication. Both names, however, are 'denotative': each denotes a particular person. At the same time, it should be noted that an individual person or thing may not be restricted to one identifying name or expression. The descriptive title 'James the First of England' refers to the same historical personage as does 'James the Sixth of Scotland'.

It is important to distinguish between a collective noun and an abstract one. In our present context, abstracting is an attempt to embrace in one expression all the characteristics of the members of a group (of things, creatures or anything that can be perceived or thought of) which distinguish them from members of any other group. For example, the characteristics of all members of the cat family could be summed up in the term 'felinity', those of the dog family by 'caninity', and so on.

There is sometimes a danger of confusion between a collective term and an abstraction which may obstruct the process of successful communication. For example, when we say that the board of directors of X Company Limited decided to act in a particular way, it is implied that there was sufficient agreement on the matter when the several members of the board came together to discuss it and that the statement is an adequate reflection of the views of all the directors. So long as we are thinking of the board as a gathering of individuals, whether they be unanimous in their views or not, we are using 'board' as a collective noun. But if we envisage the board as an 'entity' doing something, deciding in its own right or character, divorced from its composition of several people, we have stepped into an abstraction. An expression – a symbol – 'the board' – has become endowed by our imagination with the characteristics of a person who or which completely replaces the individuals who, severally, comprise and empower it.

Through our lifetime of experiences we have, for the most part, developed our thought processes and thought patterns to such a degree that we are often able to form our judgement and express it very quickly indeed, perhaps almost instantaneously, if we have some prior knowledge of the subject-matter. That is, we have at our mental disposal a highly developed complex of classificatory, abstractive, identifying and judgemental techniques and criteria which we can often apply with little or no hesitation. Sometimes, however, our thought processes are not so habitually constituted, and it may take some deliberative and positive attention to aspects of the forming and formulating of a value judgement before we are willing or prepared to express it.

The immediate point at issue, however, is that the process of abstracting – that is, of setting aside some of the known or presumed characteristics of a perceived 'object' – is frequently used; it is one that we imbibe, so to speak, from acquiring the communication skills needed in living within our own culture. Other cultures may not require the same degree of abstraction.

Some of our most deeply held and highly cherished views and attitudes are expressed as abstractions of a high order – patriotism, honour, glory, compassion, solicitude, beauty and many others; but so also are many of those that we despise (or are usually expected to despise) – treachery, infamy, selfishness, greed, sloth, vice, and so on. Our culture appears to be riddled with abstractions. What we should bear in mind is that these views and attitudes are based on and expressed in abstractions, and that we should recognize them for what they are; in particular, that they are often far removed from specific referents to which we can point or of which we can have actual experience. By concentrating our attention on certain characteristics we inevitably ignore others and so we are apt to distort the object of our attention as an object of our experience.

If one creates an abstraction for purposes of intellectual argument, it does not thereby become anything more than an abstraction. If it is a symbol for something that exists, it remains a symbol; it does not itself become something that exists outside thought. For instance, 'government' is a symbol which represents people who, through their position of power or influence, manage the affairs of some social unit – a country, a business, a hospital, a church, a club. Each of these is a symbol for people. And the relationships between the people concerned is the important thing to explore, and these are rarely, if ever, simple.

Abstractions have legitimate uses:

1   In logical (for instance, mathematical) systems to promote and/or test rationality of thought. But this use does not extend to anything outside the system, that is, it is intellectual only.

2   As symbols or shorthand references to, but not substitutes for, things or persons in the world of life and activity.

There are differences between what we perceive as 'facts' and what we conceive as abstractions. Facts can be verified or refuted by investigation, whereas abstractions are, simply, believed in. In their interpretation or description, some people are often prone to distort facts in support of their belief.

Abstractions are often more powerful as instruments of influence than facts. People, as 'nations', go to war and die for abstractions, though individuals may sometimes fight over their interpretation of facts. In truth, however, the only matter of fact which can be resolved by fighting is which is the stronger party – and that can turn out to be a matter of belief.

Classifying perceptions, as a process, involves the development and recognition of abstractions and concepts. One of the most prevalent and most dangerous myths (or fallacies) is that, once we have given something a name, whether it be an ailment, a social movement, a religious sentiment, a philosophical concept, an organism, a mechanism, or whatever else, we somehow understand it, and use it as if everybody else agreed with our interpretation. However, giving something a name serves to help people to identify it and communicate about it, *only so long as they can agree consistently* on its characteristics. It does little in itself to enhance understanding, and so contributes little towards cure or development or coping. A name has no power in itself, nor, indeed, any meaning. Any such meaning or power comes, rather, from the communicative process in which it is consistently used.

The success of an exercise in communication depends on the realization by the several parties of the part played by each one's frame of reference and whether each is able and willing to identify and allow for any differences that may exist, if those differences cannot be eliminated. And this depends

> largely on whether each party to the communication is prepared to report back what he in fact receives. The feeding back of such information is essential, if any difficult communication is to be kept on the rails and I wish that our social and moral code impressed it in each one of us as a primary duty.
>
> (Vickers 1955: 80)

One of the dangers of abstraction – at least in the English language, and, perhaps, in others also – is that, having arrived at a symbol by abstracting from many of the details which characterize the specific referents, we are then tempted to personify the abstraction, and portray a concept as something or somebody with a will of its own and the capacity to do things to carry them out. The temptation proves only too often to be too strong to resist. Our world is full of such personified abstractions;

they are among the most powerful of our social symbols. But, when we consider them dispassionately, we can see that they exist, and that they act – in whatever way they do act – only in our minds. Their 'actions' are the actions of (in most cases) people, either as individuals or identifiable groups.

We consider it a worthy aim to help people to think 'behind' the abstraction which they have become so used to taking for granted in their experience and to recognize abstractions for the concepts and nondoers that they are. And, as for ourselves, we have to watch our own use of symbols closely, for, admittedly, we do not consider ourselves completely free – yet – from the habits of intellectual attitude and usage which we have absorbed through our own experiences.

Relevance for accountants

The foregoing discussion appears to lead us to this position: before two individuals or units of experience (human and human, human and animal, animal and animal, creature and creature) can communicate, they must have some things in common. For instance, man and dog (or horse) must have somewhat similar nervous systems, vertebrated anatomies, and so on; insects and animals can communicate annoyance or threat in such a way as to be 'understood'. When *everything* is in common, however, no deliberate communication is necessary; understanding is complete, and automatic or innate; but this can surely only occur within a given organism, and even then the passage of time may result in the development of differences.

This suggests that communication occurs where both similarities and differences exist between the communicating parties. The greater the extent of similarities, the greater the likelihood of successful communication.

On a little reflection, the relevance for accountants of this discussion becomes clear and commonsensical. In the process of communicating, the functions of accountants may vary: in some instances they may be the preparers of messages or be responsible for their preparation; in others they may, in effect, serve as the channel whereby messages are transmitted; and in still others they may be recipients of messages which have to be interpreted for use, whether by themselves or by others.

Hence, accountants need to be flexible enough in their attitude towards communication to be able to fashion their initiatives and responses according to the function they are carrying out from time to time. This may not always be an easy task or a comfortable position, but it needs to be faced as part of their vocational and professional responsibilities. If they are to attain and maintain professional and social recognition and their own communal self-respect, accountants must ask themselves the question: When we prepare our messages, with whom are we trying or intending to communicate? And they need to ask this question in specific terms and not in confusing generalities. For instance, the notion that reports can be prepared as 'general purpose financial statements' is a nonsensical proposition. It has no meaning for any user of an accounting report. For, in using any such report, the user has specific aims in mind, and, in using the report, seeks answers to specific questions. The report may or may not be capable of providing such answers, and part of the technical skill of analytical accountants lies in their capacity to elicit answers which the preparers may not have been aware could be so found in the contents of the report.

With internal reports, where the recipients often have access to the preparers, many of their questions can be precisely formulated and the form of reports can be designed to provide specific answers. In this area, it is rare to find reference to 'general purpose reports' or any equivalent expression. In the field of published reports, however, where the users cannot be identified so readily, assumptions have to be made by the preparers or on their behalf, and it is in this area of accounting that most reference is found to general purpose reports. But the expression, and the notion behind it, are, to use a simile, like plastering over a gaping hole in the fabric of communication. There is, indeed, a dilemma.

On the one hand, some of the recipients of published accounting reports are known or strongly suspected to be technically incapable of analysing much of the detail contained in almost any such report. On the other, some recipients, who are technically capable, can scarcely be satisfied by any amount of detail that could be provided. And between these edges of the range, there may be an extremely large number of shades of difference in capacity. The preparers, then, are constrained to make some assumptions about the audience to which they can address their reports. And in recent years they have, at least in the case of published corporate reports, been guided or directed by the issuing of 'standards' to which they are required to conform and which have been developed by some authoritarian body of people, whether recognized as community legislators or not.

The availability of these standards, however well-intentioned they may be, does nothing to remove the dilemma or to solve the problem; they are merely part of the plastering process. There is still a gulf between the requirements of the users of these reports and the capacity or willingness of the preparers to meet them. And, indeed, the preparers, in many cases, are required to provide so much detail in supporting notes to the accounting reports that they must be presumed to be attempting to communicate only with their technical peers rather than with most of those who are known to be recipients of the reports. And, in some instances, it is questionable whether those peers can extract sufficient fully relevant information from the reports to answer their specific questions with confidence.

It is not yet known – or knowable – whether the problem can be solved, but, whether it can or cannot, the first step is surely to pose the question and not to hide it or run away from it. It will probably not go away merely by being ignored. In Chapter 16 we offer some suggestions for dealing with this dilemma.

Another aspect is that accountants, whether practitioners or academics or serving in any other position of responsibility, should be conscious of the extent to which they use abstraction and generalization in their communications. Take one instance for illustration. 'Money' itself is a symbol often used in both general and professional communication. As a word, it is used as a generalization for all those devices and instruments which facilitate exchanges of goods and services between people wherever they live and wherever the exchanges take place. As a generalization in this sense, it includes and accommodates any of a large and growing family of media, from coins and tokens to electronic transfers of entries on computer tapes or disks, to providing credit facilities or promises to meet obligations at some future time or for some future contingency. At the same time, since the various kinds of money are used to facilitate the exchange of goods and services, they represent or express not only those goods and services, but also undertakings, rewards for past services, promises of future services, including the transfer of goods themselves. But 'goods' and 'services' are also symbols of what in fact is a multifarious group of human or natural artifacts and identifiable activities. ('Natural artifact' may be a strange expression to use here, but it appears justifiable in the sense that an object, though found in nature without human effort, becomes an artifact if it is deemed to be useful to humans.) Further, the exchange of goods and services is often referred to as 'commerce', which is a form of communication in which people are brought into agreement through the use of accepted symbols of their intentions and attitudes.

It is also worth noting that a particular obstacle to effective communication arises when writers or speakers refer to 'reality' as if it is a perceptible phenomenon in itself. Unfortunately, it is not; the word is a symbol for an abstraction which is a mental construct depending on the process of communication for its conveyance of any meaning at all, and each one of us has to apply an individual, subjective interpretation of its significance; and this significance is privy to each one of us. In other words, what any human being regards as being 'real' (in his or her own interpretation of 'real') is derived from and depends upon the experience, accumulated or selective, of that particular human being. Many of those who talk or write about something 'representing reality' may well be trying to escape from ignorance or lack of intellectual persistence or penetration by using words which, on analysis, convey little or no positive meaning.

One important aspect of this general situation is that the person who records occurrences may not be (and, under many current systems often is not) the user of the data initially recorded and subsequently processed in the system; for example, the accountant may not be the decision-maker. But if the record is to be effectively used by the decision-maker, the recorder has to interpret the occurrence or phenomenon and use symbols which can be useful, when processed, to the decision-maker.

8 Units of activity – occurrences and ventures

> It is with common daily affairs that I am now dealing, not with heroic enterprises, ambitions, martyrdoms.
>
> (Bennett 1913: 67)

Occurrences

In parts of the discussion to date, the word 'occurrence' has been used without a detailed consideration of its meaning in the overall context of this work. When we say that accountants record, report and interpret occurrences and relationships arising from them, we should try to clarify what meaning is intended. Questions that arise are: What are 'occurrences'? Are they the same as decisions? If they are, does this necessarily imply implementation, or merely formulation? The nature of occurrences is the subject-matter of this chapter; decisions are discussed in Chapter 11.

In an earlier work (Goldberg 1965: Ch. 8) the unit of activity was taken to be the 'event', which was defined as an occurrence which can be distinguished from other occurrences by virtue of differences in time, place and/or character. This is not quite satisfactory; it is, at least in part, tautological, and, as well, it seems to be trying to give objectivity to events which they do not, and perhaps should not, have if we are to be consistent in linking accounting with people. If the activity is human activity, the events or the occurrences have to be performed or initiated by people, or, at the very least, have an impact on people. A natural phenomenon may, of course, occur, but, whatever its nature or extent, it can only become of accounting interest – or even of social, economic, political, journalistic or family interest – when, and if, its existence and impact are noticed by some human being(s). And even more so for activity carried out or contemplated by humans themselves.

Does the recognition or contemplation of an activity amount to an occurrence or event? Perhaps it does, in that it represents a decision made to recognize or contemplate it, and, for an accountant, to measure its impact or extent, whether known or envisaged. Various units of measurement may be applied, and herein lies the possibility of a new perspective.

The phenomena of accounting – what accountants 'deal with' – are occurrences expressive of or representing purposive activities. In an animistic, metaphorical form of putting it, one might say that accounting deals with purposive occurrences. This is why consideration of decisions is important in understanding accounting. For it is possible to account for intention as well as activity so long as a suitable mode of expression can be found.

It also suggests a reason for distinguishing between accounting and statistics. Statistics may deal with any occurrences, whether purposive or not; it is possible and proper to list, aggregate and analyse records of occurrences that represent or result from what we call chance or non-purposive influences or, at least, influences which we do not so far understand, as well as doing the same for purposive occurrences. In this sense, accounting might well be interpreted as a subset of statistics with specific procedures appropriate for a particular spread of phenomena.

However, conceptually, the processes of accounting would not necessarily be restricted to human activity alone. It is conceivable, but not necessarily practicable, that one could set up an appropriate accounting or information system for, say, a squirrel, to provide details from time to time of the progress of its hoarding activities and its subsequent consumption of its inventory, or for a hive of bees, because, (if judged by our human concepts) they are engaged in a purposive activity of gathering, accumulating and processing materials. Whether such creatures have some sort of analogous information system embodied in their perceptions is something which presumably has not yet become communicable to us humans.

What kind of occurrences do accountants select as appropriate for the exercise of their functions? The writers of most of the early treatises on bookkeeping directed the interest of their readers to the advantages of the system they were presenting (usually the 'Italian' method of double entry) for business dealings, although some included reference to its virtues for personal affairs as well. In all cases, however, the occurrences selected for bookkeeping treatment were financial transactions to be recorded in the currency of the realm; if any asset or liability or transaction were measured in any other currency it was to be converted to a common unit of financial measurement for subsequent bookkeeping treatment. This approach persisted for a long time and still remains, to a considerable degree, in most of our current text-books. These expositions took little, if any, notice of the need or applicability of accounting for non-business purposes, even though accounting records were, of necessity, being made and used by many non-business institutions, such as governments, parishes and other ecclesiastical units, and trade or craft guilds.

The complexities of trade, commerce and industry which arose from the Industrial Revolution and which were developed by the exercise of the ingenuity of numerous business people, revealed inadequacies in a purely cash recording to portray an accurate measure of net 'financial' result from periodical business activity, and the 'accrual' notion was applied as a remedy by bringing to account in a given period any deferred or expected elements of revenue or outlay which could be rationally viewed as appropriate to the period under review even though the cash impact would be felt in some other period. Not only were accrued debtors and creditors, and inventories on hand brought to account, but depreciation and amortization of long-term assets and the writing off of intangibles as well. In other words, occurrences which had financial implications as well as those which were being directly financially expressed were taken to be the subject of accounting treatment.

The unit of measurement for all these occurrences was still the currency of the realm, which caused little difficulty so long as the unit retained reasonable stability in terms of its purchasing power, that is, in the expression of earlier economic writers, as a 'store of value'. But in times of rapid or extensive variations in this measure, and, in extreme cases, its collapse, as occurred during the rapid changes of the twentieth century, retention of the currency of the realm created serious difficulties for measuring what many accountants saw as an appropriate and 'true' result of business or, perhaps more precisely, financial activities.

During the twentieth century the directors of many companies resorted to *ad hoc* revaluations of some of the companies' assets, whether upward or downward, to express recognition, from time to time, of the effects of the fickleness of the medium of exchange and its instability as a store of value. In addition, many academic and professionally organized accountants attempted to institute a systematic adjusting mechanism for business units to overcome this deficiency of the currency in the periodic public reporting of business enterprises, especially companies and corporations. Lack of agreement on details of any proposed system, absence of governmental compliance for taxation purposes, doubt on the part of many of the businesspeople affected and even of many professional and some academic accountants, and some naivety in 'marketing' strategy by its proponents, contributed to deferral, at best, of introduction of any such system, and, possibly, its demise and relegation to the curiosa of history.

Thus, the answer to the question of selection of occurrences has traditionally been that accountants have chosen financial transactions and those occurrences which have or are deemed to have ultimate financial expression.

Whether this financial constraint should continue to govern accounting procedures, and, if so, whether and how accounting procedures should dominate the description of recorded characteristics of occurrences are worthy of reconsideration.

The mode of expression used by many accounting writers has for some years been widened to cover economic occurrences, but 'economic' has usually been either taken as understood and accepted, or defined to relate to the notion of scarce resources. As already noted, scarcity of a resource has been the recognized reason advanced for its being in demand and this demand is evidenced by offering some other resource in exchange; a scarce resource requires a price for its acquisition. Hence, the notion of exchange, which is so greatly facilitated by the use of money as its medium, is implicit in the use of 'economic' by those who seek to determine what accountants should account for. (Cf., for instance, Thomas 1969: Ch. 1.) Thus, in essence, the adoption of an economic interpretation of occurrences has made little difference in their recognition, in advocacy or in practice, as being, at most, an adjusted financial expression of activities.

It is questionable, however, whether adoption of this point of view, with its constraining effects on the interpretation of an accountant's functions, is completely justified. If we go back to the earliest extant records of modern man, those of our ancestors in the Tigris-Euphrates valley and their neighbours, of some five or six millennia ago (cf. Schmandt-Besserat 1992), the symbols there used have been interpreted to relate to commodities which may have been scarce, and which may and very probably did have 'value', but the value may well have been a value in use ('utility'), which economists have long distinguished from value in exchange ('price').

There are also instances in more recent times showing that barter still operates where a generally accepted medium is not readily available, and a more direct exchange of goods for goods takes place (cf. Baxter 1965, seriatim). Indeed, the currently widespread custom of proffering and accepting a used appliance or vehicle as a trade-in on a new one is an example of at least partial barter. It might be argued, of course, that these latter exchanges take place through an imputed price being applied to the goods in question, and that the value placed upon them reduces the amount of cash (or equivalent) resources to be paid for the newly acquired commodity. While this may be true in many instances, the trade-in value is often subject to an expectation of usefulness rather than subsequent exchange, and in such cases market value is not likely to be a significant factor. In some cases, a trade-in value may be used to provide a discriminatory discount of the general retail price of a commodity. It is also of interest that the practice of bartering in parts of Australia during depressed economic conditions caused some concern to the Australian Tax Office, because of the difficulty of distinguishing the extent and value of taxable income from non-taxable acquisitions. (Lau and Brennan 1991: 7)

One significant point about barter, however, is that, when it occurs, one commodity is valued directly in terms of another, and this valuation does not need to be fixed either from time to time or between any one of the parties to the exchange and other people who are not parties to it. While this might modify the accounting for such dealings it would not necessarily mean that they are not accountable occurrences.

A further instance arises where the medium of exchange is subject to rapid and violent fluctuations, as has occurred in several countries during the twentieth century, when the market for commodities and, often also, services, reverts to a series of barter arrangements. The lack of stability of the medium of exchange as a store of value as well as a measure of value can be interpreted as the reason for much of the economic adversity and distress in the twentieth century in many countries, and this, in turn, has given rise to attempts to devise means of measuring and offsetting the effects of this instability. Some further aspects of measurement for accounting purposes are discussed in Chapter 13, where the so-called fundamental accounting equation is critically examined.

There seems to be no reason why an individual or a particular group of people should not keep a record of the quantity of commodities which are to be used rather than exchanged. For instance, if a resource is not renewable or replaceable, whether temporarily or permanently, it is none the less valuable because it is unobtainable and therefore without a price; in such circumstance its use may be strictly regulated, and its monitoring, through some kind of inventory recording, could readily be seen as an accounting function. The purpose and justification for such recording would lie in the need to monitor the usage of a non-renewable resource in order to make it last as long as possible and/or to ensure that it is used in the most effective way according to some agreed criterion. Examples could arise when supplies are strictly limited, as in cases of exploratory expeditions or sieges in military operations or, indeed, in long-term and not-so-long-term conservation of some of our planet's exploitable natural resources.

In fact, when accountants 'account for' depreciation of long-term assets, they are trying to measure the use and/or the using up of resources which have a limited life of contributing to the operations they are quantifying, and because the unit of measurement for their quantifying is a monetary one they quantify the usage in the same type of unit; they feel constrained to determine a monetary value of the periodical 'depreciation' for any such asset. What is necessary, when we think about it a little, is that the resource, whatever it may be, shall be measurable, whether precisely or in reasonable estimate (for example, equipment in years of productive service or units of output) and that the usage shall also be measurable in the same quantifiable unit.

While these considerations suggest a widening of accounting functions to cover usable as well as exchangeable resources, an even wider coverage might be contemplated to include the mere accumulation of resources, whether they are generally considered of use value or exchange value. To be sure, it may be rare for anybody to accumulate any resource that is neither scarce nor valuable, but it is conceivable that one person alone should regard some particular kind of resource as collectible and therefore of 'value' only to him; he might be the only collector in the world to accumulate such things, but if he maintained a record of his acquisitions it could well be regarded as an accounting record which would gratify his awareness of the growth in his collection from time to time. And such a record may have no monetary content at all.

Many resources, especially consumption goods, whether durable or non-durable, are acquired purely for use and are used up in the process of use. Until the moment of acquisition, such a resource has a value in exchange, but once a final consumer acquires it for use the price paid is irrelevant so long as the acquirer does not have a change of mind about the purpose for having it; the benefit gained is from its use and no variation in its price is relevant. Of course, the price of similar resources may differ from that paid, but, in relation to the use of the one acquired, any such price is also irrelevant. The price paid is a 'sunk' cost, and cannot be 'recovered' in any specific sense; it may, however, be matched by some benefit derived from its use, but this benefit may not necessarily be measured in the same units as the price paid. The very purpose of many items of equipment, for example, is to convert what is put into them to a product that is very different in nature and composition from the input.

Thus the essence of an accountable occurrence is the acquisition (through exchange, gift, inheritance, dispossession or discovery), and either the disposal (through exchange, gift, bequest, loss or use) or accumulation of a resource which is considered to be of interest by a particular unit of experience who engages in or is affected by such occurrences. The only requirement, so far, is that the resource shall be measurable.

However, we do have to note some constraints on the acceptance of the notion of measurability in this context. If the record is to serve only one person's gratification for knowledge about the occurrences relating to the selected resource, that person can use whatever unit for measuring which he or she deems suitable to the purpose. But if that person wishes to use the record as an element in communication with another or others, then the unit for measurement has to be understandable by and acceptable to that other or those others as well, and this means some consensus, which in turn implies a kind of social outlook (cf. Goldberg 1965: 175ff.)

The resource is not necessarily a commodity or physical good. It may be a service or a form of energy; for example, it may be the service of a skilled professional practitioner, the strength of a labourer, the time of a computer, the duration of a lease; so long as it is measurable it may qualify for consideration as an element of an accounting occurrence.

What is the purpose of measuring? Why do we measure things – or want to measure them? From the viewpoint of the individual – the unit of experience – perhaps the reason is a subjective judgement, in terms, ultimately, of whether one is better off or worse off if there is more or less of some perceivable thing or experience. The better off and the worse off need not be in financial or economic or even social terms; they may be, for instance, merely in terms of satisfying one's curiosity or an emotion of some sort.

The basic question to ask is: If there are more of x, is one likely to be better off or worse off? If the answer is the former, then one has to measure x in some way to find out where or whether there is more or less of it. If one is indifferent to the quantity of x, then one surely would not need to contemplate its measurement. But, even if one is merely curious to know, then measurement is required to satisfy that curiosity; and the presumption is that satisfying curiosity, and putting one's mind at rest, is a good thing for that unit of experience. If one's indifference is complete, there would indeed be no incentive to measure x, and, since the measurement of x would have no purpose, one would not measure it. This need not preclude any one else from measuring *x* or anything else of interest to particular individuals. Hence, we come back to a subjective interpretation of purpose of measurement.

If an individual wishes to communicate with somebody else about the quantity of *x*, even in terms simply of more or less, there must be agreement between them on their respective interpretations of the terms they use to communicate – in both words and numbers: the words, to identify *x* so that they can understand each other's subject-matter, that is, they must agree that *x* symbolizes the same *kind* of things for both or all of them; and the measuring unit (numbers, more than, less than, equal to) so that they can agree on the result of the measuring process when it is carried out. A significant point is that, for the most part, so long as the current view of accountants is restricted by the requirement to translate all occurrences into financial terms, the measurement of results lies in purely monetary terms; for example, efficiency is normally expressed in terms of financial result irrespective of other measures possible.

If the basis for measurement is broadened to include some non-monetary characteristics, it should be possible to improve the usefulness of the ensuing information system to incorporate other measures of monitoring the progress of or changes in the unit of operation concerned. This will, to be sure, require a broader viewpoint for accountants in selecting the characteristics to be accounted for, and this may well involve the exercise of a broader judgement.

An occurrence, for accounting purposes, expresses or represents some change in circumstances. In this context, expression and representation are intended as alternatives and not synonyms. If an activity takes place and it actually effects a change, we would say that it is an accounting occurrence which can be expressed. If, however, an activity is only envisaged or even imagined as changing relevant circumstances, it can be represented as an accounting occurrence. In the former category, implementation of a decision would be accounted for; in the latter, any stage prior to implementation may be brought within the range of accountability and the accounting processes. Thus, estimates or anticipations of future occurrences (for instance, such varied issues as long-service leave, budgets, treatment of doubtful debts, etc.) can be and are part of the legitimate field for accountants to explore, equally with the processing of transactions which have taken place between two or more discernibly distinct parties.

In many cases, if a particular characteristic of an occurrence is not recorded at the time of happening, it may be exceedingly difficult, and often impossible, to retrieve it later with complete accuracy.

The expression that an occurrence is something that 'happens' or takes place, needs further analysis. 'Occurrence' is the word we use for an inference which we make from our observation of what we deem to be a change in some aspect of our environment or self. The 'deeming' may be an interpretation of actual observation or of contemplation of presumed or assumed observation. But whichever it is, whether the observation is actual, presumed or assumed, it is of change; if there is no change, there can be no occurrence or activity to observe.

It may be helpful to put it this way: We observe (or contemplate) a change. So far as we can understand them, natural forces are operating continuously to effect change, even though some changes take place so slowly or on such a small or great scale that they are beyond the capacity of human intellect so far to detect them. But the progress which scientific endeavour has made in recent times points away from a completely inert universe or any part of it. However, human observation is limited by the capacity of the instruments it can use to observe (whether actually or in contemplation).[1] In many cases, the change itself is termed an occurrence; these changes are often referred to as natural events or occurrences. Examples would be an opening in a particular part of the earth's surface as in an earthquake, or the flow of a wave as part of an incoming or outgoing tide at a particular spot on the seashore, the fall of a specific object from the sky to the ground under the force of gravity, the emission of steam from a kettle as its content of water is heated to boiling point, and so on. The last-mentioned is an example of the use of natural forces in a humanly devised implement, but is no less an example of natural forces in operation.

If we wish to understand the change, to bring it within our capacity to 'explain' it to our own, inner, satisfaction, which involves making it appear to be compatible with our previous cognitive experience, we shall seek a causative element from which the observed change can be inferred to have come. In such cases, the causative element is regarded as the initiating occurrence and the 'effect' as a consequential occurrence.

The position may be further complicated by the possibility of inter-mediate occurrences between the initiating and the observed 'final' ones, as well as the interaction and interdependence of elements or forces and occurrences. In other words, there is rarely certainty at any time or in any instance of a clear, sole one-to-one correspondence of an initiating element and a subsequent or consequent occurrence; the proximate cause is not necessarily the only initiating element for any observed occurrence. There may be other, further removed, causal influences.

In support of the suggestion for broadening the basis of measurement for accounting purposes, the views of some writers on different types of systems are of interest.

Sorter's 'events approach' (1969) and Ijiri's 'multi-dimensional account-ing' (1966, 1967) may be considered here. Both Sorter and Ijiri had similar objectives in proposing systems of accounting that were intended to overcome a number of 'valuation' problems of conventional accounting

---

[1]Note that in saying this we recognize both the limitations of the instruments themselves and those of the users: a more skilled or more practised user of a particular instrument would normally be capable of observing more than a less skilled or less practised one.

which resulted in limited information for users. In pointing to these similar objectives Cushing (1989b) concludes, however, that: '. . . multi-dimensional accounting is generally limited to the same event set (exchange trans-actions) utilized by conventional accounting' (Cushing (1989b): 33).

In considering the definition of relevant events, Cushing initially restricted his list to those having 'direct financial implications', but then pointed out that: 'Under a broader concept of corporate accountability, events that are primarily non-financial in nature could also be viewed as relevant' (p. 32).

Included in his examples were 'product engineering data', 'ecological data', and 'personnel assignments'. Also of interest are the examples of 'non-events', given by Cushing, which included accruals, cost and revenue allocations, and depreciation.

In our view, at least some of these 'non-events' could be considered as purposive occurrences that express or represent a change in circumstances. For example, when an accountant assesses depreciation of a long-term resource, the procedure is one of interpreting and measuring the influence of such things as use, deterioration, obsolescence, market price, demo-graphic change, or any other seemingly relevant aspects; the purpose of the assessment is to provide information for those people whose activities may be affected, directly or indirectly, by it. For example, the assessment not only affects pricing of goods and services, but also has its place in any report which purports to measure periodical financial performance; the procedure is rarely just an exercise in mathematical dexterity; it is most likely a purposive occurrence for some particular unit(s) of experience. Therefore, it seems to be an appropriate occurrence to be accounted for.

The definitions of an event and a non-event (as proposed by Cushing) and our definition of what accountants deal with – purposive occurrences – can be viewed as follows. A data-base approach to designing an information system, of which accounting (in its currently accepted interpretation) is a part, would emphasize the separation of the description of data from their processing. The stage of data description involves the identification of occurrences (and their characteristics) that are of interest to a community of users, including accountants. These occurrences, both financial and non-financial, are what we believe Cushing describes as 'events'. They may be purposive since they have been identified as being required by users; and they express a change in circumstances, because a change has caused the 'event' to happen. It is about that change that data are recorded. However, the process of accounting goes beyond the identification of occurrences and their characteristics. Events, in the Cushing sense, may deal with occurrences, whether purposive or not. Most are likely to be purposive, but it is conceivable that some users will specify the need to collect data about occurrences, whether purposive or not. The data stored about occurrences specified by accountants are for use in subsequent accounting procedures. Accountants will use the data in a data base to produce information and undertake procedures that are purposive to the appropriate unit of experience. These procedures, such as the calculation of depreciation, represent purposive occurrences for an accountant.

With an appropriate data-base system, which emphasizes the separation of the description of data from their subsequent processing, those users who want to use data unencumbered by further accounting procedures may do so. The accounting procedures and their results can be kept quite separate from the data used in those procedures. Measurement in non-financial terms should be considered if we are to improve the resulting information for users. However, it is useful to separate the occurrences about which we record data from later purposive occurrences arising from procedures. This separation can be made conceptually and physically. A conceptual model about the occurrences to be described initially can be developed before any attempt is made to implement it, for example, using computer hardware and software. Once implemented, the initial recording of the data about occurrences can be physically separated (on data files, for example) from the results of those occurrences that are purposive for accountants. Both the initial data and the processed results will be available to a user.

Ventures

Occurrences as single happenings have little significance in themselves. Significance can only arise in a relationship between occurrences which have or are perceived to have some common characteristics. Such a set of occurrences, which may range from as few as two to a very large and, at times, indefinite number, comprises a venture.

In carrying out their accounting functions, accountants record occurrences, but they report ventures.

Three examples of some very simple ventures would be:

(a) John buys a pen   Occurrence 1
     He sells it   Occurrence 2
     _____

(b) Mary buys a postage stamp   Occurrence 1
     She uses it on a letter   Occurrence 2
     _____

(c) William buys four postage stamps   Occurrence 1
     He uses the first stamp   Occurrence 2
     He uses the second stamp   Occurrence 3
     He uses the third stamp   Occurrence 4
     He uses the fourth stamp   Occurrence 5
     _____

These are all ventures of a simple type, namely, the acquisition and disposal of a resource. Each venture is completed when the 'physical' resource acquired has been totally disposed of. However, time elapses between occurrences, and in some ventures this time between the initial and the final occurrence may be considerable or even very great.

Each venture can be considered before the final disposition; in each of cases (a) and (b), after Occurrence 1 but before Occurrence 2. In case (c), after Occurrence 1 and at any point before Occurrence 5; for instance, after the third stamp has been used, the position is that, of the initial acquisition of four stamps, three have been disposed of and one is still available for use; in other words, after Occurrence 4 the venture has still not been completed.

At this stage attention has been directed solely to the inherent or 'physical' characteristics of each resource. The 'value' or monetary tag ('price') has not arisen. Neither has the matter of intention. For instance, in case (a) John may have acquired the pen intending to use it himself, but that intention was displaced by the need or the opportunity to sell it. There are, however, instances in which an intention, such as the formulation of a decision, is taken to be an accountable occurrence and thus the start of a venture, or even an occurrence within a venture. Thus, in case (c), William may decide to take one of the stamps, all of which he had acquired for postal use, for his personal satisfaction rather than its designed social function of facilitating communication. This occurrence, although one of disposal within a venture of acquisition-cum-disposal, constitutes a different kind of use from that of the other stamps acquired by Occurrence 1; this form of use would warrant different accounting treatment from that of the other stamps acquired at the same time.

Many ventures are the results of decisions; they express the activities which constitute the implementation of decisions. Ventures are composed of occurrences which involve human activity or which impinge upon human experience; a venture comprises a set of occurrences which are perceived (by humans) to relate to the interest or concern of some unit(s) of experience. While it is difficult to think of a venture which is not the result of a decision or a series of decisions, it is not claimed here that it is impossible or unimaginable. It is suggested, however, that, although most ventures arise out of decisions to undertake some positive activity, it should be recognized that the intention behind a specific resolution may be varied before complete implementation is carried out. The course of implementation may change or may be aborted; however, this in itself would require another 'decision'. Some further aspects of decisions are examined in Chapter 11.

But the facts that occurrences may have several characteristics, some of which may not come under consideration when particular decisions are made, and that these characteristics may be subject to recombination in unforeseen or unintended ways, suggest that occurrences may create or adhere to relationships not comprehended or not adequately allowed for when a given decision is arrived at. Thus, while a given decision makes it necessary for occurrences ensuing from it to be accounted for in terms that are specifically envisaged in whatever venture may be clearly intended, it is also possible that they may become parts of other ventures not foreseen or intended when the decision was being formulated or, if recognized at all, were regarded as not sufficiently relevant or material to warrant distinct recognition in the decision-making process. To the extent that these neglected characteristics do, in the outcome, constitute or contribute to relationships which may become relevant or material, they begin to constitute unforeseen ventures which require recognition for the production of information. It is by this means that improvement in the development of decisions can take place.

Thus the notions of both occurrences and ventures are potentially fruitful concepts, worthy of exploration not only in their theoretical aspects but also in their practical applicability for enriching the performance of information systems.

There is some ground for regarding the concept of the venture as being more fundamental for commercial activity – and perhaps for other social undertakings – than that of a time period. For instance, in his account of the 'great chartered companies', Hannay pointed out that the Portuguese explorations of the African coast prior to the rounding of the Cape of Good Hope by Vasco Da Gama were 'creeping voyages . . . made slow not only by the quality of the ships and the inexperience of the crews, but also by *the necessity to enable each cruise to pay its expenses* by trade in gold dust, ivory, and slaves . . .' (Hannay 1926: 8, emphasis added. In Hannay's account the dates of 1587 for the rounding of the Cape and 1598 for the reaching of Calicut appear to be misprints for 1497 and 1498 respectively.) Each voyage was, in effect, a self-contained venture, financed, according to Hannay, by foreign, that is, non-Portuguese, capitalists such as bankers of Italy, Germany or the Netherlands.

In writing of the English East India Company, he stated:

> The practice of forming syndicates for each voyage was a makeshift proper enough to the very early days of experiment, but not as a permanent arrangement. One voyage might be out before the other was back. They fell across one another, and as each had its own factors, and put them at a chosen port of trade, it naturally came to pass that competing agents were left face to face, with no common authority to compel them to work together. Being human, and often very human, they came to loggerheads. . . . It was no less inevitable that muddle should insinuate itself into the Company's accounts. On one occasion, indeed, the Governor and his council had to confess that God alone knew to whom a sum of money they had in hand rightly belonged. Such excellent men of business as they were came speedily to the conclusion that there must be a change of method. In 1613 it was decided to form a joint stock for four years, the amount being £418,691, to be paid in four equal instalments yearly.
>
> (Hannay 1926: 180)

Eventually, the notion of a fixed term of investment gave place to one of indefinite (and, hopefully, perpetual?) investment, and the concept of long-term continuity with 'arbitrary' divisions into operating or 'accounting' periods of one year or less became the accepted norm; this became the traditional practice which spread from commercial enterprise to private and individual activities (especially under the requirements of an annual income tax). Governmental undertakings, under the political requirement of annual accountability to parliament, are also subject to a similar concept.

Accounting period

The term 'assumption' or 'convention' has often been used to describe accountants' use of a specific accounting period in carrying out the processes of accounting. What is often overlooked is that, if this is taken to be an assumption that accountants make or that is imposed on them by circumstances (social or individual) outside their sphere of influence, there is a further assumption *behind* that of the accounting period which should be recognized, namely, the concept of continuity of change, of which a time period is a measure.

As human beings we accept, and we have to accept, as a fact of living, that everything is subject to change, and our concept of a period of time is simply a measure of our perception of change. For social convenience we agree on a conventional unit by which to describe the passage of time, and this agreement has attained the status of a universal, objective unit among us. But to many of us occasions arise when we apply a subjective measure by which we say that, for each of us, 'time passes slowly' if we perceive little change in our environment, or that it passes too quickly if the perceived changes are considered too many for us to feel comfortable with.

We also accept that changes are, for the most part, explicable. This is a reflection of our human capacity to adapt, so to speak, our perception of occurrences which constitute a change to conform to our current sum total of experience, or, in other words, we lay a claim or a hope to understand them. Another way of putting it, however, would be that something which changes does so in the course of becoming something else. This may seem like a truism, and indeed it is, but it is worth raising because it introduces the positive aspect of change, namely, the concept of 'becoming'.

Thus, starting a venture is an embarkation on a course of becoming – a voyage during which and by which some change will be made through occurrences which will take place. The period may be long or short, but the situation at the end will differ from that at the start. Within a long period for the whole venture, it may be necessary or convenient for human purposes that interim assessments of change be made, but we should recognize that these are interim assessments and, in relation to the whole venture, tentative until the full termination of all those occurrences which constitute it.

It seems that accountants rarely ask how, in their procedures or in their thinking, they portray this aspect of 'becoming'. At the same time, however, we should recognize that the notion of continuity is, itself, an abstraction from a succession of separately identifiable occurrences. The occurrences in a venture are linked to each other, but, if they are to be recognized, they have to be identifiable; each has to be distinguishable from all the others. If we seek to interpret activities in terms of time periods, and view those taking place in one time period as distinguishable from those taking place in another time period, what we are doing is imposing a concept of continuity upon a collection of ventures, some of which are likely to be in course of operation (that is, 'continuing') at the beginning or at the end of any particular time period.

Both the notion of time and the notion of the venture are based on the perception of change, and the perception of change is through our observation of occurrences. Whether we link occurrences as elements of ventures or as elements of time periods is a matter of classification, which as already noted (Ch. 4) is a human technique devised for human understanding and communication.

It might be going too far to say that continuity is an illusion and that therefore the accounting period is an assumption based upon an illusion, but continuity is an abstraction and our use of specific time periods is a human and arbitrary means of applying a human technique of classifying observable occurrences for human purposes.

In practice the concepts of the venture and the time period are both significant; both have to be translated into accounting procedures. There may be and almost always is overlapping between them in even the most simple series of accountable activities; it is rare for the durations of a venture and an accounting period to be identical.

It might be more precise to say that for particular purposes one of these concepts may predominate over the other, in accounting thinking and in accounting procedures, with, nowadays, a more widespread predominance of the period over the venture. But even this requires considerable qualification, for in many highly significant areas of decision and policy the notion of the long-term venture, with its requirements of great capital investment, is often predominant over that of the time period involved, which may be several accounting periods.

Where the accounting period is shorter than the venture time, the accounting interpretation is in much the same situation as that of the 'creeping voyages' of the sixteenth century: when results could not be determined until the voyagers were back in their home ports with the clearly observable and calculable results of their activities during their long period on the seas and in foreign lands.

Some years ago Gilman pointed out some examples of the 'transition from successive to overlapping ventures' which have taken place in the twentieth century:

> In the early days of automobiles their manufacturing and marketing conformed somewhat to the successive venture type. As automotive manufacturing practice became standardized and as effective distribution channels were developed, individuality as between one car and another was practically lost. With the introduction of the modern production line, automobile manufacturing now resembles a continuous

stream like the manufacture of soap, breakfast foods, matches or razor blades. . . . The manufacturing of airplanes is even now undergoing the transition from a series of separate ventures to continuous production.

(Gilman 1939: 74)

Recombinant characteristics and recombinant occurrences

We wish to emphasize that each perceptible occurrence of vocational interest to accountants is that it has more than one accountable characteristic. Hitherto the accountant has generally restricted his notice to the monetary aspects of occurrences, with an exception for records of 'physical' inventories, and even in these the physical terms of the records are often justified by reference to their financial implications. We suggest here that occurrences are themselves composed of more than one characteristic and that there is now available in attainable technology the means for recording and subsequently classifying, summarizing, reporting, analysing and inter-preting occurrences in a much richer and more effective manner than has been possible under a monetary-driven recording process.

The way in which this can be done may be termed the recognition of recombinant characteristics. Each occurrence is seen to have several charac-teristics which can be recorded and stored in an appropriate and adequate manner for subsequent extraction and recombining into sets for com-parison and analysis that will provide decision-makers with a greater amount and more varied arrangement of information to guide them than is currently recognized.

Even within the set of monetary characteristics there is a variety of perceptible measures that can be adopted for processing in the accounting system. The base of value for each occurrence, for example, may be the immediate sum outlaid or received, or some translation of that into a more current measure of cash equivalent, whether of purchasing power in terms of other commodities or of replacement of goods or equipment. Dis-cussions between accountants over several decades have revealed a variety of alternatives to what has come to be known as historical cost for accounting interpretation of occurrences. Thus one or even more than one of the alternatives to the presently generally accepted historical cost model could be incorporated into the recording procedure for each occurrence, the formula for translating each monetary amount being set in motion when the occurrence takes place. In this way it would be possible to have, simultaneously, continuous records and timely reports on a number of different bases of price-change formulae.

We wish to emphasize that each of these 'values' for given occurrences could be incorporated into an accounting information system so long as it was recognized as feasible and of interest to users; since an occurrence has – or may be perceived to have – multiple characteristics, it can be treated according to each characteristic. Of course this would give multiple results for any one set of occurrences, and this would serve to reinforce the point that the interpretation of occurrences is a matter of human outlook and human activity. There is no reason to suppose that any occurrence has a single unequivocal outcome because only one of its multiple characteristics is selected for accounting treatment. A good example exists in the trend in Australia to impose financial criteria on assets held in cultural collections in which non-financial objectives are manifestly significant to the social purpose of such collections (Carnegie and Wolnizer 1997).

Another possibility would be to incorporate into the information system a number of 'what if' directives so that the likely effects of alternatives to the actual occurrences could be traced, at least to some extent, without disturbing the handling of the data about the occurrences themselves. This would increase the extent of available information, if not the competence of the people called on to act upon it. Further, what has occurred may have occurred differently. An alternative may be interpolated into the system and its likely effects inferred by analogy or deduction according to a formula.

As observed already, an occurrence involves change. It may be a change in location, time or condition of something or somebody. An occurrence is a change that can be perceived by somebody, who has an interest in perceiving it; it is an interpretation of or inference from what is perceptible. The perception does not necessarily have to be contemporary with the occurrence; it may take place after, but obviously not before, it. However, occurrences may be anticipated or foreseen, but these do not become actual occurrences until they do happen, and if steps taken in anticipation are effective, the eventual occurrence may turn out to be different from that foreseen.

Some instances of characteristics other than the traditional monetary measurement which may become accountable would be derived from a recognition of objectives, such as the pursuit of the least consumption in a given process of non-renewable resources, the least use of pollutant substances in manufacturing processes, the safest procedures and conditions for workers, the safest or most wholesome product for consumers or users, and so on. At least some aspects of these are measurable, and therefore can be brought into measurable and accountable relationships.

These characteristics are not those normally recognized as 'economic' phenomena, taken by most accounting writers to be essential underpinning for any accounting procedures; they are, however, important social aspects of human activity, and, if they can be accounted for in a useful manner, such accounting should not be precluded on the ground that they are not yet admitted into an economic-driven accounting theory. If the technology is available and could be developed by accountants there would seem to be no reason for not applying it to increase social benefit.

Significance of occurrence and venture

For accountants, much of the significance of these concepts of occurrence and venture lies in appreciation of the inherent complexity and variability of the characteristics of the former and the flexibility of the latter.

Consider a simple example. An area of floor space is acquired for the locating of several pieces of equipment of different dimensions and different kinds. The acquisition of the space and its disposal constitutes a venture of spatial dimensions as well as one of financial resources (such as the amount of rent to be outlaid from time to time). Hence, in addition to any record to be installed and kept for the monetary transactions, another record can be set up for the spatial allocations to the several pieces of equipment. This recognizes the spatial characteristic of each piece of equipment, as well as that of the floor in total. Each piece of equipment would have, in addition to a monetary expression for the costs of its operation and for a 'valuation' of its output, 'quantitative', but non-monetary, expressions of those costs (e.g. units of power, time, human effort, material used in operating it, idle time, and the like), and output (number of articles produced, or quantities of materials processed, etc.).

These are all characteristics of the occurrences of using the equipment, and the function of recording of each one could be applied to broaden the base of information about each piece of equipment. In this sense, the acquisition and use of a piece of equipment could be viewed as constituting not only one venture, but several ventures, or, at the very least, one venture expressible in several different ways according to its various aspects.

Further, however, not only could each piece of equipment be viewed in this multiple way, but each type or mode of characteristic which the several occurrences display could also be segregated, if required, and aggregated, to constitute a kind of venture in itself. For instance, the use of, say, electric power or water (or both) could be related to each use of each piece of equipment and assessments made on a base of information in ongoing records derived from the analysis of recombinant characteristics of occurrences.

The concept of occurrence is a simple one in itself, but each occurrence has a number, perhaps an indefinite number, of characteristics which may prevent it from ever being 'totally' recorded. At the same time, available technology exists to record occurrences in much greater and more useful detail than is usually applied. We suggest that accountants should seek these details in a positive exploration of the social aims of the individuals and groups of people who make up a society. This will, of necessity, involve judgement and ethical decisions – or, at the very least, ethical attitudes. For example, accountants will need to assess, say, purposes of individuals and groups against a backdrop criterion of social well-being; in a sense, they do this at present to the extent of considering such things as legal restraints in relation to some activities.

The concept of the venture is one of fluidity and variability. Some ventures are readily determinable, and their termination can be easily recognized. Others are, in effect, indeterminate; they may go on for a very long time before they are completed and their completion recognized.

But there is one feature which characterizes human ventures in this sense of the concept. They are all, initially at least, purposive. That is, the initial occurrence is the first step towards an intended or projected outcome. The initial intention may subsequently be varied, or the projected outcome may not ensue, but this does not alter the position that the venture was embarked upon with a purpose, which, if necessary, could usually be expressed specifically in definite and positive terms.

Some characteristics of an occurrence which may be considered for recognition include, as a non-exhaustive list: date, time, location, description of commodity or activity (sufficient for identification at any time), quantity, initiator of activity, direction of activity (=purpose), source of authority for activity (minute, written or verbal instruction, implementer's own initiative, etc.), implementer or actor, expected effects of activity or transaction, observed effects, classification (e.g. debit and credit for traditional accounting recording, duality relationships or inflows and outflows as advocated by some writers), monetary tag (price, cost, outlay), total quantity and/or cumulative outlay or intake. No doubt others can arise according to the circumstances of the occurrence. For instance, an occurrence which is, in its essence, a thought rather than an observable physical activity, might give rise to, say, an estimate of the usage life of a long-term resource, or of the deterioration likely through non-use, or wastage involved in its use. These would also be relevant characteristics in accounting for a venture of the acquisition, use and ultimate disposal of a particular piece of equipment.

From among this (non-exhaustive) list of characteristics, somebody has to select those considered necessary or desirable for recording. In most present-day accounting systems, these would be the date, description (=identification), quantity, parties or accounting classification involved (=accounts), and monetary tag (price, cost, value). The remainder are rarely incorporated into the accounting processing system; if they are noted at all, it is usually as parts of a separate, non-accounting data-processing system.

If the characteristics of occurrences are very numerous, the kinds of occurrences are legion. It is submitted that it is not possible, in a changing world, to list or enumerate all the constituents of this variety. Whatever occurrences may be examined for appropriate consideration should be interpreted and taken as examples only; they are meant to be regarded as illustrations of occurrences which do sometimes take place. In practice, the characteristics of any occurrence to be recorded need to be determined according to the circumstances at that time. This is no small responsibility for a professional person to undertake. We are, indeed, suggesting that the accounting system for many, if not most cases, can and should be broadened to include more characteristics than are now usually admitted. To be sure, this would widen the responsibility and functions of accountants professionally, but if they are not willing or able to undertake them it seems likely that some other professional people will develop a capacity and willingness to do so.

Clearly, whatever additional characteristics are to be accounted for, those currently included in accounting processes will need to be continued. Present accounting practices can readily incorporate these. But, as an illustration, it may well become a responsibility of particular people to monitor the control exercised over specific types of activity, for example, to ensure that excessive quantities of pollutants are not emitted into the natural environment. Those characteristics which quantify such emissions from occurrences may then have to be distinguished and brought into an information system. If such characteristics are identified at the time and place of the occurrence, they could become the subject of accounting treatment. This implies a recognition that some of the current emphasis upon the sanctity of the bottom-line result needs to be spread further afield to effects of accountable occurrences upon other aspects of living in a society where the natural environment has turned out to be, itself, a scarce resource. As members of a responsible social profession, accountants could well turn their minds in this direction.

Appendix to Chapter 8[1]

Ventures

A series of occurrences (not less than two, but often many more) linked by a common measure and a social or economic objective into a meaningful relationship constitutes a 'venture'. For example, the receipt of a quantity of goods and its piecemeal issue to various production jobs until it has all been disposed of constitutes a venture; so does the purchase and sale of a commodity or a specific number of articles, and the building of a bridge.

These examples are simple and straightforward and may be considered as representative of 'determinate' ventures. A determinate venture is a series of occurrences for which there is a determinable result. If you buy a television set and a radio and later sell the television set, you cannot relate the sale of the television set to the purchase of the radio to get a venture, but only to the purchase of the television set.

Many series of occurrences, however, are not so easy to determine, in the sense of setting boundaries or limits on them. For example, consider the acquisition of shares or stock in a company. Dividends are received on the shares, perhaps regularly, perhaps irregularly; the amount of the dividends may be subject to fluctuation; the shares may be disposed of after a short period or they may be held for a long time, perhaps being transferred from one shareholder to his heir or to the trustees of his estate after his death for the purpose of holding them as a charitable trust in perpetuity. Of course, the shareholding will terminate when the company itself is wound up, but the contemporary social framework is such that the end of such a venture is virtually indeterminable. Or take the purchase or erection of a building. Rent may come in regularly, with some fluctuation in amount from time to time; the building will require maintenance and repair and may eventually have to be pulled down. The title in the building may pass successively from generation to generation, and we can, in fact, see

---

[1] Taken from Goldberg 1965: 89–95. Some variations in terminology have been made to accord with that used in the present work.

buildings in the old world which have been standing for hundreds of years and which will, it is to be hoped, last for hundreds of years more. The end of such a venture is also indeterminable. And what of the land on which a building is erected? Here is something in respect of which maintenance and repair do not apply – it simply exists, and will continue to exist indefinitely, so far as practical human conception can tell.

So far as a particular human being is concerned, we could, of course, say that all the ventures in which he has concerned himself terminate at his death. *His* shareholding or *his* title to land is no longer his when he himself is no longer here. In this sense, all ventures of human beings are determinate. But if the holding is in the name of a corporate body, which has had an indeterminable period of existence endowed upon it by law, the venture, once more, is indeterminable in so far as the corporation *may* endure beyond the life of any presently living person. It must be recognized, however, that this indeterminacy is a result of a legal convention which gives to corporate bodies a continued existence within the existing social system. A change in the system – such as took place in the supersession of feudal society – might well involve the cessation of the life of many corporate bodies which at present have no foreseeable end. (In some countries, admittedly, there are in existence corporations which have survived from feudal times; this does not invalidate the above propositions – we merely have to extend the period back to pre-feudal days or, say, the Roman Empire, and we can safely say that none of the then existing and functioning bodies now exists.) Thus, even for the corporation, it is reasonable to conceive the termination of all its ventures, if we are prepared to extend the period of time sufficiently far.

The difference between a determinate venture and an indeterminable venture is thus one of degree and, basically, one of time. The distinction between them is nevertheless convenient for purposes of exposition and analysis. Thus the activities of a corporation may be regarded – until it has ceased or is about to cease to exist – as comprising an indeterminable venture which is composed of a vast number of determinate ventures beginning and ending at numerous and various points of time within its life, overlapping and interwoven in a complex pattern. The accountant's task is to segregate each of these ventures for appropriate accounting treatment, but at the same time he has to determine the relationships between the various ventures and assess the overall result of their interactions. For example, the purchase and sale of each commodity, the acquisition and use of each long-term asset, the issue and redemption of each debenture, are determinate ventures within the life of, say, a company; each one represents a strand in the cloth of overall activity which we call the life of the company. The accountant should not only record each one of these ventures, but he should also relate each one to the others so far as is applicable, determine the result of such interrelation and consider whether the result is satisfactory and what future action the result suggests. Some writers would appear to deny that this last is a function of the accountant as such, averring it to be rather that of managers or directors or government heads; but there is much to be said for the view that the accountant, who should be more familiar than anybody else with detail behind the result, is in the best position to at least recommend and advise on desirable policy (even if he is not given the executive power to carry it out), any recommendations he may make on such matters being regarded as those of a professional expert and, although, perhaps, not mandatory, having a strong (non-legal) sanction.

There appear to be a few primary, recurring patterns of determinate ventures discernible from a consideration of accounting procedures:

(i) *Trading ventures.* Acquisition and sale of a commodity, with a resulting profit or loss on the venture. The fact that there may be various kinds of outlays incidental to the purchase, manufacture or sale of the commodity – buying expenses, freight, salesmen's expenses, advertising and the like – or that, between acquisition and sale, there may be a change in character of the product, as in manufacture, or an accretion process as in, say, a flock of sheep or an orchard, only serves to make a particular venture or series of ventures somewhat more complex, without disturbing its fundamental character.

The basic pattern is that a commodity is acquired at a cost of $\$x$ and is sold for $\$y$, the difference $\$ (x \sim y)$ being the measure of profit or loss on the venture.

The pattern recurs, in accounting procedures, under such various disguises (among others) as consignment and joint venture accounts, job cost finding, liquidation and realization accounts.

(ii) *Usage ventures.* An article is acquired and used for a more or less specific objective, the elemental pattern being of the form: Of 100 units of a commodity acquired, 40 are disposed of on objective x, 25 on y, and 35 on z.

The pattern will be recognized as applying to such various procedures as inventory records, pastoral, i.e. live-stock, accounts and long-term asset accounting. What is commonly called depreciation might be explained or, at least, expounded, by saying that when, say, a machine is acquired, it represents a quantum of units of service which are allocated on a usage basis (time being an approximation to usage in many cases) to relevant objectives; a similar representation could apply to 'amortization' of, say, a lease or a copyright, and to 'depletion' of, say, a mine.

(iii) *Financing ventures.* Resources are obtained, whether in the form of commodities or money, and a commitment for their subsequent return, in the same or a different form, is entered into, with or without an interim compensation for availability.

This type of venture covers a wide range, but in each case the three fundamental occurrences can be distinguished.

In the case of an ordinary credit purchase of goods, there is first the occurrence of obtaining the goods and the creation of the liability to pay for them, and, secondly, the discharge of the liability. The third element may arise if interest on the commitment is charged, especially where a promissory note or bill of exchange is an intermediate step in the discharge process, or where goods are acquired on hire-purchase (conditional sale), and the 'hiring' charges include a substantial interest element. Or it may appear as discount for prompt payment, which means, in effect, that the cost of acquisition may turn out to be less than the invoice price of the goods if discharge of the commitment takes place within a specified period; in this case, the compensation for the availability of the resources is included in the initial commitment but is rebated under appropriate subsequent circumstances. In the case of a cash purchase, the discharge of the commitment takes place so soon after its creation as to be regarded for all practical purposes as simultaneous with it.

The issue of shares or stock in a company involves, first, the acquisition of monetary resources from the shareholders, with, secondly, a commitment for an ultimate return of the resources, whether augmented or diminished, whether in the form of cash or other resources, when the company is finally wound up. There is an interim obligation to pay dividends periodically out of available profits, as compensation for the investing of the resources. Similarly with the investments of partners, while the issue of bonds or debentures or borrowing under a fixed-period loan is also closely analogous, except that the commitment for the return of the resources is fixed in amount and usually in time, and the compensation is in the form of interest at a fixed rate independent of the making of profits or losses.

Where a bank overdraft is used, as is common in the United Kingdom, Australia and other countries, the resources are acquired in the ordinary way from suppliers, but the discharge of the commitment to them is effected by an exchange of that commitment for one to the bank, and the compensation becomes payable to the bank as interest, rather than to the supplier. Thus it frequently happens that a creditor will allow a discount on being paid promptly, while the payment increases the interest charge payable to a bank because of its increasing an overdraft. The overdraft must be settled ultimately by repayment to the bank either on termination of the borrower's activities or earlier, and in turn this may involve a different financing venture, such as an issue of shares or debentures or the raising of a mortgage on some of the borrower's property.

(iv) *Service ventures.* A natural or acquired skill, of a personal nature, is made available for the benefit or enjoyment of others for a reward, which may be financial or non-financial.

This type of venture covers not only professional activities of various kinds but also those of tradesmen, agents, salesmen, sportsmen, entertainers, artists, domestics, and all those cases where personal services are involved.

(v) *Custodial or fiduciary ventures.* Resources are placed under the control or management of a person(s) who, while not being the beneficial owner of them, is responsible to another or others for their safekeeping or disposal. Trusts, charitable and educational foundations, receiverships, and some government activities will be recognized as being basically of this character, while some aspects of the accountability involved are often present in some of the other types of venture.

In any given set of circumstances, several ventures of each kind are normally being undertaken at the same time, and the character of some of the ventures may influence ventures of another type. Thus a decision to acquire a machine or a building may be affected by past or prospective financing ventures; a particular financing venture may be undertaken in order to permit certain trading or usage ventures to be carried on. Hence the accountant's task in relating each venture to its contemporaries and in determining its characteristic features distinctly from those of the others is not always easy. Isolation of each venture does not necessarily reflect a valid result, because of the interaction between different contemporaneous ventures. Nevertheless it is necessary, as a preliminary to sound decisions, to isolate each venture from all others, and it is this aspect of isolation which constitutes a basic feature of the recording process in accounting. The recording of occurrences is, indeed, a fundamental aspect of accounting, but, as is now widely recognized, it is by no means the only important aspect. As a next step, the accountant must examine the recorded occurrences and relate them to each other in such a way that the relationships so determined are significant for and relevant to the objective in view.

9 Relationships

Tse Kung asked, 'Is there one single word that can serve as a principle of conduct for life?' Confucius replied, 'Perhaps the word 'reciprocity' (shu) will do. Do not do unto others what you do not want others to do unto you.'

(Lin Yutang 1938: 186)

A large part of the accumulated knowledge of any given unit of experience comes from the observation of activities external to itself; and such activities include the behaviour of other units of experience. However, before a given unit of experience can interpret these activities as relating to another unit of experience, it must recognize (even if this recognition is based merely on a presumption) not only that such other units exist but that they can be identified as units and that each can be isolated in some way from the rest of its environment for separate observation. The capacity for such recognition, it would seem, is not difficult for us to attain; our very birth gives each one of us a separate unitary existence and at the same time begins our apprenticeship of learning that we are not independent of others around us, whom we gradually learn to distinguish, not only from our own self, but from each other as well. Further, the connection between one unit of experience and another, that is, the way in which and the extent to which the behaviour of one unit is affected by that of another, constitutes a relationship between the two units, and these relationships are important parts of the experience of either or both, according to the circumstances of any given case.

A relationship 'exists' when the presence of a phenomenon or the activity of an occurrence is perceived or conceived by a unit of experience. The phenomenon or occurrence may lie within (the organism of) the unit of experience, whose function of perceiving or conceiving is taken to be separate from other functions it may exercise. Thus, one may have a relationship with some imaginary or hallucinatory being which cannot be perceived by anybody else but which is none the less influential and, indeed, powerful for the person experiencing it. In other words, a unit of experience who or which perceives or conceives any state or happening, whether within itself or external to it, has a relationship with that state or happening.

It is truistic to say that in social matters all relationships are, ultimately, between people, and that it is the activities of people that produce relationships between them. But, truistic or not, this simple proposition often seems to be overlooked or ignored by writers on accounting.

There are many ways of classifying relationships; any classification is a human artifact, each one appropriate to a particular purpose. Some primary categories that suggest themselves include: perceptual and conceptual relationships, direct and indirect, active and passive, conscious, sub-conscious and unconscious, intellectual and emotional, deliberate, habitual and instinctive, and so on. Some of the relationships which are or may well become significant for accountants are briefly discussed below. These relationships may be identified and classified in various ways.

One basis of classification might be regarded as methodological, under which relationships could be considered as either 'observational' or 'interactive'.

Observational relationship

The relation between one unit of experience and another or between it and a non-experiential 'object' may be termed 'observational' if the process of observing in itself does not affect the behaviour of the observed in any discernible way or to any discernible extent. This is a relationship which pervades most scientific observations or, at least, is normally presumed to underlie them. In recent years, some scientists have expressed doubt about the universality of such pervasion in their field.

By adopting the techniques of scientific observers, many writers on accounting – especially those who carry out 'empirical' research projects – make this presumption, often, it seems, without recognizing that they do so. In many cases the individual researcher may appear to be widely separated from the phenomenon being measured or circumstances or situation under observation. But, if there is any trace of a feeling or belief or 'hunch' in the attitude of the observer that there is or may be something 'wrong' or something that needs to be corrected or even if there is any trace of the contrary, namely, that the observations are of something that does not require any change, the relationship goes beyond that of pure observation into one of observation influenced by opinion, that is, with an element of a value judgement. On this ground, the path of empiricism strays a little.

Indeed, the very positing of a hypothesis by which the 'behaviour' of observed activity is to be gauged is, essentially, an expression of a value judgement of the way in which the observed should behave in conditions or circumstances laid down, explicitly or implicitly, by the hypothesizer in formulating the hypothesis. Conformity of the observed behaviour with the hypothesized behaviour is taken as evidence of the validity of the hypo-thesis; non-conformity as evidence of its non-validity (and therefore as ground for its rejection or modification) or of some fault in the observing process (occasioning, perhaps, re-observing or varying the conditions of observation). In either case, the element of value judgement in the hypothesis is not relinquished. This does not mean that the observer is consciously or deliberately distorting or even influencing the observations, but it does mean that the criteria by which the observations are judged or measured are, unavoidably, subjective in origin and reflect the attitude of the observer as a unit of experience.

Observational relationships frequently arise in practice. Examples are (a) a supervisor watching and assessing the performance of workers under his charge; (b) a marketing executive of one organization observing the market strategy of a competitor or of an agent or subsidiary; (c) an accountant observing the efficacy of a computer program to meet the requirements of a particular user.

Interactive relationship

An interaction may be defined as the creation of or a change in a relationship between two or more (observable) units of experience. In carrying out the procedures of accounting, accountants do observe and attempt to measure relationships between units of experience. These relationships comprise the result of an interaction between units of experience and usually give rise to further interaction between them. While observation of the activities which give rise to these interactive relationships is required for recording data about them and applying appropriate accounting procedures, the activities are observed from a particular point of view in each case, and the accounting treatment will be affected by the point of view adopted. Indeed, for most of these interactive instances, the point of view adopted for each unit of experience is the reverse of that of the other involved: any given transaction between two units of experience is reflected in the accounting records of each as the reverse of its treatment in the other.

One feasible approach is that the functional activities of accountants are concerned with 'resources', taking this word in a broad sense to include such things as personal skills, strength or knowledge as well as physical objects, whether movable or immovable. Accountants purport to trace the acquisition or incoming of various kinds and quantities of resources, the ways and extents to which they are 'dealt with' to change their character or location or applicability and their ultimate disposal or transfer to another destination. All of this could be expressed in terms of the creation of and changes in interactive relationships.

Another basis of classification of relationships would recognize the socio-legal-economic characteristics that a number of relationships embody. These would include relationships such as indebtedness, ownership, possession, use or deployment, trust (fiduciary), consumption, and accessibility.

Indebtedness

Perhaps the most common and longest-standing relationship to which the procedures of accounting are devoted is that of indebtedness. Indebtedness arises whenever two or more parties are involved in actions or situations which entail obligations or commitments on either or both parties, that is, when they enter into a transaction: one is a debtor, who is under an obligation to meet some commitment to the other, a creditor, who is entitled to receive from the debtor the benefit of fulfilment of the commitment. The debtor is indebted to the creditor.

Indebtedness occurs as a result of two factors: (a) a lapse of time, whether it be short or long, during which (b) a state of trust exists between the parties involved in the relationship. The lapse of time may be so short as to make the state of indebtedness virtually instantaneous (as in a cash sale) or so long as to make it virtually perpetual or, at least, without a foreseeable end within the duration of the existing culture of the community (as in a 'perpetuity' or annuity for an indefinite period into the future).

It may be of passing interest that the terms 'credit' and 'creditor' are derived from the Latin *credo*, I believe, I trust. Also derived from the same Latin root are such words as 'creed' and 'credibility', while we also in English use 'credo' to intimate a system of personal beliefs. This reinforces the suggestion that the notion of trust and trustworthiness is not only widespread but also deep-seated in the relationship of indebtedness.

Indebtedness may arise from a multitude of circumstances: from trade, borrowing, investment, trusteeship, marital agreements, court proceedings, taxation, levies, pledges, gambling, and so on, wherever somebody undertakes or even appears to undertake an obligation to do something for the benefit of another. For traditional accounting purposes, the commitment is measured and recorded in monetary terms, but this is, fundamentally, a convenience in our modern socio-economic conditions. In pure barter circumstances, however, a monetary measure would not be available, and the commitment would be expressed in terms of commodities or services. (See, for instance, Baxter 1965: 22, in which delivery of a quantity of oats and rye gave rise to a request for a shipment of bibles, testaments and psalters; Mair 1748: 25, where the entry 'Wares received Dr. to Wares delivered' is prescribed for barter when the goods received and delivered are of equal value, in which case, it may be noticed, the notion of a common medium of exchange is not avoided.)

Ownership or proprietorship

The relation between owner and resource is subject to the social or cultural constraints in which humans find themselves. We should not take our own notion of personal and private ownership as being either universal or inevitable.

An alternative view is exemplified by the Bushmen of the Kalahari desert. According to one investigator, the lives of these people are too precarious to permit quarrelling between themselves, so that they deal with disagreements by removing their causes. As a result 'the few possessions that bushmen have are constantly circling [*sic*, meaning 'circulating'] among the members of the group'. Bushmen always share their objects, food and water with the members of their band, 'for without rigid co-operation bushmen could not survive the famine and droughts that the Kalahari offers them' (Thomas 1968: 22). The author illustrates how it is done:

> No one cares to keep a particularly good knife too long, even though he may want it desperately, because he will become the object of envy; as he sits by himself polishing a fine edge on the blade he will hear the soft voices of the other men in his band saying: 'Look at him there, admiring his knife while we have nothing.' Soon somebody will ask him for his knife, for everybody would like to have it and he will give it away. (Thomas 1968: 22)

The relation between the possessor or handler is, in truth, an expression of a relationship between that individual and other members of his band. In much the same way, what we regard in our more complex and sophistic-ated society as an inalienable right of ownership of an object is, in fact, a right against the potential claims of other members of the group, that is, a social right. But this right is often limited or restricted according to per-ceived social needs; we are used to living with prohibitions which refine and restrict our rights to do as we might otherwise like to do with what we consider to be our own property or belongings.

In broad terms, within the Western culture which constitutes the environment for this work, ownership is a socio-legal relationship by which it is commonly recognized within a given community that people have a right to do what they desire to do (with communally agreed limitations) to or with anything in their possession or at their disposal. The limitations are important; for example, ownership of, say, a building does not normally confer a right on the owner to burn it down for the purpose of collecting its insured amount, or to allow it to create a danger to another or others or to any other property, or to use equipment in it which emits poisonous gases into the atmosphere or sparks which might start a fire, and so on. In effect, the right is not absolute; however, to the extent that it is exercisable, that is, legally recognized, it is exercisable, ultimately, as against any other person in the community.

There are degrees of ownership. The highest degree – if it were practic-able would be an absolute right to dispose of property (in a wide sense); this would be equal to the greatest possible interest which a person can have in property. For example, the discoverer of an uninhabited island in, say, the Pacific or Antarctic Ocean. But this right would be meaningless in that no forum exists in which it can be recognized unless and until the discoverer has some contact with other human beings. Immediately a forum is set up, others come into the picture, and, in effect, society comes into existence. And, as soon as we have society we have restrictions on many rights of individuals, including the right of ownership.

Ownership, then, expresses the rights against other people (including others via the state) which a person may have in the disposition of his property; it is also the ability to exercise such rights in the property as are not prohibited. Some aspects of ownership may be vested by an individual in another or others, as in the case of a trustee, director or agent.

Legal disputes arise where the right is questioned. The right may be asserted by an individual or group not only against other individuals or groups within the community, but also against the community itself (under the nomenclature of the Crown, the people, the government, etc.) and vice versa.

Possession

'Possession' and 'ownership' are sometimes used interchangeably, but there is also a sense in which the two symbols refer to distinct relationships. For instance, when a thief takes possession of another person's watch or jewellery without the owner's consent, he does not thereby gain a social or legal recognition of any right to its ownership; indeed, he may be said to dispossess the rightful owner, and incurs the displeasure of not only the owner, but of most of the community as well; if he is caught, he could be liable to substantial punishment for acting outside a generally accepted code of behaviour.

Behind this, clearly, lies an acceptance by most of the community of the notion of private property, a cultural concept not universally applied, but widespread in those communities with which we are most familiar. And, in such communities, while there may be some property which is seen to belong to all the people in common, that is, to the community itself rather than to any individual or to any smaller group than the whole community, it is usual to set up a fictional or notional 'being' or 'person' for legal recognition as an ostensible owner for purposes of enforcing a legal or social right analogous to that of private property; for example, 'Crown' land is deemed to be possessed by the government of the day on behalf of all – or the vast majority – of the people in the community for the benefit of all and to the exclusion of those who might want to exercise non-communal rights to it. Despite this, however, the thief, while not having a legal or socially recognized right, has a capacity, while the goods are in his possession, to use them or dispose of them according to his wish and according to the opportunities available to him, whatever the consequences may be for him.

Thus, in the present context, it is appropriate to recognize a relationship, which can be called 'possession', to describe the condition of having a capacity, apart from any socio-legal right, to handle, or use or dispose of usable or disposable resources. For the most part, the resources are physical objects, but there are instances where rights and evidence of rights may be included in this category; for instance, the recognition in law of the right of adverse possession, under which, after a lapse of time, the undisputed occupancy of a piece of real estate by somebody other than the rightful owner may give a good title of ownership to the occupier, even against that rightful owner.

Again, it is common for owners of material objects to delegate or assign to others a capacity to use one or more of such objects freely or, at least, with wide powers of use, short of disposal, so long as they are in 'possession' of them. For instance, the owner of real estate – a building or a rural block of land – may lease it to a tenant who can use it in any reasonable and fitting way so long as the lease is in operation, without having a right, which is reserved to the owner, to sell or otherwise dispose of the property.

Use or deployment

Closely akin to possession, perhaps, there is a relationship by which people, other than the legal owner(s), have the capacity and the right to use resources in specified social or legal circumstances. For instance, equipment sold under a 'finance lease' or instalment purchase agreement is physically transferred from the vendor, who retains the legal title to it, to the purchaser, who has the right to use it while in his possession, until the final instalment of the amount due under the agreement has been paid, at which point the title is transferred to the purchaser, who thereby, but not until then, becomes the fully recognized owner of the equipment. The agreement may, however, embody some restrictions on the extent or mode of use by the purchaser during the term of the agreement.

Fiduciary

A fiduciary relationship arises when a person, often known as a fiduciary or trustee, is responsible for the custody or administration, or both, of property belonging to another person. As a legal relationship, the 'person' in either case may include other-than-sentient human beings as well as individual people; thus, we could have an incorporated company acting as a trustee for another incorporated company, or an incorporated company as an executor of the will of a deceased individual. Functionally, however, the performance of the fiduciary duties and the meeting of the fiduciary responsibilities can only be carried out through activities of individual human beings. They, and not the incorporated companies, are the units of experience who can actually perform the requisite functions, whatever the expressed legal attitude may be.

There is an element, and often, perhaps, a fairly strong element, of fiduciary relationship in some of the other relationships already noticed. For instance, an employee who has the custody of a piece of equipment owned by an employer has an obligation to use it with reasonable care for its intended purpose; a director of a company is in a fiduciary relationship to members to take care and use diligence in performing the duties of a director; nevertheless, neither of these would be regarded as officially a trustee in the normal, legal sense.

The most obvious instances in which this relationship has attracted the attention of accountants over many years are the legal relationships of a trustee in bankruptcy, a liquidator of a company in winding-up procedure, a receiver appointed to supervise operations in a situation of financial difficulty, and an executor and/or administrator of a deceased estate. These are legally recognized fiduciary positions for which legal rules and procedures have been developed to a considerable degree over a long period.

Although many of the procedural aspects of the accounting for these functions are well settled, there are still some intriguing questions of theory that may be asked. For example, in the case of a trust estate for a deceased person, from whose point of view are the accounting records to be kept? Although the resources which form the subject of the estate did belong to the deceased, that person can no longer be considered to have any viable interest in them after death. The executor, who is appointed under the will or by a legal process, has the custody of the resources that once belonged to the deceased and is charged with the duty of carrying out the deceased's wishes as expressed in the will; however, unless the executor is also the sole beneficiary, the deployment of the resources must be undertaken for the benefit of others, namely, the beneficiaries; and, even so, the primary obligation is to any unpaid creditors of the deceased, including, it may be noticed in passing, any taxes or other imposts due or becoming due to the government of the day.

Is the paramount point of view that of the beneficiaries? It may be suggested, with some semblance of legitimacy, that the resources, though subject to prior claims, are or will eventually become the property of the beneficiaries. While this may be true, there are different kinds of beneficiaries recognized at law, and the interests of those who are tenants-for-life and those who are remaindermen could well be in conflict; the former are entitled to distribution of income from investment or deployment of resources during their lifetimes, while the latter are entitled to the outcome of realization of the resources on disposal after the interest of the former has ended. While it is possible for some beneficiaries to be both tenants-for-life and remaindermen, the potential clearly exists for clash of interest in other cases. Should the accounting problem of determining the point of view be subject to such an issue?

Can the problem be avoided by setting up a notional unit, which we may call, say, the estate, and keep or purport to keep any records from 'its' point of view? Perhaps this might be attempted, but it is difficult to see whether or how it would resolve any of the problems. The relationships involved are between people, and the trustee is required to develop and maintain records which reflect these relationships. Even if we accept that the beneficiaries are, in some nebulous way, equivalent to the owner(s) of, say, a business enterprise, we have to recognize that the primary aim of a custodian is functionally and economically different from that of an owner or manager of a business; the primary custodial aim is to preserve and distribute the resources rather than to increase them as a capital growth. There is a fundamental difference in point of view between an owner and a custodian in this sense. This is a facet of the culture in which the accounting with which we are familiar is carried out.

It is interesting and instructive to consider a little the position of a trustee, one of whose cardinal duties is, as was pointed out many years ago, 'to take as much care of the trust property as being a prudent man of business he is accustomed to take of his own' (Birrell 1912: 25–6). The requirement for a trustee to be prudent is linked to a positive, albeit a somewhat vague economic or social criterion of a man of business dealing with his own property. There is an implicit acceptance not only of the legal recognition of private property, but also a presumption of due care and caution in deploying it. Thus, if a habitual gambler were to become a trustee, he would not be permitted, in the eyes of the law (or of his fellow citizens) to apply the same attitude to the trust property as he would have to his own; he would have to keep his gambling activities strictly apart from those as trustee. And, if the previous owner of the trust property had been a gambler (and even if the trust property embodied accumulated gains from gambling) this would not permit the trustee to engage in gambling as trustee of that property. In this sense, the criterion of prudence is an 'objective' one, and, even though it might not be precisely measurable, there is a considerable body of legal evidence – in our cultural inheritance – to assist in its determination in specific instances.

Command

Several years ago the notion of a relationship of 'command' over resources was introduced into the accounting literature. (Goldberg 1965: Ch. 9, Secs. VII, VIII). It was there stated:

> It is . . . suggested that . . . we should direct our attention to the function of control which can only be exercised by human beings. It is submitted that the unit of experience and outlook for accountable activities is a human being or small group of human beings who has or who have the power to deploy resources over which they have economic and, in certain cases, legal control, whether or not such legal control constitutes a right of ownership.
> . . . the term 'commander' is used to signify the person who has such command over resources. This notion enables us to arrive at a realistic interpretation of the purposes and functions of accounting without recourse to artificial abstractions.
>
> (Goldberg 1965 pp: 163)

While this presentation emphasizes an economic interpretation of this relationship, it is, in fact, a broader, social relationship which embodies duties and responsibilities to social mores and standards of behaviour which may take their place alongside and even, in some cases, transcending those of adherence to a direction from an immediate superior within a particular organization.

Some aspects of this relationship are further considered in Chapter 11.

Consumption

Where a resource is consumed, that is, where it loses completely any residual usefulness for its user, we may say there is a relationship of consumption as a separate category of deployment or use. Many expense materials, including such a wide variety as postage stamps, waste materials (like cotton waste or lubricating oil), energy (gas, electricity, fuel, etc.), occupancy costs, advertising, have a common characteristic that their use involves their 'using up'; once used, there is little, if anything at all, that can be used again. This relationship is not restricted to such ephemeral or evanescent resources. In a sense, it also applies to many long-term resources; the difference is a matter of duration. While the instances mentioned above are short-lived resources, a piece of equipment which can be used over many years can nevertheless be completely used up at the end of that period; the relationship of consumption lasts longer, but is functionally no different from that of a piece of rag.

Underneath all the technical and quantifying endeavours of accounting writers on topics such as depreciation, for instance, there lies this relationship of consumption. In passing, it may be noted that recognition of a residual value for some resources slightly qualifies, but does not remove, the relationship; it merely envisages a minor adjustment to the final disposition of the resource; that is, rather than saying that the resource totally loses its residual usefulness, we add a phrase, such as 'except that in some cases there may be a salvage or disposal value'; the expression used above in its entirety still stands, namely, the resource 'totally loses any residual usefulness for its user' in applying it to the purpose for which it has been used. In some cases, indeed, consumption of an asset may continue beyond the time when any quantifying of its value in normal accounting measures is available, that is, after it has been 'written off'.

Accessibility

Underlying many of the recognized relationships, including such legal ones as ownership, is that of accessibility or availability, which exists wherever a resource can be used or enjoyed by an individual or group of people, whether subject to legal or customary restrictions or not. The international waters of the planet beyond the recognized national coastal limits comprise a storehouse of fixed and mobile resources which 'belong' to no specific human beings until claimed through some legally recognized human activity. Even before any such recognized activity occurs, however, anybody who sails such an area has a relationship of accessibility to the resources which abound beneath the surface. In recent years, also, the human exploration of space beyond the earth's close atmosphere has made accessible and potentially available resources of which as yet most humans know little. At a less elevated level, so to speak, or on a more mundane one, many governments claim a right of ownership of land on behalf of the community which they represent or purport to represent, some of which they declare to be accessible to anybody within the community under relatively very slight restrictions on their activities. This also often applies to some buildings and, for instance, collections of art or craft or books or scientific or historical material and the like; some of these are made freely available to visitors for their use, education and/or enjoyment.

The relationship of accessibility is often considered to be as valuable as that of ownership; for instance, some students would regard access to reading material in communal libraries as more valuable to them than their personal ownership of books and periodicals, even if they could afford considerable personal acquisitions; again, for many people accessibility to publicly-owned parks and gardens is the only way for them to enjoy more than a minute area of horticultural effect, and accessibility to zoological establishments their only source of acquaintance with the fauna of other regions.

Other relationships

There are, of course, other important relationships which rarely impinge directly upon the accounting aspects of one's experience. Some of these would be citizenship, marital and familial relationships, educational (pupil–teacher) and so on. In some circumstances, however, even some of these may have a bearing on others which do affect accounting processes.

There are also relationships which, often, cannot be adequately expressed in words; they may be emotional, instinctive, embodying sympathy, anti-pathy, phobia or bonding. For instance, one may experience a sense of wonder or beauty or awe or peace and serenity in the presence of some natural phenomenon for which available symbols may be incapable of communicating the experience effectively, however much one may try to express it. Such relationships are not subject-matter for accounting, but they exist nevertheless and are powerful in particular circumstances in affecting the activities of people; accountants should be aware of them and recognize their potential capacity to influence accountable activities.

All the relationships which are recognized for treatment in the account-ing processes are relationships between people; the means of recording them is often the only available or the only acceptable evidence of a particular relationship. Viewed from this aspect, data recorded about occurrences, whether in the form of conventional accounts or in data-base systems, are instruments of social record.

A hypothetical, but nevertheless interesting and possibly fruitful, question might be suggested here. If we imagine a Robinson Crusoe, a marooned and solitary human being with no opportunity for developing social relationships with other humans, we might well ask whether he could have any need or desire to make a record of any kind which might be of any use to him. Certainly, no record of indebtedness would be of interest:

he would not owe anything to anybody but himself, nor would anybody else owe anything to him. The question of ownership would scarcely arise: he could regard himself as owning all or nothing, since there would be no other human being to contest or support his claim to any part of the island or any object in it. However, after experiencing the vagaries of weather and seasons, he could well decide that a record of supplies of food and other provisions as available, as produced, and as consumed might serve a useful purpose in meeting changing circumstances arising from the natural habitat in which he found himself. If he knew how to do it, he might well set up some kind of inventory record. The relationship he would be interested in would be that of procuring, using, and consuming resources of whatever kind he considered less than plentiful beyond his requirements. In other words, he would be concerned with keeping some sort of score of scarce resources, which is at the heart of the perceived field of economics. Perhaps this is the common ground between economists and accountants which should be explored by them conjointly.

Multiplicity of relationships

In many cases, some of these relationships are only conceptually distinct. For example, in a modern company, a shareholder may also be, simultaneously, a director, a borrower, a lender, a customer, a supplier and an employee of the company.

As a shareholder, the relationship is that of owner

As a director, it is that of $\left\{ \begin{array}{l} \text{fiduciary} \\ \text{deployer of resources} \end{array} \right.$

As a borrower with, for example, a housing loan, it is that of debtor

As a lender (debenture holder), it is that of creditor

As a customer, it is that of debtor

As a supplier, it is that of creditor

As an employee, it is that of deployer

One function of the accounting processes is to keep these relationships distinct and account for each one separately from the others. Traditionally, this is achieved by using separate accounts for each relationship for each individual and adherence to a detailed classificatory identification of persons, resources and functions.

One of the purposes behind an accounting system is to have records and reports which reflect relationships and, if possible, to measure them. It is the relationships that underlie the point of view from which the accounting processes are carried out. Also it will be necessary to ensure that the method of recording enables accountants to identify relationships that are suitable for a particular purpose without inhibiting the identification of other relationships for other purposes. Traditionally, indebtedness and ownership have been the most common relationships dealt with in accounting procedures, although other relationships have an influence in some circumstances. For example, cost accounting often reflects the relationship of use or deployment, while the fiduciary relationship is an overriding factor in trustee and liquidation procedures.

One of the challenges facing present-day accountants is to explore the means of making accounting procedures and products express other relationships which have social significance. In order to do this it may be necessary to recognize or even invent appropriate means of measurement, whether financial or non-financial, not usually available in current accounting practices.

Appendix to Chapter 9

Observational and interactive relationships

The process of observing can be carried out only by a unit of experience. Hence, an observational relationship can only exist where there is not less than one unit of experience to do the observing.

If there is more than one unit of experience, the one or those being observed may or may not be aware of being an object of observation.

(a) If the person or object is not aware, the act of observing may be construed as not affecting the observed person or object.

(b) If, however, the object is aware, he, she or it may be indifferent to or affected by the act or process of observing. If indifferent, the circumstances are equivalent to (a) above; if affected, there are interactive relationships.

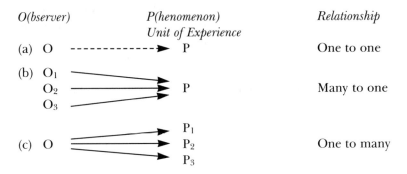

O(bserver)	P(henomenon) Unit of Experience	Relationship
(a) O ------------▶ P		One to one
(b) O₁, O₂, O₃ ⇒ P		Many to one
(c) O ⇒ P₁, P₂, P₃		One to many

If P are activities of, say, people who are also observers, (P-O) that is, people who are units of experience, then:

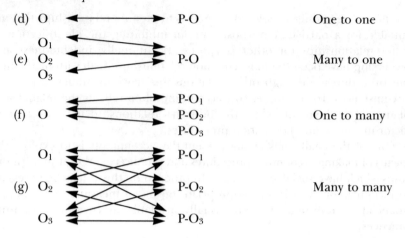

In so far as the term 'relationship' has or implies some positive or activating sense or connotation, we can interpret this series of symbols thus:

(a) implies only one relationship: that of O with P

(b) implies three relationships: O_1 with P; O_2 with P; O_3 with P

(c) implies three relationships: O with P_1; O with P_2; O with P_3

(d) implies two relationships: O with P-O; P-O with O

(e) implies six relationships: O_1 with P-O, P-O with O_1; O_2 with P-O, P-O with O_2; O_3 with PO, PO with O_3

(f) implies six relationships: O with P-O_1, P-O_1 with O; O with P-O_2, P-O_2 with O; O with P-O_3, P-O_3 with O

(g) implies eighteen relationships: each of O_1, O_2 and O_3 with each of P-O_1, P-O_2 and P-O_3; each of P-O_1, P-O_2 and P-O_3 with each of O_1, O_2 and O_3

In effect, the relationship between each O and each P-O could be interpreted as one relationship looked at from opposite points of view.

Another way of regarding interactive relationships is to think of them as being created or developed by volition, that is, at least one of the units of experience involved in the relationship acts purposively towards the other or others in the relationship.

Consider a relationship of, say, relative weight, such as 'x is heavier than y'. Is this a relationship between x and y? At first sight it may seem obviously so. But, on reflection, is it not rather a relationship between an observer, say, A and x, and a relationship between that observer and y? In other words, somebody – a unit of experience – must be there and capable of observing both x and y and assessing their respective weights. Hence the initial statement can be expanded to reveal the implication more explicitly:

> A observes both x and y and perceives (or judges) that x is heavier than y.

The stated relationship becomes a statement of observing and perceiving, even of judging or measuring, all of which are processes of, at least, animate creatures, and, within the context of this work, of human activity.

The further point that may be noted – in passing, almost – is that the search for or contemplation of a causal relationship between observed phenomena, even between natural occurrences or states of being, is based on a human concept of 'cause'; it is humans who attribute a relationship between what they perceive as a causal occurrence or force and a subsequent occurrence or state. Even though the observations may be interpreted as being unaffected by human activity, the perceiving and interpreting processes are human activities.

While interactive relationships can be created or developed only between animate creatures, observational relationships can arise between one unit of experience and an inert object or some form of natural force. Consider a landslide or a flow of lava from an active volcano. These could hardly be regarded as completely inert objects because they are moving; their motion, which we perceive as observers, is interpreted by us, as conceivers, to be caused by forces of nature whose operation we may understand to the extent that it fits in with and is acceptable within the framework of our accumulated experience (or knowledge). Anybody in the path of the slide or flow would quickly develop an observational relationship towards it, which would be motivated by a desire to get out of the way as quickly as possible. But the relationship is not interactive in the sense that the force of nature or the slide or the flow has – at least as far as we can at present tell – a volitional or conscious purpose in directing a particular course for the natural activity. That is to say, while P, the phenomenon, may not be affected by the process of observing, O, the observer, is likely (in some circumstances) to be affected by his interpretation of what he observes. O sees the flow of lava, interprets it as being a danger to him if he stays where he is and is motivated to get out of its path. Does this constitute an interactive relationship? It is certainly a reaction by O, based on his interpretation of what he observes, but hardly an interaction if the flow of lava is unaffected by anything the observer can do.

Perhaps accountants of the future will explore relationships with close attention and in greater depth, and determine whether some of them may serve to broaden their perception of their legitimate field of interest.

10 The unit of operation and the notion of command

Is this a dagger which I see before me,
The handle toward my hand? Come, let me clutch thee:
I have thee not, and yet I see thee still.
Art thou not, fatal vision, sensible
To feeling, as to sight? or art thou but
A dagger of the mind, a false creation,
Proceeding from the heat-oppressed brain?

(Shakespeare, *Macbeth*, Act II, Sc. 1)

Introduction

In the previous chapters in this Part we have sought to emphasize that the vocational processes of accountants are essentially concerned with the activities and the results of activities of people, who have been termed 'units of experience' in order to avoid discrimination or connotation of bias or prejudice (Chapter 6). It was also pointed out that the process of accounting is, as it has always been, one largely of communication between two or more units of experience (Chapter 7), that the occurrences which happen in the lives of people are its perceived subject-matter (Chapter 8) and that these occurrences create or affect the relationships between units of experience (Chapter 9).

In applying accounting procedures an accountant traditionally focuses attention upon a specific, holistic unit in terms of which particular occurrences are observed, interpreted, recorded, and further processed. It is convenient to apply a term such as 'unit of operation' to distinguish such units. For instance, if a practitioner, say, an accountant, not only conducts his professional practice, but owns or leases some land on which he grows carnations and tulips for sale in a horticultural market, and, at the same time, has an ostrich farm, each of these interests – the practice, the horticultural land, and the ostrich farm – may be regarded as a distinct unit of operation. The accountant – the unit of experience – may be the sole proprietor and beneficiary of the activities involved, but may wish to maintain the distinction between the occurrences applicable to each interest. Thus, the circumstances relating to each interest would be distinct from any others and could become a focus of attention in accounting for them.

The notion of such a unit is a fluid one in that it may range from the separate interests of a single human being through those of a group of people to a legal-fictional 'person', such as an organization or institution, and to such artificial, conceptual concoctions as a cost centre, a fund or a trust estate. Some of these units comprise collectives of people acting together, to a greater or less extent; some are intellectual inventions, that is, abstractions, 'on behalf of' which specifiable people are regarded as acting.

The numerical procedures of accounting are, in any given case, consistently applied to a specific, identifiable unit of operation, whether natural or notional, to express relationships between it and other units of operation and, as required, between its own constituents (sub-units).

Before considering the unit of operation in any detail, it is desirable to discuss some of the relationships which are relevant to the attitude and activity of accountants.

Entity

On the Entity theory
An accountant is a grave man
Whose work is very serious.
Some think that, like a cave man,
His gods are most mysterious.

And yet, behind his calm visage,
Behind his thoughtful mien,
There lies a psychical mirage,
A self-hypnotic lien.

For he believes in entities
(As loved by metaphysicians);
Confused in their identities,
He thinks they make decisions!

But let us not assert he's lost,
Nor that he's not clear-seeing;
It's just that he prefers the ghost,
And ignores the human being.

Accounting writers sometimes confuse the unit of operation with the unit of experience. It is true that sometimes these seem to be identical, in that the unit of experience – an individual human being – is the focus of accounting attention, that is, the occurrences which impinge upon and constitute part of the experience of that human being are the subject-matter of accounting procedures which encapsulate relationships directed towards that individual.

However, even in such cases as this it is frequently advocated that, for purposes of exposition, a fictional entity, which becomes a purely accounting vehicle of thought, should be set up as separate from the living sentient human being. Such a creation is called 'the business', 'the concern', 'the firm', 'the enterprise', 'the household', 'the reporting entity', or the like. These are what we term 'units of operation' and, indeed, if a natural person has more than one such set of activities, it is necessary to do something like this if a distinct accounting is to be made for each separate unit of oper-ation. Often, also, the unit of operation is quite different from the unit(s) of experience; for example, an incorporated company is a different unit of operation from the shareholders or the directors or the creditors or any other natural persons who are units of experience.

Even when accounting is carried out for a natural individual human being, the focus of attention for accounting purposes is now commonly posited as a conceptual, non-natural being which has been created for the purpose of recording data about occurrences and applying accounting procedures. For instance, if an individual human being embarks upon, say, a commercial career, the business activities are accounted for on the hypothetical presumption that they are distinct from any other social and private behaviour and can be segregated for observation and appropriate subsequent accounting treatment. Indeed, such an individual may embark on a variety of activities each of which can be accounted for separately, so that an individual can be viewed as being involved in and involved as several separate units of operation for accounting purposes. Adoption of such a view is often useful in the exposition of double-entry procedure; it can be compared with the fiction of a legal as distinct from a natural person; it can be used as a kind of short-form reference to many socially recognized operating organizations of various kinds, that is, of groups of people with specific common relationships.

Nevertheless, while it has its uses, it is also open to abuses. One source of these is the often-evinced tendency to ignore or forget that 'entity' is not a symbol for a unit of experience. For instance, when people speak or write about a 'reporting entity', they cannot mean that the entity, which is purely conceptual, actually compiles or provides a report, but that some living human being, capable of operating whatever instruments and procedures are required, compiles and provides a number of statements about occur-rences which have been experienced by people, and the results of such occurrences in terms of relationships between people. The reports may be provided in the name of the entity – whether it be a cost centre, a branch, a company, a government department or an entire government – as a short-form title of identification of the people of the relationships, but it is not the entity itself which prepares or provides the reports. An entity cannot *do* anything. Confusion in this respect enables some people to carry out questionable and sometimes unlawful activities in the name of an entity, and shift any penalty from themselves (for instance, as a director or officer of a company) on to the innocent and trusting members of the 'entity' who were unaware of the unsatisfactory activity. The endowment of human characteristics on a fictional concept can lead to confusion as the path to further abstraction takes us away from the observable units of actual experience, who are the only ones who can arrive at or implement decisions and undertake activities. It remains, and cannot but remain, a symbol. To overlook or forget this is to slide into an unfortunate animism which has enabled some people to use the symbol as a mask for activities detrimental to their fellows and even, sometimes, to themselves. During business and financial cycles, with their recurring crises of confidence, the activities of many people are greatly affected – to the extent of being governed – by fictions of this sort.

To be sure, an 'entity' may comprise a group of people, but this does not make it any less fictional, nor does it give it, as an expression, symbol or concept, any actuating power. If anything is done, it is done by people who act in the name of a group of people, or on their behalf; they may use the symbol of the entity as a representation of those on whose behalf they act. This is by no means a novel suggestion. Devine expressed very concisely and directly the distinction that is being emphasized here:

> While the assets may 'belong' to the entity and the reports may be about the entity's activities, it is people who have needs and objectives. The accountant monitors the effectiveness of the entity in terms of the needs of these important people. Which people and which of their needs? It is our contention that the importance of various people (e.g., bankers and owners) varies as economic conditions vary, and when liquidation is imminent the importance and the dimensions of the entity approach zero.
>
> (Devine 1985: Vol. IV, p. 87)

When we talk about assets belonging to, or controlled by, an entity or to anything or anybody else, we are expressing a legal relationship; we are recognizing certain social rules set up by members of a community for the governance of particular aspects of their behaviour. The rules may go back to times long past; some of them may have become complicated through the cumulative impact of changed circumstances; this does not make them any less a social statement designed by people for the regulating of activities between people.

Some objections to the 'entity theory' are:

1   The existence of an entity cannot be examined objectively, much less verified. That is, it is a gratuitous assumption.
2   The notion of an entity 'point of view' does not apply to the whole field of accounting. For example, analysis must be made from a personal, human point of view, such as that of a shareholder, creditor, auditor, manager, and so on. In management accounting, we often forget about the enterprise or the whole organization as the entity, and about the proprietor also, but we may set up other entities such as cost centres or production processes as foci of accounting attention.
3   An artificial entity cannot prepare records. Somebody prepares the records; somebody (and it may be somebody else) uses reports. Should

not the records be kept and the reports be prepared from the point(s) of view of those requiring them?

4   Suppose a man keeps no accounting records. He then employs an accountant to establish and maintain such a set. When is the entity created and what is its nature? Is it created, as Gilman insisted (Gilman 1939: 52), when the accountant sets up the double-entry records? If he backdates them, is the entity created at the moment of setting up the records or *as at* the opening date of the records, or *as at* the beginning of the activities which can be accounted for, which would pre-date the double-entry records? Must the records adhere to double-entry procedure? Or can an accounting entity exist without double-entry procedure, or, for that matter, without any formal accounting records at all? If it can, what kind of creation is it?

Our objection to the entity is not that, in itself, it is merely an accounting fiction, but that, in its application, accountants have too often taken it, and have been allowed to take it, too far – much further than has been good for the community in which it has been applied.

In endowing the entity with a personality which they know it does not possess, accountants have interpreted it as having powers which human beings alone can have. Accountants are not alone in this: lawyers, and others also, have done the same; indeed, it has become a commonplace feature of much modern socio-economic activity. As already suggested, some of this activity has not necessarily been socially or culturally beneficial. But in many cases where a company or corporation is recognized as a 'person' it is for the purposes of imposing upon it responsibilities as well as powers. It is the assumption or presumption of powers and the negation of responsibilities that has enabled some businessmen, on the advice of lawyers and accountants, to manipulate the legal and accounting use of the entity notion to their own improper advantage and to the disadvantage of others in the community.

No amount of argument or postulating can make an entity, which is something created in the human mind, exist (in the sense of having an organic life in which change, whether progressive or retrogressive, can be observed) or do things in the same way that people exist and do things. Any such changes that are alleged to be observable and observed are illusory if they are attributed to actions of the entity itself, for it is only to the activities of people that such attribution can explicably be made. For instance, when we say that XY Company makes television sets, we mean that a number of people (employees), selected by certain other people (personnel officers) and working in a factory on materials bought by certain other people (purchasing officers) make and assemble the several parts which constitute television sets, which are sold by certain people (salespersons) to customers who will eventually remit payments which will be recorded by certain people (clerical workers) and deposited by certain other people (cashiers) in a bank for the improvement of an indebtedness relationship evidenced by a specific bank account; all these people operate under the general direction of certain identifiable people (directors and managers); and all these activities are carried out in the name of XY Company, and produce impacts on other members of the community to which they all belong and on the environment in which they all live.

The word 'company' was originally a collective word; literally, it indicated those with whom one shared one's bread (from Latin *cum*, with, and *panis*, bread), and it is still used as a collective noun in some of its applications, for instance, a military company, or a theatrical company, usually is meant to convey the sense of all the members of the particular group of people, although it does not now carry the initial implication of eating together. Even in some of these instances, however, it has had an abstractive connotation imposed upon it, so that it is often doubtful whether, in speaking of a theatrical company, for instance, the intention is to refer to the members as a whole or the abstract 'entity' to which the name, and little else of substance, refers.

In an article on early balance sheet classification, Baladouni quotes thus from the 1782 Report of the East India Company:

> . . . unless the Sum due from Government for Saltpetre, as well as that due for Goods sold . . . be speedily paid, your committee conceive the Company cannot discharge the . . . Debt . . .

and

> . . . the company will soon be embarrassed in their Operations for Want of Current Cash, unless some relief can be obtained from Government.
> (Baladouni 1990: 39)

The use of the verbs suggests that the directors at that time thought of both the Committee and the Company as each comprising different individuals with separate conceptions and potential embarrassments, and not as unitary entities.

In carrying out their procedures, accountants have to select and record observable occurrences or phenomena, and in doing this they have to adopt a point of view. Practical circumstances dictate the point of view that has to be adopted. To assert that this point of view is that of a fictional or notional or conceptual 'being' of some intangible nature is a flight into fantasy; to convert such an assertion into practical procedures is virtually impossible, for a specifiable relationship must be identified in order to recognize and record the occurrences or phenomena. And to do this, the entity, or whatever other notional term might be used, has to be 'endowed' with a positive human capacity to do things as human beings can. In most instances, this point of view is that of owners or members with a proprietary relationship to the resources and commitments fictionally attributed to the entity itself.

There is some ground for considering the notion of a legal or accounting entity as an anti-holistic view of man. If an entity is regarded as being separate from any human beings, for instance, in the case of a business, distinct from any owners, customers, suppliers, lenders, borrowers, managers, employees, financiers, etc., it is possible and, indeed, desirable to record multiple relationships between 'it' and any human being or other 'entity' with whom or with which 'it' may have dealings. These relationships may be regarded as functional, and, in a particular case, for example, as already suggested in Chapter 9, an identifiable person may have multiple relationships in a company, at a given time. In such a case, it is conceivable that, say, a director could sue himself as a debtor or borrower and to justify his action by arguing that he was protecting the interests of shareholders one of whom would, of course, be the defaulting debtor or borrower. To do this is equivalent to denying or ignoring the fact that the particular person, while having more than one relationship with the 'entity', is, as a unit of experience, a whole living person.

It is not intended to decry this capacity of accountants to distinguish between the several functional relationships which individuals may have, but to bring into the open some of its implications which seem to be often overlooked.

In the initial exposition of accounting procedures the notion of an entity seems to fill a need. It is, surely an abstraction, and if we continue to use it we should at least ask: At what level of abstraction is it? By what referents can it be brought back to a more realistic view?

One serious drawback in using the notion of the entity is that it is or rapidly becomes a stultifying notion. Acceptance of it as a complete abstraction inhibits further examination of its nature or constitution as a unit. Since, as an expression, its meaning is simply 'being', it cannot be analysed unless it loses or is bereft of its abstractness; if it loses its abstractness, it loses its meaning and becomes something else. If it is recognized as a lazy abstraction which hides referents which can be expressed in human terms, then these referents can be examined as individuals or groups of people whose characteristics in particular cases can be either objectively and, at least to some extent, dispassionately determined, or be assessed by means of an admitted value judgement. Either way, our knowledge of humans is capable of growth and development, whereas our knowledge of abstract 'being' is stultified by its metaphysical origin and existence.

Hence, if knowledge about the functions and scope of accounting processes is to develop, they have to be explored in terms of human activity, not in terms of an abstract or fictional being with no recognition of the essential human referents which alone can give it any continued justification. In other words, an entity is something accounting writers and jurists have created as an accounting fiction. What they have not created are the people who deploy resources or do the work that has to be done to produce the goods and services that people use and desire. It seems reasonable to object to endowing an entity with powers which it cannot exert except through people.

It is possible, of course, to embrace a concept of some kind of bio-social entity, which could be defined to include companies, corporations, and various other organizations on a basis designed for such a purpose, and to develop a rationale that would then justify endowing these entities with natural characteristics to give them a semblance of social organisms. However, no matter how far we should go in developing such a concept, it would remain a human intellectual construct, and would be no more a matter for objective observation than the individual units of experience comprising it and the relationships between them, at least with our present instruments of observation and analysis. Hence, even with some such bio-social entity, the observable behaviour would be that of the human units of experience who constitute it.

Acceptance of and adherence to the notion of the entity are acts of faith, not observation of identifiable phenomena or even recognition of a 'self-evident truth'. Its adoption amounts to an unproven and unprovable assertion of something unseen and unseeable, a figment of metaphor or fancy. It does not arise from logic or from philosophy, but from metaphysics. By being given a name, which means inchoate being, it has had thrust upon it an unjustifiable load as a verbal and conceptual workhorse. The loads are heavy indeed, too heavy for such a characterless concept to bear successfully; its back is breaking under its burden.

The difference in terminology may be illustrated in the case of a shelf company. So long as it remains a shelf company, it may well be regarded as an entity, which is there, which exists, but nothing more. As soon as it is used as a means of doing something, such as attracting resources from investors, or as a title for a trading organization, it becomes a unit of operation with a recognition that particular units of experience – human beings – are involved in carrying out activities under a registered name as identification.

The notion of command

There may be less objection to referring to, say, a cost centre or a branch as a separate entity, so long as the abstract and fictional nature of the term is consciously recognized and remembered and not confused or, even worse, fused with the people responsible for conducting the affairs of the cost centre or branch, for it is they whose performance is in fact being recorded and monitored for analysis and evaluation in some form or at some time.

There can surely be no admission or acceptance of any notion of sub-entities or super-entities. In so far as an entity *is* at all, it is itself; it is the whole of itself; it is indivisible; it is not and cannot be composed of parts; and it exists in thought and in thought alone. To speak of sub-entities is to fly in the face of respectable and acceptable use of our language and to muddle our process of thinking. To put it figuratively, the notion of the entity, like any other notion, may have a job to do, and, in its limited field, it may do that job fairly well. But it should not be overworked to the point of exhaustion and distortion, as it often seems to be by accountants. For instance, if we portray the CDE company as an entity and it creates or acquires the FGH company as a subsidiary, the FGH company is no less an entity than any other; and, if the CDE company joins with a JKL company in a consortium, this is no more an entity than any other. Sub-entities and super-entities are nothing more than figments in our language and in our thoughts.

It was in order to avoid such obfuscation that the notion and expression of 'commander' was suggested some years ago (Goldberg 1965: see Ch. 9 above). It seems to have attracted little notice from accounting policy-makers in particular. Some writers were adversely critical (for example, Gynther 1967), and some even converted it to the proprietorship notion (Meyer 1973; Lee 1980). It was, in fact, an attempt to direct attention towards a more realistic interpretation of accounting occurrences than can be vouchsafed by the adoption of an imagined entity endowed with personal powers in order to provide accountants with a theoretical justification for their accepted procedures. The attempt obviously failed, since the accounting literature is as saturated with the notion of an entity, with the capacity to undertake and carry out activities, as ever it was. It seems that, to use a metaphor, nobody in accounting academia took it up and ran with it. As a result, it has lain largely idle and unused; whether it is unusable has not been established.

The commander has, or is given, control of resources, in the sense that he or she is empowered – and is usually expected – to deploy those resources. The resources may comprise recognized rights in relation to other people as well as tangible assets of various kinds. In some instances the manner in which and/or the extent to which a commander may deploy these resources may be subject to specific restrictions imposed by agreement or by law or by some equivalent authority. This interpretation is based on a recognition that relationships of people to resources are not solitary, and that resources are not merely owned by specific people but are also used by people, some of whom, at least, may not be the owners. When there is identity of owner and user, the relationship of sole proprietorship may pertain, although even in such instances the sole owner may appoint other individuals to exercise, in part or, perhaps, completely, the function of use or deployment of the resources.

Thus the notion of command and acceptance of commandership as a relationship between people and resources is a recognition of a function which is in fact carried out by virtually everybody at some stage in some way, and, for most people, frequently.

There is also a sense in which 'resources' can be interpreted to include those qualities and characteristics pertaining to an individual's own self. In this sense, a commander is able to deploy, as available resources, such personal traits as skills, strength, charm, patience, and so on. (It might be noted, incidentally, that some personal characteristics in this category may not necessarily be advantageous in the pursuit of the commander's own objectives.) We suggest that the exercising of this function is important in society and is worthy of the attention of accountants who wish or are required to record, process, report upon, interpret and validate movement of and change in resources, whether for an individual, or for a group of people.

The lack of recognition and adoption of this notion of commander may have been due to lack of clarity in exposition or to misunderstanding of it by readers, with a strong possibility of both. A third possibility, namely, that it was rejected because it was wrong and did not fit the facts, does not yet seem likely, since there has been little real examination and debate of the issue.

In double-entry recording the commander has to recognize claims to assets and restraints against them; in terms of any measure of value, the equation Assets=Equities (i.e. Claims) is applied. In commercial accounting, it is generally accepted that the principal aim of carrying on operations is to increase the available resources without increasing external claims to a greater extent, whence it follows that any net increase is available for internal claimants, that is, the proprietors, other owners, or members of the organization. If and where a state of insolvency is reached, the aim of a trustee in bankruptcy or a liquidator is to realize the assets to the best advantage and pay off the claims of creditors (external claimants) so far as is practicable and equitable in accordance with prescribed legal procedures and guidelines. In a receivership, the aim is to increase resources up to a point where specific claimants can have their claims satisfied, after which the management of the resources may be restored to those from whom it had been taken.

It is the function of a commander to deploy resources. This function usually, but not necessarily, embodies a socially recognized right to apply and use these resources; 'not necessarily' because, as already noted, a thief who does not have a legal right to ill-gotten resources is nevertheless able to deploy them as effectively as anyone who has an indisputable legal right to do so. In some cases, the function includes a duty to deploy certain resources in a particular, specified manner not contrary to the public interest.

In a well-organized society, rights involve responsibilities. Both rights and responsibilities are concepts of social relationships. We suggest that one of the important tasks for accountants is to devise means of 'dealing with' the evidence for the exercise of these rights and responsibilities. This may greatly broaden the scope and function of the work of accountants. At the same time, if accountants can devise appropriate techniques for meeting these requirements, it would raise their work from a solely, or at least primarily, individual–client or individual–employer orientation and emphasis to a social orientation through which a broader and more judgemental approach would need to be developed in the interests of social equity. Questions to be faced would include: What are the obligations of client or employer in relation to:

(a) other people in society, which may raise health, safety and other social, legal and political, as well as financial, issues;

(b) the environment in which they and others live and operate, which may raise issues of physical, chemical and biological impact on social resources?

On this kind of approach, the commander is basically a steward, with considerable responsibilities beyond the purely financial ones and, in some circumstances, beyond the sole-client orientation. Only human beings, not entities, can be commanders.

It is suggested that one important problem for any accountant is to determine who is the commander in relation to what resources in each particular situation, and to fashion the accounting procedures and the accounting results accordingly. It is to this relationship that the term 'unit of operation' is intended to apply. Such a unit becomes a focus of attention because it is recognized that 'operators' are human beings; the use of 'unit' is meant to suggest a wholeness embracing the occurrences which constitute the operation. In many instances, the unit of operation is equivalent to a venture, as envisaged in Chapter 8. This may involve a potentially more complicated structure of accounting records than is usually encountered at present, but one which would be better adapted to the social, and, indeed, the economic needs of a complex society. In essence, however, it would probably be more directly oriented, and, therefore, more readily understandable than much in the present kind of system.

To take one example, what actually happens when a company is formed? A number of individual human beings, say, A, B, C, etc., suggest, either directly or through an intermediary, such as an agent or broker, to a number of others, say, S_1, S_2, S_3, etc., that the latter should transfer some of their resources (usually money) to them, to be used by persons D_1, D_2, *et al.*, whom A, B, and C suggest to S_1, S_2, and S_3 as being fit, proper and desirable people to act as directors in whose advantageous handling of resources all can have faith. In return for this transfer of resources, S_1, S_2 and S_3 hope to receive either a regular amount for an indefinite future period or an accretion in the value of resources returnable to them at some future, usually unspecified, date, or typically both. D_1, D_2, usually receive a salary, fees, and other emoluments in return for their endeavours to increase the resources entrusted to them. If successful, they also benefit from an accretion of prestige which may be reflected in other simultaneously held directorships, political or social appointments, admission to exclusive clubs, favourable publicity and other forms of evidence of modern success. D_1, D_2, employ people to produce goods or services, or market them, or perform other social or economic functions in the course of which the resources (goods and services) acquired through deployment of the contributions of S_1, S_2, S_3, etc., are used.

For accounting purposes (though not, in the current state of the law, for legal requirements) it would be valid to postulate that the directors of, say, a company have the records set up to reflect their point of view. After all, it is the directors to whom the resources of shareholders and suppliers are entrusted, and it is they who determine in what services and goods and to what extent those resources shall be applied. We suggest that this would put the directors in an analogous position to that of Gilman's hypothetical slave. But the point of view of the directors is neither that of an impersonal entity nor that of the owners, yet it is a human point of view – the point of view of the human being who manages and controls the resources in question. The records could be kept by the directors *from their point of view in their capacity of commanders or managers of resources*, with adequate recognition of social responsibilities as well as purely ownership-oriented duties. Thus the point of view of the commander would also cover the position of trustee, sole proprietor, partners, committee or board members of clubs, societies, charitable or educational organizations, and municipal and other government instrumentalities. If S_1, S_2, are identical with D_1, D_2, we would have a partnership; if they are different, we have a company.

If the net resources are increased, the hopes of S_1, S_2, S_3, for a regular return are likely to be fulfilled, and D_1, D_2, are likely to be confirmed in their position of managing the contributed resources of S_1, S_2, S_3. If the net resources decline, the hopes for a regular return are likely to fade, and, if the decline continues, the shareholders may find their company becoming economically non-viable and a target for take-over, liquidation or receivership.

The relationship of use or deployment, which underlies the notions of command and commander, as used in the present context, is often akin to that of responsibility, and is present in some common accounting procedures. For instance, the purpose behind inventory recording is to provide evidence so that the activities of those responsible for the acquisition, storage and disposal of commodities can be monitored and, if necessary, controlled. In this respect an element of the fiduciary relationship is also usually involved. A discrepancy in the records raises the question of what can be done about it, and the answer is to instruct somebody to find who is responsible and to take remedial action. That is, somebody is sought to bear responsibility for the occurring of the discrepancy or for removal of its cause or both.

If we say that the commander has 'command' over resources, we need to clarify what we mean by 'command' and by 'resources', even at the risk of seeming to be repetitive. 'Command' is the symbol used to signify a capacity to do certain (specified or specifiable) things, such as to move some physical objects from one location to another, to use them in some way, to influence other people to act in particular ways, for example, to devote their strength or knowledge or personality or appearance to a prescribed purpose or service. This capacity adheres to and is exercisable by individual human beings or small groups of people who are able to carry out decisions. In other words, commanders are people who make or have the means to implement decisions. The capacity to implement decisions is not necessarily a legal right, although it is often derived from and supported by such a right, especially that of ownership; 'possessory' rights can provide a capacity, and often a duty and a responsibility, to deploy resources where the right of ownership belongs to another. Even if a possessory 'right' is not recognized, the fact that certain resources are at the disposal of a specific person for a limited time or under particular conditions enables that person to apply the resources in accordance with the stipulated conditions. As noted in Chapter 9, the use or application may be unlawful, and not to be condoned socially, but this does not alter the fact that command over the resources is held.

If we were to say that a commander is able to exercise a use-function over resources, we should be close to the mark. However, if we shortened this to say merely that a commander can use resources, this might be inter-preted as implying a selfish or self-oriented purpose in the use, whereas in this context the concept of command is intended to be neutral. Admittedly, commanders may use resources for their own (presumed) benefit, but if the use is for somebody else's benefit or even to their own detriment, this does not lessen the capacity to exercise the use-function. It is the function of use and the being able to exercise it that makes the commander.

The analogy of, say, a racehorse may be apposite. Commonly, several different people have a relationship of close interest in each horse, some of them being the owner, the trainer, the strapper and the jockey, apart from a general body of punters, bookmakers, racing officials, and so on. Leaving this latter, general group aside, the relationships of the former group may be briefly outlined. The owner, obviously and by definition, has a legal, ownership right to sell the horse or relocate it to a different trainer or, if the horse becomes ill or seriously injured, to have it put down. The trainer is engaged by the owner to take care of the horse, and design and supervise its training program for its races; this involves the trainer in having actual physical possession of the horse and providing appropriate accommodation, food, exercise and so on while the horse is in his care. Of course, the trainer usually has several, perhaps many, horses in his care and under his supervision, and owned by various owners, at any one time and over any given period. The jockey usually is engaged to ride the horse in a particular race on a particular day. The horse is under his sole charge immediately before and during the race, but the jockey's immediate relationship does not extend beyond this period; each race is a distinct and different engagement, and a specific horse may have a different jockey for each of its races, or it may have the one jockey for all or most of them. The relationship is one of intimacy for the duration of each race. The strapper normally has a continuing day-to-day relationship of care of and attention to a particular horse or a very few horses, but very rarely rides it in a race.

Each of the four people would be entitled to refer to a specific horse as 'my horse', even though only one – the owner – is legally its owner with a right of disposal. The possessive pronoun can thus imply more than the single notion of legal ownership. Each of the four would be a commander in the sense presently intended here. In one sense or another, each of the four has 'command' or control over the environment and activities of the horse; each has, in perhaps different senses, a right or a function of access or 'use' or direction.

The point of this analogy is that the notion of a commander is a fluid concept, except that it always refers to and emphasizes the existence of a human being. In addition, the function of command can be diffused, often without any reduction of responsibility for any party in the relationship because of such transfer. Some implications of this are considered in Chapter 11.

In order to meet the requirements of each commander, it is unlikely that any one set of data would be adequate without being overloaded with non-required information. Each type of commander would require information appropriate to particular functions; information directed towards satisfying the needs of other commanders would be superfluous and probably wasteful from the point of view of each commander in turn. In an accounting setting, each (identifiable) commander would need a separate view of data about the unit of operation, activities undertaken by him or her and their results – data related to and adequate for the express and identifiable purposes of each commander.

The analogy, like any analogy, has limitations. In this case, the horse, as a sentient animal, exists apart from the ministrations of owner, trainer, strapper and jockey. But it is to their ministrations that it owes its character and identity as a racing horse; it is their care and attention and purposefulness which provide it with distinctive, individual characteristics as a competitive creature in a specialized kind of environment. We submit that the limitation does not invalidate the suggestion made from the analogy.

Whether a commander owns all, some or none of the resources to be deployed, the function of command is unaffected. It is the exercise of this function which gives rise to the relationships in which accountants are vocationally interested.

Each contributor of resources is a commander of those resources until they are dedicated (that is, made available) to another commander for use and deployment according to the latter's judgement or instructions. Apart from these contributed resources, each contributor remains the commander over any other resources at his or her disposal. However, by exercising a personal knowledge, skill and experience as a commander over the acquired variety of resources, the initiating commander, acting in the role of what is commonly recognized as an entrepreneur, uses and deploys these resources for a gainful objective (not necessarily financial improvement) which may be more or less clearly expressed and comprehended. The objective of gain may be clearly defined, in a commercial setting, as in an increase of personal monetary resources or a net-after-tax accretion of shareholders' funds, or it may be less specifically envisaged and stated in non-financial terms or qualitative terms such as in improved teaching standards and conditions (for an educational institution) or an expanded distribution of needed goods to distressed people (for an eleemosynary body) or the enhancement of the cultural, heritage, scientific and educative values (for a public museum) to take but a few examples.

In exercising command over a variety of available resources, a commander often delegates command over some of them for more or less specific deployment towards a specific or general objective. The more precise the comprehension and assessment of the objective, the more clear and decisive the understanding of the use and deployment of resources is likely to be by such delegatees, who, in turn, also function as commanders.

Sole ownership by the commander of all resources to be deployed is rare. For example, if electric power or light is used, the resources required to generate and transmit it to any particular commander are almost always owned by some body other than the user; similarly with public transport, telephone and other communication processes. If employees are engaged to work, there are usually restrictions on the command over the resources provided, which the commander has to recognize and comply with, such as health and safety requirements, leave entitlements, and the like. In other words, in a society, command is not absolute whenever other people are involved.

The following appear to be relevant propositions:

> A commander is not necessarily the owner (of resources) but he or she might be.
>
> A commander is not necessarily a manager but he or she might be.
>
> A commander is not necessarily in a fiduciary position but he or she might be.
>
> A commander is not necessarily an employee but he or she might be.
>
> A commander is not necessarily an agent for another but he or she might be.

Within an organization (a group of people with some common interests) command over resources may be delegated from people in one rank to people in a rank below them. In this respect there may be a 'hierarchy of command' over resources, but this does not of itself make those in the lower ranks managers in the normal sense of that word.

Above all, however, whatever other circumstances apply, a commander is a living, human being.

In any non-static set of circumstances, which surely would be pertinent even in a so-called 'static' society, since people must always do something to keep alive, people act as a result of decisions made by the various units of experience comprising the group. It is therefore appropriate for accountants, whose vocational efforts are directed towards these activities and their results, to become aware of and to be concerned with the steps by which decisions are made and carried out. These, and considerations arising out of the structure of decision-making, form the subject-matter of the next three chapters.

11 A dissection of decisions

And thus the native hue of resolution
Is sicklied o'er with the pale cast of thought.
(Shakespeare, *Hamlet*, Act III, Sc. 1)

(Decision-making among the Persians)
If an important decision is to be made, they discuss the question when
they are drunk, and the following day the master of the house where the
discussion was held submits their decision for reconsideration when they
are sober. If they still approve it, it is adopted; if not, it is abandoned.
Conversely, any decision they make when they are sober is reconsidered
afterwards when they are drunk.

(Herodotus 1954: 69)

Introduction

In his seminal book, *Administrative Behavior*, H.A. Simon referred to the
'anatomy of decisions' (Simon 1957: 60) and provided a masterly analysis
of decision-making which became a basis for developing a fresh field of
intellectual endeavour in ensuing decades. While we do not pretend to
have a comprehensive knowledge of the rich literature of decision-making,
we offer an approach somewhat different from, but, where apposite, complementary to, numerous studies in decision theory and practice which have
been carried out in recent years.

The product of accounting nowadays is frequently justified in terms of its
contribution to decision-making; 'user-friendliness', 'decision usefulness'
and similar expressions have become part of the conventional vocabulary of
accountants. Many learned researchers have devoted much resourcefulness
and many resources to investigating the (mainly) psychological aspects of
decision-making, and have produced many valuable propositions for the
experts in their respective fields.

At the same time, there does not seem to have been presented to accountants a clear and concise treatment of those aspects of decision-making
which most closely affect them in developing their own criteria for application of their skills.

In this and the next chapter some analysis of the process of making
decisions is presented. This chapter considers in lay terms what we see as

the process of arriving at a decision, and the next raises some significant issues, in relation to decisions, that accountants should, in our opinion, be aware of.

The decision function

We all make decisions. Our lives are a continuous course of making decisions. Even if we choose to do nothing about a given situation, that can be regarded as making a decision. Most of the decisions we make are probably short-lived and not important in their effects; most do not have financial implications. On the other hand, the importance of some decisions is not truly apparent at the time they are made; when their effects are known, some may turn out to be more or less important than was envisaged at the time of making them. However, they can only be made in the light of circumstances as known and anticipated at the time, but these may not turn out as interpreted or expected.

In this and subsequent chapters we distinguish between 'making a decision' and taking action to implement it, but first we have to indicate that we do not consider that all our actions are necessarily the result of making a deliberate, conscious decision. We recognize that some actions are 'reflex' actions, which are a physiological and constitutional response to a particular circumstance in our immediate environment. Thus, if somebody throws a missile at our eyes, we involuntarily close them as an act of self-protection, and, when a doctor taps a particular spot near our knee, a knee-jerk reaction, which is automatic and not controlled, is what he is looking for.

At the same time, some of our actions are taken as a result of a habit, which was initially formed on a basis of conscious and deliberate choice but repeated often enough to have become unrecognizable as a conscious and deliberate response among available options. These habitual actions may appear to be automatic, and they are often embedded in our subconscious mental workings, but they are not necessarily physiological or constitutional, as reflex actions are, and may be varied, if required, by appropriate de-habituating activity.

However, the decisions that we are most aware of, are those conscious and deliberate ones which face most of us at some time or other, and they face some of us often enough to warrant examination and an attempt at elucidation of what they comprise.

The process involved in these acts of deciding is that a person is faced with a set of circumstances in which the selection of one course of action is to be chosen from two or more possible or available courses, for instance, whether one should work through the lunch hour and complete a project, and so gain the commendation of the recipient of a report, or fulfil a social engagement for lunch and defer completion of the project at the risk of an unpleasant glare or a possible reprimand from an expectant recipient.

In making the choice, the chooser has to follow a course of reasoning somewhat along these lines: If I choose to do *A*, the likely outcome would be X; if I choose to do B, the likely outcome would be Y; I prefer X to Y, therefore I should do A. At this point the chooser has made a decision, but it is worth noting that the 'making' of the decision involves the judgement 'I should do A'. We propose to use the word 'resolution' and the verb 'resolve' to indicate clearly this stage of the process of decision-making. Expressions such as 'making a decision', 'taking a decision', 'arriving at a decision', 'coming to a decision', are synonymous but often carry an implication of action taken to implement the decision arrived at, as well as the 'arriving at' which we suggest is a separate and prior course to implementation.

A resolution, then, is a proposal (suggestion, recommendation, advice) resulting from investigation and/or analysis (contemplation) of known facts and expectations. It involves the selection of one out of two or more options for proposed action arising from such examination.

The reason behind any desire or requirement for a decision is a felt need or wish to alter the status quo, that is, some dissatisfaction or unease with existing circumstances.[1] In some cases, such as continuous monitoring of activities or processes, an idea (or the notion) of potential improvement of the status quo implies a possible rather than an actual or positive dissatisfaction.

In the absence of some action for change, the status quo will continue. However, a proposal for change may sometimes be regarded as less beneficial in some respects than continuance of the existing state; in such a case a resolution may be to make no change, that is, to do nothing or take no action. To illustrate, a particular human being might cogitate thus: If I am walking in the countryside for pleasure and exercise, I should be content to continue walking unless or until I begin to feel tired, or a small stone gets into my shoe and I feel discomforted as a result, or I feel thirsty, or I see a scene that attracts my interest, or something occurs to cause me to wish to change my current state of progression. If the wish or need is felt strongly enough, I shall stop or change my action into that of running or creeping, whichever is more appropriate to my interpretation of the situation. The sequence is that of unease or dissatisfaction with the status quo, investigation into the cause of unease or dissatisfaction, analysis of the situation, consideration of options available and their relative beneficial outcomes, resolving to adopt one of the options, and carrying out the resolution. A subsequent stage is that of reviewing the outcome and assessing whether it has been in accordance with my expectation.

Whether the resolution is in fact turned into action involves some motive power, such as a strong will (will power) or great energy, which will transform the 'should do' into 'does', to convert the aspiration into performance. We use the term 'implementation' and the verb 'implement' to indicate the carrying out of selected choices of activity. Expressions such as 'taking action', 'acting',

---

[1]This aspect has been noted by other writers on accounting; Cf., for instance, Chambers (1966) p. 20 and the footnote references to Dewey and von Mises.

'carrying out a decision', 'acting on a resolution', and the like, are synonymous for what we term implementing or implementation of a resolution.

Thus, the symbol 'decision', as it is commonly used in both ordinary conversation and the academic and professional literature, is replaced here by symbols representing two components, each of which is subject to further analysis. This division can be compared to that of Simon who described the decision-making process in three phases – *intelligence, design* and *choice*. (Simon 1960).

For Simon, the first phase, intelligence, involves searching for and identifying things that require change. In our deliberations, this is matched by investigation comprising analysis of the status quo to identify those elements that may require change. This is the start of the process of deciding – an investigation that may identify where we believe we can make something better than the status quo. In undertaking that investigation, the investigator has to make some judgement on the relevance of the elements being investigated. In one sense, a feeling of dissatisfaction with the status quo and deciding to undertake an investigation to make something better is coming to a resolution: in this case, resolving to investigate in an attempt to identify the problems. 'If I am dissatisfied, then I should undertake an investigation' is a resolution; but it is only the beginning of the process by which the feeling of dissatisfaction may in the end be allayed by removing or changing the source of dissatisfaction.

Simon's second phase, 'design', typically involves developing and analysing different courses of action in coming to a resolution. Once a problem or a source of dissatisfaction has been identified, investigation and analysis will enhance our understanding of it. The results of the analysis need to be interpreted. Only after interpretation can a 'choice' (Simon's third phase) be made – that is, selecting from the courses of action identified through investigation, analysis and interpretation. It is in this phase that a resolution is formulated. The resolution is made: 'I resolve to undertake the following action(s).' However, that is where Simon's model of decision-making appears to end.

After investigation, analysis and interpretation, a resolution may be formulated that nothing be done. It is possible that the analysis indicates, in the judgement of the decision-maker, that the status quo is the best available alternative. On the other hand, it may be resolved that to overcome the dissatisfaction, a change is required. The action of carrying out a resolution is its implementation.

In summary, our examination provides the following components of what might be termed the decision function:

Component 1

(a) A feeling of unease/dissatisfaction with the status quo.
(b) Analysis (including interpretation) of the composition of the status quo and the relative relevance of its elements.

(c) Consideration of choices available for change, including assessment of potential/probable/possible effects of each choice.
(d) Making a judgement or resolution in accordance with the above steps.
(e) Formulating the resolution arrived at.

Component 2

(f) Implementing the resolution, that is, taking some action to carry out the resolution.
(g) In a continuing state of affairs, monitoring the effects of implement-ation, producing either satisfaction with the new status quo, in which case no further change need be contemplated, or unease with the new status quo, in which case the functional cycle starts off again at stage (a) above.

This process of coming to a resolution and implementing it is con-sidered in a little more detail below.

Resolutions

Not all resolutions are arrived at on a basis of or through a process of rational consideration of the circumstances. Apart from reflex reactions and habitual responses, many resolutions are based on a predominantly emo-tional reaction to perceived circumstances rather than on a reasoned analysis of them. It is sometimes difficult to distinguish these from habitual responses, but there is a difference, at least analytically. Frequently, a person coming to a resolution regards it as being based on reason without realizing the considerable, if not predominant, emotional content of the process of arriving at it. And a pseudo-justification of the thought sequence, often referred to as rationalization, may take place. It is beyond the scope of this work to explore in depth the impact of emotional content in the process of arriving at a resolution, but the possibility and potential strength it may have in any given set of circumstances should not be overlooked.

The process of arriving at a resolution, or 'resolving', is often a complex procedure. It has been explored to some extent in the literature of inform-ation systems, in which a number of different stages are often distin-guished.[2] We consider the process of arriving at a resolution by examining the stages of 'investigation', 'analysis', 'interpretation', and 'formulation'.

Investigation

'What is wrong with the way things are at present?' This is the basic ques-tion that initiates the whole process of decision-making. If there is no occasion to have any change in the status quo, no dissatisfaction, no

---

[2]See, for example, the collection of articles in Galliers (ed.) *Information Analysis*, 1987.

unease, no discomfort, no pain, no malaise, no hunger, there is no reason to even think about making any sort of decision; indeed, one would hardly be in a state to do so, for the probability is that, in such circumstances, one would be beyond living, in this world at least. In order to continue living, all creatures must satisfy some basic wants, and must do something, however little or, indeed, however pleasurable, to meet them. To the extent that this activity is conscious and deliberate, these creatures are engaging in a change of their status quo; the expectation is one of either improvement of the known present state or minimization of its deterioration.

Humans can apply intelligence of a high order to examine the circumstances in which they find themselves and to develop systematic procedures to help them to understand; we do not always exercise this capability. The question of a need for change is not always asked specifically; for example, if an ongoing review operates, the question may not be raised regularly on, say, a daily or weekly basis, but this does not mean that it is not there. For instance, behind any review or audit there is recognition of the possibility that somebody's expectations might not be fulfilled, and this is based on a 'feeling' that dishonesty, incompetence, inexperience, accident, human frailty or change of conditions or personnel may occur. If there is absolute confidence, there is no need felt for monitoring or review. But it appears that most of human experience – at least in worldly matters – belies such absolute confidence.

The recognition that the existing state of affairs is not completely satisfactory is often a sentient rather than an intellectual one; it is a 'feeling' of unease, and of the possibility of improvement. David Hume put this clearly and simply as long ago as 1751:

> It appears evident that the ultimate ends of human actions can never in any case be accounted for by *reason*, but recommend themselves entirely to the sentiments and affections of mankind, without any dependence on the intellectual faculties. Ask a man why he uses exercise; he will answer, *because he desires to keep his health*. If you then inquire *why he desires health*, he will readily reply, *because sickness is painful*. If you push your inquiries farther and desire a reason *why he hates pain*, it is impossible he can ever give any. This is an ultimate end, and is never referred to any other object.
>
> (Hume 1751: 129)

Since then, echoes of this view, sometimes modified, sometimes amplified, have found expression in the literature and the practices of economists and accountants, among others. For instance, von Mises put it this way in 1949:

> The teaching of praxeology [the 'science' of human action] and economics are valid for every human action without regard to its underlying motives, causes, and goals. The ultimate judgments of value and the ultimate ends of human action are given for any kind of scientific inquiry, they are not open to any further analysis. Praxeology deals

with the ways and means chosen for the attainment of such ultimate ends. Its object is means, not ends.

(von Mises 1949: 21)

Even if we were to refrain from further pursuit of this element of emotional content, however, there are difficulties enough in determining what is meant by the use of such terms as 'reason' and 'rational' as applied to a course of thought processes by which an individual person or a group of people would arrive at a resolution.

If we consider 'reason' and 'feeling' against a background of evolution, it could be suggested that both are instruments of evolutionary development; that is, that both are elements of decision and action and that they are both utilitarian in purpose, in the sense that they are 'directed' towards the preservation and continuity of the individual and/or the species. They may be different in the way they function, but they are not contradictory in purpose; rather are they complementary to each other, at least for humans in most cases. Indeed, one of the most pleasurable experiences a human being can have is that of intellectual excitement, when the two seem to be completely merged.

However, they can be distinguished from each other. It is some aspect of feeling that seems to be required to initiate the process of examining the composition of the present state of affairs, that is, to observe it in detail, to identify its elements, to classify them and to perceive patterns in them, to analyse and interpret them, to deduce conclusions from them, and to formulate an anticipation of the results of any proposed action. This anticipation also is itself a feeling – a sensory experience, at first imagined or remembered, and later, if the action is undertaken, experienced either as it had been anticipated or as it turns out differently. This last proviso, however, conceals a further function of feeling, for, before any action can be undertaken, the 'actor' has to be motivated to undertake it: he has to 'feel' strongly enough to do something positive. Hence, we should recognize that, while emphasis may be put on the examination of reason and rationality in the course of coming to a resolution, our feelings provide an important and inescapable component; no decision and no action is wholly or automatically intellectual or, in a narrow sense, 'rational'.

Thus, after von Mises states that '[H]uman action is necessarily always rational', he immediately rejects the expression 'rational action' as pleonastic, since '[W]hen applied to the ultimate ends of action, the terms rational and irrational are inappropriate and meaningless' (von Mises 1949: 18) In effect, he seems to be saying that all human actions are rational by definition, and, further, he goes on to argue that no human being is in a position to 'substitute his own value judgments for those of the acting individual'. In other words, one might just as well say only that 'Human action is' or 'Human action takes place'.

The course of his logic seems a little obscure here. He states that all human action is directed to satisfying some end, that is, some desire of the acting man. Nobody else can judge the values of the actor. Therefore, human action is necessarily always rational. But he also asserts that 'rational' and 'irrational' applied to the ultimate ends of action are 'inappropriate and meaningless'; it would seem to follow that to say that something is rational in a situation in which that term is inappropriate and meaningless is to destroy all sense in which the initial statement could have any communicable meaning. In other words, he is talking what looks like non-sense. To make sense, 'rational' must be given some meaning in relation to human action. Otherwise, it would be equally sensible to say that human action is necessarily always irrational, or that human action is neither rational nor irrational. Indeed, there is a sense in which this last pro-position could be acceptable. If we distinguish action as implementation *alone*, and rationalizing as applicable to mental processes *alone*, then human action, needing a motivating influence for implementation, may be taken, not as a rational step in itself, but *as a result* of a process of ratiocination in developing the non-rational (that is neither rational nor irrational) but motivating factor to trigger the action.

The process of investigation may be lengthy or short, cursory or in depth, with great knowledge or little, carried out with the utmost care or without, with expertise or without, with cooperation or hostility from others, with a firm objective or a vague one, under a specific directive or a nebulous one. The number of varieties of combination of such factors as these (and no doubt others) can be very large and it would be foolish to attempt to exhaust the possibilities available. And it is the combination of factors that determines the degree of rationality, in the sense of taking into consideration as many as possible of the relevant circumstances and apply-ing a process of reasoning to them. However, while the degree of rationality may be in question, its essential presence is not; it is a rational process; it is 'sensible' in that it 'makes sense' and is laudable by people with sound judgement in such matters.

However, in the end, there is a strong and perhaps inescapable ele-ment of approval by a respected group of people; or, to put it another way, the accolade of rationality is granted, not by the individual who makes the resolution or undertakes the implementing action, but by another or others who can assess it according to accepted rules of judge-ment. In short, rationality is a social, as much as an individual, attain-ment or accomplishment.

If one were wishing to carry out the most detailed process of observation possible into virtually any set of existing circumstances, there would be, practically, no end to the number of points to which attention should be paid. The limits lie in the capacity of the observer to think of the criteria to be applied for their inclusion or exclusion; that is, the criterion of rele-vance for selection is determined by the observer or by someone to whom the responsibility for determining has been delegated.

Important parts of the process of 'rational' observation (using 'rational' in the sense of applying techniques which have given successful or satisfactory results in past investigations) are the identification and classification of elements comprising the set of observed circumstances. Here much depends upon the capacity, knowledge and experience of the observer as to whether the classes and the criteria for inclusion of elements in them will prove to be the most useful for the purpose envisaged; this involves a kind of teleological outlook for the observer who needs to be aware of the purpose in making separate observations.

Implicit in the classification of detail is a search for intelligible or 'instructive' patterns of occurrence, and it may turn out that different classifications of data may yield different levels or standards of usefulness of observations. In such cases flexibility in the classifying procedure is desirable. The perception of patterns of occurrence, whether it be by time, location, type or some other criterion, may provide insights into potential alternative courses of action. For example, the selection of observations and identification of occurrences to be recorded about ventures depends on the capacity and experience of the selectors. Any initial classification of the occurrences and their characteristics should not inhibit the use of the data by other people whose purpose may differ from that of the selectors.

These several steps in investigation constitute a counsel of perfection. In practice, many investigations are but a partial application of a potentially complete procedure. Some of the required information might not exist or be forthcoming, some of the personal capacities might be lacking, the recording of data or the analytical techniques might be defective, the perception or appreciation of the purpose of the investigation might be inadequate or faulty; these are some of the possible reasons why an actual investigation might fall short of its potential merit; and yet it might still be the best available in the given circumstances.

Short of omniscience, then, any collection of information about any given set of circumstances which require a resolution must be incomplete in some respects, and its limitations should be admitted. A call for consideration of *all* relevant data simply cannot be met, and this constitutes a limitation on any human attempt to detail all the circumstances comprising the status quo. Further, the interpretation of known circumstances in assessing their relevance is a matter of human judgement which depends upon the interpreter's knowledge, experience, attitude or known bias and other personal qualities. However 'expert' the interpreter may be, there are limits to interpretation, and these limits are human, personal and individual. Even if 'safety' is sought in statistical calculations based on a number of interpretations, such safety is, in fact, an amalgam of separate, whether similar or different, exercises of human judgement.

Another factor is that the status quo is the result of changes from previous circumstances, and even as it is being examined, is in process of change itself. Any view of a stationary state, especially in matters involving organic activity – and this, of course, includes human activity – is essentially illusory and, at best, an approximation to a very complicated moving agglomeration of related active elements or constituents. It is, of necessity, an abstraction from a huge number of perceptions. Even more, not only do these relationships extend between contemporaneous actions, they extend backward in history and may extend forward into the future. In other words, causal influences, as these are usually interpreted, not only have contemporaneous effects but may be traceable backward and forward in time, as time is humanly perceived.

The information available about any given set of circumstances is always about something which has happened, whether recently or long ago. Even something which is happening 'contemporaneously' has, in fact, happened in the instant before the perceived action makes its impact on our sense organs. The passing of time is exaggeratedly clear in the field of astronomical distance, in which phenomena seen 'in the present' are calculated and confidently asserted to have taken place light-years previously.[3] In human affairs, however, the time involved is not so great, but the difference is one of degree.

Any prognostication of future happenings is a matter of speculation, based, perhaps, on deduction from logically recognized premises but none the less speculation about what may happen; its limitations are those of the absence of omniscience, not only about the status quo in total or in general, but also about the nature of the relationships between the numerous elements which constitute it and make it recognizable.

Before an investigation begins, the investigator, or the instigator of the process, must have a conviction, whether strongly held or mildly entertained, and whencever derived, that some change in the status quo may be desirable or necessary; that is, a 'feeling' that the status quo is not entirely satisfactory. Indeed, the investigator is implicitly inclined to examine critically the existing circumstances for elements producing or promoting dissatisfaction. However, a 'sound' or well-balanced judgement (conclusion) will depend upon adequate recognition and examination of the satisfactory as well as the unsatisfactory aspects of any given set of circumstances.

In asking: 'What is wrong with the way things are at present?', there are at least three factors to consider. The first comprises the pressures which are or will be imposed from the external environment. Such pressures may be real or imaginary. In a commercial field, they include, for example, pressures from competitors. The introduction of a new product from a competitor may cause us to ask what is wrong or inadequate with the one we produce. The change in a marketing strategy by a competitor may induce us to investigate our own marketing activities. A change in government or predicted change in government policy is another example. Such external pressures which may affect our present behaviour are likely to make us consider an investigation.

Second, pressures imposed from the internal environment may reveal the need for an investigation. For example, we may discover, by accident, a

---

[3]See, for example, Eddington 1943: 93: 'The light which we now see [in the constellation Andromeda] has taken 900,000 years to reach us.'

new product or process. Until the moment when the discovery was made its existence was not evident. Such an occurrence is likely to suggest that we should investigate whether the new product or process is better than our current one.

A third pressure is the need of individual self-satisfaction. For example, individuals may feel that, unless they propose changes – often portrayed as desirable or necessary reforms – the prospects of personal advancement in their careers may be inhibited. There may be purely selfish reasons in beginning or advocating an investigation. Such reasons, and subsequent resolutions (and possibly implementation), may be quite rational from the point of view of the individual but unnecessary and/or irrational for others in the organization. Such cases may be merely change for the sake of appearing to be doing something different, which may or may not be in accordance with the expectations of superiors. This is but one example of the need to give meaning to 'rationality' in relation to human action.

In practice, the investigative process itself may be of short or long duration, narrow or extensive in scope, subject to constraints of resources devoted to it, or of zeal, knowledge, expertise, experience, attitude, honesty or personality of the investigator(s), governed by short-term, medium-term or long-term objectives, limited by the availability of required information, and subject to other influences such as bias which may restrict the usefulness of any results produced. Despite all this, some such investigation is a widespread response to a claim or requirement for a 'rational', or 'balanced', or 'sensible', or 'reasonable', or 'reliable' basis for either change or constancy.

Analysis

Analysis is usually thought of nowadays as a sophisticated investigative procedure. While not disagreeing with this view we suggest that in practice the sophistication involved is a matter of degree. Some resolutions appear to be arrived at after inadequate and/or unsophisticated analysis; we often see instances of people 'jumping to conclusions' which would have been different if more, or more mature, thought had been given to analysing the available information. Human action is far from being universally based on mature and adequate analysis of available information.

Investigation and analysis can rarely be divorced except for purposes of conceptual distinction and to do so is itself an application of the procedure of analysis. For analysis, as its philological source suggests,[4] is an attempt to distinguish between the different, separate components of a compound or complex 'unit' of some sort; that is, something which is perceived as a unit is re-observed, so to speak, as a complex of interacting, but distinct components. In analysing the unit, we proceed to 'break it down' into what we conceive to be separable parts.

---

[4] From Greek words meaning 'up' implying distribution, and 'loosen'.

In the progress of scientific development in the last few centuries, the application of analysis has given us more and more unravelling of the components of our perceived worldly objects and of the relations between them, particularly, for example, in physics, chemistry, biology and kindred fields of scientific endeavour. At the same time, relationships between what our predecessors regarded as unitary structures have been examined as if they applied to component parts of greater structures, and this has developed into a study of macro-structures or cosmic universes. This has been noticeably fruitful in such areas as physics and astronomy; an analogous development in the social sciences does not seem to have been so successful as yet in providing completely satisfying explanations, reliable predictions of happenings or fully acceptable policies.

The process of analysis itself can be analysed; it can be examined to reveal a series of components which can be regarded as a rough sequence of steps or stages. Some of these are:

(a) Envisaging the possibility of the perceived unit being composed of or constructed from component parts, and imagining or 'conceiving' their nature.

   It must be presumed or imagined that the unitary object or situation can consist of distinguishable components, and some notion of their likely composition has to be entertained. In some fields of enquiry there is now a long history of progressive analysis which has, in recent decades, provided an accelerating rate of investigative activity; this has happened particularly (as in physics and other 'hard' sciences) where international and interdisciplinary communication of ideas and knowledge has taken place freely and openly.

   We use analysis as an instrument of intellect in trying to understand phenomena, that is, to bring observed activities into the ambit of our accepted experience (accepted by us as individual units of experience). If we are satisfied that we understand something, or accept it whether we 'understand' it or not, we are not usually concerned with analysing it, except to justify our acceptance of it or to induce somebody else to accept it. However, the initial notion that a perceived or conceptual unit is made up of distinguishable components may be derived from any of an innumerable variety of sources, some of which may not be identifiable in particular cases; its generation is one of the remarkable activities of the human intellect. Some of the terms which have been applied to it are 'inspiration', 'imagination', 'lateral thinking', and the like.

   Accepting the possibility of a unit being analysable is usually very quickly followed by forming a hypothesis about how the component parts are related to each other.

(b) Devising means of observing whether the components can be separated or otherwise distinguished from each other. This may include experimenting or using other means of observing. To do this involves some hypothesizing about the relationships between the envisaged components.

Indeed, the conception of a hypothesis, however tentative or likely it may be, often appears to be simultaneous with the envisaging of the possible existence of the components themselves. However, this is not necessarily so, and the case for regarding the process of hypothesizing as a distinct intellectual step can be supported by this consideration: if an initial hypothesis about the relations between component parts is not supported by subsequent observations, the need for a different hypothesis becomes apparent, and a deliberate intellectual effort is needed to provide it, while at the same time there is no change in the composition of the unit itself. That is, the hypothesized explanation of the relation between the components, whatever it may be, is distinct from the observation and identification of the components themselves.

(c) Observing the relationships between the components in their inter-actions.

The test of whether the component parts do exist and operate as envisaged lies in devising or using situations in which they can be observed as they operate. Performing an experiment is one means of constructing conditions in which such observations can be made and recorded, and a successful experiment is one which can be repeated, particularly by other people or in other locations, and give the same results as first attained or others consistent with them. Where experimentation is not practicable, other means of providing appropriate observations have to be devised if the hypothesis is to be supportable and convincing.

(d) Formulating a model or pattern of the interacting relationships, especially incorporating causal interactions.

Part of the process of analysis (and it must be reiterated that the steps or stages are not necessarily sequential in their occurrence or incidence) is formulating a model or pattern of the relationship between the observable components which gives the unit its characteristic existence or behaviour. The questions that arise are: How does component A affect component B? Why does it have this effect; what is there in the distinct components that produces the effect? What is being sought is a causal relationship.

(e) Predicting behaviour in specific circumstances, that is, setting up a working hypothesis.

If we consider that we have found a causal relationship between com-ponents, we can make a working hypothesis and predict an outcome from a proposed course of action. In effect, we have to say: If we do A and B, then the result will be R; or if we can comply with P and Q conditions, then the outcome will be S. And in either case the result will be *R* and *S because* the relationship between *A*, *B* and *R* or between *P*, *Q* and *S* is as we have expounded it in our working hypothesis.

(f) Testing the prediction(s) by observation through experiment or otherwise.

Where an experiment is possible, it is presumed that the antecedent circumstances (for example, in the terms of the previous paragraph, the doing of *A* and *B* or the compliance with conditions *P* and *Q*) can be attained and the actual result can be compared with that predicted. If the observed, actual result turns out to be as predicted, then the experiment can be regarded as 'successful'; it provides evidence to support the hypothesis. If not, the details of the experiment, including the way in which it was performed, must be examined as well as the process of reasoning used in making the prediction. In some cases, another or a different kind of experiment may be devised.

The use of controls or controlled conditions has been recognized as essential for experiments to be acceptable in modern scientific endeavour. This involves having a set of objects, creatures or even humans which or who are not subjected to the experimental 'treatment', in order to compare the effect(s) of the experiment on an untreated set as well as on those treated. There is an implied prediction that there will be a difference in the respective states of the two groups after the experiment has been concluded. If there is no such difference, the worth of the experiment or the validity of the hypothesis would be in doubt.

Where an experiment is not possible or practicable, the conditions in which the observations are made should be as close as possible to those envisaged when the prediction was made. If the circumstances of the actual observations differ materially from those prevailing when the prediction was made, the whole procedure becomes merely an intellectual exercise, with, perhaps, potentially illustrative and recreational value, but little more. If a prediction is fulfilled, the tentativeness of a hypothesis is reduced, but is never eliminated. It may well be a basis for further analysis, of which there seems to be no end in empirical investigation.

Analysis is essential not only for invention and innovation, but even for appropriate maintenance and repair, of unitary objects. For, if we wish to keep an operating unit continually performing its allotted task, we need to know how it is constructed, what its components are and how they work in relation to each other; for instance, in a mechanism, what parts to oil, and how often, what energy is used and how to provide it, what signs of potential fatigue or failure to watch for, what steps may be appropriate to forestall or minimize ineffectiveness, what parts are replaceable, and so on.

For innovation, we should want to know whether different parts could be substituted for those in use to improve performance of the mechanism or reduce its operating cost; for this a knowledge of the operation of the various parts would be needed. Similarly, for invention, an analogous knowledge would be required before a different kind of unit could be constructed to perform a given task better than an existing one or to do something that no existing unit can do.

These are all based on an understanding of how the components of a present unit relate to each other in contributing to the unit's performance. This applies to all structures whether mechanical but also to electronic, organic, social, cosmic and includes conceptual units.

Interpretation

Investigation and analysis are conceptually antecedent to interpretation, which includes assessing the importance of the several factors regarded as relevant to change in the status quo. However, although we are here using 'interpretation' as at a specified stage, the function of interpreting is also present within the stages of investigation and analysis. In the course of interpreting, we are confronted with symbols, and interpreting involves elucidating what these symbols signify in terms understandable to the recipient or observer, and this, of course, depends upon the recipient's corpus of experience. Thus, interpretation can and does take place as part of any stage of dealing with data.

It should be remembered that the time involved in the several stages may, in any given instance, be extremely short (or extremely long) and the stages themselves may not always appear to be disparate except for conceptual consideration.

In assessing the relative importance of factors, a method of weighting is likely to be required. This may be a formal method; for example, a number of experts may be engaged to investigate what they regard as relevant factors in arriving at a resolution, and may have an agreed formula of weights based on their previous experience. By contrast, the weights may be assessed by a single interpreter who may arbitrarily give one factor double the weight of another.

The relative attraction of options may be determined by a process of sequential pairing of assessed options. Each option is paired with another and the less attractive is discarded until one is selected as the most preferred. This process may range from being very fast and seemingly effortless and intuitive to being long, laborious and diffident. The use of computer programs which incorporate this capacity make it possible to use what may appear to be simultaneous, multiple comparison, but this effect is, in fact, a result of extremely rapid successive comparisons of paired factors.

The purpose of the interpretation is to formulate a resolution, which is essentially a statement of advice or suggestion to act in a particular way. The advice may be expressed in a brief imperative or in a long, reasoned argument, which sets out other options as well as the one preferred for action, or in something in between.

Whether an interpretation is correct or not depends very much on what we mean by 'correct'. If we mean that the interpretation incorporates the result(s) of a process of logic, its correctness will depend upon the validity of the reasoning applied, and that is a matter of conformity to long-established rules. In this sense, an interpretation may be correct irrespective of what results may ensue from action taken in accordance with it. On the other hand, if by 'correct' we mean that action taken in accordance with the interpretation produces the (favourable) result forecast (or avoids an unfavourable one) then its correctness cannot be determined until the effects of the action can be assessed; it can only be a tentative assessment until then, irrespective of the validity of its logic. Further, some actions which have been taken on the best advice available at the time of decision may turn out to have secondary effects which were not foreseen but which proved to be deleterious, while some actions may have beneficial effects additional to those anticipated as the basis of the action at the time.

It must also be recognized that, while the above analysis may suggest a somewhat detailed and logical process that is painstakingly undertaken over a period, there are many instances in our everyday life in which the human brain operates so quickly in investigating, analysing and interpreting the circumstances of a desire for change and arriving at a resolution that action appears to be almost instantaneous, or at least with a minimum of delay. For instance, an individual human being may think in terms like these: if I wish to cross a road and see a vehicle coming, my assessment of the feasibility of crossing will include a calculation of the speed at which the vehicle is travelling in the direction of my path, the time it will take it and me to get to a collision point, and a process of logic which will produce a resolution whether to wait or to attempt the crossing. All this is done in a very short time. If my observations, reasoning and calculations are accurate and valid, I shall be able to make the crossing successfully, that is, safely, and my decision and my action will prove to have been correct, despite the short time it took to decide and act. However, if my observation, calculation or interpretation had been faulty in any way, for instance, if I had failed to see another vehicle travelling in the same direction or had miscalculated the speed of the vehicle or of my own walking capacity, or if I had tripped on the way across, then no matter how sound my logic may have been, the unobserved or unforeseen circumstances, while not invalidating the train of reasoning, would prove the crossing to have been a serious mistake and in that sense incorrect.

However, there are many situations in which it is not possible to assess whether a decision has been correct or incorrect, the best or less than the best. Suppose X resolves to renovate his home. He goes through the processes of investigating all the available data, analysing the information and interpreting the results; he obtains several quotations from builders, and chooses one builder to carry out the renovations, which are duly completed. There is never any way of knowing, with certitude, that X has made the best or 'most correct' choice. Even if he is very well satisfied with the outcome, it is for ever conceivable that one of the other builders may have done a better job. To say that a particular decision was the most correct or the best possible is often little more than an unsupportable assertion.

Further, there is no way of knowing if the weights assigned to factors considered in interpreting are correct or not. The interpretation of the factors that have come from the analysis is crucial to the final resolution (and implementation of the decision). The weights in one particular instance may be quite different from those assigned to the same or similar factors in another. The specific interpretation depends on the judgement of the interpreter.

What we have been discussing may also be couched in terms of the process of communication. We discern our observations as sensory perceptions: we see things or hear them or feel them or taste them or even smell them or experience an imbalance or unease which may be difficult to specify. A large part of our learning experience has comprised developing a technique for applying appropriate symbols to the multitude and variety of our sensory perceptions. To a large extent, 'appropriate' in this context means communicable, either to other human beings or to oneself at some other time, and this in turn involves an agreed adherence to a constant usage of the symbols adopted.

Whatever the origin of language or signs may have been, the implicit or explicit agreement on usage by people within a communicating group is an essential aspect of its and their functioning, today as always. Hence, when we say that observation, analysis and interpretation of circumstances and the relationships between them are involved in the process of arriving at a resolution, we are also saying that a process of communication is being carried out in all stages. Any difference between, say, investigator and instigator in recognizing or using specific signs and symbols, or any change by either in such recognition, could lead to an unintended resolution, and, subsequently, to a misdirected action.

The decision-maker's interpretation of the information collected and analysed during the investigatory stage may depend on how the collected information is communicated to its interpreter. Also, in many cases, there is a fine line between different options based on perceived needs, and economic or other considerations. Hence, communicating advantages and disadvantages, or benefits and costs, or pros and cons, of any option proposed by the interpreter to the decision-maker is important to enable the latter to make a more, rather than a less, informed decision.

Another point that emerges is that the process of coming to a resolution involves the creation of information: the sensory perceptions are clothed, so to speak, in communicable terms. That is, they are portrayed in the guise of information which is intended to be understood by the receiver in the same way as it is by the sender. This means that interpretation is an act of interpreting information transmitted from one to another *about* sensory perceptions rather than an act of interpreting sensory perceptions themselves, for sensory perceptions are privy to the perceiver alone, and one can, at best, only describe or portray them in communicable expressions; one cannot transmit or transfer them directly at firsthand.

This raises the question of what kind of information can be and should be provided for a resolution to be made, and this brings us back to the matter of relevance. Also, it brings us back to the process of recording – the ability of users of information to foresee and specify their own requirements and so to identify the occurrences (and their characteristics) to be recorded; how those occurrences and characteristics are to be identified and classified initially; and the likely effects that such classification may have on their availability for use in the future.

Formulation

The interpretation of information, generated through observation and analysis, will normally provide a set of options graded in a scale of priority according to desirable or required effects. On this basis, a resolution can be formulated in a manner intended to induce action. The formulated resolution may be a suggestion, a recommendation, a piece of advice, an imperative, an exhortation, perhaps even only a gesture; whatever its form, the intention is to produce some specific action. The formulation has come from the investigation, analysis and interpretation of the data available for that purpose; its content depends on data available and suitable for investigation, analysis and interpretation.

Formulating a resolution based on a considered interpretation of available information embraces an anticipation of the results of a proposed action. Whether such action will occur in the form suggested or recommended depends upon the will, the willingness, the capacity, the experience, and the judgement of the person who has to perform the action. If that person is also the investigator, analyst and interpreter, that is, if only one person is involved, the likelihood of action being carried out as formulated may be great; one of the main obstacles could well be no more than a tendency towards procrastination. If different people are involved, the actor's interests and characteristics could provide additional obstacles to the performance of the formulated action.

Although the foregoing treatment may portray the formulation of a resolution and its performance as a rational process, rationality itself is always a relative concept. The kind of reasoning which people are able to apply often differs between individuals, and between people of varying cultures; indeed, the actual reasoning which an individual uses may vary according to experience or stage of development, or the particular circumstances at a given time, or relationships to other people or to the environmental situation, and the like.

Implementation

Arriving at and, even, formulating a resolution do not, in themselves, have any observable consequences. A resolution is and remains an internalized, and, often, purely a mental occurrence. This is as true for the resolution of a committee, board or cabinet recorded as a minute of its proceedings as for an individual hopefully 'making up his mind' in a resolution at the turn of a year. Just as the individual has to follow up resolve with a fortifying of the will and strength to act, so too must the group have an executive person to ensure the carrying out of its resolution, and that person has to have the power and capacity to enable the envisaged action to be taken.

Implementation is the carrying out of the activity involved in order to effect the change in circumstances envisaged in a resolution. Although resolutions may be said to be observable in the sense that their formulation can be recorded and noted, only actions are observable in the sense that they have any discernible effects; it is only when something has been *done* – rather than when a thought has occurred or a resolution has been approved – that any change can be detected in the set of circumstances in which the activity has happened. Certainly it is only the extents and effects of actions that can be measured and positively assessed, although this does not necessarily mean that all such effects are precisely measurable.

In observing actions and their effects, many questions become pertinent in trying to assess them. Some of these are:

- Were the actions carried out in accordance with the formulation of the resolution?
- Have the effects of the actions been in accordance with those expected in the formulation of the resolution?
- What, if any, unforeseen circumstances have arisen to affect the validity of the resolution after formulation?
- Can any of these matters be measured, and, if so, how and with what results?
- Can responsibility or credit for any variance of experienced effects from those anticipated be attributed to specific actions or individuals?

One point to note is that a resolution is always formulated to promote or stimulate proposed *future* action (or, in some paradoxical situations, future inaction). Although it may be or may purport to be based on past experience (and this must be so since it is only the past which is knowable in any effective sense), a resolution expresses an intention to change the status quo into something different in the future.

As it was put some years ago: 'The outcome of a decision always takes place in some future period. Put in another way, the behavior pattern chosen by a person takes place *in fact* after the decision has been made' (Carzo and Yanouzas 1967: 326). At first glance this may seem to be an obvious, truistic statement. Certainly the first sentence appears to be undeniable. On closer examination, however, the second sentence does not seem to be saying quite the same thing in another way. If 'behavior pattern' means a sequence of actions which is consistently followed, and if it is chosen by the person consciously and deliberately formulating the sequence to be followed, the choosing could take place when the 'decision' or, in our present terms, the resolution is expressed, or even earlier. Indeed, the nature of the resolution may be influenced, perhaps to an overwhelming degree, by an established pattern of behaviour. The second sentence of the quotation is not necessarily consonant with the first, but this may have arisen because of the lack of distinction between the formulating of a resolution and the carrying out of its intended action. Perhaps the authors meant that the behaviour itself always takes place in the future, that is, after a resolution has been accepted, in which case the expression is truistic.

If one wished to use the term 'decision' to embrace the processes of observation, analysis, interpretation, formulation and implementation, that is, as a complex of steps or stages, then one could say that a decision can be described and identified in terms of certain characteristics such as its relation to space (location), to time (date) and to various other circumstances (such as people involved, equipment or resources to be used or changed, services to be acquired or provided, and so on). We could also say that every decision has more than one characteristic.

Every decision is unique in that in at least one of its characteristics it differs from any other decision. (Many decisions differ in more than one.) At the same time, no decision can be different from all other decisions in all its characteristics, that is, at least one of its characteristics is the same as a characteristic of some other decision. This implies that in at least one of its characteristics (and, in most cases, more) it can be related to and compared with some other decision; this, in turn, permits classification and, in this sense, no decision is unique.

There is, admittedly, a sense in which 'coming to a decision' or formulating a resolution could be regarded as an 'action', but, as has been suggested, it would be an action of thought or emotion; it would not, in itself, produce any change in any thing outside the particular unit of experience. To produce a change in some thing or some body outside that unit of experience involves action of a physical, mechanical, electronic or organic kind and not merely of an 'internal' kind; action of this kind is required to implement a resolution.

However, viewing decisions in this way may tend to endow them with a conceptual individuality and existence which they do not have. No decision can be made without a decision-maker; no set of circumstances can be observed without an observer; it takes somebody to analyse the information derived from the observations; the interpretation has to be made by somebody; a resolution is of necessity made by people; and it is implemented by the actions of people. It is not, as yet, a valid objection to this to say that some of these steps can be made by machines or non-human devices; if this is possible, it is only through human ingenuity, and the devices are performing their tasks because they are imitating the thought processes of their creators; the limitations of the maker are echoed and perhaps in some cases intensified in the limitations of the device.

In recent years expert systems have been devised and developed, and it may well be asked: What about the case of an expert system which embodies the expertise of several different experts? It is claimed that some, at least, of these have been shown to perform better than an individual expert in an identifiable field. Among the pertinent questions that may be asked are these: What is the criterion by which the performance is judged? On what is it based, and who judges it? Is it set up and judged by a completely unbiased, though thoroughly knowledgeable, jury? If more than one expert is involved, are all the participatory experts from different areas of expertise? If they are, who decides what areas are to be included or excluded? If not, that is, if more than one has the same kind of expertise as another, either the views of all with the same kind of expertise must agree, and there is redundancy of effort, or, if they disagree, what basis for selection of one over another view is adopted, and why? Questions such as these do not necessarily invalidate the development and application of expert systems but they may cast a little doubt on the intellectual purity of the concept. In short, an expert system does not of necessity or by definition eliminate the frailties of humans, but it may reduce the risk of their incidence somewhat. At the same time, however, the limitations of some devices (for example, computer programs) may well be less in scope than those of some of their users would be without them in coming to a resolution or working out details of implementation. But it still remains true that the concepts of decision-making are statements of relationships between the human contributors to the whole process rather than identifications of separate components analogous to the parts of a watch which could be transferred from one watchcase to another with equal usefulness.

This discussion suggests that the greater the amount of reliable relevant information communicable at each stage of decision-making, the greater the likelihood that resulting actions will be satisfactory for the purpose of the decider. The term 'feedback' is often used to symbolize the making available of this communicable information. The essential point is that information is necessary to monitor and assess any action and its effects.

The stages distinguished above correspond to those recognized in other spheres of human activity. For instance, Sir Paul Hasluck, in dealing with the relation between social scientists and politicians, suggests that some social scientists have a role of 'observing, recording and analysing what governments are in fact doing and how they are doing it and bringing some scientific accuracy and detachment to that process' (Hasluck 1986: pages unnumbered).

One aspect of implementation that needs to be recognized is that the way in which a resolution is carried out often depends largely on the character, personality and training of whoever does the carrying out. In this respect the whole of the experience of the implementer comes into play in determining whether tact, persuasive power and flexibility are or are not to be preferred to stubbornness and hardline attitudes. In this area it is difficult to see how a non-human device can be developed to take over what has up to now been a very human activity. But this does not necessarily mean that, say, alternative strategies based on differentials of this kind could not be computerized for potential use in some foreseeable cases. Even so, however, the selection of the approved strategy would surely reflect the characteristics of a human selector. In addition, implementation, in the way a resolution formulates it, is not always an easy task. The formulation of a resolution depends on the information available to the formulator(s) at a given time, while its implementation has to be executed at some later time. During the interval, some circumstances may change to such an extent as to make the pre-resolution information wholly or partially obsolete or inadequate, or the purpose behind the resolution may have altered so as to make the resolution itself, or the way in which it was formulated, out of date.

However, while resolutions, until they are fully implemented, are alterable or even subject to rescission, actions carried out cannot be undone; the only modification possible lies in their effects. While a resolution remains unimplemented it can have no effects, but the effects of an action can only be modified by other actions; they are not expungeable or rescindable by any resolution which does not lead to specific further action.

The expression 'decision-maker', as it often seems to be used in the current literature, is a vague and possibly misleading term. It usually appears to conjure up a vision of a strong, active, dynamic and vigorous individual. On analysis, however, the formulation of a resolution may be the work of a far from resolute person, indeed, a visionary; it is the implementer who needs to be the resolute and strong individual. However, many resolutions may require tact and care in their implementation if the purpose behind them is to be fulfilled, and this may in turn require, in some instances, a flexible approach rather than a headstrong one.

Whatever approach is called for, there has to be a motivating factor to link a resolution with its envisaged implementation; the implementer has to be 'moved' to action. The motivating factor may be one of reward, such as salary, commission, social recognition, promotion, and so on; or it may be one of fear, such as demotion, loss of rank or income, social degradation, or the like; it may be one of self-gratification or ambition; it may be any one or more of a complex of such elements. Whichever of these it may be, it is fundamentally a matter of feeling, that is, an internal initiator. Thus, however discerning the observations may have been, however accurate the information compiled from them, and however valid the reasoning in the consequent analysis, the implementation of a formulated resolution requires an essentially emotional impetus to set it in motion. Our actions, if they are to be recognizably deliberate, and hence 'rational', depend on motivation, however strong or weak, for their performance.

The significance of the discussion in this chapter lies in the recognition that accountants should be aware that coming to a decision is often a complex and diverse process, even when it appears to be quick, simple and direct. If they are aware of this and understand and appreciate the structure of the deciding process, they should be in a sound position to explore and devise appropriate means to observe and record a variety of occurrences in the first place, and, later, to devise adequate means of monitoring the implementation of decisions arrived at.

Levels of decision

Decisions may be made at various levels. At the top are policy decisions made by policy-makers. These are direct expressions of the objectives or ideals in mind for the individual, organization or government. In the corporate world the appropriate persons to make policy decisions would be the board of directors, so long as all is going well; if not, the creditors might decide as a matter of policy to carry on the business under a receiver or to put it into liquidation. In the realm of politics the Cabinet should be the policy-maker, but, in a modern democracy, subject to such mandate as the people might have given. Next come executive decisions made by the hierarchy of executive officers. These are the decisions necessary, or thought necessary, to carry out the policy laid down. The executives in charge of the several divisions of the business, the ministers at the head of the several government departments, determine what actions have to be carried out. These decisions are expressions of policy. Then come administrative decisions, made to express the routine for ensuring that the actions decided upon are carried out. These are the day-to-day decisions of the administrators of business or government.

At each level, a decision represents an attempt by humans to exercise control over the actions of other humans towards certain ends, as in the movement of materials, the use of resources, appointment or discharge of employees or contractors, and so on.

For any individual or group of people, the decision to change the status quo may vary from almost trivial to extremely serious, even threatening to life or to the existence of the human species.

Decisions and command

The functions of the commander can be seen most specifically in the implementation of resolutions, for it is in this stage that action has to take place, and it is a commander who has to do the acting. This is where the concept of command becomes operative. It is the implementer at each level of implementation who has or is provided with resources for deployment in order to implement a decision. It is in this way that the relationship of command over resources (interpreted in a wide sense in this context) is linked with the function of implementing a decision, because, without somebody with required resources available, no envisaged implementation can take place. Further, unless one has command over resources, including the ability to direct the activities of people (perhaps especially so), one cannot have decisions implemented; without command over the means to implement it, a decision (or a resolution) is no more than a declaration of hope – an intention without will.

Where many people are involved in implementing, say, a policy decision, each person has to be able to deploy resources appropriate to the activity required for the implementation as envisaged in the resolution.

Questions which each commander is likely to face include:

- Are the resources under my command sufficient to attain the objective(s) of the decision to be implemented? If not, how do I obtain them?
- If a particular resource under my command has more than one application, to which use shall I put it first?
- If more than one resource under my command can be used for a particular objective, which resource shall I use?
- Are any risks attached to either over-use or under-use of a particular resource, and, if so, can it be (a) measured, (b) limited or avoided?

This leads to the possibility that the notions of command and commander become readily applicable to accounting for decisions at any level. Indeed, if applied in the several stages of arriving at a decision, it could well focus attention on the means required to attain any desired change in the status quo, for the question would be raised: Are the required people and resources available to attain each objective in the several stages of performance?

At the same time, it should be noted that, along with resources and the means to apply them, come duties and responsibilities, between individual people, and between each commander in the group and in the society in which the activities of all have any effect. Some of these may be specifically documented by contract; others may be implied by custom or social usage.

Hence, the opportunity to account for decisions, and especially their implementation, may give to accountants a basis for a reorientation of their attention towards the notion of efficiency and effectiveness in the application of resources, particularly in a social or communal context. Thus comand in this context is not a narrow economic concept, but a responsible and active function operative in virtually any society.

This is a direction for exploration which we commend to potential researchers. It is also the underlying motive for discussing the process of making decisions and the notion of command.

12 Relevance and reason in decision-making

Who shall decide, when doctors disagree,
And soundest casuists doubt, like you and me?
                              (Alexander Pope, *Moral Essays*, Epistle i:i, Line 1)

Relevance

The adjective 'relevant' and the noun 'relevance' have been used in accounting and associated writing for a considerable time. Although some writers
have set out to define the terms, it is far from certain that readers interpret
them in the same way; their precision and clarity cannot be taken for
granted and an attempt to apply tests of relevance in a particular case
raises some troublesome questions.

One difficulty is what relevance applies to: Does it refer to an occurrence
or to the result of or information about an occurrence? Or, indeed, about
one's perception about one or other of these? This is a philosophical or
analytical matter which needs to be addressed before we can progress far in
trying to communicate successfully.

We are, let us say, observing a set of circumstances in order to come to a
resolution about a proposed course of action. The circumstances are many
and diverse. Which factors are to be regarded as relevant and by what
criteria? We submit that the selection of some factors as relevant and the
exclusion of others as irrelevant depends upon the observer's experience of
past occurrences and an appreciation of the objective(s) of the proposed
action, together with an acceptance that any pattern of past occurrences is
extendible in the future. This pattern is an expression, so to speak, of a
relationship between disparate or, at least, distinguishable factors within
the set of observable circumstances; the relationship is one of influence,
that is, factor A influences (or has influenced) factor B and the latter is
considered certain or likely to be important in determining the resolution
to be arrived at.

The term 'relevant' usually means assisting in and influencing an activity
or process, or contributing to an effect. The relevance of a particular factor

may be deemed to be high or low; if it is high, this means that it is thought to be important; if low, then it is regarded as not important. Thus, some identifiable factor, while admittedly present and contributing to an effect, may not necessarily be important, because other contributing factors are regarded as more important.

The kind of influence is that of either causality, wherein one factor causes the other, or conjunctivity, in which the presence of one factor is always accompanied by the presence of the other; in the latter case we normally and naturally presume an underlying, further factor which causes them both. If this is so, then the notion of causality is inescapable in interpreting the concept of relevance. Even if we admit chance or randomness as a factor, we do not deny the existence of a causal factor; we are only admitting that we do not know or perceive it and certainly cannot identify it for the time being.

Another question is whether relevance lies in the eye of the observer or is inherent in the factor(s) observed, irrespective of the observer or, indeed, of whether it is observed or not. The question could be answered in an analogous manner to that used in the ingenious pair of limericks on philosophical idealism,[1] but in this form of answer its importance is not great: if there is no question of communication or interpretation it does not matter if any factor is relevant or not; relevance can hardly exist if there is no reason why it should be considered, or if it does exist, then it cannot be important unless or until it is recognized as having existence, and the recognition gives it, for human purposes, its existence.

Some writers, admittedly, have set out to provide a definition. For instance, Chambers gives us the following:

> Relevance of information is the property by virtue of which inform-ation is serviceable in the adaptive process at a point of time. Relevant statements, being objective statements, do not relate to or contemplate any specific or potential choice or future situation of an actor. Relevance is a general property; its reference is any and all of the actions available to an actor at a given time.
>
> (Chambers 1966: 149)

---

[1]There was a young man who said, 'God
Must find it exceedingly odd
To see that this tree
Continues to be
When no one's about in the quad.'

'Dear Sir, your astonishment's odd,
I'm always about in the quad,
And that's why the tree
Continues to be,
Since observed by, yours faithfully, God.'
     (Frequently quoted, see, for example, Bibby 1978.)

and

>7.25   Relevance is the property by virtue of which a statement, singular
>or aggregative, has potential for selecting responses in an actor
>at a point of time.
>
> (Chambers 1966: 164)

As they stand, these propositions do not carry a strong conviction of
clarity. It is difficult to see how a statement, whether relevant or not, can be
said to have potential for selecting anything. Surely exercising any potential
and making selection are processes involving some activity, by living
creatures or by devices designed by living creatures, and not merely by the
existence of statements.

However, if, as seems more likely, a less transitive use of verbs was
actually in the writer's mind and that his intended meaning was that a
relevant statement is one which contains information which can be used in
the adaptive process at a point of time, it does not follow that 'relevant
statements do not relate to . . . any specific or potential choice or future
situation of an actor'. Surely, it would be rather the reverse: *only* relevant
statements relate to a choice or future situation of an actor; if there is no
relationship, it is indeed difficult to see how any statement can be relevant,
for the relevance is itself a relationship. Anybody engaged in an adaptive
process at any point of time would surely have some specific objective in
view, otherwise towards what or away from what is the adaptation to be
directed if the time and effort are not to be completely wasted?

It is not clear, further, whether statements include information or whether
information is made up of statements, but this probably does not matter
very greatly, except that it would be strange if, say, non-relevant statements
could be made up of relevant information or relevant information of
irrelevant statements.

Relevance is something that is, in a sense, discovered, but, before it can
be discovered, its existence or presence has to be envisaged or suspected.
For instance, knowledge about the relevance of smoking to lung cancer, or
the sun's rays to skin cancer are the result of discoveries of recent decades.
The relevance of microscopic organisms to disease could not be more than
imagined – and, for most people, even less than that – before the invention
of the microscope.

Relevance cannot be determined beforehand. It may be suspected; it
may be intended; but it cannot be imposed or fore-ordained. The question:
Is such and such relevant? is, essentially, unanswerable before the event.
The more appropriate question is: Do you think such and such is likely to
be relevant and, if so, why?

Relevance is not something *contained in* a 'factor', a quality of it, but
rather a relationship between things or activities. The history of science is,
to a large extent, the story of numerous instances of the discovery of relevance between things and activities, not previously thought to be relevant

to each other. The story also encompasses many instances in which a presumed relevance has been discovered to be false.

Can there be degrees of relevance? Or, is it rather that if a factor is relevant it cannot be irrelevant? If a factor has any influence, it is relevant. But the influence may be material to a greater or less extent. Hence, something may be relevant but not material, which is a way of saying that there can be degrees of relevance. Another way of putting this might be to say that materiality is the measurement of relevance.

If relevance is described or defined as a quality of information and if this means that it is something inherent in the information, then this is an untenable proposition, because by its nature information is the result of a human activity which produces it; whether something is known to humans about anything else, be it human or non-human, depends upon the human process of observation, discovery, interpretation, communication, record-ing, preserving (of evidence), and the like. Its relevance is relative to some part of these processes, and the judgement that some information is or is not relevant is part of the process of interpretation, and can only be made when the purpose of the interpretation is considered in relation to the information available or sought.

Information in itself is neutral, neither relevant nor irrelevant. Perhaps this is what Chambers really had in mind. The 'relevance' of information is necessarily related to the use made of it. The provider of information cannot *foretell* its relevance; he may speculate or hold an expectation (perhaps justified) that it will be (or will not be) interpreted by the recipient as being relevant. Its relevance lies in its interpretation and use.

Since information in itself is neither relevant nor irrelevant, its relevance can only be judged when the purpose of the information is known and taken into consideration. In determining the relevance of particular information, we engage in an attempt to examine its causal influence on human actions; if we conclude that it is likely to have or to have had such a causal influence, then it is judged to be relevant *to that action or to those actions*; otherwise, it is deemed to be irrelevant. The relevance lies in the relation, not in the information itself. The human actions may be future ones, as in the process of decision-making, or they may be past ones, as in historical interpretation.

This is why experience (that is, knowledge and interpretation of things past) is significant in determining whether information in any particular set of circumstances is to be judged as relevant or not. Interpretation of relationships of causal influence in past series of occurrences produces an intelligible pattern of such relationships for circumstances which have not been concluded and whose outcome is yet to be experienced; this outcome may be affected by action yet to be undertaken as a result of decisions still to be made.

Perhaps the essential point is that the relevance of something, *A*, to an event, *E* (or a situation or state of affairs), cannot be *tested* until the event itself takes place or even later. It may be suspected in advance (or in retrospect), but the confirming or refuting of it depends on some kind of testing (experimenting, in a sense) which cannot be completed until an event of type E has taken place. This suggests that 'relevance' is a term used to symbolize a relationship between A and E, rather than a quality or characteristic (if there are such things) of either A or E. In practice, the attributing of relevance can often be attained through regular or continuous monitoring of factors and effects in the several stages of the decision process; its assessment or measurement depends on the judgement of the monitor.

In the design of a data-base system, for example, the use of data depends on the recording of it in the first place. (Indeed, irrespective of data-base considerations, if data about an occurrence are not recorded when the occurrence takes place, then they are not available unless they can be derived or estimated when they are needed.) Does the recognition that data should be recorded mean that the data are 'relevant'? While relevance is not a 'quality' of data, not something that can be determined *before their use*, the recording of data suggests that somebody expects, suspects, imagines or speculates that they may turn out to be relevant in the future. It is its use that determines whether or not a datum is relevant. However, before it can be relevant, someone must foresee that we need to observe and record it. This is the basis for the stage in data-base design that is known as 'requirements analysis'.

Davis (1982) considers that:

> There are four major reasons it is difficult to obtain a correct and complete set of requirements:
> 1   The constraints on humans as information processors and problem solvers.
> 2   The variety and complexity of information requirements.
> 3   The complex patterns of interaction among users and analysts in defining requirements.
> 4   Unwillingness of some users to provide requirements (for political or behavioral reasons).
>
> (Davis 1982: 474)

One of the constraints 'on humans as information processors and problem solvers' is their ability (or inability) to foresee the future. How do users know what data they need (and therefore deem relevant) in the future? Whether or not a datum is deemed relevant will depend on the requirements of a user in the future – whether that datum can be used in the relationship with other data to assist in the decision-making process. Yet, in many cases, observations about occurrences can only be made at the time of happening. Once it is past, it may be difficult or even impossible to remember or reconstruct relevant data. We may suspect that something may be relevant in the future (and therefore should be recorded) but we will not know if it is relevant until it has been used for a specific purpose, or, if absent, its non-availability is regretted when the time for action arrives. 'The variety and complexity of information requirements' may result from a lack of 'knowing' on the part of a user whether data are likely to be relevant or not. There may be a temptation to record data in case it becomes relevant in future, leading to a recording of much data which may never be used and therefore never become relevant. The third difficulty referred to by Davis relates to the communication problems likely to arise between those responsible for designing a data base and those attempting to foresee the possible future relevance of data. The fourth difficulty is a quirk of human nature; the non-recording of data because of such un-willingness may result in resolutions being made that omit relevant factors.

The role of reason in decisions

The role of reason in making decisions has been implicit or explicit in the above discussion. We have distinguished between two significant functions:

(a) Arriving at a 'conclusion', that is, considering information and formul-ating a resolution (recommendation, advice or instruction) and saying, in effect, 'this is what we (or you) should do'. This is or could be or should be based on reason and reasoning, such as noting the several factors which influence a particular situation, weighting them in relation to each other and in relation to an envisaged objective, and, as a result of rational analysis, arriving at a proposal for action. 'Rational' here means 'in accordance with accepted rules of logic'.

(b) Implementing a resolution requires doing something intended to affect the situation. It is here that motivation is involved – one must be 'moved' to action. A.N. Whitehead pointed out many years ago that the basis of experience is emotional. (Whitehead, 1948: 205) Reasoning, of itself, stays in the mind; it does not lead to action. If action is to be taken, the resolution reached under (a) must be reinforced by some kind of motivation. However, it should be noted that we often use the word 'reason' in the sense of motivation, for example, when we ask: 'Why did John take a taxi?' and we accept the answer: 'His reason was that (='Because') he wanted to get there as quickly as possible'. Now John may have reasoned thus: 'If I am to get there as quickly as possible, I shall have to take a taxi. I do want to get there as quickly as possible, therefore I should (or must) take a taxi'. And he might himself say: 'My reason for taking a taxi was that I wanted to get there as quickly as possible'. But his action – the actual taking of the taxi – depended upon his *wanting* to get there as quickly as possible. If he hadn't wanted to do this, his reasoning would not have had any effect on his actions. And wanting or wishing or desiring is an emotion. Indeed, surely the person who wants nothing will do nothing.

Even if the ultimate resolution is not to change the existing circum-stances, any investigation into the factors comprising or affecting the status quo would have been motivated by a feeling of unease, discomfort, danger or the like. While the investigation may be undertaken according to the rules of deductive reasoning or according to the rules of empirical science or to those of any other system of belief, it remains, if no action at all is taken, an intellectual exercise. The resolution arrived at may, indeed, even say that no action should be taken. In this case, the initial feeling of unease, discomfort, danger, etc., is either seen to be unnecessary, and, consequently, removed or greatly diminished, or is dwarfed by the prospect of greater unease, discomfort or danger, etc. (if any action be taken), and, consequently, borne, with or without good grace, with or without grumbling or complaint. In this sense, what is seen as inaction has an emotional content.

A pertinent question to raise is: Why should a writer write in this way at all? It may seem to be 'rational' to the writer to do so (in whatever sense of 'rational' we may wish to use), but this does not answer the question. If the writer were merely content to think out the logic, it would probably not be necessary to write it out. But there are two points. First, many writers find that the actual process of writing helps the progress of the train of thought, whether it is logical or not. And, second, a writer may *want* to have a record of the argument or of the process of thought which he or she may *wish* to recall some time, when he or she might *want* to convince somebody else of the strength of the case or of the vividness of the thoughts. That is, any positive attempt at communication involves some emotion, however slight in degree it might appear to be. Further, a writer or an artist may feel uneasy until relieved by activity involved in at least trying to express those troublesome emotions in communicable symbols.

What is a good decision?

People are continually implementing decisions all around us, and we ourselves are engaged in it, too. We cannot avoid being influenced by the actions of other people as well as by our own. How can we tell whether the decisions upon which these actions are founded are 'good' or not? What do we mean by a 'good' decision?

Several possible answers may be considered:

1   As already suggested, a decision may be judged to be good if it has been made in accordance with the recognized rules of logic as developed in the so-called Western culture and philosophico-scientific tradition over many centuries. Such a decision could be called 'rational' in a strict sense of that word.

    If the person making the resolution is the only one involved in implementing it, the decision is likely to be assessed as good at the time of performance, because of its rationality. But this assessment may differ from that held by others who contemporaneously observe the impact of the decision, or by the person concerned, at a later time with the benefit of hindsight. If the envisaged result was in measurable units, then an outcome which attained the envisaged number would be regarded as strong evidence that the decision was good; if the envisaged number was not attained, the shortfall would detract from the goodness of the decision. However, this is a simplistic means of forming a judgement, for, often, an envisaged result, even if regarded as measurable, may have other factors contributing to peripheral or ancillary or environmental effects not foreseen, or disregarded as unimportant in arriving at the resolution, and thus neglected in its implementation. In such cases, although a decision may be regarded as having been good in the sense of attainment of an envisaged and measurable result, it may be unsatisfactory when other criteria than such a precise measurement are applied.

2   A good decision may be one that turns out to be 'right', in the sense of giving the result that was envisaged and desired when the decision was made.

This seems to be the sense in which Simon, Smithburg and Thompson would have judged the behaviour of administrators when they wrote several years ago:

> Before an individual can rationally choose between several courses of action, he must ask himself: (1) 'What is my objective – my goal?' and (2) 'Which of these courses of action is best suited to that goal?'
>
> (Simon *et al.* 1950: 58)

In this respect it should be noted that in every resolution there is an implied prediction, namely, that if the action suggested is carried out, certain identifiable results will follow. If the action is taken, and the results turn out as forecast, then the decision was 'obviously' a good one. But this overlooks the possibility of a non-causal relationship between the elements considered in forming the resolution and those contributing to the result; in other words, the prediction may be correct because of coincidence or accidental forces. Even if the outcome is not as forecast, the decision may be deemed to be good so long as the variations from the forecast (for example, 'variances' in the language of management accounting) can be acceptably explained; the meaning of 'acceptably' here being largely a subjective matter.

3   A good decision may be one that takes into account, with 'proper' balance, all foreseeable relevant information. The determination of what is a proper balance is a subjective assessment, depending upon the knowledge and experience of the person making the determination, while, as we have seen, the relevance of many influences cannot be determined until after a decision has been implemented. Thus, such 'good' decisions can turn out not to give the desired or forecast result because of unforeseen occurrences for which the decision-maker should not, perhaps, be blamed.

4   A good decision may simply be one that the person charged with assessing it agrees with, representing, in most instances, one that that

person would have made in circumstances the same as or similar to those faced by the decision-maker at the time.

It is easy to see that some of these criteria may be in conflict in particular cases. For instance, a decision which may be considered good because it has been logically determined may turn out to have deleterious results, while a fortuitous result may provide support for a decision that was illogically made or which neglected to take into account some otherwise foreseeable elements which may have influenced the action taken.

Another question is: If the result of implementing a resolution is affected by the skill or the will of the implementer, does this affect the goodness of the resolution so implemented? For example, an architect who has to prepare plans for redesigning the interior of a building must make many decisions on factors affecting the redesign: the size, position and shape of the rooms, the best way to use the floor space of each room to fulfil the purpose of the alterations, and so on. There may be many options available; the architect uses judgement and experience to *resolve* to design it in one way rather than another. The result of the resolution is a set of drawings. From the architect's viewpoint this may be considered as the implementation of his resolutions. But the plans are handed to a builder for actual implementation of the architect's intention, that is, to build the interior of the building *exactly* in accordance with the architect's plans. The builder has no part in deciding how to design the interior. However, during the implementation of the plans, the builder may *resolve* that some things should be changed, in accordance with his experience, and so implements not the architect's plans but a modified version of them. In this example, the will of the implementer (the builder) affects the 'goodness' of the resolution arrived at by the architect. The question whether or not the builder's decision to make changes to the architect's plans is 'good' or 'right' or not is likely, in the end, to be judged by the architect and/or the owner of the building.

This matter of criteria is one for adoption by policy-makers, who should consider it consciously and deliberately, with all of its difficulties, in addressing their attention to the decisions they have to face.

Accountants and decisions

Accountants are concerned in the decision processes in several ways. Whatever else they may do, they are involved in preparing and furnishing information; they are involved in communicating. They are involved in collecting, portraying and conveying data as a contribution to formulating resolutions. This does not mean that all resolutions are based only on information supplied by accountants or on what are usually regarded as accounting data, but that many resolutions do have a component of accounting information and to that extent and for that reason accountants are involved in the formulation process. In addition, accountants often provide information on the results of the actions taken, whereby those results may be measured against the implied or explicit prediction of the resolution; in other words, accounting information is often used in assessing the goodness of decisions. This is not always recognized explicitly and may contribute to an inability of accountants to realize the extent of their responsibilities. One aspect of this is the incorporation of accounting concepts, such as profit, into the criteria for assessing the virtue of decisions. If these criteria are based upon information provided by accountants who have interpreted occurrences or situations according to their knowledge and expertise, and the measurement of such goodness is made by accountants with a similar background and experience, the risk of intellectual insularity is not only possible, but serious. Just as the formulations of resolutions are founded on information, so are the consequent actions monitored from information; to the extent that such information in either case is provided by accountants through accounting processes, accountants are involved functionally and responsibly in several of the stages of deciding.

In collecting and providing information, accountants have to make resolutions on several matters, some of the most important being the kinds of occurrences and their characteristics that are to be recorded, and, if they are measurable, the most appropriate unit(s) of measurement; the relationships that may exist between the occurrences and their characteristics; the form in which the data about occurrences are to be recorded; their measurement, including what is or are likely to be the most useful measured result(s) for the specific user(s); the level of aggregation of occurrences and the most appropriate way to aggregate them; and the form of report to users. One important aspect of providing information in this connection is its timeliness, that is, it should be available to the prospective user(s) before it is too old to be of use in arriving at a resolution. This applies to any decisions with which accountants are concerned, such as reports to managers, owners, investors, creditors, guarantors, employees, or any other decision-makers perceived to be involved. (For a discussion of timeliness in relation to financial corporate reporting, for instance, see Carnegie 1990: 11–13.)

In order to arrive at satisfactory accounting resolutions, accountants should consider the requirements of the subsequent decision-makers and the precise decision(s) for which the information is being provided, any external influences such as legal requirements and socially approved (or socially condemned) activities and apply their knowledge, experience and judgement in contributing to the decision to be implemented. Hence, if accountants are to discharge their professional and vocational responsibilities creditably, they need to understand the nature and implications of the whole process of arriving at, implementing, analysing and evaluating significant decisions in the elaborate web of the organizational or social fabric.

Rational decisions: rational actions

In addition to the nature of a decision and analysis of what is involved in making and implementing it, another point that arises is: Since the word 'rational' is so frequently used in trying to communicate about decisions and actions, and since 'rational' decisions and actions are, so far at least, the most amenable kind to 'explain' and 'understand' or 'accept', some of the senses in which the word is and can be used should be further examined.

One writer who has raised some doubt is Kindleberger who asked:

> What does it mean to say that markets are rational? Is it assumed that most markets behave rationally, or that all markets behave rationally most of the time, or that all markets behave rationally all the time? Which formulation one adopts makes a difference. It is much easier to agree that most markets behave rationally most of the time than that all markets do so all the time.
>
> (Kindleberger 1978: 25–6)

He accepts the proposition that 'rationality in markets in the long run is a useful hypothesis', and that people act as if they were rational in the long run, so that economic activity should be analyzed according to that hypothesis. However, his studies of economic history produced some doubt. As he points out:

> Manias and panics, I contend, are associated on occasion with general irrationality or mob psychology. Often, the relationship between rational individuals and the irrational whole is more complex . . . Mob psychology or hysteria is well established as an occasional deviation from rational behavior . . .
>
> (Kindleberger 1978: 28)

> . . . euphoric speculation, with stages or with insiders and outsiders, may also lead to manias and panics when the behavior of every participant seems rational in itself. This is the fallacy of composition, in which the whole differs from the sum of its parts. The action of each individual is rational – or would be, if it were not for the fact that others are behaving in the same way. If a man is quick enough to get in and out ahead of the others, he may do well, as insiders do, even though the totality does badly . . .
>
> (Kindleberger 1978: 34)

> . . . Markets can on occasions . . . act in destabilizing ways that are irrational overall, even when each participant in the market is acting rationally.
>
> (Kindleberger 1978: 41)

It does not take much thinking effort to conclude that the word 'rational' has multiple meanings, and many writers seem to use it without regard to the possibility that their use or interpretation (if they have a clear one in mind) may not be that in the reader's mind. (Cf. Goldberg 1964.)

We submit that the question: What does 'rational' *really* mean? is a nonsensical question. The word 'rational' relates to the way of thinking; it is a symbol of a concept. Its 'meaning' can only be determined by trying to find out what message the user intends to convey and we do this by considering what we know about him or her and the context within which the word is being used. Often this is far from easy, and, in any case, we are always apt to put upon it a meaning which reflects, in part at least, our own use of it. We suggest that 'rational' has little, if any, objectivity of its own as a symbol in communication.

'Rational' may mean different things to different people, and it may signify different things to anybody in different contexts or in different circumstances. Like so many expressions we use in communicating, it has a fluidity of interpretation which may result in difficulties in transmitting intended meaning with precision. We all have our own rationality. Even if one adopts another's, it becomes one's own by adoption. It is accepted and adopted because it is compatible with the adopter's experience to date. It may be rejected later and in hindsight if experience is contrary to expectations, but that is another matter; at the time of adoption there is compatibility.

'Rational' is often contrasted with 'emotional' and 'rationality' with 'feeling'. It was suggested earlier that it is 'feeling' – specifically, a sensation of disquiet about the way things are – that initiates the processes which constitute decisions. The anticipation of the results of proposed action is itself clearly a feeling – a sensory occurrence – which at first is imagined or remembered, but later is experienced, either as anticipated or as different from the expectation.

Within the sequence of processes in arriving at a decision, reasoning will usually have been applied, so that feeling and reason (or rationality, in the sense of a process of argument in accordance with agreed logical steps), far from being contrasted with each other, should be viewed as complementary, at least for human activities. As pointed out earlier, if we consider them from an evolutionary point of view, both are ingredients of decisions and actions which are utilitarian in purpose, being directed towards the preservation and continuity of individuals and/or species. While they are different from each other, they are complementary in objective. Indeed, it is possible to 'feel' an intellectual excitement in cogent reasoning; in such an experience of excitement, the two seem to merge.

In considering the criteria for assessing the 'goodness' of decisions, it was suggested that rationality was one which might often be applied. Philologically, 'rational' is derived from a Latin ancestor, *ratio, rationis*, which meant (i) a reckoning, computation or account, and (ii) relation, reference, respect (to a thing), or judgement, understanding, reason, from which it came to be used to signify a theory or system based upon reason and the process of reasoning. Through its ancestry, it is related to such words as 'rate', 'ration', 'ratify' and 'reason'. (In Italian, *ragioneria*, derived from the same ultimate source, means 'accountancy'.) In current usage, some implicit sense of reasoning is always present.

However, we are not primarily concerned with philological or dictionary definitions, but rather with those conceptual usages by which it may influence our thinking and interpretation. A generalized expression of rational thinking, which we all use quite frequently, is: 'If A, then B.' This is a short and symbolic way of saying that if, and wherever, certain antecedent circumstances, namely A, exist or occur, it follows that a certain result, namely B, will also occur. The antecedence and the result need not exist or occur in a time relationship – they may be contemporary – nor need they be related in a space relationship – they need not differ in their occupation of space. The relationship needed is that of causality: an acceptance and recognition that it is because of A that B arises.

We need not go so far as to say that we can only have an acceptable reasoning process when we say: If, and only if, A, then B. This may be required for some sequences of reasoning, but not all; for instance, where A is one among several influences contributing to B. Further, the expression If A, then B does not necessarily exclude such an additional expression as: If A, then C, where C is something different from B. But the recognition of a causal relationship between the antecedent proposition(s) or expression(s) and the derived conclusion or result is necessary for admission to the family of logical thought processes. So much so, that Mankind, as a species, is frequently differentiated from other species (perhaps not always correctly) by the presumed universal presence in all its members of such a capacity for this kind of thinking.

Reasoning is bound up with explaining. When we 'explain' some natural phenomenon in terms of reason and communicate about it with our fellows in terms that we believe or hope they will understand in the same way as we ourselves do, are we not attributing a kind of reason either to the organism whose actions are being observed and explained (if the phenomenon is organic) or (if inorganic) to some invisible intelligence who or which has arranged a sequence of occurrences which can be interpreted by means of human reason? For instance, if we explain, say, the dance of a bee as a means of telling its fellows the whereabouts of an exploitable resource – its direction and distance – then doesn't this suggest that the bee has been involved in some process of reasoning? It has encountered and sampled the source of benefits; it has arrived at a conviction that it has had an adventure which, or the result of which, must be recounted to its colleagues, *so that* they may verify the richness of the source and exploit it for the benefit of the hive? To put it down to the bee's instinct alone may be technically correct, but it does not explain anything, and only plays with a word. If the instinct involves a recognition of purpose and an activity which communicates and promotes this purpose, then, one must ask, how does it really differ from the underlying basis of human reasoning?

Consider another, simpler and more commonly observed example of an individual who can speak in the following way: I am digging in my garden and with my fork I turn over a clod of earth and soon see a worm squirming and slithering to get down again below the surface. I explain this to myself by thinking (and perhaps saying) that the worm dislikes the warmth, the light and the prospect of increased danger it has been exposed to. But I must recognize that it is capable of making a choice. It had been quietly and legitimately going about its normal activity of living in its dark, cool habitat, when, suddenly, without warning and, from its point of view, with no justification, it has been catapulted into an antagonistic environment, dazzlingly light (which it probably can only sense by some other means than seeing) instead of dark, warmer or, possibly, if a frost is on the ground, colder than is comfortable for it, but, above all, dangerous, for the upper world is the one where birds and other predators operate. If the worm doesn't 'know' some of these things in some way, how can we explain its endeavours to go back to its normal safe (or less unsafe) habitat? If it does know them, then it has some kind of reason: 'I am in a strange, nasty place, therefore I must go back underground.' Of course it will be said that the worm cannot think this way; it cannot verbalize as we humans can. And, of course, this is clearly true. But words are used to communicate thoughts, not to have them; words are, after all, mostly symbolic. The worm's reactions are chemical, it will be said; but so are ours, when we feel too warm or too cold, but we have symbols for our feelings, whereas, so far as we can tell, the worm hasn't. We have words to express our feelings – or some of them; *we* presume that the worm hasn't or, if it does, it is in a kind of language that is incommunicable to or by us.

It should be emphasized that, whatever view is adopted about the function or province of logic, it occurs only within the minds of people (and, perhaps, of some other organic creatures with which we can scarcely communicate at present).[2] We may be able to examine our own thought processes consciously and directly, but we can only discover another's through communication. In order to communicate with others and to consider whether their thought processes, as they report them to us, have an affinity with our own, we need to have agreement upon the symbols which we use in communicating. Much of our language, whether written or spoken, is attributable to this requirement; even some gestures may serve in communicating reasoned thoughts, although this is less common than their use in communicating feelings.

What we are principally concerned with at this point, however, is what we mean when we say that an action or a conclusion is rational if it is based on

---

[2]In recent years television viewers have been able to see humans communicating with chimpanzees and gorillas through a vocabulary of words and/or signs conveying a cognisance of understanding by both sides of the species differential.

a reasoned or logical sequence of thought. Over a long period, rules of the discipline of logic have been developed as part of our culture, whereby the validity of the thought processes and the resultant conclusion(s) can be assessed according to the extent of compliance with those rules.

As with so many words in our language, 'valid' and 'validity' are not without their semantic difficulties, which the dictionary does not completely dissolve. For instance, a typical entry for 'valid' has as one of its group of meanings:

> valid . . .
> 2. Founded on truth or fact; capable of being justified, supported or defended; not weak or defective; well-grounded; sound; good, e.g., a valid argument or valid objection.
>
> (Webster 1926)

The words are derived from the Latin *validus*, strong and *valere*, to be strong, and are philologically related to 'value', 'valiant', 'avail', 'prevail', and 'convalescent', among others.

It is important to distinguish between two of the uses of 'valid' and 'validity', which are often confused. As the dictionary suggests, 'valid' and 'true' are possible synonyms, and there are contexts in which they could be interchangeable. But there are others in which substitution of one for the other would give a completely erroneous interpretation, and one of these lies in the field of logic. Within the accepted rules of logic, a conclusion may be valid, or 'true' in one of the senses of 'truth', if it is derived from an agreed set of premises and an accepted line of argument; that is, it can be logically true or valid. But, in another sense of 'true', namely, that of being in accord with some observable or empirically acceptable data, the premises, and the conclusion may have no relation to truth at all. That is, if we adopt different criteria for according validity and truth, relating the former only to the force of argument and the latter to some empirical content of observable 'fact', we can have a perfectly logical set of thoughts about something which has no truth content whatsoever.

This may be put in another way. The word 'truth' is a symbol like any other word. When we say that something is true, we are saying that we accept something we perceive as being compatible with our total experience to date or with our state of mind at the time of perception (for example, as under hypnosis or hallucination) and we apply the word/symbol 't-r-u-e' to it for the purpose of communication if required. Whether we use 'valid' or 'true' or any other adjective to describe it, a conclusion derived from a purely mental exercise does not have any truth in relation to empirical observation of sense data. If it is to have any 'truth' in relation to the facts of sense data, a relation of such truth to sense data must be established in the first place in the premises from which the conclusion is derived; factual 'truth' in the sense of conformity with observable sense data cannot be manufactured in the processes of thought, however strictly logical they may be and, therefore, however logically valid any inference drawn from its premises may be.

The process of reasoning needs to be discussed because it often involves conceptual obscurities which should, at least, be recognized, even if they cannot all be cleared away in universal agreement or to everybody's taste and satisfaction. Whether we accept an identity of meaning between 'validity' and 'truth' should depend upon the context in which they are used and upon the intention of the user in that context; each of these words has multiple meanings and shades of meaning, and the user, whether transmitter or receiver of a message, should, at least, be conscious of this and try to guard against any innocent misinterpretation of the intended meaning.

Further, a corollary of the possession of multiple meanings by a word or phrase is the likelihood that a user will sometimes slide unintentionally from one meaning in mind to another. The context often reveals this, and, if it is recognized readily, little or no harm in interpretation may result; but, if the context does not readily reveal it, it is more likely that the recipient will not interpret the message in the way intended; if this happens, communication between the parties is not successful.

In what follows, we try to be consistent in our usage by restricting our intended meaning of 'valid' to apply only to conformity to the recognized rules of logic, so that 'validity' relates solely to arguments arising in the course of reasoned thinking, while our use of 'true' and 'truth' involves reference to some 'facts' or experience which can be observed and/or empirically tested for their or its existence.

Something more than adherence to the pure logic of the case is needed to warrant the acceptance of behaviour in any kind of social setting. For one thing, if everybody always relied on logical thinking alone, no action would ever occur; all would starve through lack of applying valid conclusions, because it obviously requires some physical activity to pick up a fallen fruit rather than to stop at the thought that it would satisfy our hunger *if* we were to do so. To put it another way, we can say that reasoning is the conscious exercise by the mind on logical processes. Not only can logic not tell us anything about any 'real' world, it cannot tell us (even though it may purport to) whether or not any such world exists. Only experience can tell us this. With this criterion, reasoning, and hence rationality, is embedded in thought; it is mental, and not experiential.

However, 'rational' may be interpreted in other senses. An action or a conclusion may be termed 'rational' if it is presumed or expected to optimize results, that is, to get the best results possible within the restrictions imposed by known or expected circumstances. We are here using the words 'optimum' (noun or adjective), 'optimize' and 'optimization' in their current usage in common language and not in any technical sense; they are symbols respectively for 'the best or most favourable degree, quantity, etc.', 'the process of attaining the best or most favourable degree, quantity, etc.', and 'the attainment of the best or most favourable degree, quantity, etc.' As so used, the concept is far from clear-cut and raises many questions of interpretation, not the least of which is whether one can have a concept of an optimum without implying a means of measuring it. It would seem that if it is to be operational as a criterion by which to judge the *extent* of shortfall or shortcoming, measurement is required; but perhaps if one can be satisfied with knowledge of the *existence* only of such shortfall or shortcoming, comparison without precise or even fairly close approximation may well be sufficient for one's purpose. However, if we start with an agreed measure of hoped-for results (reverting somewhat to the earlier meaning of 'optimize' as being always optimistic), it is possible to measure the extent to which a result attains or falls short of the expectation. But there is an innate difficulty here: If the expected result is attained, what is there to say that the goal should not have been set higher or further or greater than it was?

Any such interpretation immediately raises several questions. What results are to be optimized? Whose optimization is involved? What criteria exist by which to assess optimization? Can there be degrees of optimization, and, if so, how can they be measured?

An initial point is that the mere use of the notion of an optimum result (or, indeed a result of any kind) implies an action of some sort. If this were not so, the interpretation would have no more existence in a world of observation and experience than that of any exercise in fruitless thought sequences (for which an apt expression exists in 'day dreaming'). The action may be imagined, and the result of that action may be imagined, but even in this mental exercise the result is seen to be that of some activity. The thinking may run on some such line as: 'If we do this (or if we refrain from doing that), then the result will be so and so, and this result will be the best possible.' But our thoughts are focussed on the prospect of *doing* something which will alter an existing set of circumstances.

The best (that is, the optimum) for whom? Or for what? A point of view is implicit in this interpretation, and this needs to be specified. In many cases, perhaps most, it is that of the actor (or by people who are perceived to represent such actors, as in a professional body, trade union, or the like) or of the one who arrives at the conclusion. In such cases the situation seems to emphasize the notion of self-interest (in the sense of selfishness). But some other's point of view may be paramount; this happens in many social problems when conclusions may have to be arrived at and actions under- taken for the benefit of people whose category may be specified but whose personal identity may not; indeed, they may belong to a generation still to be born. This does not preclude the desirability of or necessity for arriving at conclusions or undertaking actions which are envisaged as giving the 'best' results.

Whatever stance we adopt in relation to point of view, the problem of measuring optimality is present always. Fundamentally, it is an insoluble problem, for, once a given action is undertaken, no other can take its place simultaneously; even if a particular activity is suspended after it has commenced, the fact that it began cannot be effaced completely, and the longer a course of action continues the greater its impact is, in general, likely to continue. Since no more than one course of action can be taken in the same place or in the same circumstances at any one time, it is only possible to see the effects of that one course of action; to consider what the results of any other would be or would have been is speculation and not observable. One can only compare an imagined 'what might have been' with what is, for there can be only one 'what is'.

Somewhat akin to, but not identical with, the notion of optimization is the interpretation of 'rational' as fulfilling expectations. If the result of a particular action is seen to be that expected at the time of deciding to take it, that action may well be interpreted as having been rational, as would the decision to take it. This interpretation also has its little problems. If the result falls short of that expected, does this affect the rationality of the decision or action? Can a decision or action be partially rational? Is there a scale ranging from complete irrationality through mostly irrational, neither irrational nor rational, somewhat rational, much more rational than irrational, to completely rational? If so, how are the divisions to be detected if not from a measurement of the result? And, if this, is it sensible (or rational) to contemplate such an interpretation?

Another aspect of this interpretation is that the rationality of a decision or action cannot be determined at the time of deciding or acting. It can only be judged afterwards; sometimes not until long afterwards. Strictly, on this interpretation, no conclusion, decision or action could be claimed in advance or contemporaneously to be rational, from which it could be argued, perhaps somewhat speciously, that rationality cannot exist! Without going quite so far, however, it seems that such a problem could claim attention.

Another problem is a matter of timing. A result which may appear to be in accordance with expectations at one time may later, because of changed conditions, turn out to be averse to them, so that what was seen to be rational earlier may later be seen to be otherwise. Can it be said that rationality is an elastic concept, or that the expectation for the result is elastic or should be so regarded? If the latter, would any resolutions ever be made or action undertaken under the guise of rationality? If a resolution or action is to be interpreted as rational only in hindsight and in the light of its outcome, would not this mean that no rational resolution could be known to have been made and no rational action would be known to have been taken until the ultimate outcome is known? And would not this virtually destroy any possibility of applying the concept of rationality to any *proposed* resolution or action? In other words, it would not be rational to propose a rational action (on this interpretation) because we could not judge in advance whether it would turn out to be rational or not!

A related issue is that of the identity of the beneficiary of the decision or, more importantly, of the action. For a result which may benefit one person or group may be detrimental to others, and the expectations of people often conflict either at the time of the resolution or at that of the action or subsequently. Sometimes the conflict does not become evident until the action or some part of it has taken place; when it does, the wisdom, and, as likely as not, the rationality, of it is brought into question.

Another problem is that, in considering the circumstances for making a resolution, those which are seen to appertain to the proposed action must be selected. These are only a proportion, and sometimes a small proportion, of all the circumstances which could be altered from their existing state into something different. Some assumptions necessarily have to be made that many circumstances will remain unchanged or that any change will not be great enough in extent or direction to seriously affect an expected outcome. In other words, an assessment of the relevance of known circumstances has to be made. But this assessment may be seen as misguided or may be misinterpreted when subsequent events take place. There may be blame to be attached to those who frame the resolution or take the action. The result may be different from the expectation wholly through an unforeseen and, for humans in their present stage of development, unforeseeable, change in influential circumstances. Does such a failure to achieve an expected result mean that the resolution when made or the action when taken was not rational? If what was done was the best that could have been done in the then known circumstances, what more could be required to regard it as rational?

Another criterion of rationality is whether an action or a proposed action conforms to the norms of conduct for the members of the group to which the implementer of a decision belongs. The customs and mores of most groups, especially large communities, are often numerous and complicated, and a great deal of the learning process of individuals within such groups is taken up with absorbing the customs into their individual experience. In modern communities, aberrations are frequent. Many of the customs and mores become incorporated into the laws of the community; compliance with these becomes compulsory under imposition of sanctions. Indeed, in some legal systems, including those based on British law, a criterion of 'the reasonable man' has been a measure of actions in many a case brought into the courts for decision. The question 'What would a reasonable man have done in the circumstances?' has been the basis for interpreting and measuring the effects of the actions of individuals. This standard is far from precise in varying circumstances or constant over time, but it has been applied with, presumably, sufficient success to have made it endurable and widely acceptable. The concept of the reasonable man may also be applied to some of the customs commonly observed by individuals, but without specific legal compulsion and prescription of penalty for non-observance.

In essence, this interpretation of rationality is a normative one. Whether something is rational or not depends upon whether it conforms to what a 'normal' person within that community would think or do according to the mores of the community, whether these are specified in law or only recognized in custom. It is a reflection of a system of thinking and, almost certainly, subject to change over time or through variation in social circumstances, and subtly inconstant in perceptibility at any time. It has a low content of objectivity and a high risk of variability in application. It is closely related to 'common sense'.

One of the dangers in applying this interpretation arises if it is extended too widely without some countervailing influence. The mores of the group may become debased or distorted under the influence of such things as propaganda, stress or fanaticism; and standards of behaviour change through any change in the attitude of a sufficient number of members of the community to jeopardize the comfort or, in extreme cases, the safety and existence of others. It may well be an element in such social phenomena as mob hysteria, bull markets on the stock exchange, fanatical political demonstrations, ethnic or racial feuding, and others. Activities undertaken in such circumstances may reflect the mores of the group at the time, but are far divorced from those of 'a reasonable man' as envisaged in the calm contemplation of British law in which it is currently widely accepted.

Another point to notice here is that, since many customs have become enshrined, so to speak, in the law of the community, a view is widely held that any action which does not specifically break a legal obligation or is contrary to a widespread and widely known custom, is not irrational or unacceptable. Indeed, an attitude of 'beating the system' may become not only tolerable, but applaudable, throughout a community or a smaller group within it, even though it is demonstrably inimical to the interests of the community as a whole or of a substantial proportion of the people.

Akin to this interpretation, but not quite the same, is that personal one by which an individual takes the view that he himself is the 'reasonable man', and that his own actions, thoughts and trains of reasoning constitute the criterion by which those of others are to be judged. The word 'rational' means what the assessor agrees with. It is often embodied in advice such as 'what I would do if I were you . . .' or 'What I would do in those circumstances . . .'. Such expressions convey a frankly subjective attitude, which may be partially 'justified' by the holder by a rationalizing process of reference to some criterion such as reasoning or experience. This means, in effect, that rationality lies in the mind of the interpreter; it is very largely, and perhaps wholly, subjective. Although this interpretation might be widely denied, it is probably applied in many instances. One suspects that many arguments, conclusions and explanations are accepted or denied on a criterion of whether they satisfy one's own standards for acceptance. Indeed, in any specific instance, it is virtually impossible to avoid such an individualistic stance. Wherever and however our criteria for assessment of the validity or truthfulness of another's statements or actions have been derived, they have to become our own if we are to use them in judging others. If we are to understand anything, it has to satisfy *our* reason and be in accord with *our* experience. If our own criteria are the same as those of many of our fellows, then our judgement will be as theirs; if they vary then our judgement will probably stand out from theirs with prominence and perhaps with denunciation. Expression of a dissenting judgement is usually uncomfortable and sometimes dangerous; it frequently requires courage, especially if it has to be maintained in the face of a hostile 'conventional wisdom'. At bottom, however, it is the source of intellectual progress. But it may also be the basis for retrogressive change if the views of enough people in a community can be directed away from a tolerant to an intolerant attitude for non-conformers. Herein lies a dilemma.

Within the communities of our Western culture, the conventional wisdom, which embodies the rationality of the majority, runs behind the rationality of some individuals whose outlook would draw the conventional wisdom forward after it. At the same time, however, that same conventional wisdom is likely to have left behind it the views of some whose intellectual attitude is nostalgically reactionary. There is, so to speak, a continuing tug-of-war between the minorities (and, in a specific instance, they may not be restricted to just two) for the minds of the majority, that is, for the conventional wisdom or accepted norms of behaviour of the community. In this context 'majority' may not mean simply numbers of individuals; it may consist of just enough people with the power or influence to control the affairs of the community or an identifiable group within it. Neither are our comments restricted in application to those communities in which political 'democracy' is observed; the significant environment is one of culture rather than political institutions.

Consideration of these various interpretations of 'rational' and 'rationality' and their implications leads us to the view that what we can observe around us is a scene of different and sometimes conflicting rationalities. People apply different criteria of rationality: from each other, and even of their own at different times or in different circumstances. There is no absolute criterion for determining the rationality or the extent of rationality of anything done or proposed to be done. Social problems arise from conflicting or competing rationalities. *A*'s view may differ from *B*'s, not because one is rational and the other irrational, but because each is rational according to the holder's interpretation of rationality. It is the interpretations which differ.

Many writers have emphasized the importance of rational behaviour, which nobody 'in his right mind' would be likely to deny. However, this in itself does not clarify its meaning or its implications. To take one example from a well-known work, Alvin Toffler makes this statement:

> Rational behaviour, in particular, depends upon a ceaseless flow of data from the environment. It depends upon the power of the individual to predict, with at least fair success, the outcome of his own actions. To do this, he must be able to predict how the environment will respond to his acts. Sanity, itself, thus hinges on man's ability to predict his immediate, personal future on the basis of information fed him by the environment.
>
> (Toffler 1971: 319)

He then discusses the problems of how much 'sensory impact' we can absorb and the limitations of human capacity to deal with information. Toffler does not discuss in any detail what he means by rationality, but he suggests that irrationality consists in people acting against their own clear interest, with the further assertion that '[e]ven the most stable and 'normal' people, unhurt physically, can be hurled into anti-adaptive states' in times of crisis as might arise in a fire, flood, earthquake or the like. He thus presents two criteria: accordance with self-interest, and non-adaptation to customary social behaviour.

Not only is our view of rationality complicated by the possibility of different criteria for assessing its presence in particular or general circumstances, but it may recede even further from simplicity and clarity by acknowledging that some behaviour may be regarded as rational in some circumstances but not in others. In this sense, rationality is relative. For instance, if one is told that somebody is interested in collecting small pieces of paper which had been made to serve a particular function once and once only, so that cancellation makes any one of them incapable of repeated use, the rationality of that person's behaviour might 'reasonably' be doubted, if that were all that is known about the circumstances. But if we were told that these pieces of paper were gummed and perforated and had varying pictures, designs and values imprinted on them and that their function had been to ensure the passage of mail, the possibility of their providing pleasure through contemplation of their appearance or information about their scarcity value would almost certainly remove any such doubt; this is, indeed, a matter of gaining more data about them. At the same time, if any of these pieces of paper is unused for the purpose for which it was designed and even if it is in perfect (or 'mint') condition, it gains no value for its use in that function, but, paradoxically, it may gain greatly in value so long as it is not used for its intended purpose. In other words, its gain in exchange value may increase so long as its nominal value in use for its initial purpose is not varied. This is the general rule with these pieces of paper; there are, occasionally, instances where the face value of an unused stamp may decrease over time, but these do not occur often. And there are also instances in which a used stamp may command a higher price than the unused one of a particular issue; this also occurs but rarely. The point, however, is that a function is imposed upon these pieces of paper which is different from that for which they owe their existence, and, even though some issuing authorities exploit this secondary function (collectability), the use of these stamps in their primary function remains the basis and justification for the secondary function.

From one point of view, philately might be regarded as a non-rational behaviour: why spend time or energy on collecting small pieces of paper that have little intrinsic value until they are used in the function for which they have been made, and no such intrinsic value once they have been used? From another, the collecting of such specimens may give pleasure in contemplation of their design, organization or completeness in series, or of increase in value by reason of their relative scarcity, and may turn out to be a valuable and portable store of exchange value; what could be more rational behaviour?

This is but a familiar illustration of the relativity inherent in the concept of rationality; rationality is the (form of letters in our alphabet which we use to express the) relationship between certain perceived behaviour and our assessment of it in the light of our knowledge of the circumstances and according to the criteria, based on our experience, which we are able and willing to apply to it. It is we, the perceivers, who interpret the relationship according to the criteria which we are disposed to accept and adopt.

With such a variety of interpretations of rationality available, it is small wonder that there should be considerable differences in opinions about it. But, however one defines 'rational', surely it cannot be rational to close one's eyes, and, worse, one's mind, to the patent existence and power of both non-rational and irrational behaviour that goes on around us continually. In social affairs, Man's instinct has, for the most part, prevented him so far from relying chiefly on reason for any big decisions. Emotions are more powerful than reason in inducing action. When it is a case of national actions, such as wars, elections, selection of governments and the like, emotional factors are paramount in getting things done. It is emotion which uses 'reason' as a tool. For instance, accuracy and truth are only too frequently displaced by propaganda directed by people filled with emotion, often linked with self-interest, rather than the equitableness of reason.

Recognition of the variety and complexity of the notion of rationality is important in any attempt to interpret the activities of people which constitute a 'market' in any commodity or in any instrument of finance or exchange. Those acting in a market rarely act 'irrationally'; most of them act according to their own criterion of rationality, which may differ from those of other operators; indeed, they must be different, since their expectations of the outcome differ. If this were not so, there would always be minimum or no market activity. Thus it is not a matter of *A* acting rationally and *B* acting irrationally because his actions differ from *A*'s; they may both be acting rationally but according to different criteria, for instance, their reaction to particular influences may differ according to their interpretation of circumstances, and there is nothing irrational about *B*'s behaviour at all. Again, the outcome for each of them may turn out to be precisely as each had anticipated, which, according to one criterion of rationality, would ensure that they had both acted rationally.

In contemplating any particular action or decision, the most important question to be asked, perhaps, is not only whether it is (or was) rational or not, but what criterion for rationality has been applied. Was the action taken or the resolution arrived at consciously? Was it deliberate? Was it reasoned? Were all relevant interests represented? Was it based on a clear anticipation of its outcome? Was it based on conformity with the environment of social mores or custom? These are the kind of questions that need answers before judgements on rationality can be adequately supplied.

The raising of such questions may make the formation of judgements more complicated and perhaps more tentative, but they would also be more penetrating, more substantial, more understanding (in the senses both of more comprehending and more tolerant), and more defensible; they would clearly be less mechanistic or automatic. If, for example, we wish to incorporate human expertise, judgement and experience in a computer program (such as an expert system), a consideration of the questions raised above should assist in ensuring that we are not just making automatic an already inadequate decision-making process. In any computer-based system, there is danger in accepting results that may rely on human thought processes that are quite inadequate in the first place. If we are to automate the way in which humans come to resolutions, it is important that the automation does not lessen the need to question and take into account how the reasoning is undertaken.

One further point needs to be raised as a general observation. People tend to believe in their own rationality, which is founded on and derived from their own experience, and to doubt the rationality of anyone else which is not in agreement with it or which they themselves cannot somehow reconcile with it. The position that this discussion leads us to is that each unit of experience develops its own criteria of rationality based on its experience. Perhaps there is in humans an innate capacity to reason, but if there is it is one that can be and is developed through the experiences to which it is applied by the individual. Perhaps, also, there is a limit to this innate power, but this is something we cannot tell until we come to it, each one for oneself; and this is something which cannot be communicated by any reasoning process in itself to anybody else. If it is communicable, it must be by some other means. In brief, the unit of experience is also the unit of rationality.

It would seem to follow that no two people are likely to have precisely the same criteria for assessing rationality, whether in themselves or in others. However, units of experience with similar experiences (including, very importantly, being brought up within the same cultural environment) will be likely to have very similar criteria for rationality. Hence agreement about what is rational behaviour may vary according to the extent of similarity of experience of those involved in the process of agreeing or disagreeing.

It is several decades since Viscount Samuel, while acknowledging that 'reason itself may err' and that 'intellectuals are often found to be wrong', seemed to obtain comfort from opining that mistakes of reason 'can be detected and remedied by the process of reason itself; indeed, if rational methods are consistently applied, sooner or later they must be detected and remedied'. (Samuel 1939: 62) What our current analysis suggests is the paramount importance of consistency in the process of 'detection' and 'remedy' of mistakes of reason, for if different 'detectives' have variant criteria of rationality their respective processes of detection may well produce varying 'explanations' of the mistakes and varying prescriptions for the 'remedies' required. In economic, social and ethical matters, the differences may have serious implications. Of course, Samuel was then contrasting reason with intuition, both of them expressions of great abstraction; he was seeking to have reason applied to rescue us all from the dangers of absolute authority, which he somehow linked with intuition.

Appendix to Chapter 12

Hamlet as decision-maker

As an example of some aspects of decision-making and implementation, consider the case of Hamlet, using his own words and those of other characters in the play.

Hamlet's first appearance is in Act I, Scene 2 (I, 2), and his first words are an aside when the King addresses him as 'cousin' (meaning, more strictly, perhaps, nephew) and 'son' (more specifically, step-son). This aside is 'A little more than kin, and less than kind'. This is, at the very least, a grumble; it betokens an assessment of less than complete satisfaction with his current situation. He is being chided for perpetuating his mourning for his father's death and for his intention to return as a student to Wittenberg, whence he had come to attend the funerary rites for his father and the subsequent marriage of his widowed mother to the present King.

When his mother, the Queen, also pleads with him to stay in the court, he agrees to do so. But, when left alone, he voices his dissatisfaction with the state of affairs and exposes (to the audience) his reasons for his unease:

> Oh that this too too solid flesh would melt,
> Thaw and resolve itself into a dew!

He is clearly not happy about his father's successor, either as a king or as a husband for his mother; but he can see no way to do anything to redress the circumstances in which he finds himself: 'But break, my heart; for I must hold my tongue.'

Directly after this revelation (to the audience) of his discomfort, his student friend, Horatio, appears and tells him of the apparition of his dead father at the walls of the castle. Hamlet seems ready to believe, but cross-examines Horatio and his companions, Marcellus and Bernardo, who were on guard when the ghost appeared. Apparently this evidence of his father's ghost engenders in his mind a hypothesis of foul play as a cause of death, and he makes a resolution to speak to the ghost if he can:

> If it assume my noble father's person,
> I'll speak to it, though hell itself should gape
> And bid me hold my peace.

In his interview with the ghost (I, 5) Hamlet hears an accusation of his father's murder, and forthwith pledges speedy action:

> Haste me to know't, that I, with wings as swift
> As meditation or the thoughts of love,
> May sweep to my revenge.

Later in the scene, however, when he is in the course of swearing Horatio
and Marcellus to secrecy, he anticipates his future odd behaviour. This
suggests that he expects that implementing his decision of revenge is going
to require some indirectness of approach, and he recognizes that the King
is astute and powerful.

In II, 2 Hamlet is playing mad, or at least unhinged and unpredictable by
'normal' standards of behaviour. Polonius suggests it is because of unrequited love for his daughter, Ophelia, and proposes that the King and he
hide behind a curtain to observe Hamlet in conversation with Ophelia. But
before they can do this Hamlet enters and, finding Polonius alone,
exchanges badinage with him, and later, with Rosencrantz and Guildenstern
who tell him of the arrival of a group of actors who have come to entertain
the court. Hamlet arranges for a particular play to be performed.

When alone once more he berates himself at his failure to implement his
resolution of revenge:

> Why, what an ass am I! This is most brave,
> That I, the dear son of a father murder'd,
> Prompted to my revenge by heaven and hell,
> Must, like a whore, unpack my heart with words,
> And fall a-cursing, like a very drab,
> A scullion!

And he decides to incorporate into the play to be enacted a scene which he
conceives will produce overwhelming evidence of the King's guilt or
innocence. Presumably up to this stage his resolve was not supported by an
overwhelming motivation for immediate action:

> I'll have grounds
> More relative[1] than this; the play's the thing
> Wherein I'll catch the conscience of the king.

In III, 1 what is possibly the most widely known of Shakespeare's many
speeches occurs, namely, 'To be or not to be'. In it Hamlet sets out some of
the problems involved in and arising from delay or failure in implementing
a decision. Even though, in an earlier scene (I, 4) he told Horatio: 'I do not
set my life at a pin's fee', now he is concerned in, at least, the after effects
when life has ended:

> what dreams may come
> When we have shuffled off this mortal coil,
> Must give us pause;

---

1 Nowadays we would probably say 'relevant'.

Is he rationalizing his lack of action to implement a decision, or is he questioning the decision itself? Whichever it is,

> Thus conscience does make cowards of us all;
> And thus the native hue of resolution
> Is sicklied o'er with the pale cast of thought,
> And enterprises of great pitch and moment
> With this regard their currents turn awry,
> And lose the name of action.

After this, he puts on his mad hat and is quite nasty to Ophelia. His words to her have been overheard by Polonius and the King, and the latter announces his intention to send Hamlet to England. The King is shrewd enough to suspect some reason for Hamlet's behaviour other than or additional to his formerly unrequited love for Ophelia.

Act III, Scene 2 is the scene in which Hamlet is convinced that the ghost's account of his father's murder is substantiated by the King's obvious discomfort at the poisoning scene within the play. Left alone with Horatio, Hamlet observes: 'O good Horatio. I'll take the ghost's word for a thousand pound. Didst perceive?' Hamlet had told Horatio some detail, at least, about his conversation with the ghost and asked him to watch the king at the poisoning scene, which, in his view, has provided corroborative and convincing evidence of the King's guilt.

Rosencrantz and Guildenstern come to convey the Queen's request (or demand) for Hamlet to see her and explain, and Polonius reinforces the request. While alone, Hamlet tells us he is all worked up: he is ready to use harsh words with his mother, but will not offer any violent action: 'I will speak daggers to her, but use none.'

In III, 3 the King tells Rosencrantz and Guildenstern to get ready to accompany Hamlet on a voyage to England; Polonius goes to hide behind the curtain to overhear Hamlet's session with the Queen. The King prays – or, rather, he kneels but finds that he cannot pray because of his guilt. Hamlet sees him kneeling and is tempted to kill him then, but refrains, being restrained by the thought that if the King were killed while purging his soul he would not be damned and condemned to hell. An opportunity to carry out a resolution is not taken; implementation is deferred.

Hamlet has a session with the Queen (III, 4) and has some caustic words for her. She calls for help; Polonius, behind the curtain, echoes her call, and Hamlet 'makes a pass through the arras', thinking it is the King, and kills Polonius. Thus, he has taken action to implement his resolution, but it turns out to have been misdirected and merely serves to complicate the state of affairs further. Polonius' death could, perhaps, be interpreted as death by misadventure, or the killing as murder through inaccurate implementation.

While Hamlet is showing the Queen her shortcomings and telling her that it was the present King, now her husband, who had murdered the previous one, the ghost appears once more to him, but not to his mother, to remind him that he has not yet implemented his resolution to avenge his father's death.

In IV, 3 Hamlet learns of his forthcoming journey to England, and the King tells the audience of his 'instructions' to the authorities in England to dispose of Hamlet there. This journey is obviously a change in the circumstances for Hamlet, and, although it does not alter the resolution he had made, it presents a change in his opportunities and in the manner of implementation.

However, in IV, 4 Hamlet is on his way to the ship for England, and, after meeting the captain of the Norwegian army of Fortinbras, soliloquizes on his failure to implement his resolution:

> I do not know
> Why yet I live to say 'This thing's to do;'
> Sith I have cause and will and strength and means
> To do't.

A little before this, in the same soliloquy, he has an observation about reason:

> Sure, he that made us with such large discourse,
> Looking before and after, gave us not
> That capability and god-like reason
> To fust in us unused.
> ['fust' means to go mouldy; to smell or taste ill from mould.]

In IV, 5 we are shown Laertes returning to Denmark in a passion of resolution and readiness to avenge his father's death. This may be meant to be a contrast to Hamlet's indecisiveness in his implementation of a father-avenging resolution. The King implicates Hamlet in Ophelia's madness as well as in the murder of Polonius. We then see Horatio receiving a letter from Hamlet, who has escaped from the ship but is held by a pirate gang. (IV, 6)

At the burial of Ophelia (V, 1), who has died by drowning, Laertes leaps into the grave for a last embrace, and Hamlet, coming out of hiding, impetuously jumps in also and they grapple in the grave. He does a bit of boasting and outbidding of Laertes in his love of Ophelia; he cannot understand why Laertes should be so cross at him. The outbidding is one-sided, since Laertes has said nothing to him except one curse. Perhaps Hamlet merely forgot that his victim, Polonius, was the father of both Laertes and Ophelia. The King arranges a duel between Hamlet and Laertes.

In V, 2 Hamlet tells Horatio about his voyage towards England and how he changed the instructions for his execution on arrival into a similar fate for Rosencrantz and Guildenstern. He has no remorse for this: 'They are not near my conscience.' He has implemented a minor resolution; he must stay alive to implement the main one, so this action is a necessary part of the overall strategy.

He also seeks Horatio's moral support for the resolution to rid the world of the King:

> He that hath kill'd my king and whored my mother,
> Popp'd in between the election and my hopes,
> Thrown out his angle for my proper life,
> And with such cozenage – is't not perfect conscience,
> To quit him with this arm?

Horatio merely observes that it will not be long before the King gets news from England about the fate of his messengers.

Osric arrives with a challenge from Laertes, which Hamlet accepts, telling Horatio that he can win, but is uneasy about it. 'I shall win at the odds. But thou wouldst not think how ill all's here about my heart.'. However, he shrugs it off: 'It is but foolery; but it is such a kind of gain-giving as would perhaps trouble a woman.' (He does not know that the King has arranged for Laertes to use a poisoned foil and for him (Hamlet) to drink a poison when they pause between passes.)

Soon the climax and the conclusion are reached: the duel with Laertes, in which both are killed, the King is killed by Hamlet, and the Queen by the poisoned drink intended for Hamlet. Hamlet has at last implemented his resolution but is himself destroyed in doing so, and so, too, are several others.

> Horatio is left to tell the story:
> And let me speak to the yet unknowing world
> How these things came about: so shall you hear
> Of carnal, bloody, and unnatural acts,
> Of accidental judgements, casual slaughters,
> Of deaths put on by cunning and forced cause,
> And, in this upshot, purposes mistook
> Fall'n on the inventors' heads . . .

From this point of view, a series of bad decisions and faulty implementation. Or, in modern parlance, a literal case of overkill.

The question arises: Was the initial decision a good one? Whatever the answer, by what criteria and from what point of view are it and its outcome to be assessed? For instance, from the point of view of Fortinbras of Norway, who seems to have thought he had some claim to Denmark, the outcome may well have appeared fortuitous, if sad. Think of all the unlucky innocent victims: Polonius, Ophelia, Rosencrantz and Guildenstern, Laertes, perhaps even the Queen. All dead because Hamlet was not good at either arriving at a resolution or implementing it once made. In modern vernacular, we should have to conclude that Hamlet was in truth a bit of a wimp.

Where did Hamlet go wrong? Was his data base faulty? Was his investigative method unsound? And what about his judgement and timing? Would he have done better if he had understood more about the process of decision-making? And if so, how and to what extent?

We can recognize some of the elements of the state of affairs which evidently irked Hamlet and made him uneasy. His father was dead. His uncle was King. His mother had remarried too hastily. He himself was being kept at court against his wish to return to the University in another town in another country to resume his studies or at least to experience a different way of life from that at court. We do not know whether he was wondering why he was not king in succession to his father or whether he regarded his uncle as a usurper. Presumably Denmark did not then have a constitution by which succession to the throne was ensured by primogeniture. Hamlet's uncle is the King, and not a regent during the minority of the Prince.

Hamlet was 'canny' enough to feign madness, fairly convincingly, apparently, for many of those at court, and that is a sign of maturity rather than the naivety of youth. After all, if we are to believe what we are told in the grave-digging scene, he was not a teenager. He was old enough to be a student at a university with mature fellow students, such as Horatio; he could remember Yorick giving him piggy-back rides. Such memories of Yorick could scarcely go back to before the age of three or four years of age, and, according to the grave-digger, Yorick had been dead for twenty-three years. So, Hamlet was in his late twenties, unless the grave-digger's information was wrong or Hamlet's memory was at fault and he was mixed up about what may have been a succession of jesters at his father's court.

While Hamlet may be a case in which accounting information is not directly involved or relevant, it serves to show up a number of matters about the making of decisions. It also shows some of the essential features of evidence required before arriving at a resolution: the evidence should be not only acceptable (into one's experience) but verifiable. Hamlet is willing to accept the evidence of the Ghost, but cedes the possibility that it may be an evil spirit, luring him into trouble. He therefore seeks, and gets, what he regards as confirmation through the performance of the players.

A question that may well be raised is whether Hamlet would have been more likely to do better if he had had available the technology of an expert system or a more extensive data base. This question may be unanswerable, but it is of interest as suggesting or implying that, when and where a decision is required, the experience, the perceptions and biases and the character of a decision-maker are significant, as well as the kind, amount and reliability (or verifiability) of the data available. This is a question that accountants need to recognize as pertinent to situations frequently confronting them.

Part III

Constraints

13 The accounting equation reconsidered

> It is giving much too extended a sense to the notion of an equation to suppose that it means every kind of relation of equality between any two functions of the magnitudes under consideration.
>
> (Comte 1822: 50)

As we look back on accounting developments over the past century or so, we can discern a complex paradigm (to use T.K. Kuhn's useful term) to help in understanding them. It comprises the so-called accounting equation, which has become a basic factor in introducing and expounding the 'theory' of accounting procedures, the venerable double-entry procedure itself, and the balance sheet which expresses directly the accounting equation at specific dates for specific units of operation or foci of attention. These are examined in this and the next two chapters.

Since early in the twentieth century the presentation of the study of accounting in terms of a pseudo-mathematical equation has steadily become more frequent and more popular among accounting writers, at least in the English language, so that it is now virtually universal among them. It is often known as the 'balance sheet approach' and, although its origin goes back to the nineteenth century at least (for example, Cronhelm, 1818: 8 ff.) it has become predominant in accounting literature only since the 1920s in the USA and subsequently in other regions. However, it would be rare indeed nowadays to find an English language introductory text in accounting that did not employ it as part of its basic presentation of the field of study.

The equation, which is regarded as fundamental in accounting thought and practice, is variously expressed in such forms as:

$$A(\text{ssets}) = E(\text{quities})$$
$$\text{Assets} = \text{Claims on Assets}$$
$$\text{Assets} = \text{Liabilities} + \text{Proprietorship}$$
$$\text{Assets} = \text{Liabilities} + \text{Owners' Equity}$$
$$\text{Assets} = \text{Liabilities} + \text{Shareholders' Funds}$$

and similar propositions.

Until a few years ago[1], balance sheets are sometimes set out in the form of:

What we Own *less* What we Owe *equals* Our Net Worth

or something equivalent to such an equation. This is often regarded as a simple or non-technical way of presenting a balance sheet which shows the result of the operations undertaken by those people who have been responsible for conducting the affairs of an enterprise and who have to report from time to time to those to whom they are legally or socially responsible.

The overwhelming importance and ubiquity of this equation does not seem to be questioned; it is accepted as an expression of a universal, self-evident and undeniable truth. It is rarely examined for its innate logical or semantic implications.

Let us consider the expression: A(ssets)=E(quities). As has been pointed out, over some six decades this equation, in its various forms, has developed into the 'fundamental' proposition in expounding accounting thoughts. It underlies the teaching of the recording procedure, the preparation, analysis and interpretation of periodical accounting reports, and is, virtually, all-pervasive in discussions in accounting theory. The long-standing search for 'principles' or a 'conceptual framework' has been largely directed towards expressions of the components of the equation – assets, equities (that is, liabilities and proprietorship) – and recognition of or agreement on the meaning and coverage of each, with a direction towards the appropriate means of measuring each kind of item comprising each component.

However, little, if any, attention seems to have been paid explicitly, at least by accounting writers, to the consideration of the connecting link between the components, namely, 'equals'. What do we mean when we say that 'Assets' equal(s) 'Equities' (or 'Liabilities plus Proprietorship')?

Let us first consider some possible related meanings which do not apply. We surely do not mean that assets are identical with equities, for that would entail that we could substitute 'equities' whenever we have 'assets' without altering the meaning of any proposition which contains the word 'assets'. If we say that a particular building is one of X's assets, can we also say that that particular building is one of X's equities? If we can, then we are saying in the equation that assets are assets, which is an obvious tautology, and we can scarcely proceed further in using it. But we do proceed to divide equities into external equities, that is, liabilities, and internal equities, that is, proprietorship or ownership. Then we have to consider whether we can say that that particular building is an external equity, in which case we acknowledge that an asset is a liability, or that it is an internal equity, in which case an asset is an item of proprietorship. We do not mean either of

---

[1]More recently, text-books for accounting students in Australia seem to have fully adopted the standards set out in the Statements of Accounting Concepts as an infallible guide for accounting practice. This is considered further in Chapter 16.

these statements; they would be contradictory to the development of further propositions from the basic equation. Hence it may be concluded that 'equals' does not mean 'identical with'.

A similar argument can be applied if we regard 'equals' as meaning 'synonymous with'. In this case we are clearly dealing only with the use of words. This means, in effect, that if one word is synonymous with another, each could be substituted for the other in a statement without changing the meaning of the statement (or its import). In other words, if we meant that 'assets' and 'equities' were interchangeable in statements about either, each could be viewed as a definition of the other. And again, the expression: 'Assets equal(s) Equities' would be tautological.

If we wish to convey a meaning that something is the same *in some respects* as some other thing without being identical with it, we may say either that it is equal to it or equivalent to it. In each of these words 'equal' and 'equivalent' there is some element of sameness and some element of difference between the things which are equal or equivalent to each other.

In some expressions the characteristic of equality of one with the other is implicit in the manner in which the two are compared. For example, if we say that six plus four equals ten the characteristic of being ten is implicit in the expression 'six plus four' because the system of numbers which we customarily use is based on an acceptance of conventional meanings of 'six', 'four', 'ten', 'plus' and 'equals'. These symbols, in their respective significances, are part of our experience, and we accept each one as having that same significance for any future experience we may have. In other words, the *rules* under which a comparison takes place are agreed on beforehand.

There is, however – at least generally – a positive, if sometimes subtle, difference between the perceived significance of 'equals' and 'is equivalent to'. If we say that 'six plus four is/are equivalent to ten', there is no implicit omission in the statement, for we are prompted to ask: six what, four what, and ten what? While 'six plus four equals ten' implies a uniformity in all relevant characteristics of whatever the numbers can be attached to, so that, for instance, six fowls plus four fowls equals ten fowls, there is a suggestion, at least, of some difference between the nouns in the expression when we use 'equivalent to'. So if we say that six fowls plus four dogs are equivalent to ten pigs, we imply that some criterion, other than number alone, is available for measuring equivalence. That is, equivalence implies what it suggests philologically, namely, that there is an equality between the two sides of the equation in some respect other than the number of each item involved.

Now, when we say that 'assets equal equities' we do not normally mean to say that if we have a given number of assets we must have the same number of equities. To say that six assets equal six equities would not convey any of the meaning that is intended. But numbers are, indeed, involved, and they are attached, with virtually no exceptions, to a monetary symbol. And the intended meaning is that if one side of the statement is expressed as $x of assets, then the other side of the equation has to be expressed as $x of equities, and vice versa, irrespective of whatever characteristics each or any of the assets or equities may have or may be perceived as having, and irrespective of whether or not the $ sign is interpreted as being constant in terms of any other characteristic which any of the assets or equities might have. The equation is essentially a statement in monetary terms.

This point could also be expressed in pseudo-philosophical terms as follows: There is a class of things or objects called assets which can be measured, and a different class of things or objects called equities which can also be measured; when the measurements are compared they will be found to be equal. Whether a statement of this kind can be accepted as a statement of fact in any given instance obviously requires that the unit used for measuring the two classes shall be the same unit and that it shall not vary from one to the other or within either class of objects. In other words, to have the measurements of the two classes comparable, they must be in the same unit. This would seem to be obvious and unexceptionable.

But then we might raise the question: why should we compare them at all? Why should we expect the two groups to be equal? Is an arithmetic equality the kind of knowledge we seek or the form of communication that is helpful and fruitful? For arithmetic equality, or, perhaps even more specifically, arithmetical accuracy, is what is necessarily implied by this equation of itself; little more is, strictly, vouchsafed, whatever the unit of measurement might be. By accepting A=E, one thing we also accept is that if we increase A, then we must also increase E to the same extent; similarly, if A is decreased then E is also decreased to the same extent. Further, if a part of A (or E) is increased or decreased within an unchanging total, then another part of A (or E) is to be decreased or increased to the same extent.

These are purely mathematical, indeed arithmetical, propositions, and their 'truth' is the validity of mathematical reasoning; they are expressions of a symbolic-logical system which has its own internally consistent rules of procedure. The validity, however, applies to the numbers we may use as the symbols rather than to any other characteristic of particular instances or types of Assets or Equities. For, when we use 'A' we are saying 'for any number which may be attached to the totality of particular items which constitute recognizable and measurable assets in any given case', and when we use 'E' we are saying 'for any number that may be attached to the totality of particular recognizable and measurable claims on those assets', and when we use '=' we are saying that the number which we attach to each of those totalities at any given time shall be the same number. The process of attaching numbers is a human, logical one, and part of the culture into which we have been born and which we inherit. Its validity is a logical one; it is a certainty imposed in an *a priori* proposition or series of propositions.

When we consider further about the proposition 'A=E', we can see that it is not the same kind of truistic statement that, say, '4=4' is, for that should really be expressed as '4≡4': 'the symbol "4" is identical with or is the same as the symbol "4",' or 'the number "four" is identical with or is the same as the number 'four'.' This would be matched by A≡A or E≡E. In other words, when we say that A equals E we are also implying that there is some difference between A and E. But when we say: A=E, we are substituting *number* ($ or £ or Yen or Dm, etc.) for A and for E; this is what is *implied* but not stated.

Is it like '6+4=10'? Or, perhaps, '6+4=7+3'? This implies some classification within the two categories on either side of the equation. This raises the problem of additivity, which has been the subject of attention in the accounting literature for some years. In most cases the discussion seems to have been directed towards finding a means of satisfying the requirements for equality. The implication of validity for 6+4=7+3 is that the articles (or items or components, etc.) to which each of 6, 4, 7 and 3 are attached shall be the same articles, for example, apples, or apples of equal size or weight or ripeness or some other agreed-on characteristic. But if we were to vary this and say, for instance, that 6 apples+4 oranges=7 bananas+3 pears, the proposition takes on an obvious ludicrousness, which it loses if we retreat to a more general relationship, such as 6 pieces of fruit+4 pieces of fruit=7 pieces of fruit+3 pieces of fruit. Thus a generalization of some kind in the sort of things to which the mathematical symbols are attached is essential for the relationship of equality to hold good. In the proposition 6+4=7+3, this generalization is implicit, but not non-existent. (Cf. Devine 1962, I: 159.)

Another approach is possible. We can say 6+4=10, and 7+3=10, and 10 10; therefore, by substituting for 10 in each equation, we get both 6+4=7+3 and 7+3=6+4. This, of course, arises simply from the several ways in which a number, in this case ten, of articles can be grouped *for the purpose of counting*. They may not necessarily be the same kind of article if the purpose of the grouping or the counting is merely to determine number and not other characteristics of each distinguishable group. For instance, a group of ten people may comprise 6 males+4 females, and, at the same time, 7 adults and 3 children. This could be shown in matrix form in more than one way:

	M	F	T
A	6	1	7
C	0	3	3
T	6	4	10

	M	F	T
A	5	2	7
C	1	2	3
T	6	4	10

	M	F	T
A	4	3	7
C	2	1	3
T	6	4	10

	M	F	T
A	3	4	7
C	3	0	3
T	6	4	10

Clearly, the number '10' or 'ten' cannot be applied to either males or females or to either children or adults; it can apply only to another characteristic which all have in common, namely, that they are all human beings ('people'). Sex and age are classifications within the identifying class of 'people' to which the notion of 'ten-ness' applies.

However, our exploration need not end at this point. In the usual approach, equities are regarded as claims on assets. The implication is that the primary class for attention is that of assets.

There is nothing wrong with this approach except that it tends to shut out another approach which may prove to be fruitful. Suppose that, instead of expressing the equation as A=E, whereby our attention is focused *first* on assets, we turn it around to E=A, so that attention is focused first on equities. Since the provision of resources is most generally in the form of funds or access to funds, that is, cash or credit of one sort or another, and, even where resources are provided in kind, it is customary to regard a commitment in monetary terms as appropriate, we can use 'F' to represent the provision of funds in a liberal interpretation of 'funds'. If we use 'R' to represent financial resources as a more generalized symbol than 'assets' (A), we can get F=R, that is, the providers of funds have provided funds to the same extent as the measure of resources into which the funds have been or are to be converted.

It should be noted that the word 'funds' frequently represents a form of resources; in that interpretation R=R, which is undoubtedly a 'truth' but at the same time a fruitless tautology. In order to give 'F=R' any sensible meaning, we have to differentiate between funds and resources. It is true that if the funds provided were never transformed into some other kind of resources, the statement would remain at F=(R)=F (where '(R)' represents potential or intended or notional resources), or F=F, or, perhaps more succinctly and, indeed, more correctly, just 'F'. If funds are not used, there is little point in trying to say anything about them except that they are not used. It is only when they are put to use that they become significant at all.

Equities are usually defined as claims on assets; and when we ask why they are such claims, the answer is that they represent claims which have arisen from the provision of resources. More precisely, each of the items which comprise the class of equities is a representation (or a symbol, if preferred) of a claim due to some identifiable person, natural or legal, who or which has provided or is deemed to have provided resources, usually, but not necessarily, cash or credit funds, for the purpose of acquiring assets or at least benefits of some kind.

A person who owns or controls no assets may borrow funds from somebody else in order to acquire assets, and one who has some assets may buy more or borrow more. Or one without assets may borrow an asset itself. Or a person may have acquired an asset as a gift or an inheritance at no cost and use it for any desired purpose. In each instance there is, functionally, a provider of resources and a user of resources. In some cases the provider and the user are the same person, whereas in others they are different persons; the former is an 'internal' claimant on (or residual equity-holder in) assets; the latter is an 'external' claimant (or creditor). The former constitutes proprietorship or ownership; the latter liabilities.

However, the recognition of a claim is a social usage; it arises from, and is a recognition of, the fact that a person does not live or act in complete isolation. For one who is totally isolate, the concept of a claim has virtually no operational meaning, since a claim is a form of obligation which can only be to or from some other person, group or representative of others. Thus if, for example, a woman has inherited a sum of money which constitutes her sole asset, the answer to the question of who has the claim on the money, which she rightly regards as *her* asset, is that *she* has a claim as against any other person in that community; and this is because the right of personal and individual possession is recognized in that society. Money is an instrument of social activity. It is of no use to a person if no other people are interested in it. Hence the woman's claim is a recognition of the (social) right, against others in the society, of the possessor of the money to use it as she desires, subject to any social constraints that may be in force and enforceable.

The significant concept for the moment is that of the provision of resources and it would be useful if we could use 'P' to designate such provision. But, in this context, 'P' is customarily used to designate proprietorship, which represents only one category of providers of resources. However, another word for 'provider' is 'supplier', so we can use 'S' to represent the suppliers or providers of resources, and, if we use 'R' to represent resources as a more generalized symbol than 'A(ssets)', we can get: 'S=R', that is, the suppliers of resources have provided resources to the same extent as the measure of resources which have been or are to be used.

Even so, there might be some slight ambiguity as to whether 'S' symbolizes the suppliers, that is, the persons (the human, active beings or the social units on whose behalf and/or in the name of which they act) or the supplies, that is, the sort of resources supplied. This ambiguity could be resolved by using, say S_l or S_p for suppliers, and S_2 or S_r for supplies, or 'S' and 's', as required. The distinction becomes significant when we begin to classify either the suppliers or the supplies. For example, suppliers may be classified as internal/external, or according to residualness in their claims, (the degree or type of security for the indebtedness), whereas supplies may be classified according to a temporal measure of usage, such as immediate/short-term/medium-term/long-term, or regular/sporadic, or for stock-piling/specific orders, and so on.

In most cases, resources are supplied in the form of monetary resources. Non-monetary supplies, however, are not unknown; for example gifts and bequests of books to libraries, paintings or sculptures to art galleries, machinery or equipment to a museum, while, donations to appeals for assistance to distressed people are often called for in kind as well as in money. Such supplies are resources in the hands of the recipient(s); we could express it as:

$$S=R$$

or:

$$S=F=R$$

These monetary resources can be applied in various ways to provide assets; hence:

$$S=R \rightarrow A$$

where $\rightarrow$ symbolizes 'can be converted into'.

In a physical sense, 'converted into' would have no monetary, and, often, no numerical signification; in terms of monetary exchange (price), it could have both.

One feature of this approach is the recognition that the suppliers of funds (or other resources) are people (even if some of them act only in the name of or on behalf of some legally recognized but artificial entity), the recipients are people (ditto), and those who use the funds and use the resources into which they are converted are also people.

The suppliers can be classified, and the classification is another process carried out by human beings. The basis of classification to be adopted depends upon the purpose of the classifier; indeed, the whole purpose of classification is a nominal one, that is, putting names to perceived categories within a class of objects, or, in other words, a process of definition. As suggested in Chapter 2, there is little in classification itself which provides new knowledge, but it might become a step in assisting observers to ascertain new knowledge.

As already noted, the term 'assets' came into the English language as a secondary idea; it is an anglicized version of the French *assez*, which means 'enough' or 'sufficient', and its initial meaning was to indicate the wherewithal to meet the claims upon a person or an estate.[2] Only later did the superficial or apparent plurality of the word in its English appearance give rise to a singular form and the notion of 'an asset' developed. The point of recalling this here is that, by adopting the suppliers of funds or even the funds themselves as an element for primary attention, we are not doing something that is extraordinarily novel or revolutionary, but, rather, adverting to a historical development of some centuries ago.

If we adopt the approach of $S=A$, and at the same time recognize that, with few exceptions, the resources supplied are in a monetary form or expressed in monetary terms, then, for each unit of resources there is a moment of time at which

$$S_2=R=A$$

---

2 For an interesting discussion of historical aspects of several words frequently used in accounting literature, see Parker 1994: 70–85.

and that moment is the point of acquisition of an asset. At that moment, the appropriate measure for the asset is that used for measurement of the funds required to acquire it; in other words, its cost price. But from that point on, the use of many so-called assets bears little relation to their acquisition costs, or to any other monetary measure in a primary sense.

An asset is acquired for a purpose of use, which, for many assets, is physical or organizational, rather than purely monetary. In the course of such use any monetary expression attached to it is largely meaningless in relation to its use. An item of plant or equipment – say, a machine or a truck – is acquired for the purpose for which it was constructed, namely, to fulfil its part in a process of extraction or production or transport or storage or even administration, and neither its usage nor its product is directly measurable in monetary terms, but rather in some 'physical' unit. The character of the equipment is not altered by its use, and neither is its product, but over a period its 'efficiency', measured by such things as an increasing tolerance between moving parts or duration of processing time or failure or fatigue of particular parts, may decrease, so that some maintenance is required to keep it operating and prevent it from becoming completely inoperable. This is quite apart from obsolescence. To put any kind of monetary measure on either the use of such assets or their product is simply to use a surrogate for the appropriate, but more complex, measure in 'physical' terms of the activity which takes place in using such assets. It needs to be recognized that, as such a surrogate, it is inadequate for depicting what the actual deterioration of the particular asset has in fact been.

The accounting equation could be expanded into:

$$Sl \rightarrow S2 = F = R \rightarrow\!\!\!\!\gg A$$

where

Sl	symbolizes	supplier of funds, i.e. human beings
S2	symbolizes	supplies of funds
F	symbolizes	funds, i.e. monetary resources
R	symbolizes	resources in a generalized sense
A	symbolizes	assets in a particularized but collective sense, i.e., $A=A_1+A_2+\ldots A_n$
$\rightarrow$	symbolizes	provide(s)
$=$	symbolizes	is synonymous with, or can be defined as
$\rightarrow\!\!\!\gg$	symbolizes	produces or can be converted into.

Something like this represents more accurately what is taking place when we normally think of A=E or E=A. In effect, it is a statement which says: A number of people, who can be identified if desired or required, have provided supplies, which can be classified in more than one way, of funds, in a general or collective sense, which can be quantified and re-stated or defined as resources, which in turn can be converted into several kinds of assets which can be distinguished from each other and traced through their respective 'behaviours' or subsequent histories.

The task to be performed by an accounting system is that of setting up, maintaining and controlling the accuracy of records of S_1, S_2 and A, measuring of each of which may well involve the use of different units. (The accounting system which performs these tasks may be only a part of a larger 'information system' applicable to a set of occurrences or ventures.)

The notion of commander applies to S_1, the people who supply funds. It also applies to any person who, as commander, operates as the subject unit of operation, so that:

$$S1 \left\{ \begin{array}{c} \longrightarrow \!\!\! \Leftrightarrow \\ S2 \; = \; R \end{array} \; C \right\} \longrightarrow\!\!\!\longrightarrow \qquad A$$

where

C	symbolizes	a commander
$\longrightarrow\!\!\!\Leftrightarrow$	symbolizes	has dealings with

Or, more simply,

$$S1 \left\{ \begin{array}{c} \longrightarrow \!\!\! \Leftrightarrow \;\; C \\ \longrightarrow \; = F \; = R \end{array} \right\} \longrightarrow\!\!\!\longrightarrow \qquad A$$

That is, suppliers of funds provide funds to a commander who (treating them as resources) acquires assets for use or other deployment. If the supplier of funds were the unit of operation, then S_1 would be a commander (say, C_n) who deploys some or all of the resources at his or her disposal to make them available to the commander in our equation who could be then represented by, say, C_x.

Since the application of a monetary symbol to the several elements of this statement (rather than 'equation', for the statement is more than one of equality in any sense of 'equal') uses only one of several symbols needed to provide an adequate record and subsequent reporting, it is an over-simplification of what actually occurs.

It is also important to recognize that in thinking about numbers, whether financial or non-financial we have to be careful about the meaning and significance which we attach to our numerals, that is, to the symbols we use. We are so used to the current system of numeration that we are apt to endow the numerals themselves with an undeserved meaning. For instance, we put: 37 x 3=111, and we may be attracted by the repetition of the numeral '1' in the product; but if we use, say, Roman numerals, we would get: XXXVII x III=CXI, in which the repetition of 'I' is in the multiplier, not the product. Or: 37 x 6=222 becomes XXXVII x VI=CCXXII, in which some of the symbols in the product are pairs of some of those in the previous calculation. However, 555 (that is, 37 x 15) becomes DLV, which would break any sequence of increasing symbols in the product. Or take the interesting number 142857 which, if multiplied by any number from 2 to 6, gives the same numerals in the same sequence but from a different starting point, e.g., 142857 x 4=571428, and if multiplied by 7 it gives 999999. With another system of symbols for the same sum, for instance, interesting-looking results would be unlikely to arise, just as it does not if we write the numbers in full: 'one hundred and forty two thousand eight hundred and fifty seven multiplied by four equals five hundred and seventy one thousand four hundred and twenty eight', 'fifty' and 'twenty' are peculiar to their respective expressions, while the whole numbers require to be translated into their familiar symbols before the sequence can be noticed and recognized.

This suggests that we need to be aware of the difference between the numbers and the numerals we use to depict them. The point is one of abstraction. As Bertrand Russell once observed: 'It must have required many ages to discover that a brace of pheasants and a couple of days were both instances of the number 2: the degree of abstraction involved is far from easy. And the discovery that 1 is a number must have been difficult.' (Russell 1946: 3.) But '2' and '1' are symbols of numbers, as are 'two' and 'one' or 'II' and 'I' rather than the numbers themselves. The thought – the abstraction – behind the symbol can itself only be communicated, if it can be communicated at all, by or through symbols, for instance, the notion of one-ness or two-ness. It is difficult to know whether we can ever think of any number except in symbols; it seems impossible to communicate without them. To say: 'Just think of "two" without attaching anything, not even a symbol, to it' is to ask somebody to do something very difficult indeed, if not impossible. If we close our eyes and try to think of 'two-ness', can we escape seeing a symbol in our imagination: a word or a numeral or a couple of dots or lines or some other 'objects'?

If a numeral or a word or a letter is a symbol of a number which can only be thought of in some sort of attachment to an object, even if this is only being thought of, what is the effect if we try to climb down the ladder of abstraction in interpreting the accounting equation? If we say: A (1000)=E (1000), what are we thinking of? The numbers on each side do not refer to the same kinds of 'objects'. If they did, there would be no difference between A and E and we could just as well say: A (1000)=A (1000), which would be completely tautological and unproductive. The usefulness of the accounting equation is derived from the difference between A and E, and this depends upon the ways in which each of them can be classified. If we say: CA (Current Assets) 600+FA (Fixed Assets) 400=L (Liabilities) 300+P (Proprietorship) 700 we have a statement of some ostensible usefulness. The usefulness, of course, depends upon another symbol which has to be included, namely, an indication that the symbols 600, 400, 300 and 700 refer to some accepted or recognized unit which is equally applicable to each of these symbols. (This is the essence of the price-change controversy which has engaged the attention of many accountants over many years; it has been a debate about appropriate symbols.)

However, there is an even more fundamental point. The attachment of these numbers to these categories of equation elements is an attempt to find an expression of uniformity between them. What would happen if we were to boldly recognize that

(a) assets and equities as classes are different from each other, and
(b) the categories within each class are also different from each other?

Recognition of such differences seems to be the challenge which accountants (whether professional or academic) are facing now in our complex social environment. If the problem is not solved by accountants themselves, the profession may well become irrelevant for the significant social developments of the future, for the current general interpretation of their functions is likely to be superseded, and accountants may well find themselves less adequate than others better equipped to cope successfully with the issues that are almost certain to arise.

14 Double entry – an assessment

Reporters and gangsters I have always liked, probably because they, like me, do work they enjoy. Does anybody really get a bang out of double-entry bookkeeping? he asked no one in particular.

None of us bothered to answer until Evan, sitting up groggily, said Nobody but the screwy New Yorker who faked a big profit on his company's books just for the heck of it. No motive, no financial gain personally, all in fun. Remember?

(Francis Bonamy 1943: 44)

Virtues and claims

Writers on double entry, perhaps naturally, have often proclaimed its virtues and usefulness; but it has earned plaudits also from some distinguished people in other fields. A few examples from each of these categories illustrate this.

Pacioli commended 'the system used in Venice' to his readers as a basis for understanding any other system and as an essential for businessmen who would find it impossible to conduct their business without such systematic entries because 'they would have no rest and their minds would always be troubled'. (Geijsbeck 1914: 33. Other translations by Crivelli 1939 and Brown and Johnston 1963 have similar but not identical expressions.) One of the early exponents in the English language, Richard Dafforne, described double entry, or, rather, the keeping of books in the Italian manner, as 'so exquisite a Deep-diving Science'. (Dafforne 1651: A.)

Roger North, writing in 1715, had an expansive mode of expressing his view:

The Books of Merchants Accompts are kept in a certain Method, that from the Stile and Form of the Entries, is called *Debitor* and *Creditor*; which Method is so comprehensive and perfect, as makes it worthy to be put among the Sciences, and to be understood by all Virtuosi, whether they ever intend to make use of it or no . . .

... If any one shall say, That Regular Accompting is but a judicious Application of Arithmetick to common Business; I answer, That Arithmetick is indeed necessary, and a Dexterity in the Use of it is to be made a *Postulatum* here, as being presupposed; But in Practice, Accompting is an Art of it self distinct; and Arithmetick to Book-keeping, is as Language to Oratory, or as setting one Foot before another, to the skill of a Dancing-Master.

... the *Dr.* and *Cr.* is pure and perfect right Reason, and contains the whole Material Truth and Justice of all the Dealing, and nothing else; and this not only between the Accompter, and his Traffickers, but also between all the several Traffickers one with another, so far as they have intermixed in the Subject-Matter of the Accompts; and not only so, but also of the Incidents, Circumstances, and Consequences of the Traffick, such as Estimates, Losses, or Advantages thereby. And all this in a perpetual State; so as every Question that can be proposed concerning any Dealing, is answered almost as readily as demanded; and no Person can be injured, who takes his Accompt upon the stating of the books, so far as it runs: And in all times, even in After-Ages, the Transactions thus duly accompted will be understood as well, as if the same had been inquisited at the very Instant of the Writing.

(See Yamey *et al.* 1963: 5–6)

Matthew Quin, in his *Rudiments of Book-keeping* which appeared in 1779, included the following comments:

... it is a *proverb* among the Dutch, 'That none can be poor who keep their books correctly. . . . By attending to this salutary maxim, there is no doubt but those who adopt it will reap the fruits of their labour, and find themselves well rewarded for the care they have taken to walk in the paths of *moral rectitude*.

(See Yamey *et al.* 1963: 11)

In the nineteenth century, William Murray was evidently enthusiastic about its qualities:

... Whether we view the science of double entry abstractedly, or in combination with material wealth, we cannot but admire the intrinsic beauty of its principles and construction; and the further its detail, its analytical and synthetical power is studied, the more prolific in new beauties will it be found. It is, perhaps, the most beautiful in the wide domain of literature or science; were it less common, it would be the admiration of the learned world.

(Murray 1862: 47)

He went even further in his advocacy:

To all would I, then, say – pay that homage to the practice of an art which is the handmaiden of commerce – which has been shown to have merited and to have received the attention of learned men in various ages. This compass of the merchant – this faithful chronicler of his operations, which, apart from all the moral and mental imperfections under which it may have the misfortune to be placed – is a trusty record to which none need turn in vain.

Encourage, then, the practice of this art, and nurture it with every care . . . let not this vital subject fall into decay; but uphold it with commerce – with all the power of that wealth which its practice so largely contributes to centralise . . .

(Murray 1862: 47–8)

The novelist, Samuel Butler, wrote:

I wished him to understand book-keeping by double entry. I had myself as a young man been compelled to master this not very difficult art; having acquired it, I have been enamoured of it, and consider it the most necessary branch of any young man's education after reading and writing. I was determined, therefore, that Ernest should master it, and proposed that he should become my steward, book-keeper, and the manager of my hoardings, for so I called the sum which my ledger showed to have accumulated from £15,000 to £70,000. I told him I was going to begin to spend the income as soon as it had amounted to £80,000.

(Butler 1947 (first published 1903): 318)

In 1894 Cayley, the Sadlerian Professor of Pure Mathematics in the University of Cambridge, said:

The Principles of Book-keeping by Double Entry constitute a theory which is mathematically by no means uninteresting: it is in fact like Euclid's theory of ratios an absolutely perfect one, and it is only its extreme simplicity which prevents it from being as interesting as it would otherwise be.

(Cayley 1894: Preface)

Oswald Spengler expressed his views at some length:

. . . Number as *pure magnitude* inherent in the material presentness of things is paralleled by numbers as *pure relation* . . .

Similarly, coinage and double-entry book-keeping play analogous parts in the money-thinking of the Classical and the Western cultures respectively.

(Spengler 1926, I: 75 and fn.)

The decisive event however was the invention – 'contemporary' with that of the Classical coin about 650 AD – of double-entry book-keeping by Fra Luca Pacioli in 1494. Goethe calls this in *Wilhelm Meister* 'one of the finest discoveries of the human intellect,' and indeed its author may without hesitation be ranked with his contemporaries Columbus and Copernicus. To the Normans we owe our modes of reckoning and to the Lombards our book-keeping . . . Double entry book-keeping is born of the same spirit as the system of Galileo and Newton . . . With the same means as these, it orders the phenomenon into an elegant system, and it may be called the first Cosmos built up on the basis of a mechanistic thought. Double-entry book-keeping discloses to us the Cosmos of the economic world by the same method as later the Cosmos of the stellar universe was unveiled by the great investigation of natural philosophy . . . Double-entry book-keeping rests on the basic principle, logically carried out, of comprehending all phenomena purely as quantities.'

[fn. Sombart, *Der moderne Kapitalismus*, II: 119]
(Spengler 1926, II: 490. Hatfield gives Goethe's
expression as 'one of the fairest inventions of the human
mind', see Baxter 1950: 12. See also comments below,
under The Double-Entry Syndrome.)

Double-entry book-keeping is a pure Analysis of the space of values referred to a co-ordinate system, of which the origin is the 'Firm.' The coinage of the Classical world had only permitted of arithmetical compilations with value-magnitudes . . .. The Classical economy-world was ordered, like the cosmos of Democritus, according to stuff and form. A stuff, in the form of a coin, carries the economic movement and presses against the demand-unit of equal value-quantity at the place of use. Our economy-world is ordered by force and mass. A field of money-tensions lies in space and assigns to every object, irrespective of its specific kind, a positive or negative effect-value, which is represented by a book-entry. 'Quod non est in libris, non est in mundo.' But the symbol of the functional money thus imagined, that which alone may be compared with the Classical coin, is not the actual book-entry, nor yet the share-voucher, cheque, or note, but the act by which the function is fulfilled in writing, and the role of the value-paper is merely to be the generalized historical evidence of this act.

(Spengler 1926 II: 490)

. . . It was the supremacy of book-values, whose abstract system was quickly detached from personality by double-entry book-keeping and worked forward by virtue of its own inward dynamism, that produced the modern capital that spans the whole earth with its field of force.

(Spengler 1926, II: 493)

It must be said for the modern study of double entry that it requires its exponents and proponents and practitioners to think systematically. The system may indeed be a closed one, but within it the procedures have to be applied logically and accurately if it is to work satisfactorily within its constraints. In short, accountants are trained to think systematically, and this attribute should be applicable to matters outside double entry. Whether or not we think the system needs to be opened and broadened, this valuable attribute is encouraged by its study and application; it is stimulating merely to contemplate the possibility of applying it or something like it to broader social assessments beyond the restrictive financial issues to which it is currently applied.

Accounting procedures comprise a series of comparisons at various levels, so to speak.[1] At the level of recording in traditional accounts, each account is a comparison of debit and credit items; at the level of reporting, each report derived from the accounts is a comparison; the so-called matching process is a comparison.

The aim inherent in double entry is to make these comparisons mathematically valid. This is done in an essentially simple, but sophisticated and elegant way.

Observations on its origin and development

Stuart Chase cites Hogben as pointing out that mathematics began in the nomadic age to fill a need and follows this up with a number of instances of the utilitarian value of mathematics, such as the development of the differential calculus by Newton to communicate his discoveries about the movement of celestial bodies even to himself. But, it may be observed, the 'need' is not necessarily a 'practical' one – it may be purely an intellectual one (Chase 1947: 97ff. Cf. Hogben 1940: 37ff.)

We might ask: What need was double entry developed to meet? And we might assume the answer to be a practical, commercial one. What is it that double entry does that other means of recording do not do? It brings the records into a tidy, closed system in a sophisticated manner. What need was there of this among the merchants of the fourteenth century or earlier? What need is there today of this tidiness among the small businessmen or among the individual consumers? Further, is it still needed in 'transaction processing systems' in which computers are used? Perhaps the need was, and is, one of exposition. Many of the problems of modern accounting have little to do with the traditional formal recording technique of double entry – the problems of definition, recognition, measurement and valuation, for instance, are not, essentially, problems of formal recording procedures.

---

[1]The word 'comparison' is used here as the act of comparing or the state of being compared, based on the dictionary meaning of 'to compare' as 'to set or bring together, and examine the relation between, with a view to ascertain agreement or disagreement, relative proportions, quantities, or qualities; to measure or estimate one by another'. That is, it is by comparing two things or 'bundles' of things that we can establish whether or not the two are equal. Two things or two bundles of things can be validly compared only if they have some characteristic(s) in common, and it is these common characteristics only that can be validly compared. Hence comparison is an attempt to determine either equality or a measurable extent of inequality between the common characteristics of two or more distinguishable things or sets of things.

Perhaps it is almost an accident of history that the accountancy profession has developed from the bookkeepers; at the same time it is difficult to conceive of any sort of accountant in our present social environment who does not have a mastery of double entry.

The impression obtained from the available material on the history of double entry is that it is an invention of northern Italy in the fourteenth or possibly the latter part of the thirteenth century and that it appeared, more or less spontaneously, in several different places at about the same time. (Cf. Littleton and Yamey 1956: 2; Yamey 1949: 101.)

The records of the Massari of Genoa – 1340 – still appear to be the earliest extant double-entry records, although there is some question about some earlier ones. (Littleton and Yamey 1956:114ff). One point that arises here is the matter of definition and criterion. What do we mean by 'double-entry records'? A series of charge and discharge accounts which shows a debit in one account and a corresponding credit in another is only a double-entry record if that is the way we define 'double entry'. But this would fall short of a definition or criterion for any useful intellectual purpose. The essence of double entry as we have come to recognize it involves a coherent *system* of recording, wherein relevant aspects of trans-actions can be brought within the framework of the double-entry procedure. This requires the incorporation into the system of two concepts, one of which is perhaps slightly sophisticated, the other, highly sophisticated.

The first is that of proprietorship or capital. Assets and liabilities would be easy and obvious – anyone who has trade dealings, whether in the Middle Ages or in the twentieth century, would recognize assets and liabilities or resources and claims to those resources. And the notion of capital – net worth – would follow fairly easily on any periodic reflection on assets and liabilities. This would arise on occasions of death, if not sooner. That is, inheritance would involve an almost inescapable assessment of net worth. It is not a problem of great sophistication.

(As an aside, it might be suggested that liabilities – and that means credit – comprise a prerequisite for the notion of proprietorship. For without liabilities there would be only assets (that is, possessions) and while today we account for a two-fold character in assets, it is problematical whether and to what extent this would have been recognized 600 years ago, and whether it would have been necessary to do so. If all transactions were for cash or barter, only assets would be involved and these would be identical with worth.)

The second notion, however, appears to be more sophisticated; namely, that a specific increase in (net) assets contributes to total increase in capital, with correspondence for decrease. This would have required a sophistic-ated attitude to recognize the link between the results of specific occur-rences or transactions (increase or decrease in net assets) and the net result at the end of a period or a venture comprising those occurrences or trans-actions. The design and functioning of a self-balancing system, such as double entry, surely depends upon such a recognition. In other words, the sophistication lies in the extrapolation of short-period or continuous recognition of gains and losses to the assessment of long-period accumulation or erosion of capital (or net assets or net worth).

It seems reasonable to suggest that without both of these concepts operating one could hardly have records worthy of being called double entry.

Littleton's analysis remains one of the most interesting accounts, at least in the English language, of our perception of double-entry bookkeeping. His point of view appears to have been overwhelmingly significant among practising and academic accounting writers for half a century. He sets out his list of indispensable ingredients of double entry thus:

> The *Art of Writing*, since bookkeeping is first of all a record; *Arithmetic*, since the mechanical aspect of bookkeeping consists of a sequence of simple computations; *Private Property*, since bookkeeping is concerned only with recording the facts about property and property rights; *Money* (i.e., a money economy), since bookkeeping is unnecessary except as it reduces all transactions in properties or property rights to this common denominator; *Credit* (i.e., incompleted transactions), since there would be little impulse to make any record whatever if all exchanges were completed on the spot; *Commerce*, since a merely local trade would never have created enough pressure (volume of business) to stimulate men to coordinate diverse ideas into a system; *Capital*, since without capital commerce would be trivial and credit would be inconceivable.
>
> (Littleton 1933: 12ff.)

One of Littleton's 'antecedents' or requirements for the origin of double entry, or at least for its acceptance, was 'an extensive commerce in order to produce the pressure of a great volume of trade'. Further, it 'had to be a profitable commerce, for this is the best means of saving a fund of capital which can be re-employed productively and thus in turn create additional capital'. (Littleton 1933: 15.) In a similar way, the spread of the computer as a technical tool in accounting was initially due to a perceived requirement by those involved with larger enterprises for a means of readily handling increasing quantities of repetitive data. Subsequent technological developments and adaptations of both hardware and software rapidly led to a much wider spread of its use in a great variety of circumstances. However, the widespread practice of double entry in commercial, industrial and financial enterprises did not occur until the developments of the nineteenth century and the rise of an organized accountancy profession were combined in contribution to an extensive recognition of its considerable virtues. Some of its shortcomings have begun to be realized in recent years.

This view that double entry is to be interpreted as, inevitably, only fulfilled and fulfillable in a commercial or entrepreneurial, capital-oriented sense, seems to be the basic ground for applying to community-serving institutions (including government and non-government organizations) concepts of performance or activity such as 'user-pays', 'profit centres', 'commercial results', 'bottom line' and the like, so that 'standards' derived from commercial experience are being promulgated for application to universities and colleges, hospitals and welfare organizations, and others, which, at their inception and in their subsequent development, were not imbued or set up with the intention to earn or distribute profits or provide an attractive rate of return to investors, as business enterprises are. Indeed, a future observer may suggest, with some justification, that double entry and accrual accounting, in their full potential, as claimed by some, for providing information for managerial, entrepreneurial and financial decision-making, was not developed until at least the latter years of the nineteenth century, had a relatively short flowering during part of the twentieth century, and was running to seed well before the end of that century.

Littleton's inventory of antecedents may be a brilliant speculation about the origin of the double-entry phenomenon, but it is none the less a speculation. The evidence for a strictly business origin is not beyond questioning. The earliest extant records of its acceptedly full operation are those of a communal group, acting, presumably, in a governmental or semi-governmental capacity as stewards of the coffers of their community – the Massari of the city-state of Genoa. Their activities in some aspects may appear to have been commercial *according to our viewpoint of this commercial century*, but their notions at that time may have been very different from ours. While this also may be speculative, it should remind us that, in the absence of a reliable eye-witness, any evidence is circumstantial and open to varying plausible interpretations.

It is apposite to note two different interpretations of this early record from Genoa. Peragallo expressed his view thus:

> This is a typical venture account of the Middle Ages. The Commune of Genoa took a flyer in pepper. It purchased eight 100–pound lots of this merchandise, which presumably had just arrived from the Orient, at a cost of 24 libbre and 5 soldi per lot, and then, with economic acumen common to most governments, disposed of it at the price of 22 libbre and 10 soldi per 100 pound lot, sustaining a considerable loss.
>
> (Peragallo 1938: 9)

By contrast, de Roover points out in relation to this account:

> . . . there was a loss instead of a profit. Why? To my knowledge, no one has ever bothered to explain the purpose of these merchandise accounts. Certainly, it was not normal for a public administration to be dealing in commodities. The explanation is that, in order to raise funds, the City of Genoa bought commodities on credit and sold them immediately for cash at a lower price. The resulting loss, therefore, represents concealed interest. One must remember that the taking of interest was prohibited as usury by the Church.
>
> (de Roover 1955: 413)

It is very difficult, perhaps quite impossible, to learn how medieval traders would have thought about things. Questions include: Were the traders of these northern Italian states of such intellectual calibre as would be likely to 'discover' or invent an idea which is possibly about equal in sophistication to the notion of zero? What was the problem that the introduction of double entry solved or attempted to solve? What was the stimulus that gave rise to it? Was it necessary at the time? Or did it give any advantages to its users, and if so, what were they? If it comes to that, is it necessary today, and if so, how and why?

As mentioned above, one gets an impression that double entry sprang up spontaneously in different parts of what we now call Italy, but with local differences (Cf. Peragallo 1938: 1–2, and passim; Yamey 1949: 101–2). Pacioli, as late as 1494, wrote about the system of Venice, the implication being that it was different from others (but superior to them) and he had travelled fairly widely through the countryside by that time (Taylor 1942: Ch. 11 *et al.*). This was a century and a half after the Massari of Genoa, which would probably have been time enough for either local variations to develop from a common origin or uniformity to develop from diverse origins. A comparative study of bookkeeping systems actually in use between, say, 1300 and 1400 would be exceedingly useful if this were possible. Some studies of this have been made by such notable scholars as Raymond de Roover (e.g., 1955, 1956), and B.S. Yamey (e.g, 1940, 1947, 1949) but the available material is scant and the results are somewhat inconclusive.

Another point is that double entry was early tied to mathematics; a list of these connections in, for example, early treatises, might in itself be interesting. It is likely that this was no accident, and it must be remembered that the merchants of the time would probably have had little more knowledge of arithmetic and mathematics than our eight or nine year olds have today. This tie-up with mathematics might have more than passing significance in the study of origins; for example, were the basic features of double entry evolved as a mathematical exercise and speculation by those who developed the notion of zero and the present system of numeration? Perhaps we have to go further afield and further back than medieval Italy for the *fons et origo* of double entry (cf. Taylor 1942: 61).

Hallam said that reading – even among the clergy – practically died out for a lengthy period. When came the revival, and where? Hallam also stated that the import of Egyptian papyrus into Europe ceased about the beginning of the seventh century and from then until the close of the eleventh century, when 'the art of making paper from cotton rags seems to have been introduced, there were no materials for writing except parchment, a substance too expensive to be readily spared for mere purposes of literature'. In a footnote he hints that parchment was available for legal instruments. (Hallam 1872, III: 286, 289). But in any case there would be little likelihood of writing material being available for bookkeeping purposes.

Even in recent years, and perhaps contemporaneously, small traders, people in receipt of 'individual' income, and the like, seem to have no manifest need for detailed double-entry records; they might be better informed in some respects if they had them, but such improved information would probably be, and would be viewed by them as being, a cerebral luxury rather than an economic or social necessity. Indeed, it is highly likely that, if it were not for the requirements of taxation, with its annual returns, and other obligations under governmental or analogous social regulation, great numbers of them would not keep formal records at all. Those operating on a cash basis would almost certainly not be concerned with anything but their cash records – and these might well be chiefly maintained by the bank in the form of its passbook or statement. When credit is involved, records become necessary for reference purposes (a) as an aide-memoire, and (b) as evidence in cases of dispute.

Personal accounts are required. But this is still a long way from double entry. It appears that double entry had a long struggle for recognition. For some three centuries after Pacioli it was, on the whole, not required – at least for ventures by the individual. It does seem feasible that partnership ventures might involve its introduction, because the notion of investment, that is, capital, seems to be of the essence of double entry, and this is significant in partnership ventures. But another point is the notion of stewardship, and the accounts of the Massari are an expression of stewardship. Investment is present here, too, but in this case it is investment of public monies. C.A. Cooke has pointed out:

> It has been estimated that from the ninth to the fifteenth centuries the quantity of monetary metal available for business was only about one-tenth of the amount available at the end of the sixteenth century. These were the changes that produced the idea of capital as a money investment for profit which was later to be combined with the institution of corporate association.

> (Cooke 1950: 39–40)

Perhaps there is a point here that is relevant to the origin of double entry. If there is little money available, much of the trading would necessarily be of the nature of barter, and the notion of capital increment or profit would be difficult to recognize and express. Amassing of wealth would scarcely be feasible except in 'real' terms. That is, in the absence of a generally recognized unit, what was not possible was the measurement of an overall change in wealth, the composition of which was that of *varying* quantities of *different* kinds of desirable objects. It might be suggested, rhetorically, so to speak, that, because of the scarcity of some form of money as a measure of value, there may have been some impetus to have a sort of 'bookkeeping' to record increases or decreases in wealth as a 'book entry'. So far as we are aware, there is no evidence that this was done on a regular or systematic basis, although a record such as the Domesday Book appears to have been aimed at being a comprehensive and detailed record, but, since it was carried out only once, in 1086, even though for taxation purposes. Its intention as a base for measuring subsequent *changes* in wealth is most unlikely (cf. Godfrey and Hooper 1996).

Further, during this period reading and writing were rare accomplishments, and writing materials, especially paper, were scarce commodities. There seems to be little, if anything, to suggest that people thought of accumulation of wealth as the height of virtue or success, as it is widely held to be on our current social standards, and the records that we do know about, such as tallies, pointed mainly to indebtedness between people rather than accumulation of wealth.

It is only when money is sufficiently plentiful to become a generic and widely used medium of exchange that the suggestion could arise that a variety of things could be readily valued in terms of this common unit. This would be the prime requisite for the existence of the notion of capital, for, even if it were thought of in real terms, those real terms would require a common denominator to carry much meaning, so that positions or states of accumulation at different points of time could be compared. Hence, if proprietorship is a primary characteristic of double entry, it would hardly arise before the acceptance of a monetary unit, and this would not be likely to happen until there was sufficient money of some sort to be used as a genuine medium of exchange. The question arises: How did the quantity of money move in the Italian city-states in the eleventh to fifteenth centuries?

Some latter day analysis

In the latter half of the twentieth century several writers seem to have tried to dislodge double entry from its presumed supremacy in accounting. In assessing the function and use of double entry, some of their views should be considered, not only because of their intrinsic interest but also because of their influence on other writers.

First, however, we should consider a few points about the term 'double entry' itself, since some of the analytical discussion of these writers rests upon its interpretation. A concise, yet adequate, dictionary definition of the recording process reads thus (under 'double'):

> *d. entry*   a mode of bookkeeping in which two entries of every transaction are posted to the ledger, one to the Dr. side of one account, and the other to the Cr. side of another account, thereby keeping the ledger in perfect balance. Its principal object is to prove, through balancing, that all entries have been made correctly.
>
> (Webster 1926)

The term did not appear in the title of the earliest English language books on the practice. For many decades the authors of these works used such expressions as 'after the order of . . . debitour and creditour' (Peele 1553, see Yamey *et al.* 1963: 203), 'after the Italian manner' (Petri 1596:

ibid.), 'Merchants-accounts kept by debitors and creditors' (Liset 1660, ibid.: 205), 'after the Italian way of Debitor and Creditor' (Every 1673, ibid.: 206), 'according to the Italian methode' (Collinson, 1683, ibid., p. 207). According to the bibliographical list provided by Yamey, Edey and Thomson, the first title in which 'double entry' appears was in a book by William Webster published in 1719 (op. cit.: 211), some seventeen decades after the accepted date of publication of the first bookkeeping text in the English language.

While the use of 'double entry' in book titles became more common during the following years of the eighteenth century, the reference to the Italian method persisted into the nineteenth century (for example, Dilworth, 19th edition, 1806). Towards the end of the eighteenth century, the term 'single entry' began to appear in titles, often alongside 'double entry', so that authors claimed to provide instruction to their readers on the keeping of accounts by both single entry and double entry.

Indeed, books expounding 'single entry' were published throughout the nineteenth century. As one instance, one publishing firm had two books on its list for a long period (at least from 1861 to 1896), both by the same author; one bore the title *Book-keeping by Single Entry*, the other *Book-keeping by Single and Double Entry*; the latter incorporated the former with only very minor variations in the text. The 'Notice' in the *Single Entry* book included this statement:

> The work embraces Book-keeping by 'Single Entry' only. Another edition, containing both Single and Double Entry, is issued for the use of those who may require a more extensive knowledge of the subject.
>
> (Inglis 1861)

That in the other had this:

> This work embraces Book-keeping by 'Single and Double Entry'. Another edition, containing Single Entry alone, is issued for the convenience of those who may not require a knowledge of the entire system.
>
> (Inglis 1896)

This obviously popular publication contained the following definitions and observations:

> Book-keeping is the art of recording and classifying a merchant's or tradesman's daily transactions, and of keeping an account of his property and debts.
>
> (Inglis 1861: by 1881 the phrase 'in a set of books' had been added.)

> In Book-keeping by Single Entry, each entry in the Day-Book, Invoice-Book, Cash-Book, and Bill-Book, is posted or entered *once* to

some account in the Ledger; hence the term '*Single* Entry'. In '*Double* Entry' each entry is posted to two different accounts.

Single Entry is used chiefly by retail dealers, as it is more simple, and occupies less time in posting than 'Double Entry.'
> (Inglis 1861: 12; by 1881 the words 'and occupies
> less time in posting' had been dropped.)

Book-keeping by Double Entry is so called because all the entries in the Day-Book, Invoice-Book, Cash-Book, and Bill-Book are posted twice into the Ledger.

The entries are *first* posted, as in Single Entry, to the *Dr.* or *Cr.* of their respective accounts.

They are then posted a *second* time to the *Dr.* or *Cr.* of some other account. The entries first posted to the *Dr.* side of the Ledger, are posted the second time to the *Cr.* side; and those first posted to the *Cr.* side, are the second time posted to the *Dr.* side.

The system pursued in Double Entry serves the following purposes to persons in business:

1 To test the accuracy of the posting; the second posting being a check on the first . . .
2 To shew the value and quantity of Goods bought and sold during the year, or for any other given time.
3 To shew the Profit or Loss on the various departments of business.
4 To keep distinct accounts, under their several heads, of the different branches of stock in trade, and other property.

Double Entry is used chiefly by wholesale merchants and others whose transactions are on a large scale, and who dispose of goods in considerable quantities at a time.

It is less suitable for retail trades, in which there are numerous small entries; it may, however, be used with advantage to a partial extent, by posting the Day-Book, Invoice-Book, and the Cash-Book, in the manner described . . . under Single Entry.
> (Inglis 1896: 85)

A broader, more embracing and, functionally, more modern definition would be somewhat along the following lines:

> 'Double entry' is the symbol used in the English language to represent, indicate or refer to that systematized mode of recording selected occurrences (including transactions) which produces a set of articulated and arithmetically self-balancing reports about a specific, identifiable unit, whether natural, or legally, economically or socially artificial (fictitious).

The symbols we use to communicate our thoughts (and feelings also, but these are not our present concern) may represent different things according to the time, place or other circumstances to which they refer. When earlier writers used the term 'double entry' (or 'the Italian method', or the method of 'debitor and creditor' etc.) they were obviously unaware of the technological developments that have taken place in the latter years of the twentieth century; neither were they usually concerned with the production of accounting reports for distribution to a large and widespread audience of part-owners of rights to the tangible results of the activities of numerous people conducting the affairs of an ongoing enterprise such as a modern corporation or company. Hence, we do not feel entitled to argue that earlier writers were wrong in describing their self-balancing systems as double entry because they did not present a cogent theoretical justification for their procedures or because they did not envisage either modern technology or modern reporting requirements. Neither do we feel disfranchized from using the term to include procedures which have the same effect of producing a self-balancing system through a medium other than a bound volume of paper sheets in which entries are made according to rules devised centuries before.

The characteristic common feature of double-entry recording is that it provides a closed and integrated system. The specific procedures applied may differ, and its ultimate exhibited products may be presented variously, but the common feature is the arithmetical perfection of its hermetic system. By contrast, the symbol 'single entry', despite the definition (or description) of it provided above by Inglis, could be applied to any procedure, whether to any extent 'systematic' or not, which falls short of double entry. It is virtually indefinable except in negative terms such as 'less than double entry'.

In the double entry (or any other) recording process 'debit' and 'credit' have no moral or ethical implications; 'debit' does not mean good or bad, 'credit' does not mean good or bad. Any such implication, connotation or overtone has been thrust upon the words as they were brought into the common language to do non-technical work; it arises from the adoption of technical terms, with restricted technical meaning, by users in a general language who endow them with non-specific and often undeserved meanings or connotations.

Some writers in the twentieth century have sought to clarify double entry by distinguishing what was dubbed double classification (which was later converted or translated into 'classificational double entry' in conformity with the Gresham's Law tendency for bad words and expressions to drive out good ones) from a so-called duality principle (which Ijiri, followed by other writers, turned into 'causal double entry'). In essence, this distinction is between the *process* of making two entries for each occurrence (or 'transaction' or 'event') recorded on the one hand, and on the other, the *concept* that each occurrence can be interpreted as *either* (a) simultaneously increasing and decreasing separate items within one category of the accounting equation, that is, within Assets or within Equities, *or* (b) simultaneously increasing or decreasing specific separate items in each of the two categories. While the concept may be contemplated without carrying out the process, it seems impossible to carry out the process without somehow adhering to the concept, even if it be through observing rules which have been learned by rote; in practice the distinction is scarcely a difference.

In an article in *Accounting Research*, Richard Mattessich, who seems to have been one of the earliest of these writers, set forth the notion of a matrix form of recording for accounting. (Mattessich, 1957; for a more comprehensive coverage of the history of this matter see Leech 1986 and Mepham 1988.) He was addressing the matter of a model for all accounting systems, and introduced the matrix as a treatment which he claimed to be 'new in its general application in accounting' and used it as part of his introduction of a 'general and axiomatic foundation' of accounting. This was part of the grand search for a set of accounting 'principles' (which were given a succession of labels even unto a 'conceptual framework') which had begun, at least in the USA and other English-language countries, during the 1930s.[2]

The notion of the matrix for recording is interesting and is applicable with appropriate technical equipment. It is, in effect, an intriguing way of maintaining double-entry records through applying the concept of duality to the rows and columns of a two-dimensional matrix; the account titles or numbers are duplicated in the row and column, so that one entry into a two-dimensional matrix has the same significance as a double entry in two separate accounts. This has been pointed out in an earlier work (see Goldberg and Leech 1984: 89–90).

The first author to describe double-entry bookkeeping in a two-dimensional matrix is believed to be Augustus De Morgan in 1846. In his *Elements of Arithmetic*, De Morgan included an appendix: 'On the Main Principle of Bookkeeping' (pp. 180–9). According to him, the ledger was the basis for the method:

> The book in which the accounts are kept is the ledger. It has double columns, or else the debtor side is on one page and the creditor side on the opposite, of each account.[3] The debtor side is always on the left. Other books are used, but they are only to help in keeping the ledger correct. (p. 183).

and

> The only book that need be explained is the ledger. All other books, and the manner in which they are kept, important as they may be, have nothing to do with the main principle of the method. Let us, then, suppose that all the items are entered at once in the ledger as they

---

[2]A few observations on some of the other propositions in this axiomatic exposition are made in the Appendix to this Chapter.

[3]Note that a double-entry ledger does not have to be in columnar form, but the use of columns is a facilitator.

arise. It has appeared that every item is entered twice. If A pays an account of B, there is an entry, 'A, creditor by B'; and another, 'B debtor to A'. This is what is called *double-entry*; (p. 183)[4]

The two-dimensional matrix that appeared in that work was another way that De Morgan used to explain what he considered to be 'double-entry'. De Morgan's idea of double entry appears to have been that a transaction is classified twice from a different point of view – that is, an amount '. . . is supposed to appear in D's account as D creditor by C, and in C's account as C debtor to D' (p. 184).

In a more comprehensive work which followed his 1957 article, Mattessich (1964) also appears to consider that the 'double entry form' is that of the ledger. Mattessich presents 'a flow, accounting, or transaction system' in many different forms – the network form, the double-entry form, the matrix form, the journal-entry form, and the vector form – and offers a 'schematic comparison' of each. The double-entry form is shown as T accounts (in a ledger). Mattessich states that:

> The journal entry form is carefully described in Pacioli's [1494] treatise and may be older than the double-entry form. It usually consists of a data [*sic*], the name of the account to be debited, with the corresponding value in a debit-column; and . . . below this, would be stated the name of the account to be credited with the corresponding value in a credit column. (p. 94)

One could conclude from this that Mattessich considers 'double entry' to take the form of T accounts in the ledger, but that a similar analysis of a transaction in the journal is not a double entry-form. This view may be compared with the distinction Mattessich makes between the 'duality principle' (as an 'abstract notion') and 'actual recording':

> Much misunderstanding has been created among laymen by confusing or identifying bookkeeping with accounting. Yet, more confusion arises because of the accountants' failure to make a precise distinction between the act of making a 'double entry' and the idea of subjecting certain economic events to the abstract, mathematical notion of a transaction. The essence of the latter lies in a fundamentally *two-dimensional* property that permits double classification within one set of classes. Whether this dual classification is fully carried out, or only conceived mentally – or carried out merely on the highest level of aggregation, whether it is executed in T-Accounts, or in a matrix, or in form of an ordered tuple or a vector, or by graphical means of a network – is irrelevant for the *duality principle*. The decisive factor is the existence of

---

[4]De Morgan's statement is erroneous. He seems to have been confused about two different sets of records. Cf. also the quote below from De Morgan (p. 184).

an economic event dominated by a process of giving and taking, input and output, transferring out and transferring in. It is this property which creates an isomorphism between an empirical phenomenon and our *basically* two dimensional mathematical construct. (p. 26)

In using the term 'duality principle', he seems to say that the distinction between the actual recording (or the mode of making the record), on the one hand, and the mental conception, on the other, is irrelevant.

> Returning to the core of this section we may interpret the *duality principle* as the assertion that a transaction or flow has basically two dimensions: an aspect and a counter-aspect (to avoid the terms *input* and *output* which have too concrete a flavor, or the terms *debit* and *credit* which have too strong a flavor of the technical recording process). More precisely, the principle asserts that *there exist economic events[14] which are isomorphic to a two-dimensional classification of a value within one set of classes.* This basically dual property of a transaction thus generalizes and extends those empirical manifestations which are associated with the phenomenon of change. Wherever – in our attempt to depict phases of the economic environment – we explicitly adapt our model to this double aspect, we are confronted with an accounting system. The evolution of national income measurement offers an example *par excellence* that the duality aspect may, but need not be, exploited in creating and presenting statistical data. But it also shows that often, for reasons of systematization, perspicuity, and analysis, the utilization of an accounting frame works to great advantage. Thus accountancy, as a part of quantitative economics, is characterized by a special methodology and a set of assumptions which we might call 'the duality syndrome.' (p. 27)

The footnote 14 to this passage has an interesting passing suggestion:

> Theoretically it should be possible to develop accounting systems for noneconomic flow structures as well; e.g., for the transfer of liquids in a network of pipelines and reservoirs, or for the tracing of chemical substances during the metabolism of plants or animals (e.g., research with radioactive tracers in the photosynthesis), etc. These potential accounting systems do not deal with income and wealth aspects in the ordinary sense, thus cannot be addressed as *economic* accounting. (p. 27)

In a later section of his book ('Duality without Double-Entry') which discusses Quesnay's *Tableau economique*, Mattessich states:

> . . . before long business accountants too, will realise that the advantages of accounting do not depend on double-entry but on *double-classification* (which is attainable by a single entry or other means); (p. 107, emphasis added).

Thus, it would appear that Mattessich equates the notion of 'duality' with 'double-classification'. This is also borne out by his earlier definition of 'duality' as a basic assumption of accounting:

> For all *accounting transactions* it is true that a value is assigned to a three-dimensional concept (ordered triple) consisting of *two* accounts and a time instance (date). (pp. 33–4)

If we try to analyse these statements to see what message they contain for us, we encounter some difficulties. While we may accept that his use of 'event' and our use of 'occurrence' is no more than a matter of choice of words, we are left in doubt on whether the domination of an event/occurrence by the process of giving and taking, and so on, is necessary for it to be accepted as an economic event/occurrence, or whether not all economic events/occurrences are so dominated, but that such domination is necessary to bring them within the duality principle. For instance, if, in the course of walking along the seashore, a man picks up a shell and prises it open and finds a pearl inside, could this be interpreted as an economic event even though it does not seem to be dominated by any process of giving or transferring out or to have much input on the part of the finder, although he might become more 'economically' affluent by his find?

While we might well agree that an event/occurrence is an empirical phenomenon in the sense that it can be perceived as a change in observable objects (including socially agreed rights), to say that this perception can be put into the same form as a mathematical construct by the domination of a particular process appears to be a roundabout way of saying that we interpret certain occurrences as having a twofold effect in order to carry out a process of double entry (or dual recording, if that expression is preferred). In other words, we can observe occurrences, and select particular ones which we can interpret as having twofold effects from a given point of view (namely, that of recording by 'double entry'). There is an inevitable circularity involved. The duality is not a property of the occurrence, but of our interpretation of it. In fact, there seems to be no reason why occurrences cannot have many more than two aspects, nor that some occurrences may not have the two 'aspects' which make them amenable to a process of dual recording.

It is submitted that the essential element of double-entry *recording* is the capacity to provide a record which reflects the interpretation of every relevant occurrence or circumstance as having a twofold effect on two different units of record ('accounts' for a ledger or 'vectors' for a matrix). In a ledger the effects are designated debit and credit, or left and right, or in and out; in a matrix they are row and column. It is the interpretation which is the core of double-entry procedure, and interpretation is conceptual activity. The perceived evidence is simply that of change in something brought about by the observed occurrence.

Another formulation of an axiomatic structure for accounting was set out by Yuji Ijiri, who also explored the application of matrices and the possibility of 'triple entry' and 'multi-dimensional accounting' (Ijiri 1965, 1967, 1975, 1988). In 1965 Ijiri presented a set of three axioms and several measurement rules as a base for formulating a mathematical representation of conventional accounting measurement. One of these axioms, which he called *Axiom of Exchange*, states:

> For any object that is added to or subtracted from the property set A_t, an exchange *that has caused* the addition or subtraction of the object can be uniquely identified, and all exchanges that have occurred are identifiable, countable, and can be ordered completely and uniquely according to the time of their occurrence.
>
> (Ijiri 1965: 42, emphasis added)

In a book which appeared some two years later, this axiom was restated thus:

> There exists a method by which all changes in the resources controlled by a given entity up to any time are identified at that time or later and are partitioned uniquely into an ordered set of pairs of an increment and a decrement, where the increment belongs to one and only one class.
>
> (Ijiri 1967: 90)

He regarded it as an:

> amazing human ability . . . that a person is able to know a set of objects d^+ is obtained in exchange for another set of objects d^-. For example, a warehouse manager can see only goods coming in and going out, while a cashier can see only cash balance increased or decreased. But when we see the firm's operations as a whole, we are able to say that cash is increased in *exchange* for goods delivered.
>
> (Ijiri 1965: 40)

But, with respect to this example, it can surely be suggested that the warehouse manager, in addition to seeing the goods come in, would be intelligent enough to realise that they had come from a source of supply, (who would expect or have had payment or who would have donated or bequeathed them), and responsible enough to look for a delivery docket with sufficient details to warrant his acceptance of the goods; and, when the goods go out, that they go out because they have a destination which would be indicated on a requisition or some equivalent evidence datum. And a cashier, in addition to seeing the variation in the cash balance, would also be required to learn the source and destination of these movements and make some record of them, for, after all, a cashier is not merely a mechanical cash register.

When he says, further,

> we have a mechanism outside the measurement system, but which we are able to say that d^+ is obtained as a result of foregoing [sic] d^-, or in exchange for d^-

it would surely be equally 'true' that d^- is a result of or in exchange for d^+. That is, it is not a causal relationship between them; one does not 'cause' the other; they are simply expressions of a subjective (and sophisticated) interpretation which we 'amazing' human beings impose upon some *occurrences* which we can observe.

Of course, it may be suggested that if one needs, say, a motor car, and that one has to forgo cash in order to obtain it, then the need for a motor car 'causes' the forgoing of the cash. This may be accepted as 'true', but it does not follow that the entry:

Dr   Motor Car / Cr   Cash

represents the position, because the debit records not the need for, but the acquisition of, a car. The need 'causes' both the acquisition of the object and the diminution of the resource, or, to put it another way, it causes an exchange of assets. At the same time, if one is operating on a bank over-draft or on other borrowed funds, the occurrence will be represented by a simultaneous increase of both an asset and a liability, rather than an exchange of one asset for another.

The fact is that in using double-entry procedure in its normal way we do not usually recognize needs as such; it might well be desirable to work out a formula whereby we did, but that is not our present concern. In passing, it might be suggested that when King Richard the Third expressed his dire need for a horse, it might have given rise to the entry:

Dr   One Horse / Cr   One Kingdom

If he had got it, what entry would follow? (A car would have been even better, but it hadn't been invented until long after the need was expressed.)

However, the notion of causality was repeated in 1975, when Ijiri used the expression 'causal double entry' to indicate those cases in which 'the value of an increment (debit) is set equal to the value of a decrement (credit)', that is, where an entry 'clearly involves two different resources', as in an 'exchange' of cash for inventories. 'They [the two resources] are tied together because of the cause-and-effect relationship between the incre-ment and the decrement' (Ijiri 1975: 81).

This point requires further consideration because the expression 'causal double entry' and the notion behind it have persisted into some of the later literature. Hence, it needs to be emphasized that any cause-and-effect relationship between the increment and decrement does not reside in the suggestion that the increment 'causes' the decrement, or vice versa; both increment and decrement are equally and simultaneously interpretations of a result of an occurrence. The example Ijiri gave of a 'causal' entry, namely, that of debiting Inventories (increment) and crediting Cash (decrement), could be notionally, and, if desired, actually, expanded into two entries, debiting Inventories and crediting Supplier (both increments) and debiting Supplier and crediting Cash (both decrements). Debiting Inventories does not record a need for goods; it records the acquisition of, that is, an increase in, a resource. The *need* 'causes' (if that is the right word) both the acquisition of goods and the outlay of cash, if they occur simultaneously, but we do not normally record the need.

If we try to record needs, some measurement of them will be required. Suppose we do have a need for a car; what is required is a fairly firm figure for, say, the maximum amount we are prepared to pay for one. Suppose we say that we should be prepared to pay up to $120,000 for one that will meet our needs. We could then record this:

Dr	Need for Car (Potential asset?)	120,000	
	Cr Contemplated Maximum Outlay		120,000

Suppose then we got a suitable car for $118,500. The acquisition would be recorded as normally required:

Dr	Car (Asset)	118,500	
	Cr Cash (Outlay)		118,500

This is a little less than we were prepared to pay, hence:

Dr	Contemplated Maximum Outlay	120,000	
	Cr Need for Car		118,500
	Buyer's 'Surplus'		1,500

This still leaves a balance of $1,500 in the Need for Car account, which could, perhaps, be transferred to an account representing some other need or even written back to some kind of inclusive 'Capital Needs' account. When we get back to this point, we feel the need, if we are to persist with double entry, of a conceptual basic equation which couples, say, Total Needs with Contemplated Maximum Outlay as a fundamental starting point. This would approach something like a double-entry system for detailed budgeting, which might well be taken seriously in future developments of accounting procedures.

Clearly, however, the debit to Car account does not record the need; it records the acquisition of the car which satisfies the need. The outlay of cash is also an expression of the means by which the satisfaction was effected. In other words, the record as traditionally made is one of the satisfaction of a need and the price of satisfying that need; these are both effects of implementing a decision to vary a pre-existing status quo. To be sure, occurrences are, in a sense, the causes of all the entries, since they are the basis for all the recording to be made; but there seems to be little, if any, causality in the entries themselves.

In another analysis Ijiri gives us an example of:

> a man living alone in a cottage in a wood. He is hungry, but he has nothing to eat. He knows that he can go out, collect nuts, crack them,

and eat them to satisfy his hunger. But he must force himself to do this since he prefers staying in the cottage and lying down to going out and collecting nuts. Therefore he balances the *benefit* (pleasure of satisfying his hunger) and the *sacrifice* (pain of labour) which will result from his activity of collecting nuts.

(Ijiri 1967: 33)

He sets out the causal relationship thus:

Sacrifice → Goods → Benefit

where → indicates the cause and effect relationship (Ijiri 1967: 35). Presumably an appropriate entry would be:

Sacrifice	Dr		(Labour and effort of gathering nuts)
Goods		Cr	(Nuts)
Goods	Dr		(Nuts)
Benefit		Cr	(Satisfying of feeling of hunger)

If this is so, the question arises: What would be recorded for the day when the man in the cottage goes out and incurs his effort and labour, but gathers no nuts, and so derives no benefit? He will have had an 'outlay' or 'expenditure' without getting any consequent benefit. To what or to whom would he credit the sacrifice, and why? That is, we are faced with:

Sacrifice	Dr	
?		Cr

There is a loss of effort which has not created or contributed to any benefit. The 'cause' is there, but what is the 'effect'?

It may be suggested that a 'No Benefit' or 'Hunger' account should be credited. However, if the former is adopted we would have both 'benefit' and 'no-benefit' or satisfaction and lack of satisfaction being recorded in precisely the same fashion, namely, as 'credits'. If a 'Hunger' account is used, the likely increase in hunger through lack of means to abate its pangs would be treated in the same way as its appeasement.

When we reach this stage, there are but two further questions that crave to be raised: (1) Does this kind of 'logic' make sense at all? and (2) Is it worth spending further time and effort on such a game of nuts?

It is suggested that the duality of entries can only be sensibly applied if there is a concept of something analogous to a 'capital' of energy or effort or strength or vitality against which a loss or 'unrequited outlay' of energy or effort can be 'charged'. (Perhaps something not completely unlike this is a strong element in the attitude many people seem to have towards the taxes they pay.)

Subsequent writers seized on the distinction drawn by Mattessich and Ijiri between the traditional recording procedure of double-entry bookkeeping and that of what they describe as double (or dual) classification or the duality principle. Also, this distinction appears to be at the heart of later calls for the abandonment or reconsideration of elements of double-entry recording. For instance, in Chapter 7 (entitled 'Mathematics of Accounting') of their book on *Finite Mathematics with Business Applications*, Kemeny *et al.* (1962), stated, in a section headed 'Double Classification Bookkeeping', that:

> ... the important point about double entry bookkeeping is not that each transaction is *recorded* twice but rather that each transaction is *classified* twice – once as a debit and once as a credit. Another way to doubly classify a number is to record it in a matrix. The number then is classified once according to the row in which it appears and once according to its column. Since this can be done by recording the number just once, the common errors of double entry bookkeeping mentioned above cannot be made, and the need for trial balances to detect these kinds of errors is eliminated.
>
> (Kemeny *et al.* 1962: 347)

More recent examples include: Everest and Weber (1977):

> The accountant's notion of double-entry and the information systems theorist's concern with processing efficiency somehow seem to be in conflict. When traditional ledger accounts are taken up on magnetic media, input transactions must be split and two update entries generated to preserve the duality of double entry. This involves doubling the size of the input transaction file, which produces a corresponding increase in the time required for sorting and updating accounting information. (p. 341)

McCarthy (1982):

> It is a primary contention of this paper that the semantic modelling of accounting object systems *should not include elements of double-entry bookkeeping such as debits, credits and accounts.* As noted previously by both Everest and Weber (1977) and McCarthy (1979), these elements are artifacts associated with journals and ledgers (that is, they are simply mechanisms for manually storing and transmitting data). As such, *they are not essential aspects of an accounting system.* (pp. 559–60, emphasis added)

Mepham (1988):

> Even before the computer revolution, the T account model was inappropriate as a description of the firm's accounting information system. With the recent database developments it is even less suitable. (p. 377)

What exactly are we describing when we do not include 'elements of double-entry bookkeeping such as debits, credits and accounts' in the design of an accounting system? In their design of accounting systems, some of the same researchers retain the 'duality principle' in accounting. For example, McCarthy (1982):

> Duality relationships link each increment in the resource set of the enterprise with a corresponding decrement [Ijiri 1975: Ch. 5]. Increments and decrements must be members of two different event entity sets: one characterized by transferring in (purchase and cash receipts) and the other characterized by transferring out (sales and cash disbursements). The abstract notion of duality is described in detail by Mattessich [1964: 26–30]. (p. 562).

Geerts and McCarthy (1991):

> Finally, and perhaps the hardest to understand in terms of its departure from bookkeeping, there is a binary association required of every accounting event with another event: its dual transaction. Accounting theory (Ijiri, 1975; Mattessich, 1964) requires that transactions associated with resource outflows from a company (decrements) be paired with resource inflows (increments) and vice-versa. This is the duality principle of accounting. (p. 173)

Leech and Mepham (1991):

> The main argument for the retention of the 'duality principle' is that accounting concentrates on those events which can be described as resource flows, and flows necessarily have a dual aspect, i.e. a source and a destination. We, therefore, see no good reasons for departing from the duality principle for the core of an accounting system. It is recognised, however, that there will be events of interest to the accounting enduser, which cannot be described in this way. . . (p. 7)

and

> The 'duality principle' should be distinguished from the 'double entry' framework which is currently used. Given that an organisation's information system is relational in character, there are sound reasons for changing the form of the framework and this can be done whilst retaining the 'duality principle'. No longer is it necessary to retain any form of ledger. Rather, it is the matrix form which is consistent with relational database systems, as well as with application-oriented financial modelling systems. (p. 8)

To put it into perspective, the double-entry process has often been discussed in recent years with emphasis upon the 'traditional' procedure of journal entries and T-form ledger accounts, drawing criticism or somewhat pejorative recognition from some writers who have pointed out that recording by means of a matrix attains the same cumulative effect as the traditional procedure. (Mattessich 1957 Leech: 1986). However, it has also been pointed out that, while matrix recording produces equivalent 'final' or up-to-date cumulative numbers, useful especially for preparation of periodic reports of achievement and status, no details of occurrences which contribute to the cumulative total are contained in the matricial equivalent or replacement of the ledger accounts; (Leech 1986); such detail is only available in the journal or its equivalent or in the primary evidence itself. Hence, any *ad hoc* or even systematic exposition of the composition of detail has to be specifically readdressed if required. Thus the feasibility of matrix accounting depends upon the availability of computer systems if it is to perform the function of an aide-memoire or source of reliable evidence for the detail of separate occurrences provided by the traditional form of ledger.

With respect to double classification, the expression 'causal double entry' has been applied as if 'double entry' is something which exists apart from any human activity, and therefore can be conceived as 'possessing' attributes or characteristics which can be observed by humans applying or presuming to apply a form of scientific method. For instance, when Ijiri made his analysis, he distinguished between (a) increasing one asset, Inventories, and decreasing another, Cash, and (b) increasing both an asset and an equity or decreasing both an asset and an equity. It is to the former only that he applied the term 'causal double entry', because, he argued, the increase in the one caused a decrement in the other.

Whether we are dealing with double entry as a procedure or as a way of thought, if we adopt the basic classification of assets and equities and wish to preserve equilibrium between them, the possibility of variations of types of entry is strictly limited, namely:

> Increase one asset and decrease another asset to the same extent
>
> Increase one asset and increase an equity or equities to the same extent
>
> Decrease an asset and decrease an equity or equities to the same extent
>
> Increase an equity and decrease another equity to the same extent.

That is: $+A, -A; +A, +E; -A, -E; +E, -E.$

Why any of these should be singled out as being more or less 'causative' than any of the others seems difficult to understand or accept in the absence of some cogent reasoning or evidence which does not appear to have been provided so far.

Double entry is an invention of human intellect, but, despite Spengler's attribution, we do not know, with any considerable degree of confidence, and may never find out what the thoughts of the inventor(s) were at its development. On this point we can do little more than speculate. We have to imagine what the introducers of the procedures were thinking, and as soon as we start to do this we realize that much depends on who they were. If they were Italians of the later Middle Ages, can we presume, with safety, that they were merchants or bankers or others with resources available for investment? Or were they members of some religious order keeping records of dealings of a monastery carried out in the course of spreading the Word of their religion? Or could Italian merchants have had commerce with Arab traders with camel trains to convey goods over long distances in Asia and Africa to make contact with their customers, with whom they exchanged ideas as well as goods? Should our fancy go back even further, both in time and distance, to India, for a whiff of Buddhist or Hindu mysticism, or even to preliterate Sumeria, where it seems that the very invention of writing had its rationale and origin in the need for some kind of accounting records in the service of temple priests?

Spengler asserts that '[t]he mathematical vision and thought that a Culture possesses within itself is as inadequately represented by its written mathematic as its philosophical vision and thought by its philosophical treatises. Number springs from a source that has also quite other outlets' (Spengler 1926, I: 57).

Perhaps the development of double entry did not originate in response to a commercial need in the fourteenth century as is usually suggested, but, rather, as a result of mathematicians attempting to tidy up a section of mathematics into a suitable formalism. It may have been developed earlier as a mathematical exercise and was, in essence, available for the commercial and banking people when, eventually, the need was felt and, at about the same time, the physical means, especially a ready supply of relatively cheap paper, became available. But this is, at present, highly speculative.

This would mean that it didn't necessarily evolve by very gradual stages. Perhaps it explains the somewhat erratic appearance of double entry, in relatively scattered localities of Italy. It would explain its appearance in mathematical texts in the early days and the attention given to it by early mathematicians. Then, when it has become thoroughly formalized and 'useful' – or, rather, usefully employed – mathematicians (speaking broadly) lost interest in it, their job having been completed. Re-examination of the known facts about its origin is required to test this hypothesis. Perhaps it fits in with the hypothesis that the concepts involved originated outside Italy, but not necessarily with the proposition that they were 'imported' as ideas by the merchants of the time. It is at least questionable whether a fully fledged double-entry system is necessary to keep adequate records of the affairs of most of the individuals in a community, until such transactions become sufficiently complicated to require an arithmetical test of accuracy. Perhaps this is the reason for the slow progress in its application between the fifteenth and nineteenth centuries.

However, despite the absence of such formal and systematic recording, it may well be that the application of double-entry *thinking* is and often has been more widespread than is superficially apparent.

A considerable part of the discussion about double entry, dual classification, the duality principle, causal double-entry bookkeeping, and matrix
accounting appears to be about words (which are symbols of our thoughts
and intended meanings) and techniques (which are practical expressions of
our meanings according to the instruments available from time to time),
that is, about terminology and/or form, rather than substance.

Consider the following expression:

Cash/Capital 1000 $\dfrac{1}{21}$

where 1 is the page number or the row for Cash, and 21 is the page
number or column for Capital, and the custom is to place the debit or row
before and above the credit or column in, respectively, the (verbal) 'entry'
and the posting indicator. Whatever name we give this – double posting or
dual entry or twosome recording or anything else – it is evidence of a
direction to make one entry as a debit in the record expressing one aspect
of a relationship and an equivalent entry as a credit in another record
expressing another aspect of the same relationship. Whether it is part of
what we generally regard as a double-entry system depends upon the
extent to which the kind of double or dual entering and posting is
performed and whether the 'system' is ultimately a closed one with the use
of some appropriate means (for instance, an account) for the closure.

Suppose the following series of occurrences:
X has no resources of his own, but borrows 100 units of exchange from Y. He
buys goods for cash, 20; he sells them to D(ebtor) for 25; D pays cash, 24,
deducting 1 for discount. At this point a 'trial balance', after closure of sales,
cost of goods sold, and discount records to a further 'result' record, would
show:

Cash	104	
Y Loan		100
Profit		4
	104	104

The question that arises is: What happens to the 4 units by which cash has
been increased? They may 'belong' to Y, the lender, in whole or in part, or
to X, the borrower, in whole or in part; it will depend on the legal and/or
social circumstances of the particular case. Either way, with double entry the
recording system is a closed one because dual classification or dual entering
or its equivalent under any other name has been applied. What the recording process reveals is that a surplus exists and belongs to someone – perhaps
even to a taxing authority or a charity. It scarcely seems worth while spending much time and effort in beating the air with imaginary differences
arising from nomenclature. Whatever names may be used, the substance
does not seem to be affected.

Suppose a woman is walking along the seashore and sees a shell which
seems to be unusual for that location. She picks it up and, being possessed

by the spirit of double entry, wishes to inscribe the entry in the sand. She writes the 'debit' side:

Unusual Shell   Dr

This recognizes and records the 'existence' of the shell: 'There is a shell' is the essential message of this statement. But what is the other side of the entry? The entering, or, more precisely, the result of the entering is the evidence of the thinking; that is, it is evidence of the recognition and acceptance of a relationship of ownership or possession or usefulness or trusteeship or something analogous to one of these. The shell belongs to the gatherer or to some other person, or to the tribe or clan, or it will be or could be useful as a tool or to adorn a temple, or it might be pleasurable to look at or to handle or to discuss as an object of philosophy or speculation, and so on. The credit side of the entry depends upon and will reflect the prevailing thinking of the finder at the time of the occurrence.

Our position in this work is simple, and, we hope, clear. Occurrences do take place. We can all observe such occurrences, and some of us, who, through experience or conditioning, are able to do so, can interpret certain of these occurrences as having a twofold effect on selected human relationships and can record these effects accordingly. This interpretation is, at bottom, a mental activity taking place in the mind of the observer. It is not a property or attribute of the occurrence, although the observer often 'attributes' the relationship to the occurrence. But even when this attribution is wrongly made, the occurrence is not necessarily limited to this interpretation; it may affect other relationships as well as those seen to be involved in the aforesaid twofold effect.

What double entry, whether as a method of recording or of thought, does effectively, systematically and elegantly, is to formalize and articulate the notion that profitable occurrences contribute to or comprise an increase in (net) assets (or capital) and unprofitable ones tend to decrease them. Whether this is sufficient to meet the requirements of activities and aspirations of people in the world of today and their near descendants is open to question.

Some of its characteristics and limitations

We regard the expression 'double entry' as a symbol used to convey two distinct but related components of a human intellectual invention, namely, a technique and a mode of thinking applied to a function of human activity. What it 'is' is a matter of opinion and interpretation of a human activity rather than of observation of a 'natural' non-human occurrence or series of occurrences. On this basis, anybody's opinion may be as worthy of acceptance as that of anybody else, and the basis of acceptance or rejection could be that of agreement with the experience of the acceptor.

As with many other expressions in the English language, 'double entry' has no particular intrinsic meaning in itself; its meaning may vary according to its context. For example, a police sergeant reporting on a raid on a house by himself and a constable could say that they approached the house by a back door and a side window, thus effecting a double entry. Or a burglar might confess that he twice went in and out of a place by an open front door, and thus made a double entry (and a double exit). Or there might be a competition for look-alikes of a prominent person, which would bring forth a number of 'double' entries in the search for the closest look-alike or 'double'. In short, the expression can be merely the subject-matter of a word game which can be played for innocent entertainment without being substantially productive.

However, the context in which it appears (or is heard) usually makes clear the intention of the user, and the context in which it is being seriously considered here is that of the recording of occurrences which accountants regard and/or, in our opinion, should regard, as relevant to their activities as accountants.

Whatever technique is used in application, occurrences which are observed as relevant to accounting functions are interpreted as having a twofold effect, which the recorder, using a particular form of the technique, translates into formal dual entries in 'accounts' or one entry in a two-dimensional matrix, or some other variant of the formal ledger arrangement. But whatever form of technique is used, the twofold interpretation of the occurrences lies behind it.

Looked at in one way, there is no great mystery about double entry: the occurrences that are the subject of accounting record are everyday occurrences, and the units of experience who take part in these occurrences are ordinary people who are everywhere about us. Double entry can be viewed as an instrument of thought, as can any other mode of recording, and as an instrument of communication. In using the instrument the user gets into the habit of interpreting each occurrence as having two effects – one on each of two differently named categories of perceived or conceived 'objects'. The basis of forming the habit has varied from time to time. For many years, for instance, the rules were learned by rote with such injunctions as 'Debit the receiver; credit the giver' or 'Debit what comes in; credit what goes out', and texts listed examples of each for absorption into the learner's experience. In more recent years, a 'rational' exposition was developed through consideration of the 'accounting equation' that Assets equal Equities, and the rules for debit and credit were logically derived from it, so that the need for rote habit development was eliminated. It still remains true, however, that habit is formed by practice, whether it is logically based or not.

It also appears that the practice of double entry is based on an elegant theory, which was not appropriately formulated until the nineteenth century and widely accepted until the twentieth. But this does not make it a sacred text as if coming from an Almighty Being, and to be obeyed whether circumstances fit or not. Its usefulness in appropriate circumstances does not warrant the compelling of our perceptions of phenomena or occurrences to fit the double-entry paradigm where it does not make sense to do so.

In its strictest and narrowest accounting interpretation, recording comprises the processes of making entries of ('entering') occurrences in appropriate records ('journals') and 'posting' (which comprises classifying and summarizing as appropriate) entries to a set of relevant records ('accounts'). Broadly speaking, a journal is a chronological record of occurrences; ledger accounts are set up and maintained as episodic or ventural arrangements (or classification) of occurrences.

Because double entry is operated as a closed system, it provides an arithmetical articulation which enables the accuracy of the recording procedure to be tested and demonstrated; it is, in short, a self-balancing system. However, the accuracy so discernible or testable is an arithmetical accuracy only; anything beyond that depends on the data fed into the system and the propriety of classification applied in the processing of the data. In other words, the accuracy attainable can be spurious if the point of view from which the recorded data are observed is changed from a purely arithmetical one. The reason for this is that only one unit of measurement at a time can be applied for the data processed; and the most common unit over many centuries has been and still is a monetary one.

Since the operation of double-entry systems has its theoretical base in the accounting equation, $A=E$, it is subject to a prevalent acceptance of an ownership or claimant relationship in the application and interpretation of its results. Hence, our consideration of the procedural aspects of accounting has a two-pronged approach: the possibility of having multiple units of measurement in the recognition of accountable occurrences, and the possibility of viewing the ownership or claimant relationship as a particular case of a broader-based set of relationships between people and the resources they have access to.

One of the earliest exponents (if not the earliest) of the fundamental accounting equation was F.W. Cronhelm, who, in 1818, expressed it thus:

> ... when we ... abstract a Concern from its Proprietor, and place the account of Stock or entire capital among the component parts, the Concern itself is constantly neutral, consisting of a mass of relations between Debtors and Creditors, in perpetual and necessary equilibrium.
>
> (Cronhelm 1818: 8)

He displayed this in algebraic form:

> Let a, b, c, &c. represent the positive parts, or Debtors; 1, m, n, &c. the negative parts, or Creditors; and s the Stock, or proprietor's real worth. Then, as the whole is equal to the sum of its parts,
>
> $a+b+c$, &c. $-l-m-n$, &c. $= \pm s$.
>
> By transposition we obtain
>
> $a+b+c$, &c. $-1-m-n$, &c. $+s. = 0$,
>
> or that general equation, in which the whole Estate is neutral or a cypher, and includes the Stock as one of its component parts.
>
> (Cronhelm 1818: 8)

The connection between the accounting equation and the double-entry procedure may be set out in the following way. If we focus our attention on assets, we can distinguish each asset by regarding it from two points of view, namely, (i) as the thing in itself, that is, the thing that 'exists', or that which can be perceived and interpreted through our sensory organs as lying outside ourselves, and (ii) as the embodiment of a right to it (or its equivalent, such as payment for it). It is the fact that some person has a *right* to the *thing* that makes it accountable. Hence:

$$A(\text{ssets}) = E(\text{quities})$$

$$E = L(\text{iabilities}) + P(\text{roprietorship})$$

$$\therefore A = L + P$$

$$P = C(\text{ontributed}) \text{ Proprietorship} + A(\text{ccumulated}) \text{ Proprietorship}$$

$$\therefore A = L + C.P. + A.P.$$

$$A.P. = R(\text{evenue}) - C(\text{harges against revenue}) - W(\text{ithdrawals, e.g. dividends})$$

$$\therefore A = L + C.P. + R - C - W$$

$$\text{or} \quad A + C + W = L + C.P. + R$$

$$\text{i.e.} \quad \text{Left hand} = \text{Right hand}$$

$$\text{Debit items} = \text{Credit items}$$

(Goldberg 1953: 280–2; Goldberg 1957: 64–6)

Another approach in exposition of the 'principle' of double entry recording could be along these lines:

Expenses are debit entries, therefore the reverse, i.e. revenues, are credits.

Long-term (or 'fixed') assets are unexpired (or 'capitalized') expenses, therefore they are debits.[5]

Short-term (or 'current') assets have in common with long-term assets the characteristic that they stand as an ownership right of the one owner, therefore short-term assets are also debits.

---

5 A form of this argument which may be presented to, say, a student who is puzzled by the logic of double entry in the initial stages of study could be: Suppose that cash is paid out for both an expense and a long-term asset. The fact that cash is paid out suggests that both the expense and the asset have a basic characteristic in common, namely, that they will both be used up, so to speak, in due course. The difference between them is that the expense has a short-term usage period, whereas the asset has a long-term usage period; the difference in classification is a matter of timing: it depends upon the accounting period adopted. Of course there is an assumption in this argument that such long-term assets are eventually 'used up' in the course of their productive life and are acquired with that outcome in mind; a long-term asset which is not expected to so deteriorate in condition, that is, which is acquired as an investment, is not so clear-cut a case.

Liabilities are obligations 'owed' to others, that is, the contrary to assets, and therefore credits.

Capital is an 'internal' liability, and therefore credit.

Hence we get this:

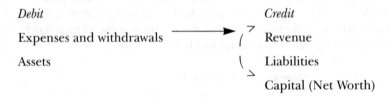

Debit	Credit
Expenses and withdrawals	Revenue
Assets	Liabilities
	Capital (Net Worth)

From this we can derive a 'Net Worth Equation':

An increase in net worth arises from an excess of revenue over expenses, i.e., R(evenue) – E(xpenses) – W(ithdrawals)=N(et) W(orth) where represents 'increase in', the converse being equally valid for a decrease.

Revenue=Increase of Assets and

Expenses and Withdrawals=Decrease of Assets or Increase of Liabilities;

Therefore:

Increase of Assets less Decrease of Assets and less any Increase of Liabilities=Increase or Decrease of Net Worth.

Thus, the system of double-entry recording is an example of an elegant mathematical series of propositions. In addition, however, it illustrates an important implicit practical lesson, namely, that, whether an individual, corporation, government or public or private institution, one cannot accumulate capital without saving out of income. For, as was pointed out above:

$$A+C+W=L+C.P.+R$$

and, if we accept this, we must surely also accept that:

$$A-L=C.P.+R-C-W$$

W is what would be, for an individual, any outlay on personal consumption; for any other unit, withdrawals by or distributions to members of the group of proprietary investors for their own personal disposition. Whatever portion of revenue remains, after charges against it and withdrawals have been deducted from it, is savings; in broad terms, it is this which constitutes and increases capital; if charges and withdrawals exceed revenue, capital is diminished. This is the basic significance of both the balance sheet and the funds statement. It took a long time for this lesson to sink in, since it is implicit rather than explicit in the theory and practice of double entry, and it is not completely recognized yet by many people who see double entry only as a traditional technique, while others can actually use it to the disadvantage of financial victims. The inherent lesson itself, however, is as old as repetitive agriculture, for the earliest intelligent and deliberate farmers must have set aside seed from a current crop to use it for sowing for future crops.

Since the application of double entry involves recording, classifying and, usually, reporting, it is useful in tracing the deployment of resources. In doing this, the record-keeping applies a 'flow' concept, depicting a conceived, rather than a fully perceived, flow of resources (or parts or elements thereof) through processes devised, if not carried out, by human beings.

Where resources are closely held or closely controlled, as may happen with some individual human beings or small groups of people, the application of double entry is not necessarily significant, although it may well be desirable to ensure the arithmetical accuracy it provides. This may have been the reason why it appears to have been neglected for sole traders before the nineteenth century – and even later – but it would have been useful in manufacturing concerns for tracing the flow of materials and the application of labour through the manufacturing processes. And where the trading or manufacturing or financing operations involved the participation of several people as a group of investors, the need to keep track of the respective shares of participants and the entitlements attaching to each would have made it almost mandatory to apply double-entry procedures to ensure mathematical accuracy. As Littleton pointed out, the corporate form of business organization required the recognition of 'the importance of maintaining a sharp distinction between capital and income' (Littleton 1933: 256). Of course, the application of a matrix as a form of technical recording may have served this purpose as well – but it had not been developed when the technique of dual entering by quill on paper became available as an instrument of communication.

Another basic function to which double entry lends itself as a portrayal of a flow concept is that of matching revenue and its related costs or charges, or, in Littleton's words, effecting 'the association of units of income and units of the cost which produced that income' (Littleton 1933: 256n). Cayley also pointed out, among his concluding remarks:

> Observe that the accounts *always* balance – and thus may be made to prove anything: if you throw £100 into the sea, the sea becomes your debtor for that amount, it would appear in the balance sheet as debtor accordingly, and you appear as neither richer nor poorer for the transaction. . . The accounts require to be kept *honestly*; viz. in the balance sheet it is to be seen that the amounts due from the several debtors represent real assets, or say assets presumably capable of realisation . . . so as to make the balance sheet exhibit the true state of affairs, and avoid the fool's paradise of a fictitious amount to the credit of Profit and Loss.

(Cayley 1894: 19–20)

It could also be suggested that two basic concepts in accounting are:

(a) the static, 'point of time' concept, namely, A=E; and
(b) the dynamic, 'period of time' concept, namely, the matching of revenue and appropriate charges against revenue;

and that the double-entry 'theorem' links the two and shows the relation between them in a systematic manner.

An asset may be defined as some 'thing' to which somebody has a right. This is a very general and diffused definition which includes several implications. For instance, a right which some one person has is, by implication, a right against some other person or persons; in turn, this implies the existence of a community in which a code of mutually observed and, presumably, enforceable obligations operates. In some instances, such a right may itself be regarded as an asset, as in a right to be paid for an object sold or a service rendered. In many instances, the implied right is one of ownership; in some, one of accessibility or use. Dual recording (by whatever name and whether by traditional manual, mechanical or electronic means or by matrix or other arrangement of data) is intellectually based upon a recognition of such a right not only to an asset but also as against others. Perhaps 'dual recognition' or, more precisely 'recognition of duality' might be a better term to describe this than such terms as 'double entry', 'dual recording', 'double classification' and the like.

Whether an asset can exist without any recognition of some right to it appears to be a metaphysical question outside the realm of double-entry consideration. If we start to think about such a thing as an asset apart from relationships such as the rights of people to it, we are getting into metaphysical questions which are either nonsensical or insoluble, or, perhaps, insoluble because they are nonsensical. We see accounting, including double entry thinking and recording, as being concerned with relationships rather than with any intrinsic 'existence' or 'reality' or whatever other term may be used to designate this nebulous concept.

There are, indeed, two aspects of double entry which should be distinguished, and each of these is the product of human thought:

(a) the technique of recording, whether it be through T-accounts in a ledger alone, or dual posting from a journal of some sort to ledger accounts, or by means of a matrix or data-base tables or by any other comparable and equivalent procedure; it is a matter of how the recording is carried out;
(b) the purpose or objective underlying the technique; it is difficult to find a satisfactory, all-embracing word to identify this, and we have just offered 'dual recognition', but it has something of a teleological view; it may, perhaps, be regarded as double entry thinking, and it represents or embraces the why of double-entry; in the current paradigm it is expressed in the balance sheet and the accounting equation as well as in the double-entry technique.

It is difficult to conceive of any purpose or excuse for intentionally making a record which has no reference or relevance to the future. When records are made without regard to the future, they are a residue – in a sense, an accidental residue – of an activity which it was not intended to record. Such are the tracks left by a living creature when it moves about (for instance, the trail of a snail as it goes about its nocturnal business of making a living) or the fossilized remains of a creature long dead. But if a record is intentionally made, its purpose or objective has, it seems inevitably, a prospective use.

Original accounting records initially belong to this category. They are implicitly, if not explicitly, directed towards future use and relevance. If one records, say, a loan to somebody, the record acts as a reminder of the identity of the borrower, the amount or object borrowed, perhaps the date of the loan and its duration, its circumstances and/or conditions. It serves as a guide to future action, and as evidence, if evidence be required, in such action. In a sense, the function of recording in accounting is based (i) on trust, in that some aspect of an activity between different people lies in the future, and (ii) on the fallibility of human memory, in that if differences of recollection or disagreements between parties arise, the record is available as evidence of expressed intention at the time the inter-personal activity took place. It is neither necessary nor fruitful to engage in any long polemical discussion about different interpretations of symbols, unless people are apt to misread or mistake the symbols or are misled into saying what they do not mean or into not saying what they do mean. It would be welcome if the endeavours of Ijiri, Mattessich and some others who have followed them were to become practicable, but we do not see a clear path to satisfactory development in that direction. Rather, we think the direction we point to is more likely to produce a successful outcome in the world of human activity with which we strongly believe accounting is, and, even more significantly, accountants are, concerned and involved.

The double-entry syndrome

History is always tentative. For instance, in accounting, double entry is and has been for some time the prevailing set of parameters. Accountants do what they have been taught to do; they act and continue to act within the constrictions provided by their education, training, intellectual capacity and vision. And, in their education and training, observance of the double-entry parameters has been the very foundation of their vocational development. This may not be a matter of great concern, but at least it should be recognized and openly admitted. For a long time now accounting has had a relationship of identity with double entry. The idea of an accountant not being thoroughly acquainted with and capable of operating a double-entry procedure is virtually unthinkable. This does not mean that accounting is not recognized as being much more than a knowledge of and a capacity to apply double-entry procedures, but it does mean that whatever further knowledge or capacity accountants have or are thought to have is additional to, and in some way dependent on, their thorough absorption of (and with?) double entry. There seem to be no recorded cases of anybody discovering double entry as a natural phenomenon; it has always been transmitted from one person to another, whether through text-book, lecture, personal instruction, or demonstration.

In his discussion of double entry, Spengler seems to have been less than meticulous about some of his facts, e.g. in ascribing its invention to Pacioli (Spengler 1926, II: 490), and he seems to have adopted the Sombartian thesis of the enormous influence of double entry in the development of capitalism. Double entry as a bookkeeping procedure can provide a superficial appearance of accuracy but no system is better than the data put into it. Perhaps the real points are that the application of double entry is symptomatic of a change of attitude towards business or financial dealings and that it became in due course an instrument through which businessmen and governments could be provided with what they considered to be information useful for their financial decisions. Perhaps the basic information required for this purpose could be derived from non-double-entry records but the elegance of the double-entry system might well have appealed to many (e.g. Stevin, Goethe, Pacioli himself). The notion of capital is surely basic to capitalism.

However, there are suggestions that many of the available early instances of Italian accounting point to the activities of groups of people acting together for commercial purposes (or, perhaps more specifically, such purposes as we nowadays regard as commercial, but which they may have linked to social or even religious objectives). Indeed, it has been pointed out (Lopez and Raymond 1955: 403n) that the word commonly used for an accounting (*ragione*) 'was used promiscuously in different meanings', one of which was that of a partnership (*compagnia*), while another, based on these two, was that of a fiscal period, that is, the period (often more than a year) when an accounting for a partnership would be carried out. Such a periodic accounting would be significant principally because of a perception that capital investment was enhanced by profitable and depleted by unprofitable transactions.

As already mentioned, double entry seems to have come into its own in the nineteenth century, although its applications were known for some centuries before that; its widespread use was an accompaniment of the rise of the accounting profession in the western communities. In the twentieth century some of its limitations and deficiencies have become noticeable.

The process of double-entry recording acts as an instrument of categorization. It helps to produce an appearance of order in, to use K.J.W. Craik's colourful expression (Craik 1943: 3), 'the untidy tangle of experience'. If we use it, we are able to select common characteristics of unique occurrences and classify them accordingly. But there are restrictions on the selection of categories for classification which constitute a basic deficiency for some purposes. For instance, a sale on credit would be recorded as:

Jan 15   Debtor (or Accounts Receivable) $ . . .

             Sales $ . . .

This expresses the selection of the date of the occurrence, the 'outside' party affected by it, the monetary amount involved, and its presumed relevant 'nature'. All the occurrences of a given day (or other period) require separate similar or analogous instrumentation equivalent to the above (however streamlined the recording system may be). Modern developments have increased the speed and quantity in handling such entries, but the information selected for processing is still much the same as it was decades ago. The use of a matrix, for instance, does not avoid posing the basic question in relation to each occurrence and the arrangement of 'account' headings in the rows and columns: What determines a debit and what a credit? Or 'in' and 'out'? Or plus and minus? Or black and red? Or whatever other contrast one may wish to use.

However, in addition to the characteristics noted, others such as time, location, sales person or department, cost of goods sold, quantity of each sale, the terms of sale, any arrangement about delivery, the existence of any legal or social constraints or warranties pertaining to the sale or the use of the goods, commission on sale, time spent in making the sale, alternative goods or other suppliers considered by the customer, and perhaps other characteristics are ignored in the double entry, and, if recorded at all, have to be handled outside an existing double-entry system. In other words, from each occurrence only a few out of many characteristics are selected in the double entry process. Even among the selected occurrences, the classification of data is limited, not only, in particular, by the adoption of a specific monetary unit as the basis for selection in the records, but also by an ignoring of some relevant characteristics that could perhaps be included in a different recording process.

While computer-based systems could perhaps do much to overcome such deficiencies, it is not likely to be successfully applicable within a strictly double-entry framework. Some kind of additional recording is probably required to handle effectively and systematically those relevant characteristics of occurrences which are not dealt with in any current double-entry system. An information-processing system is required with integrated mutual checks and balances within itself and including whatever relevant information can be derived from existing systems.

While much of the above discussion is directed towards the theory underlying double entry procedure, it also demonstrates that the procedure implies the existence of a theory of selection which warrants more examination than it can normally get within the theory of double entry itself. Simply by doing this the possibility arises of further developments in accounting by contemplating a selection of characteristics wider than those traditionally embodied in double-entry systems, but just as relevant as they are to the occurrences selected for current accounting procedures.

Further, it raises the question whether double entry is, strictly, essential and/or sufficient for meeting all of the accounting requirements of recording, reporting and interpretation of the activities of people in present-day or likely future communities. Even today such things as inventory records, share registers, plant and equipment registers, activity-based costing and the like are required and are used, outside the strict double-entry system, for recording characteristics which are not catered for within it. This is emphasized further in many organizations where double-entry records are only part of a larger data-base system which is used for recording characteristics of many occurrences.

The essence of the accounting process that this suggests lies in the practice of comparing, and of communicating results in the form of a balance. Instances arise in accounts, in which debits and credits are compared and a balance is struck; in a profit and loss statement, in which revenues and charges against them are compared and a balance of profit or loss is determined; in a balance sheet, in which assets and equities are compared and their balancing is tested; in a funds or a cash flow statement, in which sources of funds or cash resources are compared with the directions of their application and, again, their balancing tested; and in a cost/benefit analysis, in which costs, which may include non-financial outlays, are compared with benefits, which also may include non-financial gains, and a balance of net gain or net loss, often in non-financial terms, is arrived at.

This procedure comes down to (a) adding each of two 'sides' and subtracting the smaller sum from the greater, (b) the inclusion of 'relevant' and only relevant items in the comparison, and (c) consistent selection and measurement of all the single items involved in the comparison. The significance of double entry lies in its provision of a technique for articulation and in checks for mathematical accuracy. This does not make it of the *essence* of accounting, but it is and has been an exceedingly useful instrument in its contribution to the function of comparing.

Double entry can be seen as a special case of data processing, and double-entry records as one source (a very important, but not necessarily the sole source) of accounting information. Its usefulness and convenience arise from its character of articulation; its limitations lie in the assumptions necessary to make it workable. Indeed, in a sense, its very articulation, which demands a perfection of balancing, has created for accountants a syndrome – a bookkeeping or double-entry syndrome – which in large measure prevents accountants from distinguishing between perceived (or perceivable) occurrences and abstractions from them.

Double entry is, in a sense, a mechanical interpretation of occurrences and their effects; it is, in its small way, equivalent to, say, a Copernican interpretation of the stellar universe. It, too, is true or valid up to a point.

But, just as the successors of Copernicus have discovered additional forces to the purely mechanical ones of the early pioneers, so, too, is it proper to consider whether characteristics other than the 'mechanical' ones of occurrences can be discerned and explored.

Another analogy may be considered. There are aspects of the activities of a human being which do depend on mechanical actions and reactions of parts of the body, such as the movements of the joints and the bones. A skeleton is a lasting memento of the physical existence of a once-living being. But a human being is more than a mechanical contraption: chemical, biological and psychological influences are three other kinds which function in a human being. And, in a group of people, there are further social influences which are present in the interactions between humans, and these should, at least, be examined in any attempt to understand those occurrences which arise in inter-personal relationships. It is suggested that certain aspects of these inter-personal relationships are part of the subject-matter for accountants. For instance, the notion of ownership, which looms very large in the normal exposition of double entry, as in the recognition of both internal and external equities, is a concept of a social relationship. Again, modern accounting practice, although its practitioners aspire to deal only with objective and verifiable 'facts', is permeated with unavoidable value judgements. These arise not only in the attempts to place a monetary value on things owned or owed at particular points of time but also in the selection of characteristics of occurrences and in the occurrences themselves which are the subject-matter of the records. Even in the most ordinary of periodical situations, value judgements are required in estimating 'realization' values of such things as stocks of goods or debtors, in estimating the effective lives of multi-period assets and their residual contributions for the purpose of arriving at appropriate rates of depreciation, estimating an amount to be tagged on to goodwill, research and development or other intangibles, guessing at a fair and reasonable sum for transfer to protective reserves, and often many other decisions.

In a world of multitudinous, if not infinite phenomena, double entry is an abstraction into a coherent system of *selected* phenomena. Its essential characteristic is self-containment and this governs the basis of selection and measurement of the phenomena with which it is concerned.

Some of the deficiencies of the double-entry system are most noticeable when we reflect on the reporting of results which are derived from its closely integrated and articulated procedures. On a little reflection it becomes clearly presumptuous for accountants to pretend that statements can be prepared which purport to contain specific, inevitably accurate, values of things, regardless of numerous qualifications which need to be made in respect of each one of them. In other words, valuation statements can, at best, only be acceptable by some kind of consensus. The history of public discussion among accountants during the past several decades illustrates how difficult the attainment of such consensus can be, even among those who are regarded as experts by those outside the accounting profession. Indeed, in Australia, the current style of an auditor to express an opinion for corporate shareholders on the annual financial report is that it presents fairly in accordance with accounting standards (which are defined and prescribed by the setters of the standards and adhered to by the practitioners).

There is, however, one other possibility to contemplate. Most of the difficulties in the discussion have arisen from the view that the balance sheet (in particular) should be regarded as a valuation statement and that therefore it should reflect 'values', whether current or original or some other, according to the viewpoint of the protagonist. Now, behind these views is an implication that the balance sheet is sacrosanct as a statement of financial position (present and/or potential) and this sacrosanctity arises from a veneration for the procedures of double entry instilled into students of accounting from their first introduction to it as an area of study. It seems to be universally accepted by accountants that accounting has developed out of double-entry bookkeeping and that non-conformity to rules which constitute its application is unthinkable.

It is not being suggested here that there is anything wrong in adhering to the rules of double entry for the purpose of carrying out recording procedures in financial terms, or even for many aspects of the preparation of financial reports from time to time. But what must be recognized is that such adherence does carry with it some inherent limitations. For instance, in recording the acquisition of an instrument of activity, and especially a long-term asset, its price, that is, a specific measure of (financial) resources, is recorded as its cost. However, even at the time of acquisition this is only one of a number of possible measures of its value, which is not, in its essential character, singly and unequivocally determinable for even any one person. What is acquired is, say, a motor truck, or a factory building, or a white elephant; this is what is to be used, and the amount that is placed alongside its name in the book of original record is of little, if any, significance to the facts of either its use or its usability. Neither does any other amount that might subsequently be substituted for it (whether this be done within or outside the records themselves) have any overweening significance in relation to these facts. What is needed nowadays, and is likely to be needed in the future, is something analogous to an organic system, containing within itself a capacity of adaptation or modification to meet not only varying external influences but, possibly, also internal changes without losing its essential 'organic' or systemic identification.

The first step towards the development of appropriate statements may seem to some people to be a step backwards. It is a recognition of the complexity of the requirements and an acknowledgement (graceful, if possible) that the traditional accounting reports *cannot be made to answer* all the relevant questions that may be legitimately asked, by one commander or set of commanders, of another commander or set.

If, for a time at least, we try to think about reporting outside the frame of traditional double entry, some interesting prospects are opened up. It is important to stress that double entry is not being questioned in relation to the monetary recording process. At this point we are merely questioning its inevitable constraints for reporting purposes. If it is felt that a report should include information not contained in the double-entry records, that information should not be repressed; at the same time, neither should the double-entry records be distorted in order to include information that can be better provided otherwise.

There are two distinct but related aspects of the double-entry syndrome to explore in any search for improved or more highly developed information. The first is the possibility of using non-monetary units for measuring some of the relevant characteristics of occurrences; the second is to examine whether the truistic assertion of equality (between assets and equities) as expressed in the accounting equation needs to be unreservedly accepted. The former is discussed in the following section; the latter has already been addressed in Chapter 13.

For six decades or more accountants have ensconced themselves in a kind of security blanket in accordance with the attitude expressed by W.A. Paton in his classic contribution to accounting literature:

> . . . accounting is concerned primarily with economic facts – with values. Consequently a great many factors may be excluded from consideration at the outset. For example, the accountant is not directly interested in the weight, shape, volume, color, chemical constitution, or other material characteristic, of any land, buildings, merchandise, etc. . . .; in technical methods of production and other engineering data; in the number, age, race, or religion of actual or prospective employees; in the geographic location of the plant or the probable markets for product; or in the social or moral aspects of the Company's product and policies. Many interesting and important questions with respect to the nature of this enterprise and its relation to the economic community readily suggest themselves. But with most of these matters the accountant is only indirectly concerned, if at all; his sphere of interest and influence covers only certain especial aspects of the *financial* situation.

And in a footnote at this point he adds:

> This needs emphasis as there seems to be a tendency in some quarters to ignore the inherent limitations of accounting. The accountant has a specialized and relatively narrow field, and nothing is to be gained by trespassing beyond its natural boundaries. The attempt sometimes made by some accountants to express all kinds of hypothetical cost analyses in explicit accounting entries illustrates this misapprehension with respect to the true scope of accounting.

> (Paton 1922: 29–30)

Perhaps it is now no longer possible for accountants to close their minds to some of these 'interesting and important questions'.

Non-monetary possibilities

Some accounting writers have hinted at the possibility of using non-monetary units for measurement within a double entry framework. For instance, Jensen wrote in the following terms:

> ... Another tautology that accountants will agree is important is the proposition that assets equal liabilities plus equity... The usefulness and power of double entry bookkeeping is testified to by its survival since at least the fifteenth century and its continued widespread use. Viewing double entry bookkeeping this way leaves me believing that we do not thoroughly understand why it is a powerful organizing device. I am so used to thinking of assets and the claims on them, equities and liabilities, as a way of organizing thoughts about companies that it is hard to conceive of alternatives.
>
> (Jensen 1982: 20. He is using 'equity' in the sense of
> proprietorship claim, i.e. what we would regard
> as 'internal equities'.)

And in a footnote to the above he said:

> I'm left with questions like this: Why don't we organize our thoughts about the family through the double entry tautology? Perhaps one day these issues will be better understood
>
> (Jensen 1982: 20n)

The noted French writer, Balzac, may well have been a precursor of Jensen when he wrote, in relation to monitoring the activities of a gentleman's wife (and perhaps with his tongue in his cheek):

> Every evening, with the help of your friend the concierge, you should see that the number of people who have gone in tallies with the number who come out; and to make assurance double sure, by all means teach him to keep a visitor's book by double-entry.
>
> (Balzac 1908: 160. The book in which this appeared
> was first published in 1829.)

The notion of a spatial application was raised by another writer:

> It is, however, conceivable to set up a complete accounting system on a basis other than the monetary one. The idea is perhaps not very useful for practical purposes, but it would be possible to instal a set of books upon a double entry basis for, say, a building, using as the unit cubic content. The original 'capital' would be equal to the original 'asset' – total cubic capacity – expressed in terms of cubic feet. Goods stored could be accounted for in terms of this unit, the transaction involving an exchange of 'assets'. As the total cubic content of the building is

fixed, the original 'capital' would be incapable of increase or decrease, but this would not invalidate the accounting verity of the record.

(Goldberg 1944: 241–2, or Goldberg 1957: 30)

Paton, in pointing out some situations in which the accounting equation does not apply, instanced the individual human being:

> . . . the individual sometimes 'mortgages his future' and borrows sums for consumption purposes. A college student, for example, may have liabilities galore but no assets in the usual sense. Yet his creditors may consider him 'perfectly good.' The liabilities are capable of definite statistical expression in terms of sums due in the future. But there is no way of assaying the future assets. The student has a one-sided balance sheet. No equation statement is possible.

(Paton 1922: 485)

This passage may well refer to a past age of trust in one's fellow beings which is probably rarer now than then, and the credit rating of college students may be differently assessed in these hard days, but it is interesting, even if it may turn out to be somewhat fanciful, to take up his point as he put it. Suppose a student – and let us assume that he is a very ambitious student – acquires on credit $1000 worth of beer for the purposes of conspicuous consumption. At the moment of acquisition there would be the equation:

Liability (Creditor) $1000   =   (Liquid) Asset Beer $1000

After a period he finds that his holding of beer has been reduced to $300 worth, and he still owes the initial sum. The position can be set out thus:

Liability	$1000	=	Asset Beer	$300
			? Asset	700

The liability, obviously, cannot be reduced. To what kind of an asset can the amount of $700 be ascribed? It represents, of course, the quantity of beer consumed, describable, perhaps, as 'Accumulated Consumption' $700. In what sense, and this, presumably, was Paton's point, can this be regarded as an asset? An approach to an equitable equation (if such an expression can be permitted) can only be made by switching our quantifying capabilities to a different plane of characteristics, so as to get something like:

Liability – Creditor	$1000	=	Asset – Beer	$300
			Experience	700

If the student were a very convivial person, the 'asset' might be described as, say, Experience and Generated Goodwill $700. Clearly, if an accounting interpretation of the circumstances is required, it needs to be made in some terms other than the usual monetary symbolization.

It should be clear that, as things are at present, accountants deal in social fictions, just as lawyers and economists do, and to at least an equivalent extent. The practice of accountancy is based on assumptions from which a system is developed. The fact that the accounting system is developed in monetary units is due to the fact that so far nobody – not even economists or statisticians – has yet provided a satisfactory substitute for the monetary unit. Yet, the system which has been developed, and, as it has been developed, could be used with little modification in essentials and with any agreed unit of measurement.

Appendix to Chapter 14

When Mattessich argues for the formulation of an axiomatic presentation of accounting 'principles', he points to deficiencies in previous attempts to set them out, namely, that these had not gone beyond business accounting, and that 'the axioms were formulated independently of the whole axiomatic structure' (Mattessich 1957: 329). He goes on to state that 'the dangers of pressing a field of knowledge into the rigid forms of an axiomatic vice are not overlooked' (ibid.), but he does not say or suggest what these dangers are. Further, he states that despite these dangers such a purely formal method is indispensable and justified, without showing why it is indispensable or how it can be justified. He merely goes on to enumerate some 'further' advantages. We are thus left to agree with his exposition on the basis of accepting a few assertions made without cogent argument or assessable evidence.

His exposition of the matrix mode of recording is a lucid introduction, but when he presents his 'suggestions for an axiomatic basis of accounting' (pp. 340ff.), a number of doubts may arise.

His first proposition, which he calls 'Plurality Axiom' is that: 'There exist *not less than two objects*, all having a certain property in common. To the common property of each of these objects a measure is to be assigned' (p. 340). Some readers may have a slight difficulty in fully understanding what is meant here. First, the expression 'not less than two' may mean anything from two to infinity, but, whatever the number, all the objects have a common property. 'Infinity' is a human concept, which may have some mathematical usefulness, bearing in mind that mathematics itself is a collection of human concepts and has to be applied to non-conceptual circumstances to have any perceptual recognition or acceptance. One might wonder, for instance, whether it is intended to apply a measure to an infinite number of 'objects', and what kind of measurable property can be common to all of them. Perhaps some limitation was intended, despite the open-endedness of the expression. Raising this matter of infinity may seem like creating a straw man; the author may not have intended any such application. But the expression, nevertheless, is open to such a bizarre interpretation, and the straw man is no less tangible a concept than some of those which the author asks us to accept.

There is also the meaning of 'There exists'. What does the author mean by this? Is he asserting, with no more grounds than an implicit hope that it will not be questioned, that the reader should agree with something that the author has conceived in his mind and has formulated in symbols which he assumes convey the same meaning for everybody? The word 'exist' is such a flexible one when we consider it; so flexible that it is difficult to know what meaning a user is trying to convey. For instance, I see a book on my desk; I can say with confidence that it exists, because I can see it, and can touch it if I wish, and can feel the weight of it if I handle it. It 'exists' through my sensory perceptions of its 'properties'. If I turn my head away, I no longer see it, but I am confident it is still there, and that it exists, because I remember it; it exists in memory and I am confident that nobody else has come into my room and taken it away. But if I leave my room for an extended period, my grounds for such confidence may not be so strong; somebody may have entered my room and taken it away. I may still have some degree of confidence that it exists. But if the abstractor has gone so far as to take the book away in order to burn it or pulp it, does it still exist, even though it may still 'be' there in my memory? This may be old-fashioned philosophy, indeed, but it is not irrelevant when writers who aim at clarity have to use such flexible vocabulary. In one sense, of course, concepts can indeed be said to 'exist'; but is it the same kind of existence as that of a perceptual continuity such as we regard as 'physical' identity?

Hence, when Mattessich asserts 'There exists. . .' something or other, this can be valid only for those who think in the same way as he does, or, to be more precise, for those who assume that their interpretation of his symbols is that which he wishes to convey, and that the communication is successful in this sense. In other words, it is valid for those who in effect, agree with him already (that is, those who accept what he offers into their corpus of experience), or who accept the 'argument' that, because somebody can formulate (=express in symbols, including words) a concept about something, it follows that that 'something' exists or has a 'being' apart from but by reason of the concept in the mind of the sender or the recipient of a message. To paraphrase Descartes, 'I think of it, therefore it exists'.

The second proposition is titled 'Double Effect Axiom' and reads: 'There is an event which causes an increase in the property (more exactly in the magnitude of the property) of at least one object and a *decrease* to the same extent in the corresponding property of at least one other object' (pp. 340–1). One might question whether the addition in parenthesis is necessary since it seems difficult to see what any increase or decrease could be except to a magnitude of something; but this is, perhaps, merely a minor quibble. In a footnote he points out that 'increase and decrease, debit and credit, addition and subtraction, unless otherwise explicitly stated, are here to be understood in the absolute sense. That is to say, an increase, a debit, or an addition reduces a negative magnitude of a property but enlarges a positive one, while a decrease, a credit or a subtraction has the reverse effect.'

If we accept this footnote as it stands, we are tempted to relate it to the previous axiom, and ask: What does the author mean by an object having a negative property or a negative magnitude of a property? How can any 'real' or perceptible object 'have' a property whose magnitude is negative? What sort of property can it be outside of the abstraction of pure mathematics? Further, a decrease in the magnitude of a property, having the reverse effect of an increase, would increase its negative magnitude; one wonders whether this was designed to add clarity. Perhaps he was trying to cater for the difference between debit and credit, which is not the same as increase or decrease of the same 'property', but, rather, an increase of each of two aspects of an occurrence or a relationship.

To illustrate one of the possible dangers to which this kind of generalized formulation might lead, consider the following circumstances. Suppose we have three objects, a motor van, the wall of an office, and the cover of a book, which have one property in common, namely, the colour of pale blue, which can be measured in terms of the length of light waves which that colour is said to emit in certain stipulated conditions. Would an 'increase' of that property (or perhaps a 'decrease') to, say, dark blue for the van involve an increase (or decrease) in colour of either or both of the other objects? The change in colour could be measured, if required, in terms of the length of light waves. If there is any doubt about the answer, it would suggest that the axiom, as stated, is not of universal applicability; and restrictions to an axiom surely make it something less than an axiom.

Of course this is a non-sensible illustration, but it does point to the suggestion that the reader has to be willing to accept implicit restrictions in the wording of the axiom, or, in other words, be prepared to accept it because he or she already agrees with it, rather than because it contains convincing exposition in itself. The unit of measurement is the subject of a 'requirement' listed at proposition 31 (p. 346) which merely states that 'the unit ... in which the transactions and their remnants [sic] are to be expressed has to be set forth'.

Mattessich's 'suggestions' for a 'general and axiomatic foundation' consist of thirty-five propositions, comprising three axioms, seventeen definitions, eight theorems and seven 'requirements'. We do not examine these propositions further, except for one point.

One of the claims made by Mattessich for an axiomatic formulation was that it 'shows that a reality, namely what is called herein a flow system, underlies every accounting system'. (Mattessich, 1957: 329–30). 'Such a flow system', he continued, 'has certain properties and by reason of these properties is suited to accounting treatment' (p. 330). It is in this connection, he claimed, that the matrix presentation is of great help. It seems to be worth reminding ourselves that when we speak of a 'flow' in relation to accounting matters we are using a metaphor. In our perceptual world we can observe different kinds of 'flow'; without some specification, the use of the metaphor may be loose and limited. In most cases, the term is primarily associated with liquids, but it can also be legitimately applied to gases and to granular substances such as sand or sugar. Our exploration in this work suggests that any 'flow' of occurrences which accountants take cognizance of is more analogous to that of a granular substance than to that of a liquid or a gas. Each occurrence can be likened to a grain of sand and can be readily dissociated from any other, if need be, and does not merge and completely lose its separate identity in the totality of activity. The flow of sand does not affect the 'existence' of the individual grains. They may constitute a heap; they may be wetted and formed into shapes – temporarily – like sand castles (which, occasionally, is an apt description for some of the accounting reports of so-called 'creative' operators) which will collapse or disintegrate in due course as warmth and wind remove the liquid adhesive.

Mattessich, however, does not stipulate the kind of flow he has in mind. He does argue that a flow system is the 'reality' or the essence underlying the accounting system which is its 'form' of recording. He later defines a flow system formally as 'the combination and summation of several trans- actions (flows)' (p. 341), and recognizes two kinds of accounting system which he defines thus: 'A flow system for which all transactions are *indi- vidually* recorded within an accounting entity, such that the system matrix, and/or the trial balance and/or the statement(s) result(s) *directly* out of this recording process is called a *closed accounting system*' (p. 342). This appears to be a description of a double-entry system operating under a matrix flag, with a clear emphasis on the trial balance and the statements derived from it.

He continues:

> A flow system for which, because of technical reasons, the individual transactions cannot be determined and recorded, but for which an accounting entity is set up and for which, by indirect means, the system matrix and/or the trial balance, and/or the statement(s) can be con- structed such that:

$$\sum_{d=1}^{m} a_d = \sum_{c=1}^{f} a_c \pm \text{unexplained remainder} = \text{approximately} \sum_{c=1}^{f} a_c$$

> is called *an open accounting system*; $a_d(d=1\ \ldots.. \text{ m})$ being a debit balance and $a_c(c=1\ \ldots.. \text{ f})$ a credit balance at the end of a certain period; the 'unexplained remainder' is the observational error. (p. 342)

It does not seem to be quite clear just what kind of accounting system is meant here. It may be any which falls short of a double-entry system, but, if the 'unexplained remainder' can be treated as an 'observational error' which way should it be interpreted? That is, the formulated equation amounts to saying that the total of the debit balances does not agree with that of the credit balances; but which total should be accepted as correct or proper, and why? The unexplained remainder is simply to be ignored. And what sort of 'technical reasons' are envisaged?

15 The overworked balance sheet

> Many accountants have for the conventional balance sheet a feeling akin
> to reverence . . . it . . . remains the coping-stone of the accounting structure,
> proving that the foundations have been well and truly laid and the details
> carefully and conscientiously cared for.
>
> (Fitzgerald 1936: 74)

Introduction

The balance sheet is probably the most widely known product of the
accounting process. The expression 'balance sheet' is itself a technical
accounting term which has been adopted into the general language to
apply to a much wider range of statements of comparison than those to
which it is appropriate in its original technical sense. Many people appear
to believe that it can be applied to any statement of numbers, whether
financial amounts or not, which can be set out so that two sets of figures
agree in total. It is sometimes used as a social metaphor, for instance, to
compare costs and benefits related to scientific and technical developments. (Encel 1987: 4) Indeed, as an expressive term, it can be misused by
non-accountants wishing to compare any two sets of factors; for instance, a
journalist may set out to give a 'balance sheet' of some social situation and,
in so doing, display his ignorance of the metaphor he is using by referring
to debits on one side and credits on the other, exposing thorough
confusion between the characteristics of an account and those of a balance
sheet.

To a layman, a balance sheet is often a wondrous thing. Here we have a
statement which shows columns of figures ranged either (a) on each side of
a vertical line (actually ruled or to be imagined or, simply, the fold in the
middle of a double page) or (b) above and below a ruled or imagined
horizontal line. These figures 'balance', that is, the totals in the major or
final columns are the same, and this frequently strikes the layman as a
pleasing exhibit of numerical virtuosity.

When, as students, we found we had worked out a problem so that the
balance sheet actually balanced at the first attempt, were we not filled with
the pride of unusual achievement, and with a feeling of self-gratification in

our consummate (if, perhaps somewhat inconsistent and probably accidental) skill? Should it have been 'if', rather than 'when' we so worked out
a problem? The possibility of compensating errors did not arise to stain the
pure whiteness of our innocent pleasure; neither did it worry us whether
the figures had much meaning or none. They balanced, and therein lay joy.

A balance sheet has often been referred to as a 'position statement,'
emphasizing that it is a series of propositions about a social or economic
unit at a specific *moment*, by contrast with the revenue or income statement
which comprises a series of propositions about activities relating to that
unit during a *period*. Several metaphors have been used to describe this
relationship, such as the single, instantaneous frame of a continuously
moving picture, or an artificial interruption and assessment in a continuous
flowing stream, and so on.

A few points of history

To put our discussion into proper perspective, a short outline of the history
of the balance sheet as a technical document may be helpful.[1]

In brief, the balance sheet was developed from what used to be called a
balance account, which in turn was a device designed to facilitate the
opening of a new ledger – without errors or omissions – when the pages
of an old ledger were filled. The balance account was composed of the
debit and credit balances of accounts still open when all income and
expense accounts (often known as 'temporary' accounts) relating to a
period had been closed off to a profit and loss account and this in turn
closed off to some kind of proprietor's account. From this technical
bookkeeping function the balance account came to be regarded as a
statement of assets owned and liabilities owed by a unit, and therefore or
thereby a statement containing a number of financial propositions. When
the account was copied on to a separate 'sheet' of account balances and
made available for inspection outside the ledger itself, the balance sheet
came into existence.

The preparation of annual financial statements and their presentation to
members of companies arose when it became impracticable to allow all
shareholders to have access to the actual books of account. In England, by
the early years of the nineteenth century, it was common practice in most
charters, statutes and deeds of settlement relating to companies to include
provisions for annual submission of a balance sheet and income and
expenditure account for the information of members. Eventually, it became
compulsory for all companies formed under company legislation to do this
on a regular annual basis.

While the balance sheet is, in practice, clearly the product of a double-
entry system, the earliest writers on double entry (or the Italian method of

---

[1]So far as we are aware, an adequate, satisfying history of the balance sheet has not
yet been published.

debtor and creditor or other variant of expression) made no mention of a balance sheet, although the procedure of balancing was expounded. This does not mean that there were no statements setting out amounts for assets and liabilities at that time, but that these statements were not drawn from the balance account and therefore did not come under the *technical* definition of balance sheet.

Evidence of early practices of accounting are mostly fragmentary; however, in 1955 Raymond de Roover wrote about the then recent discovery of documents of the Medici bank including 'three *libri segreti*, or secret account books' covering a continuous period from 1397 to 1450, and, in addition, 'an unexpected crop of hitherto unknown documents including several partnership agreements and balance sheets' (de Roover 1955: 406). He also referred to another collection of 'the *libro piccolo dell'asse d'Alberto del Guidice e compagni* . . . a key book in which the partners recorded vital information which they wanted to keep secret' (de Roover 1955: 407).

At the same time he proffered the following criterion for the recognition of a double–entry system:

> At the end, do we have a real balance showing the owners' equity and the composition of assets and equities? Only if the answer is affirmative, is one justified in speaking without hesitation of books kept in double entry. (p. 407)

He also stated:

> The *libro piccolo dell'asse* of the Alberti Company also contains twelve financial statements – I deliberately avoid using the word 'balance sheets' – listing the assets and liabilities of the firm and ranging without interruption from October 1, 1302 to November 1, 1329. (p. 407–8)

His examination of these led him to conclude that:

> There is no doubt that these statements were drawn up at irregular intervals in order to determine profit or loss, which was then divided among the partners and credited or charged to their accounts. According to the secret account-book of the Alberti company, from one to five years were allowed to elapse between two successive settlements or *saldamenti generali*. In the meantime no partner was either admitted or permitted to withdraw. Even death did not automatically dissolve the partnership and the heirs of a deceased partner had to wait until the next settlement to receive their share in the equity and the accrued profits. Apparently each settlement was accompanied by a renewal or extension of the partnership agreement. (de Roover 1956: 124)

Whether such statements as these met the strict technical requirements to warrant their being regarded as balance sheets or not, they suggest that the notion of capital was not unknown to the bankers and merchants to whose affairs the emerging skills of the keepers of their accounts were being applied.

It should be recalled that that period was one of business expansion and population growth (prior to the Black Death of 1347–8 which ravaged Europe), and that, as de Roover put it, '[t]he trends . . . continued to favour the ascendancy of the "sedentary" merchant who, instead of travelling with his wares, conducted his business from the counting-house, used common carriers, and relied on partners, agents and correspondents to secure representation abroad' (de Roover 1956: 123). This raises the possibility that the need to prepare and provide mathematically reliable statements of position and settlement (such as would be available in a balance sheet from a double-entry system) was an active ingredient in the development of an articulated system of recording. However, it remains conjectural; the evidence available is not compelling as yet. Further, as de Roover points out, 'medieval bookkeepers often did not bother to trace small errors and were inclined to eliminate them to Profit and Loss' (de Roover 1955: 406).

It seems fairly clear that the use of a balance sheet as an instrument for regular reporting developed gradually. Hatfield, for instance, noted that 'The British East India Company prepared a general balance in 1665, but not again until 1685' (Hatfield 1915: 41); this does not necessarily indicate a balance sheet in the modern reporting sense, but it carries the possibility within it. However, William Webster, a 'Writing-Master and Accomptant', whose book on bookkeeping was published in at least sixteen editions between 1719 and 1779 (Yamey *et al.* 1963: 211), described 'The Way to make a Tryal-Ballance, or to prove the truth of your Posting' thus:

> Add up all the Dr. sides throughout the whole *Leidger* into one total, and all the Cr. sides into another; if both the said totals prove the same, the work is certainly right; for as no Accompt is ever charg'd Dr. with any Sum, but some other Accompt ought, at the same time, to be credited with the like value; so, if every Case be duly posted with its double Entry, the totals of the Dr. and Cr. sides must needs agree. But if upon such Tryal they do not agree, and no mistake is made in adding, you may be assur'd you have miss'd in posting, either by entering some parcel in both Accompts on the Dr. side, or in both on the Cr. side; or by entering only the Dr. without the Cr. or the Cr. without the Dr. or lastly, by charging the Dr. and Cr. with different Sums.
>
> (Webster 1738: 8–9)

Webster went on to describe the further procedure, namely, 'How to draw out the real Ballance of the whole':

> To do which, you must erect one more Accompt in your *Leidger*, or rather first on a loose Sheet of Paper, by the Title of *Ballance Dr. Per*

Contra Cr. to the Dr. side of which will be brought whatever *Money*, *Goods*, or *Debts* then belong or remain due to you; and on the Cr. side will appear all the *Debts* you owe to others; and by this, and the Accompt of *Profit* and *Loss* (which with *Stock* must be left open to the last) will all your other Accompts be even'd.

(Webster 1738: 10–11)

The Cash account, Goods accounts, and personal accounts ('*Accompts of Men*') are closed off to '*Ballance*' and:

all such *Accompts* as *House-Expences*, *Charges on Merchandize*, *Refusal of Bargains*, &c. as they are only particulars of irrecoverable Expences, or Disbursements which turn to no accompt, so they are all ballanc'd by *Profit* and *Loss*.

Lastly, when all other *Accompts* are clos'd, and only *Profit* and *Loss*, *Stock* and *Ballance*, stand open; to close them, first begin with *Profit* and *Loss*, and having summ'd up both the sides, and thereby found the difference, that is, your clear Gains, or Increase of Stock, ballance your *Profit* and *Loss* by charging it Dr. to the Accompt of *Stock* for the said Sum; then also adding up your *Stock*, carry the *Ballance*, that is, your neat Estate, to the Cr. Side of your *Accompt* of *Ballance*, which will make the total of the said Cr. Side of *Ballance* exactly equal to the total of the Dr. Side, and thereby fully prove the truth of the whole performance.

(Webster 1738: 12)

Finally, Webster shows 'how a new Inventory is to be form'd from the said Ballance, in order for the opening new Books':

As it is plain from the first view of the Accompt of Ballance, that the particulars on the Dr. side, are the several Items or Branches of your Estate, and the particulars on the Cr. side, the several Debts you owe; so the said particulars on the Dr. side, must in your new Books be all made Drs. to *Stock*, and *Stock* Dr. to the several particulars on the Cr. side . . .

(Webster 1738: 12–13)

Webster's exposition is interesting as showing what was presumably a widespread interpretation of current practice in the mid-eighteenth century in England. The short step from the 'loose Sheet of Paper by the Title of *Ballance Dr. Per Contra Cr.*' to a Balance Sheet showing assets, liabilities and proprietorship could be readily taken when the need arose.

The development of the joint stock company, usually under charter from the Crown in Britain and Europe, during the sixteenth and seventeenth centuries, promoted the preparation and distribution of a balance sheet to members from time to time; the period was not necessarily or regularly fixed as that of a year, but the custom arose of using it to inform stockholders of the financial condition of the company as at a particular date.

It seems likely that it was not until the middle and later decades of the nineteenth century, when large financial institutions in Britain were being asked by companies to provide funds for large-scale capital and other works for developing such structures as canals and railways, that the prospective lenders required to see balance sheets from potential borrowers as a factor in their loan applications. The balance sheet thus became a statement for analysis, and this, in turn, had the effect of greatly complicating and multiplying its implications. It was not long before potential investors were applying analytical ratios and measures, or, rather, to be more specific, financial analysts were using their professional expertise and perceptiveness to help potential investors in their decisions.

The interpretation of the balance sheet became more complex as its audience became wider and more scattered and as the stakes became greater. People applied their minds to inventing fresh instruments of credit and investment, until ultimately the structure of the operating organizations often became convoluted and spread to such an extent as to defy disentanglement in some instances.

Legislation and regulation became necessary to a larger and larger extent. There had always – or at least for a very long time – been some degree of legislation and regulation, but the story has so far always been that some people in the community have been able to devise ways of getting around or through the best provisions that the legislators or regulators can prescribe. For instance, for companies operating under the British and British-type legislation, and for those under the regulatory bodies of the United States of America and their followers, the requirement to adhere to a criterion of 'true and fair' or 'in accordance with generally accepted accounting principles' respectively has been exceedingly difficult to monitor because there has not yet been any satisfactory, universal agreement on what these phrases mean in specific instances.

Basic functions and characteristics

In its modern usage, the balance sheet is viewed as, above all, an instrument of communication, particularly between those who are responsible for the day-to-day activities relating to a given unit of operation and those who have, in one way or another, provided them with resources. It is prepared by or on behalf of the former as a message or series of messages to the latter.

Viewed from this angle, many points arise for consideration. The view of the balance sheet that is currently widespread, if not universal – at least among accountants – is that it is a representation of the accounting equation expressing the state of affairs of a specific unit of operation (ranging from each distinguishable venture of an individual human being to the complex affairs of a multinational conglomerate organization or a global governmental institution). It seems appropriate to discuss some of those arising in the preparation and interpretation of the balance sheet as it functions, or is supposed to function, in contemporary usage.

Since the two sides of an equation are required by definition to amount to the same quantities, whatever unit of measurement is used, the problems discussed in Chapter 13 above apply to the balance sheet. And, since it is, as a technical product, derived from double-entry records (whatever nomenclature may be used to describe them), it is also subject to the constraints noticed in Chapter 14.

One writer lucidly expressed the attitude of many accountants some years ago in these terms:

> The two sides of a balance sheet certainly agree, because they summarise balances which book-keeping has automatically made equal, but there is another way of explaining the equality. The assets side of a balance sheet is a review of the total fund of wealth under administration, described in terms of the concrete form it happens to take at a selected moment. The liabilities side of the balance sheet is nothing but another view of exactly the same thing, for it is a statement of the sources from which the same gross fund of wealth was derived or (what is the same thing) of the accountabilities which naturally arise in respect of its possessions. The assets are held partly because the proprietors contributed an original fund of capital, and partly because external parties have made advances, whether by way of cash, services or goods. From this point of view the balance sheet is not *made* to balance, it *does* balance.
>
> (Rowland 1934: ix)

Except for the omission of specific mention of proprietary contributions through retained profit (or better, perhaps, unwithdrawn growth in net assets), this expresses very well a positive approach to the balance sheet in a straightforward manner suitable for exposition to initiates.

The agreement of the two 'sides' or aspects of the balance sheet gives it an aura of precision and reliability which is derived from our human mode of thinking rather than from characteristics of the components or constituents themselves. There is little reason to accept that, say, a bundle of legal rights owed to external and internal claimants amounts to the same as a bundle of rights owed by others together with a group of machines, equipment, plant, buildings, and intangibles such as goodwill, capitalized advertising expenditure, and the like. This, of course, harks back to the problems of the accounting equation, which a balance sheet expresses. However, there are further specific matters that need to be discussed in its use as an instrument of communication. In the first place, two basic but separate functions or objectives may be distinguished, namely, that of a balance sheet as a custodial statement and that as a statement of financial position. The two are sometimes closely, perhaps inextricably connected, but they can be distinguished, at least functionally and conceptually.

As an essential part of any annual (or other regular periodical) report of a company or similar organization or institution, even down to a local social, sporting or charitable group, a balance sheet is required; it is usually envisaged as expressing more than one function. It is regarded, first, as a report of accountability; that is, it is seen as an answer by the governing body of an organization to its members' question: What have you done with the resources we (and perhaps others) have entrusted to your care? In attempting to answer this question the preparers are presumably presenting a statement or a series of propositions to an audience of current members, since former members would be presumed to have no longer any interest in the question and future members no right to any answer to it. In a slightly expanded but essentially similar interpretation as a custodial statement, the balance sheet can be regarded as being directed to providers of resources as a response to those people's assumed question: 'What have you, the managers, or executives, or directors, or representatives, etc., done with the resources we, the providers, have passed over to you for safe-keeping and/or deployment on our behalf?' The basic relationship involved in this view is that of trust (but not absolute and never-to-be-questioned trust), and the paramount need is for credibility, which underlies the requirement of verification and validation of the messages it contains. The relatively modern development of the profession of auditing has rested largely on this requirement.

Second, it has come to be seen as a statement of financial position. In this function, it is of interest (and sometimes of concern) to providers of resources, particularly those who have been, or contemplate becoming, long-term providers of resources, the essential question being that of assessing the security of the loan or investment and the likelihood that periodical compensation for the loan (interest) or investment (dividends or withdrawals) will be regularly forthcoming.

Third, it is seen as an instrument of analysis. This is closely allied to its usage as a statement of financial position, but other complementary and supplementary sources of information are sought, and the purpose of analysis may be broadened beyond that of purely and solely financial aspects of the behaviour of people and the financial results of their behaviour.

Complexities

In assessing the modern balance sheet, some of its complexities and their sources require examination. The term 'balance sheet' is here used in a broad rather than a narrow, purely technical sense; the discussion is not restricted to statements derived solely from complete or effectively complete double-entry records; it embraces, for instance, such reports as 'statement of affairs' and 'statement of assets and liabilities' which may still be used in relation to bankruptcy and trustee activities where double-entry or fully equivalent procedures may not have been applied.

In considering these complexities, we are not concerned particularly with the technical definition of a balance sheet. The kinds of statements we

wish to consider include those prepared by knowledgeable, expert accountants who know the difference between a balance sheet and a balanced
account, and who can recognize a statement of revenue and expenditure or
a profit and loss or income account when they see one, and are fully aware
of the distinguishing characteristics of a 'proper' balance sheet. At the same
time, we do not wish to exclude other statements, however and by whom-
soever they are prepared, which purport to convey similar information
which may influence the activity of interested parties, whoever these may
be.

Most modern balance sheets embody many complexities arising from a
variety of sources. The origins of these lie (i) in the perception, by the
preparers or presenters of these statements, of the identity and interests of
the users of the information in them, (ii) in the problems attached to
applying concepts and procedures of measuring the particular items
arrayed in the statements, (iii) in the classification, nomenclature and form
used in presenting the information, and (iv) in the need to comply with
(often complicated) requirements of statutory, regulatory and supervisory
provisions laid down by external bodies.

The common characteristic of all these statements, whether strictly
conforming to the technical definition of a balance sheet or not, is that
of presenting, or purporting to present, in relation to a specific unit of
operation, a comparison of assets and liabilities, together with a
consequential (if it has to be inferred) or inherent (if it is entailed in the
system of recording) difference between the totals of these two (group)
components.

It is worth recalling that the term 'assets', in the English language at
least, had a holistic origin, so to speak:

> The word 'assets' was adapted from the late Anglo-French 'assets,'
> which was derived through the earlier Anglo-French 'asetz' from the
> Old French 'asez,' meaning 'enough.' This in turn was the philological
> descendant of the late popular Latin 'ad satis,' meaning 'to sufficiency,''
> which the later Romans substituted for the more simple 'satis'
> ('enough') of their fathers. The origin of the English use is to be found
> in the Anglo-French legal phrase 'aver asetz' – 'to have sufficient,' viz.,
> to meet certain claims; from this legal use the word 'assets' passed as a
> technical term into the vernacular. In its original legal sense it meant
> 'goods enough to discharge that burthen, which is cast upon the
> executor or heir, in satisfying the testator's or ancestor's debts and
> legacies.' Its use up to the eighteenth century seems to have been
> rather restricted to this sense, Blackstone in 1768 describing the use of
> the word in the following terms: 'This deed, obligation or covenant,
> shall be binding upon the heir, so far forth only as he had any estate of
> inheritance vested in him by descent from that ancestor, sufficient to
> answer the charge . . . which sufficient estate is in law called assets.'
>
> (Goldberg 1957: 20)

If there was more than enough to meet the obligations to others, the difference would be an indicator, and often a measure, of what we would now call 'net worth' or 'owner's equity' or 'capital' in its sense of proprietary investment. (It may be noted, as an aside, that the word 'assets' in the English language was originally singular, but, because of the final 's' and its collective sense, it soon came to be treated as plural, and in modern usage it has, of course, the singular 'asset'.)

The origin of the word is instructive because it indicates that its early meaning was bound up with the satisfying of obligations. From this point of view, the concept of an asset may be regarded as a secondary or derived idea, rather than a primary one; the original positive or active idea was of obligations, or equities, while assets were thought of passively, so to speak, as the wherewithal to meet such obligations. However, a more positive connotation of the word has now long been in usage, and assets may be defined as those things which are perceived to have value. Anything in which value may be considered to reside, whatever its origin, may be regarded as an asset. Hence, if we were to aspire to being philologically faithful, we would never use the word 'asset' as a singular noun, because 'assets' is the 'goods or estate of a deceased person available to pay his debts or obligations; property or estate of an insolvent debtor; stock in trade and entire property of a merchant; sometimes *asset* is used as a singular – an item in one's assets' (Ogilvie and Annandale 1935). In its derivation, the word 'assets' embodies and cannot be separated from the notion of claim.

The notion of liability – that is, the idea of being in debt or under an obligation – arises out of living a non-solitary life; it is an expression of a social relationship; for the most part, it can be expressed in a specific manner and, usually, in a stipulated medium. In the culture with which we are generally familiar in Western civilization, the extent to which any one of us is in debt can normally be precisely and fairly readily measured; exceptions are rare. When we come to measuring the assets, however, it is often not so clearly cut at all. The resources acquired through incurring a liability may have increased or decreased in usefulness or in perception of their worth or may have been wholly dissipated, but none of these changes would normally affect the amount of the obligation to be discharged. With rare exceptions, the extent of change in the resource does not affect the amount of the liability incurred. Hence, if we are to adhere to the concept of equilibrium which is the very foundation of the double-entry relationship, of the accounting equation, and of the balance sheet itself, any such change must be reflected in either a compensatory equal change in some other resource or resources or a corresponding change in another liability or in some element of the residuary net worth or capital.

The direction and extent of these changes underlie many of the problems which confront accountants, both in everyday practice and in conceptual contemplation – which, incidentally, are often interactive. It is, to say the least, naive to think that these problems can be solved by a simple adherence to or substitution for a given unit or mode of measurement. Such a naivety is based on an oversimplification and/or underestimate of the complexities inherent in the approach and the procedures involved in the measuring process.

In considering the significant objectives in the preparation and presentation of balance sheets, one of the most important factors is the person or group of people envisaged by the preparer as the primary recipient(s). In fact, there are many classes of potential users and the potential requirements may be different between those classes. Further, within each class the requirements of individuals or groups of people may differ considerably.

By way of illustration, let us consider just a few aspects of this complexity. Suppose we regard lenders to, investors in, and managers within a corporation as three distinct classes of interested parties whom the preparers of balance sheets of the corporation would regard as legitimate users of the reports. Within each class there would almost certainly be individuals or groups of people (whether the members of each 'group' are in some contact with each other or not) whose requirements and interpretation of information purporting to be conveyed in a balance sheet would probably be somewhat different.

Differences between lenders would arise according to whether the loan is of monetary resources or goods – commodities for sale, raw materials, ancillary supplies, short-term or long-term consumables and possibly others – or services, such as labour, energy, professional advice and so on. In other words, any supply of goods or services on credit amounts to a loan of resources and is based on a fundamental relationship of trust between borrower and lender. A further obvious significant difference within this class would arise from the term of loan – whether payment or repayment is to be made within a short period or at the end of a longer period and whether intermediate payments, whether of interest or principal or both are to be made. Still further differences may arise according to whether a loan is secured by a claim upon assets, and if so, whether the security is a claim upon specific assets, such as a mortgage on a stipulated building, or a more general one, such as debentures issued with a general lien on assets. Even further still, some instruments of financing have been developed which partake of characteristics of both loan and investment, such as convertible notes by which the holder becomes a lender for a specified, usually long, term, and ultimately has the opportunity or obligation, according to the conditions of issue, of converting the holding to shares. So long as the holding is that of notes, interest is payable as on a loan; when and if the holding is converted to shares, dividends, with any attendant advantages and disadvantages, replace the right to interest. In some cases, holders of such notes have an option at a maturity date to convert the holding into either shares or cash repayments of principal.

These are just a few of the obvious differences within the class of lenders which suggest that some individual lenders may benefit from information in or derivable from a balance sheet which is different in some respects from that which would best serve other lenders or groups of lenders.

When we look at investors as a class of recipients, we find a similar heterogeneity within it. The people whose interests are usually regarded as coming within this class are the existing and potential shareholders of a company or corporation, partners in a firm, members of a cooperative organization or institution who have residual rights and obligations of ownership and governance. Consider the common example of a company and its shareholders.

In the first place, a distinction can be drawn between present and potential shareholders, according to whether their interests are long-term or short-term. Among the former, those who became shareholders at the initial stage of the organization's separate legal existence may have somewhat different hopes or fears (or both) from those who may have acquired shares at a later point from some of the initial shareholders. Even among the continuing initial shareholders, there could well be a difference in interest or emphasis between 'founders' of the organization, that is, those through whose positive and active endeavours the organization was inaugurated and those who, though otherwise inactive, supported the founders by contributing to the initial funds sought. The long-term/short-term distinction may apply to the future rather than to the past, and, for many, if not most, decisions about shares, the expectation about the movement in share prices is regarded as paramount for those who buy or sell shares or rights to apply for them. A person with a long-term horizon would be expected to consider the likely stability and growth of the investment held or in contemplation ('capital growth') whereas the short-term view would be focused on the likely rise or fall in the price of the shares within a short time. The situation is further complicated, however, by what obliges or induces current holders to offer their shares for sale. The circumstances affecting a long-term holder might be more serious personally than those affecting a short-term holder. The phenomenon which is often summed up in the phrase 'demand and supply' may be a vastly complicated one if it has to be analysed in a specific, practical situation.

There is, in fact, no such thing as the worth or value of a share in a specific company in any absolute sense (or for any other commodity, for that matter), even though there may be a market price at which anybody is welcome or obliged to buy or sell. Its worth or value is a personal and individual matter which can be determined only by each individual in the light of circumstances which can be fully known only to that individual. In many cases, it cannot be measured, often because no unit of measurement is available.[2]

While many of the short-term investors trade in shares as in any other commodity, namely, for the profit obtainable on a relatively rapid turnover, there are also 'investors' who may be termed 'predators' who target their

---

[2]Some further comments on value appear below under 'The Numbers and The Problem of Value,', p. 284.

share activities on specific companies in order to gain control or effective control for a takeover and subsequent absorption or dismantling of the target company. They may operate on a short-term or a long-term view, and may change their targets as circumstances change, sometimes retiring after causing considerable disruption to the target company. Since the intentions of a predatory suitor for a company are often not fully publicized when control is sought, the interpretation by such a predator of the information in a balance sheet of a target enterprise is substantially different from that of either short-term or long-term investors, or even of a rival predator.

As already pointed out, a balance sheet is intended and is usually presumed to be an instrument of communication. It consists of statements about relationships (sometimes complicated and/or multiple) between members (often very many) of a heterogeneous group of people regarding a variety (often a great variety) of objects. Since communication is about sharing of meaning, it is not irrelevant to ask: What essential meaning, if any, does the balance sheet have?

As already mentioned, the balance sheet is an expression (including measurements) of the accounting equation $A=E$ or $A=L+P$. The acceptance of the equation (by accountants and, perhaps, by others) is largely a matter of faith, and this, in a sense, warrants accounting being regarded as a semi-religious procedure, becoming almost a matter of ritual, in which attempts are made to justify acceptance of the equation as its basic tenet. For example, it may be argued that an asset has two aspects, namely, (a) the 'thing in itself' and (b) any claim(s) against it. These claims are those of ownership or indebtedness, both of which are legal concepts, or, in other words, social conventions recognized by the several members of a given society. They are not necessarily inherent in the separate existence of the asset, but in the recognition of it as a relevant resource for people comprising the social group.

And the 'thing in itself', we are told by our scientific colleagues, is in reality a process of change, or a congeries of processes of change in its various constituent parts – a process of 'becoming'. Its 'permanence' is a factor of time: not necessarily an illusion (although it may appear to be so to some observers), but based on an acceptance of a human convention dependent on the human capacity to observe. As that capacity has been enlarged and supplemented by the development of instruments of observation, so has the interpretation of the process of change in 'things' been modified.

Can an asset be regarded as having claims upon it only if and because it has been in the hands of (or belonged to ?) a claimant before? For instance, has a creditor a claim because he had previously owned the goods or services (or the capacity to provide the services) by whose sale or provision his claim had been created? If this is universally so, then the equation might be expressed:

$$Assets_1 = Assets_0$$

the difference between 1 and 0 being one of time or location (or, perhaps, transfer of title). What if somebody finds a resource which had never belonged to any human or social person before? For example, finding a nugget of gold? As a thing in itself it would have existed in its earthy bed for unknown decades and centuries, but its recognition as a thing worth having or worth digging for could only be contemplated in imagination and hope until it was actually dug up; at that point it would become a thing which it would be worth having a claim to. The possibility of using it or selling it gives it a 'value' – use value or exchange value – either of which exists only because a human being somewhere can envisage a relationship to it.

If we put the figures aside and look at some of the items in a typical balance sheet and ask: What do they mean? What do they represent?, we find several points of interest.

There are physical objects, such as machinery, equipment, motor vehicles, buildings, and the like. We are concerned with physical objects; therefore we should try to examine how they 'behave': how they are operated, how long they last, for what reasons and how they are used, how and in what circumstances they are or are likely to be disposed of. But are we really accounting for physical objects as such? Do they only come into an accounting frame of reference because they are subject to somebody's rights in relation to them? The right may be one of sole or joint ownership, or of use or usableness – as a tenant or lessee or employee – or of custodianship, as in a trust.

Once the right to a physical object is established (or recognized), it becomes accoun*table*; often, when we think we are accounting for a physical object we are, in fact, accounting for a right in relation to it. The use of the object does not affect the existence of the right, neither does the process of its being used up. Not until the object is disposed of – by sale, or breaking up, or donation, or some other means – can it be said that the recognized right is given up. In the intervening period between acquisition and disposal, does anything in the 'behaviour' of the object affect the *extent* of the right?

This is not to say that it is impossible to account for an object as distinct from any right to it. For instance, it would be possible to have a historical record – even a financial history – of, say, a piece of real estate over a period of changing ownership and/or tenancy, with due attention to extensions, alterations, modifications, revenue, expense, and any other factors relevant to the purpose of the record. Such a history could, indeed, be a highly interesting and significant document of a changing society or culture. But underlying it would be an implicit acceptance – or at least a recognition – of the existence of a succession of rights relating to it.

Some of these rights may be external. For instance, if a property is leased or some equipment is rented out, the right to use it by tenant or hirer would exist at the same time as the right of ownership of the proprietor.

A further interpretation of the functions of a balance sheet, and probably one of its earliest, is that it embodies the answer to the question whether and to what extent the activities, the results of which it incorporates, have been gainful. This is a long-standing view of its usefulness and some of the oldest extant European accounting documents have been so interpreted, even pre-dating the established double entry records (de Roover 1955: 408). Indeed, even today, where a double entry system or its equivalent is not in operation, a comparative statement of assets and liabilities at two dates is often used to arrive at a reasonably reliable estimate of gain or loss during the intervening period. It is probably applied not infrequently in determining income tax obligations of people whose financial records are short of being meticulous. It also fills a need in bankruptcy and similar proceedings. Such a statement, if not derived from double-entry records, is not technically a balance sheet, but it is conveying the same kind of information and may serve the same functions of accountability and analysis. The basic concept involved is simply that gainful activities promote the growth of capital, while unprofitable ones erode it; this is what a statement of assets, liabilities and net worth expresses, from whatever sources it is derived.

It is difficult, and probably virtually impossible, to reconcile the differing requirements of such a wide variety of users in a single free-standing statement such as a balance sheet, even when supported by a massive body of ancillary notes and details. The greater the amount of detail provided, the more difficult and time-consuming it becomes, even for experts in the discipline of analysis, to arrive at an appropriate interpretation for specific use of a particular commander/decision-maker having to make a decision on, say, a shareholding in a given company. And to argue that any one set of numbers, based on one formula of measurement, will serve all functions and users equally well, is surely to fly in the face of human experience. Human experience is based on volition as well as instinct or, even, culture; and human activity can be predicted with safety only from a position of retrospect and hindsight.

If the balance sheet contains information, then presumably the information constitutes answers to implied questions. Are we asking inappropriate questions of the balance sheet? What do we want to know from it, and why? Questions such as these have to be put before it can be determined whether the contents of a balance sheet are useful. And the answer has to come from the user, not the preparer. For instance, it may be suggested, with some assurance, that any number applied to a long-term resource in a balance sheet is likely to be irrelevant, hypothetical or fraudulent in intention, if one knew all the facts. If a piece of equipment, a machine, a building, etc. is acquired for use, its acquisition cost is irrelevant after the moment of acquisition; the use made of it has no relation to its cost; its estimated replacement cost is only relevant at the point of replacement, and, between the points of acquisition and replacement, the replacement price is hypothetical; current cash equivalent, present value of discounted cash flows, and the like, are also hypothetical and often based on tenuous assumptions. The fact is that any number is fanciful: the resource has been acquired, it is being used as intended (or not, as the case may be), and is doing a good, poor or indifferent job of functional use. Any monetary – or numerical, for that matter – evaluation is based on a fiction, or a fancy, a hope, or a fear.

A balance sheet is often expected to serve as a statement of solvency. In this capacity the primary question is: To what extent are the assets adequate to discharge the actual and/or potential claims against them? If they are fully adequate, there is no doubt about the solvency of the unit under consideration; if they are not, he or she or it is insolvent, and the extent of insolvency can be measured or estimated accordingly. This is one interpretation which can be placed on the expression that the balance sheet is a statement of financial position as at a particular moment.

For a credit supervisor, for instance, faced with the responsibility of deciding whether a prospective borrower – whether of cash or goods – should be trusted, especially with somebody else's (specifically, the lender's or seller's) resources, what points would it be necessary to know and evaluate and, in particular, to what aspects of the borrower's balance sheet should attention be directed? First would be the relation of the amount of the loan (whether a cash advance or credit for payment for goods or services or provision of a bank overdraft or providing mortgage facilities or any other means of deferment of immediate settlement of indebtedness) to (a) the borrower's resources and (b) the lender's resources. Most people would probably be more willing to lend, say, ten dollars to any of their acquaintances than ten thousand, without some sort of security or even tangible undertaking to repay, or enquiry into the prospects of recovery of the loan. In relation to somebody else's resources, if the loan is a considerable proportion of the borrower's funds, a closer scrutiny of the mode of use and the profitability and security is warranted than if the loan is merely a small amount to avoid a temporary embarrassment or to acquire an ancillary but not highly significant piece of equipment. The purpose of the loan would be significant, for example, whether it is for private or personal purposes, for the acquisition of long-term assets in a business or for current assets, and so on.

Second, the submission of a balance sheet implies that the prospective borrower is engaged in business or has a business attitude. Questions that arise are: Who prepared the balance sheet? Has it been audited by a professional auditor of good repute? An affirmative answer to the latter would engender more confidence in the information in the balance sheet than a negative one. Any auditor's report should be carefully read, especially seeking any reservations or qualifications which might be significant in this context.

The function of a position statement often goes further than this. Behind the notion of solvency there lurks an implicit presumption of imminent termination of any activities other than those for meeting the requirements of claimants. However, there is the alternative of continuing activities which will permit not only the full meeting of current claims but also create opportunities and means of improving position. In other words, what has been known as the 'going concern' convention or assumption may be applied in interpreting and, indeed, presenting the information in the balance sheet. One of the most important considerations for the lender is whether the borrower can service the debt, by meeting the periodical payments of interest and any other agreed charges or repayments of the loan. The full answer to this always lies in the future; its assessment prior to the final answer is a matter of judgement. A single balance sheet would be of little use; a series of past balance sheets (and profit and loss or income statements) could provide data about trends over the past, which may be of some use; however, extrapolating from the past to the future may express a judgement of probability but it can never eliminate the risk that an unknowable future inevitably contains.

(Note: The presupposition of a business enterprise is one that applies for most practical purposes. There is nothing to prevent any person from having a balance sheet, but very few people in their capacity of private citizens do have one prepared. From an accountant's point of view this may be deplorable, but it is a social fact. However, in very many cases, a prospective borrower from a vocational lender is almost always asked for a statement of assets and liabilities, which is treated in much the same way as a balance sheet would be.)

Third, it may be asked whether the proposed credit is an isolated loan or is likely to be a continuing debt over a long or indefinite period. For an isolated loan, one balance sheet may be sufficient, although past balance sheets could well be helpful. For a continuing loan, a series of balance sheets would be almost mandatory, so that trends might be discerned and a judgement formed of the capacity of the responsible persons (for example, managers or chief executives and the like) to meet obligations and use resources efficiently.

Assuming these points to be covered, the things to look for in the balance sheets themselves or to be derived from them would, in most cases, be particularly directed to current assets and current liabilities, and especially the following:

- valuation of current assets, and in particular the basis of valuation of particular current assets;
- composition of current assets, e.g. cumulative proportions; trend could be compared with that in other similar businesses, if possible;
- quick asset ratio;
- working capital ratio;
- turnover of debtors; this would require figures for credit sales;
- turnover of stock or inventory; this would require figures for cost of goods sold;
- turnover of stocks of finished goods may be especially apposite in some cases. In this respect a measure of turnover derived from non-monetary, or 'physical' units may be more relevant to the discerning analyst than one based on monetary amounts.

With manufacturing processes, the period of 'gestation', that is, the time taken between acquisition of raw materials and final production of finished goods, may be significant in relation to the purpose of the loan. Analogous time cycles would be the time between final production and delivery of goods sold, payment for materials purchased and receipt from debtors for finished products.

In some relatively intricate cases, the long-term assets in the balance sheet would have analytical significance and attention would be directed to a ratio of profitability, such as, for example, operating profit to operating assets.

Littleton's argument on income determination appears to be largely based on his proposition that 'everyone concerned with an enterprise has in mind some variant of the question: "How am I doing?"' He is rather severe on the balance sheet:

> It may seem that results are reflected by many balance sheet items. Buried would be a more descriptive word here than reflected. For we cannot look at the balance sheet and distinguish cash derived from operating, from borrowing, from investing. The balance sheet reflects cash in hand as of the moment, but not cash as a result of efforts made. Useful as a balance sheet may be at times as a statement of assets available for paying debts, of debts awaiting payment, of net solvency (positive or negative) it is not dynamic enough to tell of the central theme of enterprise or to suggest the trying for results and the getting of results, some negative, some positive.
>
> (Littleton 1953: 35)

While the question 'How am I doing?' is a highly significant one, surely the question 'How do I stand?' is also highly significant. As he makes fairly liberal use of analogies, perhaps this one may be useful: A runner attempting a record run over a specific distance will unquestionably be interested in his several lap times, which may be called out to him in answer to his question of 'How am I doing?'. But, at the end of his run, the question 'How do I stand (in relation to the record)?' is the significant one. And is it not, perhaps, a fact that the question 'How am I doing?' is but a short way of saying 'How do I stand now compared with how I stood before?', 'Am I better or worse now than I was a week or a month or a year ago?'. The question 'How did I become better or worse than before?' is a further question. In other words, Littleton's question 'How am I doing?' is a compound one. It is not only a question of measurement of result, but also, if only implicitly, an analysis of the forces which have produced that result. As for the result itself, the announcement in the income statement has, so far as we can see, no superiority over the announcement in the balance sheet. But, on the second aspect, that of analysis, the income statement obviously and necessarily conveys information which the balance sheet cannot contain.

Classification

Some of the complexities of the balance sheet arise out of the classification of its component items. The onus of classification lies on the preparers and presenters. In relation to most 'published' balance sheets,[3] however, they are required to adhere to and comply with provisions of legislation, governmental regulations, rules of monitoring bodies, and so-called professional standards which often nowadays have the force of law.

A heavy responsibility rests on those who design and pass or proclaim these provisions – the responsibility of attempting to ensure that the governing rules do in fact make for the improvements in communication that are, presumably, intended. One may well ask whether, and to what extent, those responsible have undertaken empirical research, for example, among users of balance sheets, to justify the mandated rigid adherence to such regulatory requirements.

For instance, a typical modern classification for a public listed company is to group items under the categories of: Current Assets, Non-Current Assets, Current Liabilities, Non-Current Liabilities, Shareholders' Equity.

Some familiar definitions of these categories appearing in introductory text-books are:

> Current Assets are those assets that are expected to be used up or sold within one year. They include cash, accounts receivable, inventory and prepayments. It is normal to list current assets in order of liquidity, beginning with cash and with inventory or prepayments. All other assets may be classified as non-current assets. These normally include land, buildings, plant and machinery and similar assets not expected to be sold in the current period.
>
> Investments in shares and debentures are classified according to whether they are short-term holdings of securities, in which case they are current assets or investments intended to be held continuously, in which case they are non-current assets. Intangible assets are non-current, because their lives are normally infinite. Non-current assets are sometimes called long-term assets and, in some instances, they are subdivided into property, plant and equipment, investments and intangibles.
>
> (Martin 1994: 267)

This author also classifies liabilities:

> Liabilities may be broken up into *current liabilities* and *non-current liabilities*. Current liabilities are those that are required to be repaid within the current year and include accounts payable, dividends

---

[3]'Published' here is used in the sense of being made available in the public domain, or open to public scrutiny.

payable, taxes payable and sundry creditors. Bank overdrafts are usually regarded as current liabilities because, legally, the bank may demand repayment at any time. Non-current liabilities include all liabilities due for repayment beyond one year. These normally include amounts payable on debenture issues, mortgages and unearned notes.

(Martin 1994: 267)

Martin also expresses owners' equity thus:

Owners' equity represents the interests of shareholders or other owners in the net assets of an enterprise at any time.

Owners' equity=assets−liabilities

(Martin 1994: 155)

One complexity that may arise is that the period adopted as the basis for distinguishing between current and non-current items may not be as relevant to the nature of activities being reported on as some other period. For example, a business having a rapid turnover of merchandise and cash resources is likely to be operated on a much shorter time-horizon than one which, say, manufactures commodities subject to a long-term credit cycle and to a possibility of stockpiling, especially by customers. Thus, the activities of a wholesale marketer of fruit and vegetables would have a different physical and financial tempo from those of a manufacturer of building supplies. Again, the complicated structure of a conglomerate organization may encompass a number of different time-horizons for its several distinguishable component subsidiaries, which cannot be effectively embraced in an overall classification in the process of consolidation for presentation of the affairs of the whole group of enterprises, as is often required under law.

Another source of complexity may be that such a classification may be incompatible with the functional characteristics of some of the activities or transactions included in accounts within the particular category of classification. For example, not all accounts receivable are necessarily current obligations; some inventories may be non-current, such as parts for early models of products. Some investments may be short-term and held for quick realization when desirable, others may be long-term, and this for different purposes, such as for production of revenue, or for ultimate capital gain or growth, or for security of supplies or outlets. This is recognized, for example, in the requirements for listing set out by the Australian Stock Exchange, which, while not defining the categories, lists their composition thus:

Current Assets: (a) Cash, (b) Receivables, (c) Investments, (d) Inventories, (e) Other (provide details if material), (f) Total Current Assets.

Non-Current Assets: (g) Receivables, (h) Investments, (i) Inventories, (j) Property, plant and equipment, (k) Intangibles, (l) Other (provide details if material), (m) Total Non-Current Assets.

Current Liabilities: (a) Accounts payable, (b) Borrowings, (c) Provisions, (d) Other (provide details if material), (e) Total Current Liabilities.

Non-Current Liabilities: (f) Accounts Payable, (g) Borrowings, (h) Provisions, (i) Other (provide details if material), (j) Total Non-Current Liabilities.

Again, the temporal distinction between current and non-current liabilities is not the only important one for a potential interpreter of the information. The relative legal security of particular liabilities is often highly significant, and whether borrowings are specifically or generally secured against identifiable assets, and to what extent, may be vital information for making some decisions. Of course, this distinction can be made in the presentation of any balance sheet, but it is a complexity which involves a recognition that security of debts may apply to both current and non-current liabilities. For instance, in a particular case, while most short-term creditors are unsecured, one may be secured by a lien upon a specific asset, and that creditor would have precedence over others – perhaps even over secured long-term lenders – in sequence of settlement if occasion arose. The revelation of this situation is not necessarily or automatically ensured by adherence to the regulatory classification.

Further, there may well be an incompatibility between the temporal basis of classification of liabilities and the functional purpose of accounts. For example, some part of the balance of an account such as a Provision for Long-Service Leave would envisage, in many instances, a definite liability for the near future – and thereby would be properly viewed as a current obligation – while the greater portion may be properly regarded as a distant, and therefore a non-current, obligation. Again, the distinction could be made in the balance sheet as presented, but there is a complexity which requires the exercise of judgement, especially, for example, at a time of downsizing, rather than the application of a mandatory rule, for an appropriate and useful treatment.

The category of shareholders' equity (or any of its equivalent expressions) also has its complexities despite its non-subjection to the current/ non-current dichotomy. It is usually regarded as a residual claim of owners after all creditors have had their claims recognized and settled. From the point of view of a lender or prospective lender, this is a reasonable assessment of the net assets of a borrower or would-be borrower; the ownership claims are to be, and should in all fairness be, deferred until those of creditors can be discharged (to the satisfaction of those creditors). However, while this interpretation may be applicable to a statement purporting to display financial position, it should not be overlooked that a balance sheet also sets out the results of the activities of, usually, many people of diversified interests and circumstances. Some of these people may be the initiators of an enterprise or their successors (whether inheritors or purchasers of initial shares), others may be supporters, or successors of supporters, of the initiators, who hold shares issued after the initial inauguration of the enterprise. Indeed, the origin of shares of a particular category usually loses its significance once the shares are issued; a share certificate is merely an acknowledgement (and thereby evidence) that an entry has been made in the records of the issuing company noting the holder's existence and the extent of the holding. These people stand, in a sense, behind the item 'Paid-up Capital' as at the date of the balance sheet; but some may have been replaced on the following day without any effect on the item itself. That is, they are not necessarily the specific people who will be involved if the residual equity has to be determined in fact and amount, or, to put it another way, an alert analyst might detect signals from a volatile share register different from those of an inert one. But the shareholders' equity also embraces the balances of certain accounts which do not represent or depict the holding of shares at all. Reserves of various kinds, and retained profits, whether legally distributable at any time or only under specific legal restrictions, are also comprehended within this category.

It is important to recognize the positive aspect of this category. It may be regarded as the functional input from proprietors into the activities and resources being accounted for. The residual claim is only a convenient means of measuring or assessing the monetary amount of this interest; it does not constitute the concept itself or any analytical view of it. It does, however, constitute a complexity, in that whatever complexities are involved in either assets or liabilities are also effective in any residual derived from them. Underlying the separate categorizing of ownership interest, such as shareholders' equity, is the notion that the relationship of ownership constitutes effective control over the resources owned and being deployed. However, in many modern enterprises effective control is not exercised by the owners but by a relatively small group of people appointed by them, very often without any opposing nominees, whether at the outset or to contest a subsequent vacancy.

The ownership of a major shareholding (more than 50 per cent of the issued voting shares, for example) certainly provides a potentiality for effective control over the resources of a joint-stock company, but, if this majority holding is widely dispersed over a range of shareholders who have little means of intercommunication, a much smaller, minority shareholding can often be equally or more powerful in exercising control. In some countries legislation has been passed in recent years to provide some safeguards for shareholders whose interests may be grossly endangered in such circumstances. Even though the proprietors delegate their (ultimate) control of resources to a small group of people who act (and appoint others to act) in the name of the company and on behalf of those proprietors, the measurement of the residual equity is an expression of (conceptually) ultimate direction. This is usually little more than a fiction rather than what can be observed to happen. As already suggested, the composition of the body of people in whom this ultimate control is purportedly enshrined (as recorded in the share register) may be continually changing, as it is likely to be in a large, widely held public company, or it might be static and narrowly fixed, as in a closely held family enterprise, or anything in between. Conceptually, however, the ownership equity is a positive rather than a negative or purely derived function.

One of the problems in corporate affairs which arises from time to time, especially, it seems, in a bullish market, is the appearance of a few 'entre-preneurs' (or corporate cowboys) who, in a sense, revolt against the concept of the residual equity, even while making use of it. As entrepreneurs, they appear to adopt the attitude that their activities, often innovative and 'smart', give them a first claim on resources, many of which are acquired through extensive and excessive borrowing. The loans are frequently made on the basis of a pledge of assets which are often overvalued or, in some instances, non-existent. Nevertheless these few operators consider that they are entitled to a first claim on resources thus obtained. If, and while, their enterprises prosper, the other shareholders prosper, and the creditors are repaid. But if, as so often happens, they are hit by difficult times, it is not they who suffer most, for they have copious resources of which they have taken control, if not ownership, to meet their requirements; it is the creditors, from whom they have acquired the resources, and/or the other shareholders, who have the residual equity (which in many such instances loses much of its worth) who bear the consequences of their machinations.

The exploits and exploitations of many of the 'entrepreneurs' of the 1980s, as of earlier recurrent times since, at least, the South Sea Bubble of 1720, can thus be thought of as a revolt against the view that, by attaining a controlling interest in the conduct of corporate activities, they thereby inherited or assumed a residual equity in the assets. On the contrary, they seem to have developed the view that their strong position and/or influence entitled them to exert a primary and favoured claim on any resources that became available for their handling. As initiators of fresh developments or new directions of activities, they satisfied their claims by diverting resources (often cash through exorbitant charges for fees, salaries, proceeds of sales of assets, and the like), leaving the residue (often very little) to creditors and the ultimate shareholders. (Cf. Sykes 1994, for several instances.)

The numbers and the problem of value

In the foregoing discussion of complexities in the balance sheet, only pass-ing attention has been paid to problems concerning the numbers attached to its component items. In fact, however, these problems have been the subject of much open discussion over a considerable period, not only among accountants, but among and with others as well. And, indeed, it must be conceded, a balance sheet without numbers would hardly be a balance sheet at all or of interest to anybody.

These numbers are expressions of valuations, inevitably subjective in origin, despite attempts to portray some, at least, of them as being supportable by objective evidence. Putting it in this way may seem to be unduly stark and controversial, and it is admitted that objectivity may be regarded as relative, and that a degree of objectivity short of absoluteness is entitled to be accepted, for some purposes, as satisfactory. However, the notion of value itself warrants further consideration.

The problem of value and evaluation in relation to ethics and aesthetics has been on the agenda of philosophic discussion for many centuries, but, despite the extensive arguments developed over such a long period, the problems seem to be as intractable as ever and as little susceptible as ever to ready resolution or general agreement. It would seem that much of the philosophers' debate has been about whether there can be such a thing as intrinsic value; that is, as Russell put it: 'A thing has intrinsic value when it is prized for its own sake, not as a means to something else' (Russell 1946: 770).

However, in the somewhat restricted field with which we are here concerned, some further discussion may be useful. If, as we suggest, we adopt human beings as the units of experience, the question of intrinsic value can scarcely arise, because any value in a thing will stem from the relationship between it and a specific unit of experience. Relevance is an essential ingredient of value, and relevance is the expression of a relationship, of which, in any given case, a unit of experience (for us, a human being or a group of people) is inevitably a part. Nevertheless, there are still problems enough.

If we ask: 'What characteristics of resources (instruments of activity) do the users who deploy them take cognizance of?' we may conclude that unless the activity is that of exchange, and because their use involves retaining them, any notion of value-in-exchange, however expressed, is irrelevant. For instance, if, say, a machine is capable of producing 100 units in a normal working week, the important consideration for the deployer of the instrument is whether it is in fact producing 100 units each week. If it produces, say, 80 units in a given week, then the idle capacity during that week can have no 'value' on any significant basis because idle capacity is simply a term for a quite unproductive instrument (in the sense of *not producing* rather than of not being capable of producing).

If the notion of value-in-use is to be applied consistently, the question: 'How is an instrument being used?' evokes the suggestion that non-use is not 'worth' anything. If an instrument is not producing at all, or is not contributing in any way to the objective of the commander, it should not be 'valued' at anything, particularly for a going concern. To do otherwise is to put a value on imagined or possible rather than on actual deployment. No basis of value is truly relevant – not cost or realization, or scrap or current purchasing power or current cost or continuously contemporary price, or any other conceivable monetary measure. Since value-in-use is the relevant concept, if the use is nil, the value is nil for the deployer. To be sure, an instrument may have a possible future use, or it may have a current active use for somebody else, but neither of these affects the value to the present user at the present time in the present circumstances. What this means is that the 'value' of an instrument of activity which is not being used may be in suspense, in limbo, so to speak, until it starts being used again.

This thought has some interesting consequences. For instance, commercial goodwill, which gains its recognition as the difference between the consideration paid for net assets and their 'value' on some more or less orthodoxly recognized basis, fails to give an affirmative answer to the question: 'Can it be deployed?' It is therefore seen to be fictitious or, if this seems to be too harsh an expression, it is the cost of expectations which may or may not be realized in the future. The price paid for a business (or a sector of a business) comprises the price of the identifiable net assets together with a price for expected or hoped-for future performance; in other words, at best the cost of an uncertain hope.

If numbers were sought to express values-in-use for specific resources, it seems that they could fluctuate upwards and downwards according to changes in circumsances, many of which would be novel in accounting thinking.

One method of calculating value-in-use of a given instrument would be by capitalizing the 'value' of its contribution towards the objectives of the organization. Apart from any other difficulties in measurement (and these would probably be substantial), it would be necessary to re-calculate this for each accounting period; strictly speaking, it could not be forecast, and so could not be calculated in advance; hence a good deal of difficulty would arise in calculating costs of operation in advance for pricing purposes. Fundamentally, however, this is not so different from current practice, whereby, for pricing purposes, costs of various kinds are anticipated; where depreciation, for instance, is conceived as an apportionment of the difference between balance sheet values of specific long-term assets at acquisition and at disposal; its computation can only be accurately carried out in arrears and its use, if any, in determining prices is an anticipatory guess.

If prices are to be set according to 'what the traffic will bear', this would merely transfer the problem from the short term to the long term, for, if a producer of goods or services is to continue production over a long period without either continuous or sporadic external subsidy to avert inevitable insolvency, the revenue received from the products has to be greater than all of the costs incurred in their production. However, if the objective is altered, and selling the resource becomes a likely prospect, from that moment a number that measures value-in-exchange becomes relevant and valid. The change is a variation of a decision previously made and implemented or in course of implementation.

What lies behind the 'principle' or notion of value? Why does any one want to know what something is worth? Perhaps these questions should be raised before any measure of value is accepted and applied.

A considerable proportion of the writing by accountants on value is probably oversimplistic, abstracted and largely inutile. By adopting economic ideas of value-in-use deprival value and value-in-exchange but limiting consideration of problems chiefly to the last of these, discussion is unduly restricted to limits which, although possibly manageable in logic, are far from fruitful in practice. The problem can be illustrated by taking an example which may not be uncommon. Suppose a man goes to an art exhibition and is impressed by many of the paintings but (for simplification) in particular by two. One painting is priced at x dollars, the other at $2x$ dollars. The aesthetic value of the higher-priced painting is certainly – for the viewer – greater than that of the cheaper one, but he has no measuring rod which can tell him precisely whether it is more or less than twice. The significant question – in accounting as in economics – is: 'What is he going to *do*?' Is he going to buy one or both? If one of them, which one and why? To buy both he would need to have available $3x$ dollars – and suitable hanging space; or he might intend to give one painting away as a gift, or even to sell one or both at some time; indeed, his purpose at this point may not be and need not be characterized by precision, strength or inflexibility. (Note that 'available' here means that the money is in hand or in prospect and not committed to other purposes.) If his resources do not extend so far, he is faced with the choice of one or other painting or neither. To buy one painting, he has to measure, somehow and however imprecisely it may be, the difference between the aesthetic values (including such complications as feelings of pride of ownership, for example) against the difference between the prices. Whatever the decision, he may later be pleased or sorry, satisfied or dissatisfied with it; nobody, not even the individual concerned, can say at the moment of action what his state of mind will ultimately be, because it depends upon future experience. It may turn out that he would part with the acquisition for neither love nor money – or perhaps for love alone, or even for money alone. His tastes and appreciation of art may change – or remain constant or deepen.

The basic point here is that in a good deal of economic behaviour values other than the generally recognized 'economic' or financial values *are* involved, but they are ignored by most of those responsible for writing on and prescribing economic policies. Many of the consumption goods in a modern industrialized society are subject to choice by purchasers on bases other than comparative price. Consider, for instance, homes (land, location, building, gardens, appliances, furniture and furnishings), motor cars, utensils, clothing, entertainment; some elements of aesthetic value (using this term here in a broad, rather than a narrow, sense) or religious value or ethical value very often enter into choice of purchase. This is well understood by advertisers but presumably not by many economists or accountants who frequently seem to insist, rather narrowly, that economic behaviour is 'rational', and then are amazed or mentally dislocated when their prognostications of behaviour are not fulfilled. (Cf. Ijiri 1967: Ch. 2, and earlier discussion on aspects of this.)

Further, as Chambers pointed out (Chambers 1966: 42) value or esteem is oriented towards the future, not the past. A thing is valued because it is capable of being enjoyed in the future, because it is capable of satisfying some expected need, rather than because it has been enjoyed or has satisfied some need in the past. Even the award of, say, a social honour in recognition of past performance implies a continuation of those qualities which produced the performance, so as, at least, not to provide grounds for regret at having made the award. The social value of an academic degree, while it is a recognition of a course of activity satisfactorily carried out, lies in a presumption that the holder will perform in a manner acceptable according to the criteria of the members of the community in which the graduate will operate. There is, it seems, always a difference between the value of something and the thing itself, and the value is a characteristic that attaches itself, so to speak, to the thing by virtue of the way in which it is viewed by members of the society in which it exists.

Something may be valued for different reasons, for instance, because:

(a) it can be sold at a financial profit;
(b) it can be used to produce a recurring financial income or as a source of self-development or for pleasure;
(c) it can itself provide pleasure from:
  • being looked at and/or handled,
  • being thought about,
  • being played with,
  • being used in making or developing desired objects,
  • being displayed to others,
  • being thought of as a possession,
  • being a family heirloom to be passed on.

It is not a question of any one of these 'values' being *the* appropriate value of a resource as an objective 'reality'. Every possible value is subjective and relative to the owner's reasons and circumstances, and, at the same time, relative to the reasons and circumstances of each one of those who may desire to have such a resource. Indeed, we might even suggest that an oft-quoted proverb could be paraphrased into: 'One man's need is another man's opportunity.' It is of such sub-elements that markets are made.

In complex societies it is not easy to unravel the standards or criteria according to which things can be valued (we are not here talking about pricing), and, indeed, different segments or sectors or even sects within a community may well apply different standards and criteria to judge behaviour and attitudes; and this means that the members of such distinguishable groups recognize and accept, whether willingly or unwillingly, perhaps even whether wittingly or unwittingly, such standards and criteria as individuals.

The notion that something has value because it can be enjoyed was emphasized by John Dewey, who also pointed out the significance of the future in the contemplation of enjoyment in the assessment of the value of anything. (Cf. White 1955: 180ff.) To say that one values something is the same as saying that one holds it in esteem; there may be, indeed almost invariably there are degrees of esteem, ranging from low to extremely high, but it is not always easy to relate the degrees of esteem of *unlike* things to each other. For instance, one might hold the writing of one author in higher esteem than that of another writer, but may find it exceedingly difficult and perhaps impossible to measure the difference in esteem between the writing of a particular author and the music of a particular composer. To be able to do this one needs a criterion beyond the range of those used for judging one's esteem for either literature or music.

Holding, so to speak, something in esteem is, surely, a personal and individual experience, and the development of criteria applied in exercising a judgement involves all the educative (using 'educative' in its widest sense) and even experiential influences which have contributed to one's life from infancy; it is, in fact, one's whole education, formal and informal; it is, further, an expression of one's whole personality and character as it stands from time to time.

Considered in this light, no thing can be said to have any intrinsic value. That is, the notion of intrinsic value is meaningless, for value is always related to somebody or something outside the thing itself. If this were not so it would mean that something could have value whether it were esteemed or not by anybody; if it is esteemed by somebody, then, by definition it has value, but if it is not esteemed by anybody, what value could it have? Even if one were to go so far as to say that something is valuable simply because it exists, because it is there, its value would be dependent upon somebody being cognizant of at least the notion of existence. What this amounts to is that the notion of value or esteem is a human concept – at least so far as we, as humans, can ascertain. And the idea of value being divorceable from particular things ('things' here including actions and attitudes to which value is in practice applied) is an abstraction of human recognition, if not of human creation. Even if we admit the possibility that value can exist in some sense apart from an object, that is, that there is some kind of metaphysical value, a step downwards still must be taken from this metaphysics towards human perception before this idea can be of any use to people outside the world of verbiage. What value can a house have before its design is conceived? What value can a painting have before it is even sketched in outline? What value could an undiscovered masterpiece have before it is discovered? What value can a 'new' species of plant have before it is known to exist?

But is it true that the notion of value is restricted to human beings? Many cat lovers, for instance, would be aware of the preferences which their pets have for different foods; and the preferences of other creatures have been used in laboratory experiments with varying objectives. It may fairly be suggested that if an animal is able to express, by its actions, a preference for some one thing as against something else, then it is thereby expressing a notion, however rudimentary, of value. And, at the other end of the scale, could it not be fairly suggested that the actions of men and women, rather than the words they utter, constitute the true expression of the values they believe in and act upon?

If we recognize this, then it may be significant to note that value arises only where there is choice, even if the choice is merely that of 'take it or leave it'. (Cf. Knight 1921: 634). Any effective ranking of values obviously depends upon being able to choose (whether notionally or physically) between them, but behind this is the more elemental proposition that what has no alternative has no value. How, for instance, can we value the sun, the moon, the stars, the tides, the south pole or the equator, about whose existence we have no choice? To be sure, we can complain about what we call a sunless day, or a hidden moon, but then what we are really putting value on or expressing (negative) esteem for is an influence on our sensory perceptions of the sun and the moon, not the existence of the heavenly bodies. We can, indeed, compare a sunny atmosphere with an overcast sky, and prefer one to the other, and say we value one more than the other, but what we are then doing is relating not to the existence of the sun or even to the existence of the clouds that come between it and us, but to the sensory perceptions in us which result from this interposition, or to its effects on the growing of crops, and so on. This is not to say, of course, that a navigator may not value the north polar star more highly than the sun for purposes of fixing his position, but this merely reinforces the point that he is in fact able to compare the two with a specific objective in mind; for that purpose the two are comparable and *therefore* are capable of being esteemed or valued *by the navigator*.

When one says that one values something highly, or prefers it to something else, one does so because one thinks that *for oneself at least* it is good rather than bad and, indeed, better than the other thing. The question still remains: From what does one get one's notion and standard of what is good? It may be noticed also that among other terms or notions which are equally puzzling and equally relevant in many circumstance are 'beautiful', 'just', 'true' and 'fair.' In other words, the 'value' of any commodity or right is a reflection and often an expression of one's perception of one's relationship to it, either as an item of use or as an item of exchange. When a price is determined at which a buyer will buy, it is presumed that the (actual or prospective) 'satisfaction' which is to be gained from its acquisition outweighs the dissatisfaction of parting with the resources which constitute the payment, while, at the same time, the seller's satisfaction from the receipt (and prospective use) of the resources received as payment outweighs any 'dissatisfaction' from being deprived of the object sold. This presumption is widespread, but it is, in fact, no more than a presumption based upon a further presumption of freedom of choice in buying and selling. There are probably many instances in which either buyer or seller is not a truly willing or totally equal participant in a bargaining transaction at the level proposed or dictated by the other party.

The significance of the question can scarcely be overestimated, for it often governs the behaviour of people, both as independent, individual personalities and as members of a group or community. For, unless (and until) we understand whence people get their notions of what is good, or right, or proper, or beautiful, or just, or true, or fair, it will not be possible to vary them by any enlightened, as opposed to oppressive, means. And it must be recognized that this itself introduces at least two other value judgements, namely, the desire or intention to vary, and the basis for determining, what is to be regarded as 'enlightened'. Perhaps it is all just an ethical or aesthetic or philosophical merry-go-round which will go on turning and re-turning until the music stops. Who is to say at what point the music is to stop?

Another aspect of complexity arises when we consider that the notion of value in use is of necessity oriented to the future. We are all surely prone to discard, or, at least, neglect, those things we own or have access to which we consider will never more be of use to us in our future activities or situations. Even if we keep something for what we think are purely sentimental reasons, such as a memento of a past experience, there is some expectation that some feelings of pleasure will ensue *in the future* by having access to it.

It follows that there must be some doubt whether a so-called historical cost which is an expression of a value-in-exchange at a particular moment, can ever serve as an appropriate substitute measure of value at any other time. Time elapses during use; the period may be short or long, but at the end of the period what has been used is gone, it is no longer available. The usefulness that remains in an instrument is a future-oriented concept.

An expectation is essentially a subjective matter. What is the evidence of a person's expectations? We can expect something, and you can expect something, but, unless we communicate what it is that we expect, you have no means of knowing it. In broad terms, we might reason in this way: We observe what somebody does, and argue: He acts *thus*, therefore he expects *such*. We might regard this as 'objective' evidence; it is not what he thinks or even what he says he expects that is important, but what his actions reveal about his expectations. But there is surely a gap in the reasoning here that needs to be shown by expanding it a little: He acts *thus*. If we acted *thus* it would be because *we* had expected *such*. We presume that he is made in the same manner as we are, that is, that his 'rationality' is the same as ours or his criteria are the same as ours are. And therefore he expects *such*.

Suppose the price of a certain instrument is $100. An individual might reason thus. I am willing to pay $100 now for it because I expect it to last five years and to produce at least $20 per year's worth of satisfaction for me. A 'buyer's surplus' could arise in at least three ways:

(a) if I pay less than $100 for the instrument, but get the same satisfaction;
(b) if I pay $100 but the object produces more than $20 worth of satisfaction each year or more than $100 in total over the five years;
(c) if I pay $100 and get $20 of satisfaction each year for more than five years.

If the circumstances were reversed in any of these cases, I should no doubt feel aggrieved and subject to a victim's malaise.

It should be mentioned that deduction from observed facts to subjective expectations may be logically dangerous. We do not know what a person's expectations are at a particular time unless we ask directly what they are *at that time and receive an honest answer*. Even asking later may produce a *post hoc* rationalization, with elements of a corrective, rather than a completely accurate, recollection of the actual expectation at the (earlier) time.

If we accept a modern view that assets, and especially long-term assets are embodiments of expectations at the time of acquisition, then discounted cash flows have this much of 'truth' in them that they express an appreciation of the aspect of the future that is represented in an asset. To take this logically, we should at the moment of acquisition bring this expectation into the records. One suggestion for doing this might be something like the following:

At moment of acquisition:

Asset (estimated to last ten years)	150,000	
Cash		100,000
Expectation of Benefit		50,000

As time and/or use go(es) on:

Expectation of Benefit	5,000	
Depreciation	10,000	
Accumulated Charges Against Asset		15,000
Expectation of Benefit	7,000	
Depreciation	10,000	
Accumulated Charges Against Asset		17,000

etc.

What this suggests is that:

(a) expectations of people are important since they are presumed to govern their activities, and sometimes do so to a considerable extent;
(b) these expectations are always difficult, and sometimes impossible to quantify adequately or appropriately, but if they are regarded as reliable and relevant and can be measured they can be accounted for;
(c) what some, and often many, people do is not inevitably in accordance with what their optimum expectations would have them do;
(d) the expectations of particular people may vary as circumstances change;
(e) the expectations of different people must be different at any particular moment if exchange is to occur.

This constitutes a complex set of circumstances, and any attempt made or procedures designed to simplify it have innate dangers. The realization of a completely adequate solution may not be attainable, but the first step in improving the current state of affairs must be to recognize and admit the complexities, and not to ignore them, hide them, or hide from them. However, even if there is no ultimate answer, the question itself needs to be asked because there is still benefit to be gained from contemplation and recognition, or even rejection of factors which may contribute towards interim or tentative answers.

When we read or hear of the value judgements of others, or when we try to understand the arguments of others when they are writing or talking about value, let us realize that what they are giving is a personal account, arising from their personal experiences and attitudes, and not – at least in our present general stage of human development – objectively verifiable facts or results of something independent of and exterior to themselves. To the extent that one agrees with them or adopts their views, one is making their values one's own. But for one's self the important thing is the development of one's own views.

Further, there are for us, and we suspect that this is true for most other people, gradations in the status of things valued. We value some things more highly than others, but this relationship of preference may change from time to time.

Again, as already suggested, the meaning of terms such as 'good', 'beautiful', and so on, resolves itself into each one of us asking the question: What do *I* mean by saying that something is good or beautiful and so on? As soon as the question is put in this way, it seems obvious that everybody else has a right, and perhaps an obligation, to put the same question. Further, we have no right to expect everybody else's answer to be the same as ours or even close to ours, nor has anybody else the right to presume to say what our answer shall be. At the same time, however, in so far as one's answers have implications of actions which do or may affect others in a community, some rules of conduct which are derived from a common agreement upon at least certain aspects of what is good, etc., become necessary if people are to live in harmony with each other; the alternative is anarchy.

One's standards of what is good, beautiful and so on can probably be gauged from one's actions more and better than from one's words, provided we can interpret these actions 'properly' or 'correctly', that is, in accordance with the influences which motivate them.

It seems at least very likely that the formation and development of any person's judgement of what is good, beautiful, true, right and so on is not a simple and straightforward process. On the contrary, it is much more likely to have had many contributing factors which have exerted influences of varying strengths at various stages of one's life and which are, for most people, probably far too complicated and interwoven to be capable of a clean unravelling in their adult life.

When we allow such considerations as these to enter our minds, it becomes manifestly ridiculous to assert that there is any measure of the value of any thing that stands absolute and incontrovertible. There is no 'truly' objective value or objective valuation. The nearest one can ever get to this is a value to or a valuation by somebody else.

We reiterate and emphasize that the very existence of trade and commerce depends upon people having different values for things. The purchase of Manhattan Island in 1626 for an assortment of beads, cloth, knives and trinkets (*Encyclopaedia Britannica*, 1937, Vol. 16, p. 388) is an extreme, but by no means a unique, example of a disparity of values. And even when one buys something from a persistent door-to-door caller which one immediately discards as 'valueless,' there is something else which the buyer values more than what has been paid for the commodity itself, namely, the absence of the caller or the undisturbed pursuit of what one was doing when interrupted.

Value in this sense, of course, is thus not by any means the same as price. Clearly, a price for something results from the interplay of relative values assessed on some kind of graded and quantified scale. To say that the price of something is a good or clear measure of its value to the purchaser (or the seller, for that matter) is not only an oversimplification but a dangerous oversimplification in many instances. For it assumes (i) that the 'market' is a fully competitive one, (ii) that the purchaser and seller both have viable alternatives available to them (namely, not to buy or sell) and (iii) that the assessments of value or esteem can be quantified in such instrumental fineness and precision as to be measurable on a monetary (or other exchange-medium) scale. In fact, however, a price is merely a local, time-specific expression of an agreement between buyer and seller to exchange something which one has for something else that the other has; in itself it says nothing about the relative esteem in which either party holds either commodity. Any relating of price to value is done by inference and this inference depends upon assumptions made in the interpretation of this kind of activity. Such interpretation is fraught with the temptations and the danger of oversimplifying complex circumstances, and hasty generalizing from inadequate samples of specific occurrences.

When the function of reporting is put in this context, the question arises whether the 'values' of assets are strictly necessary or even greatly relevant to answer the question being asked.

One possible basis for evaluating long-term assets is by capitalizing the present value of the output of such assets. But the variables to be conquered are many, including foreknowledge or estimates of future physical output which must depend upon the future demand for the products, the prices of such products, selection of a suitable rate of interest for the discounting process, foreknowledge or estimates of the outlays of contributing factors of production such as labour, materials, power, supplies, and so on. The result would be a 'value' for all the assets contributing to a recognizable type and quantum of future output, but if the value of an individual instrument is required this could only be arrived at by making more or less but inescapably arbitrary allocations based upon some more or less but inescapably subjective judgements.

The notion that a statement of assets and liabilities (and proprietorship) is an efficient indicator of the financial position of the unit to which it refers can be *valid* only if the numbers attached to all items in it are consistent with each other. Even if those in any given statement are consistent with each other they can then be *significant* only if this consistency applies over time; that is, a double consistency is required.

It is probably manifest by now that the difficulties and complexities arising in the balance sheet from the problem of value are a reflection or a counterpart of those discussed in Chapter 13, where attention was drawn to some rarely examined aspects of the accounting equation. This is scarcely surprising since the balance sheet purports to express the equation. However, the question raised in this chapter is additional and complementary to any raised in that chapter. It is: What would happen if we were to recognize that, at least for non-current assets of a going concern, any monetary expression of their value can have only a somewhat specious validity for any but a particular use in any but specific circumstances?

Accountants are traditionally and inevitably concerned with measurement. Their vocational activities embrace the recording, classifying, analysis, interpretation, and verification of measured and/or measurable occurrences. They are not necessarily the initiating measurers themselves, but, even if it is not completely true that if something can be measured it can be accounted for, it is generally accepted that anything that can be subject to the accounting process has to be measurable and, in most cases, measured. The process of measuring involves identifying similarities of specific occurrences, activities and their results.

Some of the relationships that accountants attempt to measure may be as nebulous as any other abstraction in other disciplines; but some of these other disciplines do not have to face the task of measuring their abstractions, and, in those that do, the unit for measuring is usually selected for its adaptability and fitness in the measurement process.

Measurement is desirable as a guide to judgement, and, in a way, the accounting process can be regarded as an attempt to put some objective content into subjective judgement or, in other words, is subjective with an element of objectivity. Even in arriving at a value judgement there seems to be an implicit process of measurement. When we say that *this* is better than *that*, or greener, or more beautiful, or more godly, or more ethical, we seem to have in mind a concept of a standard by which *this* and *that* can be compared, and by which divergence from or adherence to the standard can be implicitly, if not explicitly, measured. Perhaps accountants need to be realistic enough to say, in effect: We can provide relevant information, but it cannot all be expressed in a single unit of measurement or reduced to a single significant figure. Some components of their message can be measured and expressed in financial terms, but even these may not all be reducible to a uniform or uniformly applicable measure.

In present circumstances, accounting reports are, for the most part, prepared on an assumption that all users make decisions on only one basis of measurement and that the preparers of the reports know, with certainty, (or are instructed) what it is. This ignores the likelihood that some, perhaps most, users would be interested in some other-than-financial measurements applied to a variety of activities and results.

The two-faced balance sheet, or The Janus of accounting

The balance sheet can be, and perhaps usually is, regarded as a statement showing the result of activities of people who represent or comprise an accepted unit of operation and thus a focus of attention for accounting purposes. This is true: it is the result of procedures which have been applied to record occurrences, transactions and decisions that have taken place in what, at balance date, is the past. But this is only half of its function. The ventures that are regarded as being wholly in the past will have been reported in the income statement; the results of ventures which are shown in the balance sheet are those about which some expectations in the future are also held. That is, the balance sheet has a forward-looking as well as a backward-looking aspect.

Many accounting writers say that a balance sheet is a statement as at a point of time, which its title usually specifies. However, it should be recognized that that point of time, while it is the last (or latest) of a series of prior points, is also the first (or earliest) of a series of subsequent points. It is upon this perception that the notion of flows of occurrences or trans-actions is founded, and from which similes and metaphors for the balance sheet are derived. The items in a balance sheet, while they do represent the results of past activities, at the same time represent something about the future. As one writer put it many years ago:

> 'Assets are valuable on account of the future services they will render. Their market value is an appraisal of the present worth of those services. Even a relic (prized only for its past associations) really is valued for its future services as a means of preserving memory of the past – perhaps as a means of preserving a tradition.'
>
> (Scott 1925: 199)

Every account receivable represents a right to a future receipt of resources. Every acquisition has been made with the future in mind; what we pay for something is governed by considerations of future use and/or enjoyment. Even cash is a right to future command of resources: cash 'in hand' is only a symbol of future activity; e.g. a dollar now in one's pocket may 'become' a loaf of bread in ten minutes' time. Every debt, once incurred, every acquisition, once made, every payment, once disbursed, every choice and decision, once arrived at, is a thing of the past and a matter of history. At the same time, each one has its relevance to the future. Both past and future are inextricably conjoined.

Consider some of the items. The cash shown in the balance sheet is the result, as it stands at balance date, of cash flows, inward and outward, that have taken place. If we started with $100, and $10,000 have flowed in and $9,600 have flowed out, the balance is $500 and is the result of these past flows. But it is also an expression of *future* purchasing power; it means that we can use $500 immediately after balance date as an outward flow without any additional inward flow; it represents immediately future cash-paying capacity.

Debtors' balances represent the result of past transactions with numerous customers – sales to them, returns from them, cash paid by them, discounts allowed to them, and so on. But it also represents our expectation or, even more strongly, our right to future receipts from them. This forward-looking aspect is explicitly emphasized when we raise an allowance or provision for doubtful debts or for discount allowable which, in effect, modifies the result by an explicit and more or less carefully calculated or estimated deduction. Similarly with an item like bills or notes receivable – a deferment of financial settlement; this item says, in effect: We can expect to receive so much in cash resources when the bills or notes mature.

With inventories of goods on hand, the quantity is the result of procurement and/or manufacturing activities up to balance date on the one hand, and disposal by sale or otherwise on the other, but it is also the quantity which is available for future use and/or sale. The amount is the result of applying monetary tags to this quantity; it represents goods available for future disposal. The 'lower of cost or market' rule has traditionally given expression explicitly to an implied recognition of a forward-looking aspect for this item, but only in circumstances in which a policy of caution has suggested that future expectations are less hopeful than the cost figure embodies – a formal recognition of an expectation of frustrated hope, perhaps.

The case of long-term assets is even more interesting. In the double-account system, as it was strictly applied to public utility concerns in the latter part of the nineteenth century (cf. Lisle 1903: Vol. II: 396–8), the 'capital' section of the balance sheet contained the 'fixed' assets as an expression of past outlays only; these were not depreciated and were never to be written off. But, broadly speaking, this system was first modified by the introduction of calculations for depreciation and then replaced by the now orthodox inclusion of 'fixed' or long-term or non-current assets as a classification within the same statement as current assets. The recognition of depreciation and its rationalization as an instrument by which the cost of long-term assets is allocated (or 'expensed') over the fiscal periods within their life of usefulness was an admission, albeit implicit, of a forward-looking aspect for such assets. For the net value of cost less accumulated depreciation to a given date represents that portion of the cost of the asset to be charged against future operations (as Gilman's, 1939, classification made clear) just as the periodic charge for depreciation is a charge against the revenue of the period under review. Even with 'historical' costs this aspect of expectation is not only present, but dominant.

Goodwill and some other intangibles, such as capitalized expenses, have always been problems. The cost lies in the past and there is no difficulty in recognizing this; but what can we expect of it in the future? Accountants have never been happy about quantifying expectations from intangibles, except for the purpose of calculating the amount to be paid – and received – for goodwill; various rule of thumb formulae – x years' purchase of profits for example – and refined arguments based on concepts of 'super-profit' (Leake 1938: Ch. II) were devised to 'measure' goodwill when some change in ownership of a business took place or was contemplated. But they do not seem to have come up with any completely satisfying treatment for it after it has been created; again, rules of thumb, writing it off over y years by appropriations out of or charges against income or profit, have usually been prescribed without much sounder justification than prudence or conservatism. So, too, in more recent times, expenditure on research and development has been difficult and controversial. The FASB ruled that it be written off ('expensed') as incurred, but with no very convincing argument to support the ruling. However, if one considers the forward-looking aspect of such items, it becomes distressingly clear that accountants have been dodging an issue; it has, in fact, been side-stepped because it has become too hard. For do we really mean that when we reduce goodwill to a nominal figure of, say, $1, or eliminate R and D completely, there is no expectation of future usefulness from these outlays?

Liabilities have been incurred in the past whether by trading, or by borrowing. But the very term 'liabilities' suggests the forward aspect: they express the commitments that have to be met in the future; they are legal and moral obligations.

Consideration of the recipients of the balance sheet substantially reflects this dichotomy of functions, in that some users look at a balance sheet as being primarily and directly an embodiment of the results of past activities, while others regard it as a collection of signals of performance in the future; some, indeed, expect to find both. Analysis and interpretation of financial statements is founded on an appreciation of this possibility; it has become a significant function of financial analysts and advisers, especially in the corporate sector of modern communities.

As already indicated, one of the objectives which the balance sheet is intended to serve is that of a custodial statement. From this point of view it is essentially a statement of accountability and should be regarded as showing whence resources have been provided for commander(s) and how they have been deployed, rather than as a valuation statement of what a person or social unit owns and uses. In neither case, however, is the balance sheet a fully satisfactory document. Its shortcomings as a valuation statement have often been discussed, but rarely its deficiencies as a statement of resources.

The total of liabilities and capital (or shareholders' funds) does not represent the total of the resources supplied to the commander(s), because the liabilities, especially the current liabilities, are continually changing.

The form of balance sheet which starts with shareholders' funds and proceeds to show how these are represented in terms of net assets is an approach to a better statement of resources in this sense, but still does not go far enough. For, in many cases, the resources supplied by creditors, particularly long-term creditors, are virtually no different in economic significance from resources supplied by shareholders such as convertible notes. Further, some items often included in shareholders' funds may not in fact represent any supply of resources; for example, an asset revaluation reserve. There would probably be little objection to including most reserves as representing a retention of realized profit; nor would there be objection to bonus issues which merely represent a capitalized form of realized profit. The statement might take the form: The funds which we have received or retained from shareholders up to date have been so much; in addition, we have received so much from, say, bond or debenture holders who have a first charge against the assets. The total of these is represented by assets less liabilities (other than the bonds or debentures).

The notion of solvency, discussed earlier (p. 277), is bound up with that of expectation, indeed, of anticipation: the indebtedness is expected to mature and become payable, and the assets are available in anticipation of demands for settlement when the expectation becomes realized. In this respect we should draw a distinction between a statement of liquidity and a statement of net worth or capital. While both net worth and solvency may be measured as the extent of the excess of assets over liabilities, the two are conceptually different. And while an increase in solvency is also an increase in net worth, and may arise from the same activities, such as an injection of additional proprietary funds, or profitable deployment of assets, and so on, the concept of solvency is one of a relationship with external creditors, whereas that of net worth is one of an internal relationship.

The point to be made, however, is that if the balance sheet *is* to be taken as a valuation statement and the figures in it are designed to give current values or some such thing, it would surely need to be supplemented by a statement of cash flows or a funds statement covering the period since the inception of the enterprise to permit the commander(s) to answer the investor's question: What have you done with my contribution of resources? And this would have to be in terms of initial and actual money costs, until people start to think in terms of purchasing power or some other kind of 'current' (but changing) units. In present conditions the shareholder would say: I put $100 into this concern five years ago; what have you done with it? Suppose the answer is: I invested it in assets that are now worth $350. This means that the $100 has 'grown' to $350. The shareholder might well say then: Yes, but in terms of things *I* spend money on, $100 then would buy what would cost $400 now; therefore you have not dealt as wisely with my investment as you might have done or should have done. Surely this is something on which each shareholder would have a different measurement, depending on (i) the time of the investment (ii) the nature of his or her consumption pattern and (iii) his or her attitude to risk. It is asking too much to expect one document to answer comments of this sort for each shareholder or lender. And what about the lender? Irrevocably bound by a legal contract to receive, in times of rising prices, an inequitable and decreasing payment in terms of purchasing power, should not this debt, for accounting purposes of equity (and, in a broader sense, truth?) be accounted for in some adjusted terms?

Pity the balance sheet!

Criticism of the balance sheet is not a new phenomenon. For instance, Randall expressed strong language in 1962:

> To forecast the future of a company by studying its financial statements only, without intimate knowledge of the personal capacity of those who constitute the management, is like prophesying the weather without knowing which way the wind is blowing. The balance sheet is the record of the corporation's past, not a guide to its future. The best of earnings statements may prove nothing but that the company still has momentum from what has gone before.
>
> (Randall 1962: 94)

Even within the current parameters of practice, if the purpose of an annual report is taken to be that of conveying to members of a company or corporation some assessment of its directors' capacity to direct its affairs, it should include some information on the directors' expectations about the future. It may, for instance, contain some evidence in their acquisition of long-term assets; the balance sheet or some other statement could enable a distinction to be made between the acquisition of new assets, representing an expectation of increased activity, and the replacement of old assets (perhaps at enhanced prices) to maintain the current level of activity. Further, any large increases or decreases in inventories, whether of raw materials, finished products or work in process, could be explained by relating them to directors' expectations. It should also be emphasized that human resources are usually far more important for the future of any organization than physical assets, and to assume or infer that because it is rich today it will be richer tomorrow is, simply, a *non sequitur* of which history provides numerous instances.

> The investors should never think of the balance sheet as anything more than one factor, among many, to be weighed. To begin with, it does not always give a true picture even of the past. It shows how much money has been spent, but not necessarily how wisely the capital has been used. It may, and usually does, represent imaginative and bold thinking on the part of earlier leadership. Yet it may be merely the mausoleum in which their errors of judgment and their timidity have been interred.
>
> (Randall 1962: 95)

We have certified public accountants who examine the books and reassure us that the securities which the company reports it holds actually do exist. We have no certified personnel inspectors who inventory the younger executives available to sustain the company's future, no certified public psychologists to measure the brain power and test the emotional stability of those now exercising leadership.

Often, in a particular corporation, there will be one man – and only one – who is widely known to the general public. Sometimes he and the company are so closely identified, both in his own mind and that of the outsider, that they are practically synonymous . . .

Certain it is that the annual report will give no help in distinguishing the prudent from the reckless among the officers, or the wise from the merely uninhibited. The names of all will be there, but not a statement as to their respective qualifications. You will find pictures of the new plant, but not of the new vice-president. Nor will you find any explanation of why he had to be hired from the outside instead of promoted from within. . . .

I am led to wonder, therefore, whether we are as far advanced in management methods and practices as we think. We concern ourselves so much with the question of financial solvency, and so little with that of human solvency.

Actually, a good balance sheet is like the foundation for a house. It is important, but nobody lives in it. Everything that counts happens above that level.

(Randall 1962: 98–9)

Pity the poor balance sheet!

It should be clear from the foregoing discussion that the burden on most of the balance sheets prepared nowadays, whether for internal or external purposes, whether for proximate or distant commanders, is a heavy one indeed. Reliance on any balance sheet as an instrument for conveying useful accurate information is, to a considerable degree, misplaced. The problem lies not only in the inability of people to forecast with precision what is going to happen, especially to values, but in the possibility that people should believe and expect them to do so. If viewed as a statement of values, it contains many inherent unanswerable questions about value itself, and is of little worth as a statement of accountability. If viewed primarily as a statement of accountability, not only does it not provide the answers for any particular user, but many of the numbers it contains are virtually irrelevant to any particular user's interest.

A so-called general purpose balance sheet is probably of little use to any likely serious user; it is naive pretence to claim that it is. Inevitably the user needs to make some adjustments in the course of analysis to suit specific requirements; claims for more and more disclosure reflect this need. However, for particular users, the more details that are disclosed, the greater the risk of inundation by over-supply of irrelevant, though specific, data.

As an instrument of communication, the balance sheet seems to be getting very close to the limits of its capacity to inform; indeed, many balance sheets have probably gone beyond them. The multiplicity and detail of notes is often now so cumbersome that even experts are puzzled, at times, to interpret them.

Pity the overworked balance sheet!

Part IV
Loosening shackles

16 Which way? Challenges and the task ahead

Che sera, sera;
Whatever will be, will be;
The future's not ours to see;
Che sera, sera.

(From a popular song)

Recapitulatory

In the foregoing exposition we have suggested that 'accounting' is a symbol used to represent what accountants do vocationally. In this sense it is a generalization, but not necessarily an abstraction, because, although it includes several distinct functions, each can be observed as a form of activity carried out by specific identifiable human beings, either with or without the use of more or less sophisticated instruments of practice. There are, admittedly, other senses in which 'accounting' may be used, but many of these lead to abstraction and distance from observable referents for practical purposes. For instance, to say that accounting is or has been a social force is to lift it up to a level of making a concept capable of engaging in activities which, on but a little reflection, can be seen to be only exercisable by human beings.

In applying our suggested interpretation, emphasis has been on the question: Why do accountants do what they do in the way they do it? Attention has been focused or directed to accountants carrying out activities as human beings.

In Part I, we suggest some broad, underlying propositions relevant to any discussion on accounting theory and practice. In Part II, we present our view on specific ideas (perceptions and concepts) pertaining to accounting theory and practice.

The functions exercised by accountants are directed to selecting and recording specific and identifiable activities of human beings, and the resultant relationships between people to which these activities give rise. Accountants prepare periodical and *ad hoc* summaries and reports of these activities and relationships, and often analyse, interpret and/or validate (or invalidate) them.

The process of communication and the characteristics of inter-human relationships are significant features of these activities. Both of these necessarily involve recognition by accountants that both they and the people whose activities they functionally deal with are members of a community as well as being individual human beings. On this view, since communication is an inter-personal function, the preparation, analysis, interpretation and validation of reports by accountants becomes a social responsibility. Hence, accountants need to be aware of this inescapable socio-individual relationship, which may be complicated in some cases, but whose complexities may need to be simplified to meet specific purposes (both individual and social).

The activities which form the subject-matter for accountants are the result of decisions made by human beings. While this has been recognized by many writers on accounting, a simple analysis of decision-making provides grounds for some emphasis on the important but often ignored distinction between the formulation of a resolution and its implementation through positive (or, in some cases, no) activity. We recognize, but do not discuss in detail, the several levels of significance of decisions. For instance, resolutions of vision or mission may be distinguished from those of, respectively, (a) policy which seek to define, with some regard to expected circumstances, broad thrusts of change, (b) strategy, whereby these broad thrusts are converted into more closely present conditions likely to be experienced, and (c) tactics which may need to be applied in immediate circumstances to bring about activities and results contributing to the success of the strategy, policy and vision. Apart from recognizing such levels, it is outside our purpose to explore them in detail. Further, not all decision-makers are policy-makers, although their decisions may reflect a policy determined by others. This seems to be what accounting writers need to be aware of.

Part III constitutes a discussion of what we regard as the current paradigm of accounting as both a discipline and a profession, demonstrating that it no longer serves the broader requirements of accountants in the changing social environment in which most of them have to prepare for and work at their careers. The current paradigm governing the broad sweep of accounting procedures embraces the accounting equation, which appears to be the natural formulation for presenting and explaining the rules for double-entry recording, the double-entry process itself, and the balance sheet, which is a point-of-time expression of the equation. These are examined in Chapters 13, 14 and 15, which point to an inadequacy of this compound paradigm to reflect some of the significant requirements for modern accounting.

In this final part we seek not to predict the future of accountants or accounting but to suggest possible directions for accountants to take if they wish to retain a large measure of respect as active and responsible members of a community imbued with an aspiration towards an elevated rather than a depressed quality of social and individual living.

The Case of the Tripodal Paradigm

The year 1994 marked the five-hundredth anniversary of the appearance in Venice of Luca Pacioli's *Summa de Arithmetica, Geometria, Proportioni et Proportionalità*. This work included the first extant published exposition of the procedure that became known as double-entry bookkeeping. The practice had been in operation in some areas of Italy for at least several decades before Pacioli wrote, and, indeed, an earlier work showing the rudiments of double entry existed in manuscript, though it was not published until 1573 (Brown 1905: 109n; Lopez and Raymond 1955: 360, 375ff.). So, while it was befitting to celebrate the advent of Pacioli's *Summa*, it would also have been proper to spare a thought of gratitude for the unknown person or group who actually invented or applied double-entry recording for the first time.

While double entry may not have been universally applied during the ensuing centuries, by the end of the nineteenth and, certainly, during most of the twentieth century it became part of a paradigm from which most of the accounting thought and practice appears to have been derived. Its most significant current expressions – the balance sheet and the so-called accounting equation – dominate the approach to so many of the problems which accountants and those who use accounting records and reports have to face that it seems at first sight impossible to question the conventional wisdom which they enshrine.

There are signs, however, of unease and restiveness with the current intellectual status quo. Ijiri has questioned the often-asserted claim of perfection of double entry, and he has explored the possibility of so-called triple-entry bookkeeping. (Ijiri 1982). By extending what he saw as the three-dimensional logic of double entry into a four-dimensional schema, he derived not only a formula for 'temporal' (based on time as a fourth dimension) triple-entry bookkeeping, which he rejected, but also 'differential triple entry' bookkeeping which incorporated 'force' accounts as a measure of dynamic influences on the phenomena and activities which comprise the subject of recording and reporting by accountants. We are not concerned with analysing and assessing Ijiri's propositions or suggestions; we are merely noting his expressed lack of complete subservience to the double-entry template (Ijiri 1982).

In the USA, leading practitioners and academics have been concerned in recent years at the relatively low social status of accounting as an academic discipline and the failure of the educational process to provide the kind of people capable of meeting the requirements of the rapidly changing world into which they graduate. One such practitioner saw the accounting profession as being faced with a choice between 'more debits and credits for the bygone industrial age' and 'decision support for the information age' (Elliott 1991: 7).

Some accounting writers have seen in the debate on price-change accounting in the 1970s an illustration of Kuhn's expository theory of scientific revolutions, and postulated the historical cost basis of valuation as the relevant paradigm. (Kuhn 1970; Wells 1976; Cushing 1989a). Cushing, however, cogently observed that the relevant paradigm for accounting was double-entry bookkeeping itself, and he observed that 'the flexibility of the double-entry accounting paradigm was one of its greatest strengths – it offered accountants and business managers numerous choices, and provided a framework within which most choices could be reasonably explained and justified.' (Cushing 1989a: 21) He outlined several indications of the unease which adherence to the paradigm has created in application. In his view, this unease has reached a level of crisis, which is 'not only severe, but possibly fatal to accounting as a viable branch of knowledge' (Cushing 1989a: 33)

In Britain, List (1986: 44–5) advocated replacing double-entry recording and reporting by using reports prepared from information systems which incorporate a broader spread of 'attributes' of occurrence, according to the requirements of the user of the information.

In Australia, a short comment in a professional periodical suggested that 'it seems inevitable that in the next few years a complete redesign and re-weighting of performance indicators will take place in the corporate world' and pointed to the need 'to develop and find acceptance for new ways of measuring performance' of companies or practices to replace 'income-based financial figures' (*New Accountant*, 13 June 1991).

Whatever other significance these indicators may have or may have had, they all point to an attitude of unease about the adequacy of the current generally accepted model that accountants vocationally subscribe to and follow. Much of what follows is an attempt to provide a direction towards the development of a new paradigm for accounting, both in theory and in application.

The discussion in Chapters 13, 14 and 15 hints at a diagnosis of palsy in the tripodal paradigm of accounting equation, double-entry procedure and balance sheet, which is manifested in an inability to meet the provision of social information in the culture in which it is currently widely applied.

The discussion in Part III suggests that the strength of the three-legged paradigm lies in its capacity to provide a logical and consistent present-ation of the results of activities of people and relationships between them at particular points of time, and by inference and with supplementary reports over any interval between such points, so long as a simple, identifiable basis for valuation is adopted and consistently applied.

Its weakness lies not so much in its inherent shortcomings, but in its inadequacy to cope with the requirement to accommodate different bases of valuation for multiple purposes. For instance, prices are often regarded by accountants and accounting researchers as objective facts which can be observed as 'hard' evidence, that is, as reliable phenomena for empirical examination. However, a price is a result of human activity and represents a contractual arrangement for exchange between two or more people. The arrangement says nothing about such aspects of the activities as the respective individual or social strengths of the parties, or the degree of exploitation or freedom between them, or any other circumstances which may affect them before or after or at the time of the exchange. The price may be as various as the amount paid for a specific commodity, an hourly wage rate, or a professional fee for technical advice, or an insurance premium, and so on. The uniqueness of each price is rarely acknowledged but the trend of prices is often taken to be significant by researchers who derive conclusions which often determine matters of policy for future activity. The conditions and human relationships between the parties to the exchanges which the prices represent are frequently ignored or overlooked. When the influences affecting prices can be implied from the change in prices alone, the inference is very like a value judgement, and can scarcely stand as much more than a personal speculation without some further enquiry into the thoughts and expectations of the participants in the exchange process. Accounting researchers are not renowned for much of this further enquiry. But it seems to us to be a requirement for any acceptable basis for explanation of price phenomena. For several decades, much intellectual attention has been directed by accounting researchers and practitioners to a debate which seems to have overlooked the legitimacy of different purposes of valuation, and the inadequacy of the currently accepted mechanisms to develop the required means to meet variant purposes.

If a particular purpose can be identified and clearly expressed, the double-entry system can probably be successfully used to express the single basis of valuation which this involves. But if more than one purpose is envisaged, or if a purpose cannot be expressed in terms of a particular basis for valuation, the extant double-entry system and its related components of the paradigm cannot be successfully used for any other purpose than to confuse the recipients of the resultant reports. In other words, double entry is adequate if value is applied consistently – but what is this worth?

For instance, the following are two examples of perfect double entry journal entries:-

(1) Buildings   Dr . . . . . .

    Asset Valuation Reserve   . . . . . .

  To vary recorded value in accordance

  with Directors' current valuation.

(2) Profit and Loss   Dr . . . . . .

    Buildings   . . . . . .

  To vary recorded value in accordance

  with Directors' current valuation.

Each entry records a judgement of the small group of people responsible for the activities of a larger group of individuals acting in a set of varied relationships specifiable by law and custom within a particular culture. The directors may have sought the services and advice of professional valuers, who in turn would have pronounced a judgement based on such things as the location, design, age, construction, condition, purpose of the buildings in question and recent market prices for similar structures. This may be expert advice, but scarcely objective in any strict sense. Whatever the basis for the entries, each can be introduced into the accounting recording and reporting system with equal ease and equanimity. Alternatively, the directors may have responded to their own expectations of what they think is likely to happen in the future, which, equally, can hardly be regarded as objective.

A brief comment on accounting research

During the last quarter of the twentieth century a 'school' of academic accounting researchers, who advocated adherence to what they styled 'positive accounting theory', developed and applied criteria of research based on the then prevalent economic 'rationalism' in the so-called developed countries of the world. The dominance of the views of members of this school in major academic accounting journals, found a reaction through the launching of several new academic periodicals in which contrary or critical views to those of the positive accounting theorists were vigorously voiced. The principal argument of both of these groups of people is set out in the introduction of respectively, Ross L. Watts to 'Developments in Positive Accounting Theory' and Trevor Hopper *et al.* to 'Some Challenges and Alternatives to Positive Accounting Research', both in Jones *et al.* 1995 (at pp. 297ff. and pp. 517ff.).

We do not feel constrained to pass judgement on the merits or deficiencies of these antagonistic groups of researchers. However, we point out that, in addition to these academic controversies, there have appeared in the non-academic journals signs of some dawning dissatisfaction with the limitations of the current paradigm for accounting practice. For instance, Clarke has outlined some measures of non-financial performance for managers, such as customer returns and/or complaints, number of repeat orders, percentage of defects in products, number of new clients, employee absenteeism, staff turnover, and the like. (Clarke 1995: 22–3).

If we regard 'accounting' as a symbol for what accountants functionally do, then it can scarcely be interpreted as a symbol for a science in any modern interpretation of 'science'. There is little point in pretending that, when accountants are doing their vocational work, they are working as physicists, biologists, geologists or astronomers do in exploring their subjectmatters and seeking out the knowledge which lies hidden from them in the apparent infinitude of unknown variables which seem to constitute our natural environment. This does not mean accountants' functional or vocational activities cannot be studied 'scientifically', but it does mean that those studies would come within the field of anthropology, and the appropriate methods of that science should be explored and applied to observe accountants' activities and seek what information can so be gleaned.

Accounting researchers may aspire to act as natural scientists act – and it has become a fashion for many in recent years to claim to do this – but while they apply what seems to them the methods of science, they themselves seem not to realize that what they are exploring is the activity of human beings whose statistical uniformity is one of artificial (=non-natural) categorization. Much research has, indeed, now been done in 'behavioural' aspects of accounting, frequently based on techniques used in the behaviourial sciences. The question of the significance of the behaviour of the selected subjects has not often been raised specifically.

There are important distinctions between the science of nature and the social sciences of human activity. For one thing, natural scientists often assume an inherent uniformity in the subjectmatter of their observations, and can either ignore or explain away departures from uniform applications of a hypothesis. When departures from uniformity are seen to be serious enough to command attention, a fresh hypothesis is needed. Under such a regime as this, knowledge of our natural environment has expanded enormously and at a continually accelerated rate in the last three or four centuries.

There seems to be an unavoidable difference when human activity is under observation. As human beings themselves, observers cannot avoid being aware that the objects of their attention are capable of self-awareness and can and often do act as having some freedom of will as well as ingrained instincts. While some human activity results from and depends on instinctive responses, much depends on the exercise of reasoning. As has been pointed out, rational and rationality may vary between people. To arrive at a satisfying explanation of human activity, we surely need to recognize this variability in the perception and, in some cases, the concept of rationality in human activity. For instance, to take once more the example of arriving at a price for an exchange, when *A* and *B* settle on a price, it may appear that they have 'agreed' on the amount. But if *A* is acting 'rationally' because his perceived alternative to accepting *B's* price is to have the commodity rot in his possession until it becomes completely worthless and he is then to be faced with starvation, while *B* can get a comparable commodity from another source at the same or even a better rate of exchange, is there not an element of value judgement in regarding the price as the result of rational activity of both *A* and *B*? To be sure, *A* is acting rationally to accept *B's* offer, because the alternative is a dire expectation in the near future, while *B* is also acting rationally because he is getting something which he can exchange later at an enhanced rate of exchange. Both are acting rationally, and the measurable price is the result. But the modes and sequences of thoughts have little more in common than the spelling of the symbol 'rational' applied to each. The experience of the activity – the exchange itself – reflects vastly different circumstances.

In doing what they functionally do, accountants are (perhaps inevitably) faced with value judgements and choices at many stages of their activities. One of the big questions faced by an accountant is: Do I make my own choice of treatment or one selected and/or laid down by someone else, with whom I personally may agree or disagree as most appropriate or adequate for the accounting treatment?

Another problem for accountants (and perhaps for economists also) is not so much to seek benefit from scarcity of resources, but how to make scarce resources more plentiful for all, everywhere. Without going so far as to assert that accounting is a social science, we believe that accounting is consistently concerned with social activities and that its records and all that emanates from them reflect social relationships between people.

At one level, the answer to the question: 'Why do accountants do what they do in the way(s) they do it?' may seem to be simple and straight-forward: it is because they are practised in technical skills of installing, maintaining and using procedures for measuring, summarizing and reporting activities and the resulting relationships of people, whether individuals or in groups, devoted to the pursuit of identifiable objectives.

This kind of answer, however, ignores some other socially significant questions. For example, why do accountants restrict their measurement to financial units? In applying their measurements, should they adhere to or modify any assumption of invariability in their units of measurement? Should accountants use alternative or additional units of measurement of the activities relevant to accounting treatment, and, if so, how can this be achieved?

We believe that issues such as these warrant earnest attention from some of the most talented accounting researchers.

Accountants in society

Many people regard their activities as being among the most important in their community. It is probably natural for anybody to consider that what is important for himself or herself, and that is almost invariably what he or she is most interested in, is and must be as important for all his or her fellows. It is not easy to separate one's judgements from one's personal interests. In this respect few accountants are better or worse than any of their vocational colleagues, whether they be lawyers, medicos, architects, musicians, painters, sculptors, politicians, manufacturers, farmers, educators, novelists, poets, electricians, plumbers, motor mechanics, or any other. Each has a hallowed niche; each occupies that niche with a developed sense of some self-justification, no doubt deserved.

In this respect accountants have not, especially in recent years in the more advanced economies, been untowardly reticent about proclaiming their contributions to communal well-being. The days of false modesty have disappeared, and public figures are often eager to recognize the con-tribution and laud the attainments of accountants. However, the relative significance of accountants in any varied group of people is not often examined dispassionately.

When accountants carry out their accounting functions, they are usually dealing with social phenomena. Although some accounting functions could conceivably be carried out by or for an individual living in complete isolation, this would be an extremely rare situation and, while it may have some conceptual characteristics of possible interest to a speculative philosopher, it would be of little interest or value to accountants in their normal environment.

The term 'social' is used here in the sense that what the accountant is 'dealing with' is a set of activities planned or carried out by some people in some kind of relationship with others. The 'dealing with' may include activities or functions which are separate in themselves and may be performed by different accountants or by one accountant at different times or on different occasions. Not only does the accountant carry out a social activity because of a relationship between the accountant and some other human being or group whose activities he or she deals with, but also because those activities are themselves expressions of relationships between people, and the task of the accountant is to deal with those relationships, some of which can become very complicated. It is significant that each individual lives and acts separately as an individual and as a member of a group or of several groups of people. Each person is, inescapably and simultaneously, both an individual and a social creature, and is subject to both self-concern and social interest. The recognition and assessment of both individuals and their social relationships warrant attention. In earlier chapters we have emphasized our view of accountants as recorders and communicators of information about activities of people in relationship to each other. Since we use 'society' or 'community' to symbolize and generalize relationships between people, it seems reasonable to regard accountants as having a social or communal function.

Relationships between people are not only multitudinous and varied, but are subject to changes and developments which often cannot be foreseen (except in hindsight). In their vocational capacity accountants are not concerned with more than a few of these relationships, but we suggest they may properly be concerned with more than they have hitherto traditionally regarded as their customary specific and constrained field of attention. Some of these additional relationships have been mentioned or hinted at in the foregoing chapters. It is appropriate now to bring some of these together and indicate some directions in which we believe further progress lies for accountants.

Desiderata for a new paradigm

If, as we have argued, the pervading tripodal paradigm does not meet current or prospective social requirements, what kind of paradigm should replace it? We suggest some directions for exploration of issues which may contribute towards its recognition and development.

First, a recognition that any present valuation of a commodity or service is based on expectation of future occurrences and circumstances. This is so pervasive that it gives rise to at least two specific desiderata:

1   accounting for alternative values;
2   accounting for expectations, i.e. accounting for assumptions and estimates.

Second, since the making and implementing of decisions comprise such a large part of human activities with which accountants are functionally concerned, continued attention should be given to applying current procedures to accounting for specific decisions related to the responsibilities of identifiable people. This implies directing attention to accounting for ventures, as envisaged above in Chapter 8 (p. 103). This may involve recognizing more characteristics of occurrences than are usually currently recorded by accountants. Measuring some aspects of the implementation of decisions may well require recognition of non-monetary units.

Third, appropriate attention should be given to cost/benefit analysis, in which the significance of non-financial factors are adequately recognized and given due weight in assessing business, economic, social and cultural activities and policies.

Fourth, it is desirable to provide, at appropriate levels of public availability, more information about human activities. While we see developments in this direction as probably inevitable, we hope that it will be accompanied by safeguards against any intrusive violation of individual rights. The amassing and provision of information is a developing phenomenon; it may become a force for great social and individual good, but it may also carry the possibility of misuse for private gain to the detriment of many others. This may produce problems of ethics which should be recognized and faced honestly as early as possible.

Since 'rational' thought and 'rational' behaviour are so frequently used in communication about human behaviour, another desideratum is a frank recognition of varying interpretations that may be applied to the meaning of such expressions and the need for consensus between communicating parties on its meaning for them in particular circumstances and contexts. Perhaps this may give rise to a theory of relative or differential rationality!

If these desiderata are given serious attention, this in itself will amount to a considerable alteration in attitude by accountants, in practice, in education and probably in social relationships.

Norms and regulation

Since the formation of professional groups of accountants in Britain in the mid-nineteenth century, the founders of such groups and their successors have formulated and applied criteria of knowledge and expertise for admission and advancement within the professional bodies, and for observing a code of ethics and etiquette (mostly towards other members of the profession). Some of these bodies have endured and prospered, some have merged with others, some have foundered and disappeared. But it seems safe to suppose that governing groups of each one of these bodies at some time found problems of defining and formulating their interpretations of what constituted professional ethical conduct for their members and prospective members.

Over and beyond this degree of professional self-regulation, there has been a relatively continuous development of legal regulation, through specific legislation and court rulings, some of which have influenced the applied techniques and approach of accountants in carrying out their professional activities. It is obvious, too, that accountants, as members of a community, are subject to any criminal law that may apply to acts or conduct proscribed by such law. In addition, aspects of accountants' performance are affected by regulation through governmental instrumentalities at various levels of government, such as city, municipal, state and union or federal jurisdictions.

From this it appears that modern professional accountants have been introduced to and are familiar with the notion of ethical behaviour and the application of regulation in trying to ensure some measure of it. However, some aspects of ethics and regulation do not appear to have been specifically raised for appropriate contemplation.

We suggest that the essence of ethics lies in the behaviour of self-concerned individuals in relation to other similar members of their society. In operation, this embodies a multitude of difficulties and, perhaps, even incomprehensibilities. For human relationships are often very complicated; the variable constituent elements may be numerous, and their modes of combination intricate.

The desirability of regulation – indeed, the need for it – arises, from the equally elemental human characteristics of self-concern and group membership. Even within a small group, the members can operate most effectively if relationships between them are recognized and communicated among the members and adhered to. Effective communication appears to be an essential ingredient.

It may be apposite to recall here that a truly solitary human would have little to think or say about ethical behaviour: he or she would have nobody to discuss human relationships with. At the same time, such a person would have nobody to compare his or her condition with, that is, no basis for formulating criteria for social interaction. Admittedly, solitariness would not preclude the definition and recognition of, say, goals of performance, or attainment in particular circumstances, and this may require some self-regulation or self-discipline, but these could surely be seen only as a product of self-centredness and self-awareness *vis-à-vis* an absence of inter-human activities and, hence, of relationships.

At any particular time, the relationship of the individuals within a group may involve both cooperation (with other group members) and competition (with people outside it). In some circumstances, the relationship is fluid: members of a group (for instance a tennis club) may compete against each other in a club championship, and combine with them to compete against corresponding representatives of another club. We suggest that the issue of regulation of the activities of accountants requires attention that keeps such aspects in view.

At one level, the regulation of professional education and expertise is both a self-protective and a socio-protective factor. By guaranteeing a minimum standard of knowledge and competence, a professional body is offering a warranty to the rest of the community in which it is recognized that dereliction of performance by any of its members will be punishable through exercise of its own sanctions, with or without whatever punishment or penalty may be imposed by society through its (society's) own statutory and legal system.

At another level, community governments (such as municipal, state, national, international) have used statutes, ordinances, regulations, and other dicta, and, in some countries, legal decisions, to prescribe details in information provided by accountants for and on behalf of policy-forming and decision-making commanders in socially recognized groups of people (such as companies, corporations, commissions, associations, etc.) Accountants have not often been renowned for enunciating strong adverse criticism of current accounting practices, but there are some notable exceptions such as Briloff (e.g. 1967, 1972, 1976) who delivered several stinging attacks on practices in the USA.

One of the problems is to reconcile an attitude of cooperation, which is necessary to promote the aspirations of the smaller group, with the attitude of competition and protective secrecy which usually applies to the activities of 'outside' groups. Where the two sets of groups operate in the same economic field of activity, cooperation between members of different groups is unlikely. More likely is a practice of head-hunting, industrial or commercial espionage, take-over attempts, price wars, and other measures towards eliminating competition. In short, competition seems to breed anti-competitive attitude and activity – in effect, its own extinction. This may seem to be a stark Darwinian interpretation but it is one of the complexities of social human activity which should at least be explored by those concerned with or interested in accountants' activities and products. To ignore it is to admit inadequacy and/or bias and, in the long term, probably invite fruitless endeavour.

In the UK and kindred jurisdictions, the legislative prescription for balance sheets and other financial statements is to present a true and fair view of a public company's financial affairs (this replaced an earlier expression 'true and correct') but interpretation of 'fair' has been exceedingly difficult and inconclusive.

In the USA and similar jurisdictions, the expression of the criterion as being 'in accordance with generally accepted accounting principles' – a very democratic-sounding selection of words – gave rise to an extended and intensive search for principles enunciated clearly enough to command the support of all professional accountants and those influenced by published accounting reports. The long search has attracted the attention of many of the best intellects among practitioners and academics, but new problems are continually arising, and the search seems to be interminable. As Elliott put it, 'GAAP must come to terms with this more complex world if it is to retain its relevance' (Elliott, 1992: 77). At the same time, he also listed a number of implications for standard-setters (ibid).

The issue of regulation is complex and many-sided, and, in relation to the activities of accountants, warrants thorough and unbiased exploration as soon as possible. Any regulations which come into operation have implications for the education and training of vocational accountants, their level of professionalism and expertise, the source and direction of their loyalties as individuals, as members of a professional group, and as the participants in a changing society. There may be instances in which some aspects of these loyalties may raise ethical dilemmas of choice; and it becomes, ultimately, incumbent upon the individual to face and determine selection in the light of his or her experience, attitude and expectations. In some cases, pressures from varying (and possibly opposing) directions may be great and in the end it becomes an individual decision. What we are suggesting is that the individual should strive to understand and assess them. An ethical attitude cannot be legislated for by statute or any other kind of regulations. For instance, honesty in individuals cannot be mandated; even if departures from honest conduct are punishable, their detection is the prime requisite for the application of the sanction.

During the twentieth century, as in earlier periods, there have been many instances in which, through greed, errors of judgement, shortsighted expectations, inability to assess and measure changes in social conditions, some people who were able to influence the activities of others have offset the social benefits of many of the changes which have occurred. Perhaps few changes in experience – for an individual or a community – are entirely beneficial if all the factors could be known. We suggest that it is important to recognize that simple answers to complex questions are likely to be wrong or, at best, inadequate. Human beings are complex organisms. Their behaviour, as individuals or as members of groups, is not likely to be usefully categorized into simple relationships. Our most urgent suggestion is that the true students of accounting and accountants should recognize this complexity in their field of attention.

When we try to look at regulation dispassionately, perhaps we can see that it always relates to future activity, and that the regulator attempts to prescribe criteria for people engaged in certain envisaged behaviour. Regulations, in whatever form they may be communicated, always say: This is what you shall or shall not do. Most, if not all, of the regulations with which accountants are functionally concerned relate to circumstances in which some people trust others to do something in the future. The need for regulation, that is, the prescription of criteria for those carrying out the entrusted activities to adhere to, results from a recognition, based on experiential evidence, that some people are prone to succumb to human frailty in a great diversity of ways and this may affect their trustworthiness in some situations.

Perhaps the way to more socially sound regulation lies in such matters as:

- clear indication of the need for and purpose of each regulation (in whatever form);
- clear expression of the proscribed or prescribed activity;
- protection of the victim of any malfeasance or misfeasance together with compensation of victims by the perpetrators or beneficiaries of any departure from the regulation;
- ensuring that penalties and/or punishment shall be imposed on the individual human beings responsible (whether as instigators or per-petrators).

One further pertinent point for accountants is that while a considerable number of relevant litigious cases have been settled in the courts, many others have been settled out of court. Thus, the circumstances of these cases have not been subject to wide public comment or consideration. While the expedience and propriety of making such settlements in the interests of the concerned parties is not questioned here, it seems a pity, from the point of view of social justice and professional guidance, that those charged have escaped the scrutiny of judicial consideration and public discussion in courts of law.

Pointers to a way ahead

Accountants do not seem to have yet fully faced the fact that much of what they claim to measure cannot sensibly be measured in terms of a *single* measure. Any sole unit of measurement ignores or distorts many aspects of the social relationships which it purports to express. If accountants are to fulfil their purpose in society, their appropriate task is likely to become more, rather than less, complicated and diversified than it is now.

Perhaps what is needed is a recognition that in any social unit – whether small or large, simple or complicated – responsibilities necessarily and inevitably accompany rights. While essentially simple, this view has widespread and deep-rooted implications, and needs to be studied at several levels, so to speak, such as those of the individual, the professional and the social person. For instance, instead of seeking to translate non-financial items, such as, say, outcomes, into current (or even future) financial monetary units, accountants could try the reverse, that is, to translate monetary measurements into non-financial ones. If the question were asked: How is *X's* income spent – or, better perhaps, disposed of? – the oversimplification of much of social outlays would soon become apparent. Such a question is directed at the recipients of income – the end-users of many of the decisions made by commanders at every level of our economic and social activities. It might be argued that this would lead to chaos. The answer to this is that there is something very like chaos already – that is one of our major points. We have tried to explore the *fons et origo* of the current chaos, to recognize it, and to suggest means of overcoming or replacing it. But the first and essential step is to recognize its existence.

In itself, an increase of information is no more than a means of broadening the base of judgement-making. Whether the increase is used for good or for evil purposes depends not on the amount or the nature of the information, but on the intent that forms the making of the judgement. More information permits greater selectivity; selection is governed by the user's attitude, purpose and expertise, all built on experience (in a broad sense). Hence while we advocate and welcome the increase of information which an extended data base could provide, the more significant question of the purpose of decisions needs to be faced squarely as a fundamental ethical one by each professional accountant and by all accountants professionally.

Perhaps the task ahead, as we see it, may be put into some sort of focus by addressing it in relation to the broad groups distinguished in an earlier chapter. Some of the issues to be explored would include questions such as the following:

Educators

Can the educational experience in accounting be used to encourage and develop in students a capacity for independent thought and expression? If so, should any and what limits be seen as acceptable?

What should be the basic approach of educators in accounting?

What sort of graduates should the educators in any particular educational institution aim to produce?

What is the source for dedicated educators? Is it sufficient to meet expected demand and if not, how can it be provided?

Is it possible, or desirable, to develop courses in accounting to prepare graduates for their life-time careers as people with broad social affinities as well as for their first professional jobs? If so, how can it be achieved? If not, should educational institutions provide alternative or specialized courses and on what basis?

Are any maximum or minimum components of curriculum desirable or necessary? Should they be imposed on particular institutions or educators?

What steps can be taken to ensure that educators have freedom of enquiry and freedom of expression in their educational activities? Included in this aspect would be freedom to develop courses which require initiative, diversity of interests, and freedom of thought.

How can the relationships between educators and those in command of the affairs of professional organizations best be developed and maintained? We believe that these relationships are of the highest significance and need cooperation, independence and an absence of domination between the parties involved. One important aspect is ensuring that educators and researchers have freedom to experiment where and when reasonable and promising.

One point that may usefully be observed here is that the relative adequacy of procedures may not be as significant a factor now as hitherto for the discipline of accounting, but this requires much further exploration. More important is its place in and relevance to the social environment in which procedures are carried out. This depends on individual and social responsibility which in turn depends on a rigorous self-determination by each individual, who undertakes to practise in the field, of his or her motives, attitudes and aspirations, as an individual and as a member of the group(s) which he or she belongs to and can influence.

Policy-makers and Administrators of Professional Bodies

What minimum requirements of knowledge, expertise and attitude is to be prescribed for admission to membership?

What sort of leadership in the profession is desirable in the future? Can any of the requisite qualities be observed or nurtured in the education process? In this respect it should be recognized that the leaders of the profession of ten or fifteen years hence are possibly candidates for admission to membership of a professional body in the current year.

Regulators

What criteria for legislators and standard-setters should be set up? How can these be tested? Should appointments be made on a probationary basis?

Are the procedures for preparing, passing and policing legislation, regulations and standards appropriate and satisfactory? What influences do lobbyists have in the process? Do statutory regulations and standards often carry an overload or complexity of information?

Consider whether those who take on the responsibility of prescribing and monitoring the activities of others in this field, be they politicians, standardformulators, bureaucrats or interpreters of statutes, regulations or standards, should if possible, determine, formulate and declare the criteria by which they operate, so that all involved may at least be aware of the relative ethical attitude of those whose pronouncements affect their activities. The question arises: Is it not appropriate that those who seek to control the activities of others should take stock of ethical issues involved in expressions of intended social policy? Surely mankind is faced with ethical problems. And accountants need to recognize that they are in the middle of this, whether they like it or not.

Practitioners

Whatever the unit of measurement or assessment may be, should attempts be made to account for:-

- Anticipations?
- Expectations?
- Ventures?
- Multiple bases of valuation of assets and commitments?

Should freedom in the format of presentation of reports be permitted so long as it is coupled with adequate information for the derivation of alternative presentations? In other words, should the user be enabled to select the format? (Or: Let him who takes the risk select the base.)

On a particular topic, who now really appoints the auditor of a public listed company or organization? To whom is such an auditor's report now really addressed, and to what extent is it really intelligible or relevant to shareholder recipients?

For everybody interested in the matter, we suggest that it is highly likely that change in the area of activities that accountants are concerned with is going to be continuous for probably a considerable time to come. This in turn suggests that accountants, as individual units of experience operating in a social environment, need to broaden their scope and their attitude if they are to continue to meet the requirements of social usefulness.

Conclusion

Accounting is still often perceived as a minor discipline, and all the huffing and puffing will not convert it into a major one. But, having recognized this, we put ourselves into a better position to contemplate its importance. For, while it may be regarded as minor, this does not mean that it is utterly insignificant. For one thing, it is widely pervasive in any advanced society: the effects of applying particular procedures can be felt in many widely dispersed sections of the community and widely diverse kinds of activities. For another, as an instrument of measurement it could, if used wisely and perceptively, be exceedingly valuable in clarifying and sharpening concepts which are of social significance, especially in economic matters. As an exercise in logical method, it helps to develop a sensible approach to situations and circumstances, but in many cases it should be complemented by other methods of approach for the development of balanced judgement.

The general public needs to be educated about the traditional functions of accountants and especially of auditors. The image of infallibility and/or guarantee of reliability – the notion that one measure, any one measure, of results or position is available and reliable – must be modified, and the variable truth of multiplicity of purposes and interpretations needs to be faced. But before this, accountants themselves have to exorcise the myths of accounting from their own interpretations of what happens and can be measured and from their subject-matter. This is what this work is all about. For instance, what we have called a unit of operation is an attempt to provide a focus of reference. The term 'entity' is often convenient in exposition, but it has dangers if it is misused to replace talking about people. Similar objections arise with other terms such as 'cost centre' and the like which are satisfactory in their proper sense, but objectionable if misused to mean a unit of experience. Again, market prices and deprival values in themselves do not produce income, especially distributable income. If income is to be measured by the degree of betteroffness after spending, being better off is a personal assessment, determinable only by the actual sale of a commodity or a service.

In this work we could perhaps present our purpose in the form of two equations (in which → represents 'produces'):

Knowledge + Will   →   Belief
             (which is an emotion and   (which is a desire or
             provides motive power)   willingness to act)

Belief   + Means   →   Action
                                               (Implementation)

In essence, we have suggested that:-

• accountants deal with human behaviour and the relationships it gives rise to;
• human behaviour is complex;
• it is not always or necessarily rational;
• where it is rational, it may be so according to different criteria of rationality;
• accountants, like other human beings, should be modest and humble in face of the variety and complexity of human behaviour;
• the traditional units and processes of measurement are no longer adequate, (if they ever were) to meet some of the important requirements of social living nowadays.

We should examine critically what we would otherwise take for granted, and either verify or modify conventional wisdom on sound logical grounds or on exposed but accepted non-logical grounds (for example, emotional or compassionate).

What, ultimately, is the objective in accounting? Or, more properly perhaps, is there discernible a teleological purpose to which the main recognized functions of accountants as accountants are directed, whether implicitly or explicitly? One possible answer is that it is control. But control of what? Since the subject-matter of the accounting processes is the activities of human beings, it may seem logical to say that it is control of human beings in some of their activities, in relation, say, to resources of various kinds. But this may be open to misunderstanding. Some people may, indeed, use the results of the accounting processes to impose control over the activities of other people. But this attitude may seem unsavoury to some people who might argue that it is a misuse of accounting rather than its use to make it an instrument of control over human beings. To such people it may be more consonant with egalitarian views to say that the accounting processes enable people to show others with whom they have dealings, especially, for example, employees and managers, how control over resources may be attained. But what does control over resources mean if it does not mean at least exerting some strong influence over the activities of some people who have access to or influence over the use or location or movement of the resources in question? And, since resources of all kinds come from materials and forces of nature, would it be too much to say that the ultimate object of accounting is to help people to control materials, or, in generalization, to help man to control and/or manage the physical environment in which the species is placed?

But it may be claimed that man has a social environment also. The role of accounting here is not so much to enable people to control their social environment. We should recognize that each human being has a social environment composed of people. With this in mind, we could say that the purpose of accounting here is to assist people to examine and understand the relationships which make up this social environment. Hence, we might say that the fundamental purpose of accounting – in this broad, social sense – is to help all human beings to understand and live at peace with their social environment.

In recent years, however, it has become clear to many people that some parts of our natural environment cannot endure prolonged 'control' and continued exploitation without becoming impaired, that is, without undergoing reactions which are inhospitable to humans, and indeed, to other species of life. Hence, it might be even more appropriate to say that the purpose of accountants in carrying out their accounting functions should be to help people to examine and understand both their natural and their social environment so that they may live in peace with both.

Perhaps another way of putting it is this: By communicating to others information resulting from an honest 'dealing with', accountants seek to elicit the cooperation of all recognizable parties within the community concerned with or affected by the control of resources, in attaining a consensually acceptable allocation and use of those resources.

One accounting writer seemed to be aware of this many years ago when he wrote:

> Persons steeped in the habit of thinking in subjective terms . . . appear to think of social phenomena as retaining their present characteristics, that is, as remaining constant, while man learns to control them. They thereby put man outside of society. They do not seem to appreciate that an understanding of social phenomena running in objective terms would, if it became general, constitute or involve a fundamental

change of social phenomena. Such an illusion is corrected by including man in the causal process.

(Scott 1931: 131)

While the basic issues may be regarded by many as simple, and simply expressible, we do not envisage that the solution will be simple or straightforward. Much enlightened, patient and cooperative discussion and research is needed to support or refute, modify or refine; what we have here put forward.

We suggest one final point: Conventional wisdom always lags behind the pioneers and the innovators. At the end, we feel we have reached a point (or a stage) from which others may continue. We wish them well.

Bibliography[1]

Ayer, A.J.,1955, in *Studies in Communication* (q.v.).

Baladouni, V., 1990, 'An Early Attempt at Balance Sheet Classification and Financial Reporting', *Accounting Historians Journal*, June, pp. 27–45.

Balzac, H., 1908, *Eugenie Grandet*, Clarendon Press, Oxford.

Bartlett, F., (1962), in Mitchison, N., (ed.) *What the Human Race is up to*, Victor Gollancz, London.

Baxter, W.T. (ed.) 1950, *Studies in Accounting*, Sweet and Maxwell, London

Baxter, W.T., 1965, *The House of Hancock*, Russell & Russell, New York (reprint of Harvard, Boston, 1945).

Bibby, C., 1978, *The Art of Limerick*, Cassell, Australia.

Birrell, A., 1912, *The Duties and Liabilities of Trustees*, MacMillan, London, first published 1896.

Bonamy, F., 1943, *Dead Reckoning*, Duell.

Briloff, A.J., 1967, *The Effectiveness of Accounting Communication*, Praeger, New York.

Briloff, A.J., 1972, *Unaccountable Accounting*, Harper and Ross, New York.

Briloff, A.J., 1976, *More Debits than Credits: The Burnt Investor's Guide to Financial Statements*, Harper & Row, New York.

Brown, R., (ed.), 1905, *A History of Accounting and Accountants*, T.C. and E.C. Jack, Edinburgh.

Brown, R.G., Johnston, K.S., 1963, *Pacioli on Accounting*, McGraw-Hill, New York.

Butler, S., 1947, *The Way of all Flesh*. Penguin, Harmondsworth, first published 1903.

Campbell, T., 1810, *The Pleasures of Hope*, Edinburgh, Longman.

Carnegie, G.D., 1990, *Timing and Frequency of Financial Reporting*, AARF Discussion Paper No. 15, Melbourne, Australian Accounting Research Foundation.

Carnegie, G.D. and Wolnizer, P.W., 1997, 'The Financial Reporting of Publicly-Owned Collections: Whither Financial (Market) Values and Contingent Valuation Estimates', *Australian Accounting Review*, pp. 14–50.

Carzo, R., Yanouzas, J.N., 1967, *Formal Organization*, Irwin, Dorsey.

Cayley, A., 1894, *The Principles of Book-keeping by Double Entry*, Cambridge University Press, Cambridge.

---

[1]Unfortunately a few references in the text could not be located after the author's death, and are therefore omitted from the bibliography. These are Bennett (1913), Gynther (1967), Lopez and Raymond (1955), Ogilvie and Annandale (1935), Spode (1934) and Wolf (1937).

Chambers, R.J., 1966, *Accounting, Evaluation and Economic Behavior*, Prentice-Hall, Englewood Cliffs.

Chase, S., 1947, *The Tyranny of Words*, Methuen, London.

Clarke, P.J., 1995, 'Non-Financial Measures of Performance in Management', *Accountancy Ireland*, pp. 22–3.

Colantoni, C.S., Manes, R.P., Whinston, A., 1971, 'A Unified Approach to the Theory of Accounting and Information Systems', *Accounting Review*, January, pp. 90–102.

Collinson, R., 1683, *Idea Rationaria*, David Lindsay, James Kniblo, Josua van Solingen and John Colmar, Edinburgh.

Comte, A., 1822, 'Prospectus des Travaux Necessaires pour Réorganiser la Societe', in Saint-Simon, H., *Suites des Travaux Ayant pour Object de Fonder le System Industriel*, Paris.

Comte, A., 1830, *Cours de Philosophie Positive*, Vol. 1, Paris.

Cooke, C.A., 1950, *Corporation, Trust and Company*, Manchester University Press, Manchester.

Craik, K.J.W., 1943, *The Nature of Explanation*, Cambridge University Press, Cambridge.

Crivelli, P., 1939, *An Original Translation of the Treatise of Double-Entry Book-Keeping by Frater Lucas Pacioli*, Institute of Book-keepers, London.

Cronhelm, F.W., 1818, *Double Entry by Single*, Longman Hurst Rees Orme and Brown, London.

Cushing, B.E., 1989a, 'A Khunian Interpretation of the Historical Evolution of Accounting', *Accounting Historians Journal*, December, pp. 1–41.

Cushing, B.E., 1989b, 'On the Feasibility and the Consequences of a Database Approach to Corporate Financial Reporting', *Journal of Information Systems*, Vol. 3, No. 2, pp. 29–52.

Cushing, B.E., 1990, 'Frameworks, Paradigms and Scientific Research in Management Information Systems', *Journal of Information Systems*, March, pp. 38–59.

Dafforne, R., 1651, *The Merchants Mirrour*, 2nd edition, printed by J.L. for Nicolas Bourne, London.

Davis, G.B., 1982, 'Strategies for Information Requirements Determination', *IBM Systems Journal*, Vol. 21, No. 1.

DeMorgan, A., 1846, *Elements of Arithmetic*, 5th edition, Taylor and Walton, London.

Denna, E.L., McCarthy, W.E., 1987, 'An Events Accounting Foundation for DSS Implementation', NATO ASI Series, F31, pp. 239–63.

de Roover, R., 1955, 'New Perspectives on the History of Accounting', *Accounting Review*, July.

de Roover, R., 1956, 'The Development of Accounting Prior to Luca Pacioli', in Littleton and Yamey: *Studies in the History of Accounting*.

Devine, C.T., 1962, *Essays in Accounting Theory*, Vols I, II, III, the Author.

Devine, C.T., 1985, *Essays in Accounting Theory*, Vols IV, V, American Accounting Association, Sarasota.

Dewey, J., 1928, *The Philosophy of John Devery*, selected and edited by Joseph Ratner, H. Holt, New York.

Dilworth, T., 1806, *The Young Book-keeper's Assistant: showing him, in the most Plain and Easy Manner, the Italian way of stating Debtor and Creditor*, the Booksellers, London, and T. Wilson and R. Spence, York.

Eddington, A., 1943, 'The Milky Way and Beyond', in Shapley, Harlow: *A Treasury of Science*.

Elliott, R.K., 1991, 'Accounting Education and Research at the Crossroad', *Issues in Accounting Education*, Spring, pp. 1–8.

Elliott, R.K., 1992, 'Commentary: The Third Wave Breaks on the Shores of Accounting', *Accounting Horizons*, June, pp. 61–85.

Encel, S., 1987, *Scientific and Technical Progress, Who Benefits*, Academy of the Social Sciences in Australia, Canberra.

Encyclopaedia Brittanica, 1937, 14th Edition, Encyclopaedia Britannica Company, London.

Evans, B., 1955, 'Ifor', in *Studies in Communication* (q.v.).

Everest, G.C., Weber, R., 1977, 'A Relational Approach to Accounting Models', *Accounting Review*, April.

Every, J., 1673, 'Speculum Mercativum. Or The Young Merchants . . . Accompts, after the Italian way of Debitor and Creditor'.

Fitzgerald, A.A., 1936, 'Is the Balance Sheet an Anachronism?' *Australian Accountant*, March.

Galliers, R., (ed.) 1987, *Information Analysis*, Addison-Wesley, Sydney.

Geerts, G., McCarthy, W.E., 1991, 'Database Accounting Systems', in Williams, B.C., and Spaul, B.J., *IT and Accounting*, Chapman and Hall, London.

Geijsbeck, J.B., 1914, *Ancient Double Entry Bookkeeping*, first published in 1914, reprint of Scholars Book Co., Houston, 1974.

Gilman, S., 1939, *Accounting Concepts of Profit*, Ronald, New York.

Godfrey, A. and Hooper, K. 1996, 'Accounting Tabulating and Decision-Making in Feudal England: Domesday Book Revisited', *Accounting History*, Vol. 1, No. 1, May 1996.

Goldberg, L., 1944, 'The Entity Theory of Accounting', *Australian Accountant*, July, pp. 239–42.

Goldberg, L., 1953, 'The Exposition of Fundamental Accounting Procedures', *Accounting Review*, April.

Goldberg, L., 1957, *An Outline of Accounting*, Law Book Company, Sydney.

Goldberg, L., 1964, 'How Rational is Rational?' *New York Certified Public Accountant*, July, pp. 512–16.

Goldberg, L., 1965, *An Inquiry into the Nature of Accounting*, American Accounting Association, Sarasota.

Goldberg, L., Leech, S.A., 1984, *An Introduction to Accounting Method*, Longman Cheshire, Melbourne.

Haldane, J.B.S., 1955, in *Studies in Communication*, (q.v.).

Hallam, H., 1872, *View of the State of Europe during the Middle Ages*, John Murray, London.

Hannay, D., 1926, *The Great Chartered Companies*, Williams and Norgate, London.

Haseman, W.D., Whinston, A.B., 1976, 'Design of a Multidimensional Accounting System', *Accounting Review*, January, pp. 65–79.

Hasluck, P., 1986, 'The Social Scientist in a Democracy', Academy of Social Sciences in Australia, Annual Lecture.

Hatfield, H.R., 1915, *Modern Accounting*, Appleton, New York.

Herodotus, 1954, *The Histories*, translated and with an Introduction by Aubrey de Selincourt, Penguin, Harmondsworth.

Hogben, L., 1940, *Mathematics for the Millions*, Allen & Unwin, London.

Hume, D., 1751, *An Inquiry Concerning the Principles of Morals*, first published 1751; Watts & Co., London, 1906.

Ijiri, Y., 1965, 'Axioms and Structures of Conventional Accounting Measurement', *Accounting Review*, January.

Ijiri, Y., 1966, 'Physical Measures and Multi-dimensional accounting', in *Research in Accounting Measurement*, Stanford University Graduate School of Business.

Ijiri, Y., 1967, *The Foundations of Accounting Measurement*, Prentice-Hall, Englewood Cliffs.

Ijiri, Y., 1975, *Theory of Accounting Measurement*, American Accounting Association, Sarasota.

Ijiri, Y., 1982, *Triple-Entry Bookkeeping and Income Momentum*, American Accounting Association, Sarasota.

Ijiri, Y., 1988, 'Accounting Matrices and Three-Dimensional Arrays', *Issues in Accounting Education*, Fall.

Inglis, W., 1861, *Book-keeping by Single Entry*, W. & R. Chambers, London and Edinburgh, 1881a.

Inglis, W., 1896, *Book-keeping by Single and Double Entry*, W. & R. Chambers, London and Edinburgh, 1881b, 1882, 1886, 1891, 1894.

Jacobsen, L., 1988, 'Early Accounting Data Bases of the Pacific: Knotted Cords in the Ryukyu Islands', *Proceedings of 5th World Congress of Accounting Historians*, paper no. 213.

Jensen, M.C., 1982, 'Organization Theory and Methodology', Address to the American Accounting Association.

Johnson, O., 1970, 'Towards an "Events" Theory of Accounting', *Accounting Review*, October, pp. 641–53.

Jones, S., Romano, C., Ratnatunga, J., 1995, *Accounting Theory: A Contemporary Review*, Harcourt Brace, Sydney.

Kemeny, J.G., Schleifer, A., Snell J.L., and Thompson, G.L., 1962, *Finite Mathematics with Business Applications*, Prentice-Hall, Englewood Cliffs.

Keynes, J.M., 1936, *The General Theory of Employment*, Interest and Money, Macmillan, London.

Kindleberger, C.P., 1978, *Manias, Panics and Crashes*, Macmillan, London.

Knight, F.H., 1921, *Risk, Uncertainty and Profit*, Houghton, Mifflin, Boston, reprint 1940.

Kuhn, T.S., 1970, The Structure of Scientific Revolutions, 2nd edition, University of Chicago Press, Chicago.

Lau, C.K., Brennan, W., 1991, 'Battering Bible Makes Money Passe', *Weekend Australian*, August 10–11.

Leake, P.D., 1938, *Commercial Goodwill*, 3rd edition, Pitman, London.

Lee, T.A., 1980, 'The Accounting Entity Concept, Accounting Standards, and Inflation Accounting', *Accounting and Business Research*, Spring, pp. 176–86.

Leech, S.A., 1986, 'The Theory and Development of a Matrix-Based Accounting System', *Accounting and Business Research*, Summer.

Leech S.A., Mepham, M.J., 1991, 'A Relational/Matrix Framework for Accounting', 14th Annual Congress of the European Accounting Association, University of Limburg, Maastricht, 10–12 April.

Lewis, C.D., 1957, *The Poet's Way of Knowledge*, The Henry Sidgwick Memorial Lecture, Cambridge University Press, Cambridge.

Lieberman, A.Z., Whinston, A.B., 1975, 'A Structuring of an Events-Accounting Information System', *Accounting Review*, April, pp. 246–58.

Lin, Y.,1938, *The Importance of Living*, Heinemann, London.

Liset, A., 1660, 'Ampithalami, or, The Accountants Closet, being an abbridgment of Merchants-Accounts kept by debitors and creditors'.

Lisle, G. (ed.), 1903, *Encyclopaedia of Accounting*, Green, Edinburgh.

List, W., 1986, 'Exit Double Entry', *Accountant's Magazine*, September, pp. 44–5.

Littleton, A.C., 1933, *Accounting Evolution to 1900*, American Institute Publishing Co., New York.

Littleton, A.C., 1953, *Structure of Accounting Theory*, American Accounting Association, Menasha.

Littleton A.C., Yamey, B.C. (eds), 1956, *Studies in the History of Accounting*, Richard D. Irwin, Homewood, Illinois.

Macquarie Dictionary, 1982, p. 1754.

Mair, J., 1748, *Book-keeping Methodiz'd*, Isaac Jackson, Dublin.

Martin, C., 1994, *An Introduction to Accounting*, McGraw-Hill, Sydney.

Mattessich, R., 1957, 'The Constellation of Accountancy and Economics', *Accounting Review*, October.

Mattessich, R., 1964, *Accounting and Analytical Methods*, Irwin, Homewood.

McCarthy, W.E., 1979, 'An Entity-Relationship View of Accounting Models', *Accounting Review*, October.

McCarthy, W.E., 1982, «The REA Accounting Model: A Generalized Framework for Accounting Systems in a Shared Data Environment', *Accounting Review*, July.

McCrae, T.W., 1976, *Computers and Accounting*, John Wiley & Sons, New York.

Mepham, M.J., 1988, 'Matrix-Based Accounting: A Comment', *Accounting and Business Research*, Vol. 18, No. 72, pp. 375–8.

Meyer, P.E., 1973, 'The Accounting Entity', *Abacus*, December.

Mill, J.S., 1884, *A System of Logic*, Longmans, Green, London.

Murray, W., 1862, *Historical Sketch of the Science of Accountantship*, London Printing and Publishing Co., London.

New Accountant, 13 June 1991.

North, R., 1715, *The Gentleman Accomptant*, London.

Pacioli, L., 1494, 'Particularis de Computis et Scripturis', in *Summa de Arithmetica Geometria Proportioni et Proportionalita*, Venice.

Parker, R.H., 1994, "Finding English Words to Talk About Accounting Concepts", *Accounting, Auditing and Accountability Journal*, Vol. 7, No. 2, pp. 70–85.

Paton, W.A., 1922, *Accounting Theory*, Ronald, New York.

Paton, W.A., Littleton, A.C., 1940, *Introduction to Corporate Accounting Standards*, American Accounting Association, Iowa City.

Peele, J., 1553, 'The Manner and fourme how to keep a perfecte reconyng after the order of the most worthie and notable accompte, of debitour and creditour'.

Peragallo, E., 1938, *Origin and Evolution of Double Entry Bookkeeping*, American Institute of Publishing Company, New York.

Petri, N., 1596, 'The Pathway to Knowledge . . . of keeping of a marchants booke, after the Italian manner'.

Pope, 1732, *Essay on Man*, Epistle IV.

Pope, A., *Moral Essays*, Epistle i:i.

Quin, M., 1779, *Rudiments of Book-keeping*.

Randall, C.B., 1962, *The Folklore of Management*, Mentor Executive Library, New York.

Rorem, C.R., 1927, 'Similarities of Accounting and Statistical Methods', *Accounting Review*, March, pp. 10–18.

Rowland, W.S., 1934, *Principles of Accounting*, 4th edition n.d., first edition edited by Stanley W. Rowland, fourth edition revised by R. Glynne Williams, Bonnington Press, St Albans; Gregg Publishing Co., London; Editor's Introduction to 1st edition, dated September.

Russell, B., 1946, *History of Western Philosophy*, Allen & Unwin, London.

Samuel, V., 1939, *Belief and Action*, Pelican, London.

Sanders, T.H., Hatfield H.R., Moore, U., 1938, *A Statement of Accounting Principles*, American Institute of Accountants, New York.

Schmandt-Besserat, D., 1992, *Before Writing*, University of Texas Press, Austin.

Scott, D.R., 1925, *Theory of Accounts*, Holt, New York.

Scott, D.R., 1931, *The Cultural Significance of Accounts*, Lucas, Columbia, Missouri, n.d., first published 1931.

Scott, R.F., 1905, *The Voyage of the Discovery*, Macmillan, London.

Shakespeare, *Hamlet*, Act III, Sc. I.

Shakespeare, *Macbeth*, Act II, Sc.1.

Simon, H.A., 1957, *Administrative Behaviour*, New York, Macmillan.

Simon, H.A., 1960, *The New Science of Management Decision*, Harper and Brothers, New York.

Simon, H.A., Smithburg, D.W., and Thompson, V.A., 1950, *Public Administration*, Knopf, New York.

Sombart, *Der moderne Kapitalismus*, II p. 119.

Sorter, G.H., 1969, 'An "Events" Approach to Basic Accounting Theory', *Accounting Review*, January, pp. 12–19.

Spengler, O., 1926, *The Decline of the West*, Allen & Unwin, London.

Stebbing, L.S., 1946, *Modern Introduction to Logic*, Harmonsworth, England, Penguin.

Studies in Communication, 1955, Contributed to the Communication Research Centre, University of London, Martin, Secker and Warburg, London.

Sykes, T., 1994, *The Bold Riders: Behind Australia's Corporate Collapses*, Allen & Unwin, St Leonards, New South Wales.

Taylor, R.E., 1942, *No Royal Road*, University of North Carolina Press, Chapel Hill.

Thomas, A.L., 1969, *The Allocation Problem in Financial Accounting Theory*, American Accounting Association, Evanston.

Thomas, E.M., 1968, *The Harmless People*, Knopf, New York.

Toffler, A., 1971, *Future Shock*, Pan, London.

Vickers, G., 1955, in *Studies in Communication*, (q.v.).

von Mises, L., 1949, *Human Action*, William Hodge, London, etc.

Webster, 1926, *New International Dictionary of the English Language*, G. & C. Merriam Company, Springfield, Mass.

Webster, W, 1719, *An Essay on Book-Keeping*, London

Webster, W., 1738, *An Essay on Book-Keeping, according to the True Italian Method of Debtor and Creditor, by Double Entry*, for A. Bettesworth and C. Hitch, London.

Wells, M.C., 1976, 'A Revolution in Accounting Thought?', *Accounting Review*, July.

Whatmough, J., 1956, *Language: A Modern Synthesis*, Mentor, New York.

White, M., 1955, *The Age of Analysis*, Mentor, New York.

Whitehead, A.N., 1948, *Adventures of Ideas*, Penguin, Harmondsworth.

Yamey, B.S., 1940, 'The Functional Development of Double-Entry Bookkeeping', *Accountant*, November.

Yamey, B.S., 1947, 'Notes on the Origin of Double-Entry Bookkeeping', *Accounting Review*, XXII.

Yamey, B.S., 1949, Scientific Bookkeeping and the Rise of Capitalism, *Economic History Review*, Second Series Vol. I.

Yamey, B.S., Edey, H.C., and Thomson, H.W., 1963, *Accounting in England and Scotland*, Sweet and Maxwell, London.

Index

resources: accumulation 99; acquisition 99, 103–4, 119; availability 126–7; commander 140, 141, 145–6; depletion 114; deployment 50–1, 54–5, 125, 140, 141, 143; disposal 99, 103–4; exchange value 98–9, 285; funds 208; liabilities 220; long-/short-term 126; non-renewable 109; scarcity 96; suppliers 209, 210–11; use value 98–9

responsibility 141, 143, 306
revenue statement 263
revenues 245
rights 141, 248, 275
Rowland, W. S. 268
Russell, Bertrand 35–6, 213, 285
Ryukyu Islands 13

sacrifice 236
salvage value 126
Samuel, V. 194–5
Sanders, T. H. 36
savings 246
scarcity of resources 96
Schmandt-Besserat, D. 17, 97
science 30–2; analysis 158; hypothesis 35; observation 35, 118; relevance 173–4
Scott, D. R. 296, 324
Scott, R. F. 14
seashell example 241–2
selection process 17–18, 137, 251–2
self-interest 187
self-recognition 66
self-regulation 315
service industry 49–50
service ventures 115–16
Shakespeare, William: *Hamlet* 147, 195–200; *Macbeth* 132
share certificates 283
shareholders' equity 282–3
shareholding 112, 115, 273–4, 283
shares issues 115, 280
sign language 184n2
similes 87
Simon, H. A. 147, 150, 178
single entry procedures 226–7
Smithburg, D. W. 178
social context 10, 23, 28, 46

social relationships 141–2, 253, 271, 312
social responsibility 306
social sciences 158, 167
society: accountants 258, 306, 307, 312–13; ethics 110; mores 135, 193–4; ownership 128; rationality 154; symbols 91; values 288
solipsism 72
solvency 277, 299
Sorter, G. H. 48, 101
South Sea Bubble 284
space 35–6, 110, 256–7
Spade 8
Spengler, Oswald 217, 218, 239–40, 250
spreadsheet software 34
squirrels 95
stamp collecting 192–3
Statements of Accounting Concepts 204n1
statements of assets/liabilities 278
statistics 14–15, 95
status quo 149, 151–2, 155–6, 176–7, 235–6
Stebbing, Susan 26
stewardship 142, 224
store of value 96, 97–8
student/beer example 257
sub-entities 139–40
subjectivity: classification 39; experience 64–5; judgements 30, 190–1, 295; knowledge 50; measurement 100
Sumeria 12, 13
super-entities 139–40
supervision 119
suppliers 209, 210–11
supplies, non-monetary 209–10
surplus, buyer's 291–2
Sykes, T. 284
symbol: abstraction 89–90; communication 72–3, 75; experience 73; names 88; non-verbal/verbal 75, 184; numbers 213; oral/visual 74–5; referent 75; social 91; table 87; truth 185–6
symbolic logic 77

T account form 230, 237, 238–9, 248